TWENTIETH-CENTURY
DECORATION

THE DOMESTIC INTERIOR FROM 1900 TO THE PRESENT DAY

TWENTIETH-CENTURY DECORATION

THE DOMESTIC INTERIOR FROM 1900 TO THE PRESENT DAY

STEPHEN CALLOWAY

Weidenfeld & Nicolson London

Frontispiece: The Chinoiserie drawing room from Rose Cumming's
own apartment at 36 East 53rd Street, New York, 1946
Photograph courtesy of Rose Cumming Inc.

Designed by Trevor and Jacqui Vincent

George Weidenfeld & Nicolson Limited
91 Clapham High Street
London SW4 7TA

ISBN 0 297 79159 1

Phototypeset by Keyspools Limited, Golborne, Lancs
Colour separations by Newsele Litho Limited
Printed in Italy by Printers Srl, Trento
Bound by L.E.G.O., Vicenza

CONTENTS

ACKNOWLEDGEMENTS   7

INTRODUCTION **Taste, Fashion and the Way Rooms Change**   9

Before 1900   **The Legacies of the Past**   31

1900–1920   **The Avant-Garde and the Revival of Period Styles** 59

1920–1930   **The Lure of Antiques and the Modern Style**   141

1930–1945   **Pleasing Decay and the All-White Room**   213

1945–1960   **Austerity and the New Look**   285

1960–1980   **Alternative Lifestyles and Reflecting Success**   329

1980–1988   **The Cult of Design and the New Ornamentalism**   359

INDEX   403

For John Compton, scholar, aesthete, friend, who had he lived would have been the co-author of this book

ACKNOWLEDGEMENTS

This book has been several years in the writing and in that time an enormous number of friends and colleagues have given me help by drawing things to my attention, providing references, or simply discussing ideas of taste, style and fashion. Many decorators in England, in Europe and in America have hunted in their archives for material. Others in busy practice have given me their time, while several, now retired, have shared valuable reminiscences which have greatly enhanced the earlier chapters of the book.

I should like to thank in particular: Roy Alderson, Colin Amery, Ron Arad, Lady Ashton, Clive Aslet, Christian Badin, Serge Baillache, Anthony Ballantine, Mrs Jane Bayldon, Stephen Bayley, Miss Stella Beddoe, Mrs D.C. Berry, Mattea Bonnetti, Eugène Braun-Munk, Mario Buatta, Miss Ros Byam Shaw, Manuel Canovas, Mme Madeleine Castaing, Martin Chapman, Miss Yu-Chee Chong, Nigel Coates, Miss Chantal Coady, Alec Cobbe, David Connor, John Cornforth, Miss Ilse Crawford, Dan Cruickshank, Paul Delaney, Comte Ghislain de Diesbach, Tom Dixon, Alan Dodd, Martin Drury, André Dubreuil, Ray Eames, Miss Meredith Etherington-Smith, Stanley Falconer, Mrs Lilliane Fawcett, Comtesse Anne de Fayet, Mrs Vere French, Joe Friedman, Piero Fornasetti, Philippe Garner, Miss Grace Gary, Christopher Gibbs, Jonathan Glancey, Miss Georgina Godley, Miss Mary Goodwin, St John Gore, David Gould, Roderick Gradidge, Ian Grant, Henry Greenwood, Miss Sarah Greenwood, Albert Hadley, John Hardy, Robert Harling, Nicholas Haslam, David Hicks, Miss Leonie Highton, Miss Min Hogg, Mrs Stephanie Hoppen, Simon Houfe, Geoffrey Houghton-Brown, Michael Inchbald, Miss Jocasta Innes, Keith Irvine, Charles Jencks, Stephen Jones, Michael Kauffmann, Alex Kroll, Lionel Lambourne, Lady Lancaster, the late Sir Osbert Lancaster, Mrs Claude Lancaster, Peter Leonard, Miss Nicolette le Pelley, Pierre Le-Tan, Stephen Levrant, Ronald Lightbown, Stephen Long, Adriano Magistretti, David Massey, Angus McBean, Miss Pauline Metcalf, Peter Miall, Anthony Mitchell, David Mlinaric, Renzo Mongiardino, John Murdoch, Miss Amicia de Moubray, Pascal Mourgue, Lawrence Mynott, Charles Newton, Michael Parkin, Ronald Parkinson, Giovanni Patrini, Miss Amelia Peck, Mme Marie-Paul Pellé, Count Filippo Perego de Cremnago, Piero Pinto, Julian Powell-Tuck, Alan Powers, the late Mario Praz, Miss Carolyn Quartermaine, David Roos, Sir John Rothenstein, Miss Jessica Rutherford, John Saladino, Miss Bertha Sander, Dennis Severs, Michael Snodin, John Stefanidis, Miss Alexandra Stoddard, Gavin Stamp, Lord Strabolgi, Sir Roy Strong, Miss Henriette Sturge-Moore, Fr. Anthony Symondson, Miss Imogen Taylor, Stanislaus Terech, Brian Thomas, Peter Thornton, Hugo Vickers, the late Siegfried von Frieblisch, Clive Wainwright, Norris Wakefield, David Watkin, Miss Jane Wildgoose, Jean-Michel Wilmotte, Hugh Clifford-Wing, Mme Barbara Wirth, Robin Wyatt.

At the Victoria & Albert Museum many colleagues, especially in my own department, Designs, Prints and Drawings, and in the National Art Library have been, as ever, helpful and generous with their expertise. At Weidenfeld & Nicolson Michael Dover and Martha Caute gave me support at all stages of the project and as work advanced slowly showed no less continual patience. In the early stages of research Laura Suffield gave me tremendous help in searching out the visual material; later Philippa Lewis gathered important images in America; and Ian Jones was responsible for a large proportion of the excellent photographs of original drawings and early book and magazine images.

Finally, my greatest pleasure is in acknowledging my greatest debt: to my wife, Oriel, who has helped so much and in so many ways.

S.C. *April 1988*

The true perfection of Art consists less in the discovery of unknown things than in the judicious use of those elements already sanctioned by custom and taste.

Charles Percier

INTRODUCTION
TASTE, FASHION AND THE WAY ROOMS CHANGE

'We have passed from the golden age of architecture to the gilded age of decoration,' wrote Edith Wharton in 1897, heralding the rise of the interior decorator.[1] This emergence of the decorator as *arbiter elegantiarum* and purveyor of chic is one of the most intriguing of the social and artistic phenomena of our century. Edith Wharton's observation, made with her characteristically perceptive eye for nuance, pinpoints that subtle but significant change in attitudes which divides the world of the great nineteenth-century firms of upholsterers and decorators from our own: the era in which we have become ever more obsessed with interiors as expressions of individual taste, national characteristics, and cultural and social aspirations.

Towards the end of the nineteenth century, Edmond de Goncourt, one of the most refined of connoisseurs and a major figure in the Parisian art world, could write:

> I have often said that if I were not a man of letters, if I had not got money, my chosen profession would have been to invent interiors for rich people. I should have loved being allowed to have my own way by some banker who would have given me *carte blanche* to work out the decor and furniture of a palace with just four bare walls, using what I could find from dealers, artists, modern industry and in my own head.[2]

This remarkable statement by so great an admirer of old interiors as de Goncourt aptly introduces two of the major themes of this book. First, it implies a great deal about the dramatic rise in status of the decorator, from tradesman to one who meets his clients on terms of equality or even, at times, of unvoiced cultural superiority; and secondly, in outlining the interior decorator's methods as he conceived them, de Goncourt makes one of the first serious suggestions that we should consider decoration in the way that we approach the other arts: examining a room as a work of creativity and 'reading' it in terms of form, style and meaning. Here then is a man of the highest culture recognizing the artistic potential and expressive possibilities of an activity in which many of his contemporaries had failed to take any but the most superficial interest, but which in the next hundred years would come to occupy the attention of some of the finest artists and designers.

As soon as we attempt in this way to describe and analyse the appearance of any room (beyond those aspects which are purely functional) we become aware that aesthetic judgements have been made in the selection and grouping of the elements. If we pursue this examination of decoration on a comparative and historical basis, attempting to decide which examples are characteristic of their period, which are innovative and which are based on precedent, which simply old-fashioned and which created as a self-conscious revival of an older style, we find that any group so considered forms, and can be 'read' as, an episode in the history of taste. It is important however to realize that our own interest in looking at rooms in this way, as the art-historian looks at pictures, itself marks a significant epoch in the evolution of decoration; for our attitudes, formed by the legacies of the past, by the achievements of those who decorated rooms in previous centuries and by the ideals and aspirations of those who lived in them, allow us to recognize and identify with a central tradition of decoration which emerged throughout Europe and in America before the First World War.

The origins of our general attitudes to domestic rooms seem to lie, in Europe at least, much further back, in the seventeenth century. Before that period the medieval knight and his lady had repaired from the bustle of life in the great hall to the relative calm and comfort of the solar, or great chamber, and Renaissance princes had sought some hours of quiet contemplation in the *studiolo*, or small study, as a respite from a still largely ritualistic public life. However, seventeenth-century ideas of comfort and privacy, and the

Contrasts in density in the decoration
and furnishing of rooms

1. The drawing room, Eaton Hall, Cheshire,
   photographed after the refurbishing of 1882, reflecting
   nineteenth-century taste.
   Private collection
2. Dining room of a villa on the French Riviera by Djo
   Bourgeois, late 1920, exemplifying the reductivist
   aesthetic of the Modern movement.
   From Dorothy Todd and Raymond Mortimer,
   The New Interior Decoration, *London, 1929*

2

1

desire for precise visual delineations of status, brought with them firm new notions concerning the appropriateness of design and decoration to particular rooms; ideas which were further codified in the eighteenth century's more rigid definitions of Taste. In the early and mid-eighteenth century a rapidly increasing section of society achieved the means to indulge in schemes of decoration together with the leisure and a sufficient level of 'visual literacy' to enjoy them. In this milieu the 'Rule of Taste' had a strong appeal and those who subscribed to its dictates, such as the followers of English Palladianism, felt that a distinction readily appreciated by their peers was thereby conferred on their houses, and consequently on their persons.

Within this tradition individuality of thought was best expressed by subtle plays on the strict visual codes, and by what in the period was called 'wit': the apt or otherwise clever choice of a classical prototype for a given building project or scheme of decoration. Only later in the century, when the influence of the Grand Tour had declined, 'sensibility' and 'feeling' had emerged as qualities to be admired, and in anticipation of the Romantic movement of the early nineteenth century, would real originality come to be the most highly valued aspect of the creative process.

For many years it was popular to deride the 1830s as a 'débâcle of Taste' and certainly that crucial decade saw the breakdown of the 'Rule of Taste'. However, the various phases in the nineteenth century of the so-called 'battle of the styles' had the essentially liberating effect – sometimes with dire consequences – of making a plurality of styles or tastes possible, and in the great wave of stylistic revivals in the mid-century decorators came to treat the historic repertoire of ornament and decoration as a sort of dressing-up box. In this context 'originality' often consisted in little more than utilizing an obscure rather than a well-known source. An even wider range of styles entered the canons of taste, whilst old furniture and objects and exotic and colourful pieces from the alien cultures of the Orient or the Middle East became much more widely admired and collected, having previously appealed only to a small minority. The Aesthetic craze of the 1870s and 80s required everyone who would be in fashion to adopt the pose based on bohemianism and 'sensitivity' to 'beauty' preached by Oscar Wilde even as far afield as the still dangerous and largely uncivilized Midwest of America during his lecture tour of 1882–3. To be à la mode it was essential to be 'artistic' and preferable to be 'intense'; 'to burn always', as Walter Pater put it, 'with this hard, gem-like flame....'[3]

Finely honed sensibilities and an openness to the 'as-

Clearing away clutter in the 1930s

3. Bedroom of a nineteenth-century house in Highgate, London.
4. The same room remodelled, *c.*1930, by Serge Chermayeff.
   From Duncan Miller, Interior Decoration, *London, 1937*

3

4

sociative' qualities of objects and decorative schemes were the hallmarks of the leaders of fashionable taste in the 1880s and 90s. Des Esseintes, the effeminate, hypersensitive, cultured and aristocratic 'hero' of the French novelist and art critic Joris-Karl Huysmans's *A rebours*,[4] who retires from the world to create extraordinary, rarefied interiors in which to study the effect on his senses not only of furnishings but also of pure colour and scents, is the perfect expression of the decadent ideal. Huysmans, as was well known at the time, drew largely on the figure of Comte Robert de Montesquiou for his characterization of des Esseintes, quoting many of his attitudes and tastes directly, for already by this date de Montesquiou's self-conscious and dandified pose was an admirably complete statement of the rarefied manner in which a man of taste should order his life and his surroundings. Already de Montesquiou was writing curious poems about Empire furniture and about the use of colour, and his pronouncement 'a room is a mood' is perhaps, along with Edmond de Goncourt's thoughts on the creation of interiors, the most crucial for our understanding of the development of decoration and the rise of the interior decorator in the twentieth century.

These notions of style in decoration as a means of making artistic, social or 'mood' statements, and the idea that such statements are governed by the movement of fashion, leads to the oft-debated question of the extent to which interiors of all different kinds are, in any given period, subject to the influence of a *Zeitgeist*, or spirit of the age. Peter Thornton in *Authentic Decor*,[5] his pioneering study of the domestic interior in the seventeenth, eighteenth and nineteenth centuries, has described a quality which he defines elegantly as 'the period eye', which he sees principally as a measure of the degree of emptiness or clutter, or of plainness or embellishment, in interiors which people seem to find pleasing at a particular time. This is undoubtedly an interesting and helpful way of analysing decoration, and indeed long before Thornton suggested such an approach James Laver, who perhaps understood the true workings of fashion better than any other historian or observer, had pointed to the extraordinary affinity that could be discerned between costume and all the other decorative arts in any given decade. In his little volume *Style in Costume*[6] he illustrated his theory, which so neatly complements Thornton's, with the most telling visual comparisons, showing side by side, for example, a late seventeenth-century high-backed chair and a woman of the same date with her hair dressed in a tall and elaborate *fontage:* images which make identical 'stylistic statements'. Nearer our own times, there may well be an intriguing connection between the development of photography and the nineteenth century's ability to cope with a greatly increased density of detail in decoration and the other arts.

Given that interiors can be intended variously to shock or reassure, strike an avant-garde note or underline the establishment values and social position of the owner, or simply be comfortable and pleasing, we must attempt, if we would understand decorating styles, to frame the complex and ever-shifting equation which has as its main variables taste, style, fashion, image and status. It is not a problem which will be easily unravelled, but rather one which must be approached with stealth and, above all, a minute, 'Holmesian' attention to details. Only in this way can we hope fully to understand the surviving appearance of rooms and correctly to interpret what we see in original design drawings and contemporary photographs. In a sense, therefore, the real origins of this attempt to write a history of taste in twentieth-century decoration lie not only in a number of years of researching, visiting extant rooms and sifting other evidence, but most importantly in innumerable conversations with friends and colleagues, discussing this relationship between taste, fashion and style, and defending the proposition that it should always be possible to date any room stylistically – whether it is in a 'modern' (that is intentionally contemporary) idiom or in a deliberately historicized manner, or even if an attempt has been made to restore, conserve or reconstruct a scheme of historic decoration. Furthermore, it should be possible to identify each of the decorative elements that combine to make up a scheme in order to elucidate the true evolution of taste in decoration. Often it should even be possible to date specific furniture arrangements and to detect the introduction of new elements or objects into a room.

In those fortunate cases where pictures exist of the same room at different dates we can deduce a great deal from a careful and minutely detailed comparison of the images, and from asking not only *when* but *with what intention* alterations or new schemes of decoration were carried out. A number of such sequences, including groups of images of the White House and of Malmaison over a period of years, appear in this introductory section, rather than in their strictly chronological position in the body of the book, in order to shed light on this method of thinking about rooms and their decoration.

This book differs intentionally from almost all others which deal with any aspect of the history of taste and the development of design in the twentieth century, in that it is not written from either the overt, or equally importantly the underlying, preconceived view that the history of the century's art, architecture and design is the story of the genesis, emergence and triumph of the Modern movement. In following this particular thread, and insisting that 'Modern' is more than just another style like 'Chinoiserie' or 'Empire', writers from Nikolaus Pevsner onwards have effectively ignored the rich diversity of approach to the arrangement and adornment of rooms in the last eighty years, and denied to the true tradition of decoration the serious study it deserves.

To write about and illustrate so much decoration that is 'period', and so many rooms that deliberately play with the styles, furniture and other objects of the past, may still seem to many to require an apologia. The material which appears in these pages has for the most part been gathered from contemporary sources, to show characteristic examples of rooms which people found interesting in each period and, further, to try to reflect with some accuracy the proportion of modern or traditional elements which the real leaders of fashion chose to incorporate in their schemes. By this definition, therefore, a room decorated in the Empire revival style or 'Vogue Regency' manner in the 1920s was as fashionable as one of the same date showing the influence of the Bauhaus, and more 'up-to-date', by the standards of the time, than a modernistic scheme in the Omega Workshop aesthetic.

In defining avant-garde taste in this way – as the prevailing predilections and stylistic enthusiasms of the actual 'movers and shakers of society', of the more design-conscious artists and connoisseurs and of the emergent interior decorators – it is crucial to keep uppermost in the mind those factors which people themselves thought important in the creation of successful rooms in any given period. In the attempt accurately to assess this the reminiscences of a great many decorators have proved invaluable; but also, in discussion of the subject with all sorts of people whose interest has been engaged in any way or at any time by the whole business of creating rooms, it has proved fascinating and helpful to see the way in which the concerns of each period reveal themselves in the terms of description that we use. Thus when one asks about any decorator of the earlier part of the century, one is almost inevitably told that he or she 'had great taste'. Decorators of the 20s are most often characterized as having 'wonderful colour sense', which reveals a great deal about the preoccupations of that decade with colour effects, whilst the lady decorators of the sleek and monochromatic 30s seem always to attract the

Six views of the Green Room or Parlor in the White House, Washington DC, showing its changing appearance between 1865 and 1904

5. *c*.1865: with a late 'neo-classical' wall treatment and elaborate mid-nineteenth-century furniture.
6. Late 1880s: with darker, denser wallpaper and elaborate Aesthetic and sub-Renaissance furnishings. The carpet has an all-over pattern and the mantel is draped and fringed.
7. *c*.1890: the same decorative scheme but with more comfortable upholstered armchairs and sofas. Several fashionable objects such as a Japanese screen and a lamp with a fussy shade have been introduced.

6

5

7

8. 1898: a new wall treatment of sub-rococo panels has replaced the wallpaper. The screen has gone but large oriental vases on the mantel retain a *fin-de-siècle* opulence.

9. 1903: the whole appearance of the room recast by McKim, Mead & White in a grand Federal period style. A fine carved mantel replaces the ugly mid-nineteenth-century one, a crystal chandelier is substituted for the gasolier and the walls are hung with early portraits. The parquet floor is revealed and only the bearskin rug hints at Stanford White's opulence of taste.

10. 1904: the transformation to Federal period French taste is completed with the introduction of a restrained carpet and the upgrading of the furniture. The vases still remain but the only other piece not in character is the firescreen, presumably allowed to stay because of its eagle motif.

5–10 Library of Congress, Washington DC

9

10

epithet 'chic'. In the inter-war years a great many decorators are best remembered for their 'tremendous knowledge of historic style', the area of expertise which they were most often allowed to exercise, but at the same time a number of the presumably rather second-rank figures are written down as merely having had 'flair'. After the Second World War, with materials in very short supply, decorators like John Fowler were often praised for their 'ingenuity', for 'inventiveness' and, perhaps most significantly in an era of shortages, for being 'so clever at finding things'.

The main term of approbation for the designers of the post-war period, from Milan to Stockholm and from Festival of Britain London or 'New Look' Paris to New Deal America, was 'innovative'. For the 60s 'bold' seems a favourite word, at least for the early part of the decade, whereas towards the end, with the rise of a number of the famous antique dealer-decorators, highest praise went to those who 'had a good eye'. More recently we have tended to admire decorators for their 'sensitivity' and for their 'architectural approach', which aptly reflects the concerns of a newly conservation-conscious generation. Today's obsessions seem to be with 'style' and more especially with an abstract notion of what constitutes 'design'. Such period descriptions are important evidence in an area in which watertight definitions are difficult.

Obviously it is not enough merely to name the period styles which followed one another into vogue in quick succession through the century. These evolutions of fashion constitute one of the most significant strands in the history of taste: in identifying them in all their subtle variations and in setting dates on their periods of waxing and waning it has been my aim to make them the subject of an analysis on the model of, and as serious as, that which we have come to accord to nineteenth-century historicism – the period which we more automatically understand by the phrase 'the age of revivals'. Thus in looking at any of these twentieth-century fashions, such as in England the Edwardian fascination with the furnishings of the late eighteenth-century 'age of satinwood', or in France the 1930s revival of interest in the Charles X period, it is essential to hold several questions in the mind simultaneously: we need to ask just what is being copied, and why, and at the same time how accurately the original is being used or how freely and imaginatively it has been interpreted.

No historian has ever managed to treat the problem of identifying or defining styles with the felicity of the late Osbert Lancaster, the English satirist and stage designer who, in his delightful line drawings with their lucid accompanying paragraphs in *Pillar to Post*[7] and *Homes, Sweet Homes*[8], created (with a little help from his friend and fellow enthusiast the poet Sir John Betjeman) a wonderfully useful and expressive vocabulary of terms for many of the period revival styles, such as 'Stockbrokers' Tudor' and 'Curzon Street Baroque'. Many of these terms entered the language of architectural criticism, and most will never be bettered by design historians who lack an eye for the humorous or ironical aspects of their subject.

Such problems of definition are in a sense an artificial overlay created by our own art-historical methodologies for looking at the evolution of style, for in earlier times the quality of materials and workmanship or the sheer richness of effect were more frequently the criteria for judging the decoration of rooms. As early as 1881, however, Mary Eliza Haweis, an intelligent and often quirkily amusing observer of the world of design, could make a joke at the expense of those outside the charmed circle of London aesthetes who were so philistine as to be unable to identify historic styles correctly. Writing in *The Art of Decoration*,[9] her manual addressed to the woman of taste engaged in the beautifying of her home, she described how 'only the other day I was shown a French mirror (Louis XIV) by some really cultivated folks as "Queen Anne – Empire, you know – genuine Chippendale".' The problem was, she explained, that 'what people call Queen Anne fashions, with charming indifference to the trammels of dates, are the fashions of the three Georges, Marie-Antoinette ... and especially everything which came in during the Empire....' The English designer and architect William Burges, too, could not resist suggesting that in the hands of architects less devoted to the high calling of the one true Gothic style and in the rooms of the wives of successful businessmen, the words 'Queen Anne style' had come to mean almost anything anyone wanted them to mean. Ironically, there are to this day discrepancies between the accepted meanings (in terms of decoration) of 'Queen Anne' or 'Empire' in England and America.

Many informed observers who deplored what appeared to be the débâcle of taste in furnishing and decoration and the inexorable slide into meaningless historicism in the latter half of the nineteenth century laid the blame at the door of the old-fashioned firms of upholsterer-decorators. Charles Eastlake, an influential commentator and another protagonist of the reformed Gothic style in the late 1860s and 70s, who was widely read and followed on both sides of the Atlantic, spoke out strongly against this bad, unthinking historicism so prevalent in his day, claiming 'I

11

Two views of the entrance hall of the White House, Washington DC, showing the remodelling in the classical taste by McKim, Mead & White

11. The hall in the late nineteenth century with the screen in stained and leaded glass by Louis Comfort Tiffany.
12. The hall, *c.*1903, with the new colonnade and austere classical detailing in the French style.
  11,12 Library of Congress, Washington DC

13610—Remodeled Corridor in the White House, Washington, D. C., U. S. A.

12

Three successive views of Elsie de Wolfe's dining room in the Washington Irving House, East 17th Street, and a view of the dining room of her East 55th Street house, both in New York

13. The dining room in Elsie's 'unreformed' taste, c.1896.

14. c.1898: first steps in introducing the 'Old French look'. The wallpaper remains but the woodwork is lightened to a pale grey. The overmantel is now a more austere arrangement of square panes and a French bust has pride of place. The late nineteenth-century gasolier has been eliminated in favour of dining by candlelight reflected in mirror panels around the room. The ugly table has been kept, but the tablecloth is protected by a sheet of glass, which was thought chic at the time. The chairs are French and prettily painted.

13

14

15

15. *c*.1903. Several new sophistications have been introduced. The panels around the doors have been mirrored, which gives an interesting spatial effect, and a refined French white marble chimneypiece replaces the original heavy grey mantel typical of New York bourgeois taste. The sideboard has gone, but little console tables have been placed under the mirror panels.

16. The dining room transplanted to the East 55th Street house, *c*.1911. Here the effect is much more convincingly French because of the well-proportioned panelling and the even more simplified arrangement of favourite pieces. The well-placed wall clock and new chairs reveal Elsie's increasingly good eye for French objects. The decorative panels are by Monnoyer.

13,14 Photographs by Byron, the Byron Collection, Museum of the City of New York

15,16 From Elsie de Wolfe, The House in Good Taste, *New York, 1913*

16

Changing attitudes to the Empire period at the château of Malmaison, near Paris

17. Princess Hortense's bedroom, the only room to survive untouched from the early nineteenth century, photographed before 1920.
18. *Salon de réception*, redecorated and furnished to a mid-nineteenth-century density by the Empress Eugénie, wife of Napoleon III.
19. The Empress Josephine's bedchamber as redecorated to the orders of Eugénie, 'a clever and felicitous reconstitution' made in 1867, using rich and heavy mid-nineteenth-century textiles to realize the original scheme by Percier and Fontaine which had never been completed.
20. Josephine's bedchamber as restored in recent years with the emphasis on correct detail and placing of furnishings.

19

21. '*Chambre de Napoléon*', a room invented by the curator Jean Bourguignon, and decorated in his version of the domestic Empire style, *c*.1920, to house a group of Napoleonic relics originally unconnected with Malmaison.

22. Bedroom furnished by Jean Bourguignon using fabrics and furnishings by Jacob from the First Consul's bedchamber at the Tuileries Palace, *c*.1920.

23. The same 'Tuileries' bedchamber with historical corrections and additions, *c*.1935.

24. The 'Tuileries' bedchamber today, with restoration and reconstruction of period draperies carried out in the 1970s.

    17,18,19,21,22 *From Jean Bourguignon*, Malmaison, *Paris, n.d.*
    20,24 *Clichés des Musées Nationaux, Paris*
    23 *Private collection*

22

21

23

24

25

'A weakness for furnishings of the Empire period': two views of the anteroom in the Rome apartment of the writer and collector Mario Praz, showing the results of twenty years of acquisition

25. The anteroom, c.1936, as illustrated in *Decoration*.
26. The same room, c.1958, from Professor Praz's autobiography, *La Casa della Vita* (The House of Life), Milan, 1958.

26

have never met with a class of men who were so hopelessly confirmed in artistic error as ordinary decorators.'[10] Against this slowly rising tide of dissatisfaction with the traditional ideas and methods of the trade we can begin to chart the emergence of the new interior decorators.

One of the greatest strengths of the interior decoration of this century has been the freedom it has claimed to be innovative as well as to copy, to play with styles rather than imitate them in a pedantic or slavish manner, and to mix together the old and the new. This attitude was not entirely novel. Oscar Wilde, a key figure in the development of the new aesthetic sensibility, in his essay 'Pen, Pencil and Poison'[11] of 1891 correctly discerned an early and eloquent statement of the notion that 'All beautiful things belong to the same age' in the writings of the Regency painter and art critic (and, in the latter unhappy phase of his life, poisoner), Thomas Griffiths Wainewright. Wilde, who easily ignored his transportation following convictions for fraud and poisoning, was certainly influenced in his thinking by Wainewright's writings on aesthetics. This decayed dandy and aesthete should be considered today as a formative figure in the development of modern sensibilities.

Artists seem always to have played a key role in extending the boundaries of taste. In the later decades of the nineteenth century many arranged not only interesting but also visually highly effective interiors, which disproved the current theory that there was something inherently vulgar or 'tasteless' about a disparity in the styles, dates and origins of the objects and furnishings in any single room, or between the decorative treatments of adjoining apartments. Indeed, many of the finest, most pleasing and more memorable schemes of decoration created since the turn of the century have been in an eclectic style; a style unfettered by the unwelcome constraints of historicism and one which, as Cecil Beaton put it, writing particularly of the 30s, avoids both 'the Scylla of antiques and the Charybdis of an operating room sterility'.[12]

The best rooms in truly eclectic taste, such as those created in their London house in the 20s by the writers Osbert and Sacheverell Sitwell, are among the most important in terms of the stylistic development of the century, and lie at the heart of the emergent tradition of decoration (pls 255, 256). They are utterly 'original' and it is perhaps significant that the Sitwells' decoration and arrangement of their rooms with eighteenth-century shell grotto chairs, Poiret lampshades and contemporary paintings by the Vorticist Wyndham Lewis juxtaposed with blackened canvases by the then all-but-forgotten late Baroque painter Alessandro Magnasco, can only adequately be described as 'Sitwell taste'. Although amateurs, the brothers had proved themselves in their creation of rooms, as in their other varied artistic activities, to be masters of the manipulation of a 'look', essentially stylists and, because of their high public profile, taste-makers.

The best twentieth-century interior decorators have been creative artists in a way that the great nineteenth-century upholsterers were not. Firms such as Trollope's of Belgravia and Waring & Gillow in London, or Alavoine in Paris and New York, prided themselves on their capacity to decorate in any style from 'Tudor' to 'Georgian', from Pompeiian to Turkish, or in 'tous les Louis', guaranteeing the 'tastefulness' and especially the quality of their work. They also undertook maintenance work, as they were able to employ a large permanent workforce of builders, carpenters, plumbers and painters as well as upholsterers. The small exclusive firms which first began to come to the fore in the years before the First World War, such as Lady Sackville's Spealls and the Hon. Mrs Guy Bethell's Elden Ltd in London or Paul Poiret's Atelier Martine in Paris, traded on the fact that they identified a name with an individual style; they would have been most unlikely ever to have been able to produce any of their wares in large quantities and certainly would not have been capable of providing a plumber.

The origins of these firms seem to be contemporary with, and their rise parallel to, that of *haute couture* in dress, for they retailed an image which was individual not to the client but rather to the designer, like a work of art. Their immediate antecedent in England must be the firm founded by William Morris, Morris, Marshall, Faulkner and Co., which started trading in 1861 with a title that included the magic words Fine Art.[13] They were without doubt one of the first firms to exploit the distinction between 'artistic' and conventional decoration, playing on the equation between 'Art' and 'Taste', as opposed to commerce, which has always proved so useful to decorators. Morris & Co.'s customers included most notably many of the members of 'The Souls', a group of young and highly cultivated aristocrats who adopted a pose of self-conscious and uncompromising artistic sensibility. Their ideas and attitudes form an important link between the predilections of the Aesthetic movement of the late nineteenth century and 'Taste' as expressed in the ideals of the smart interior decoration of the new century, for they and their children, as members of the avant-garde, became the first crucial patrons of the new decorators. It is perhaps the relationship

27

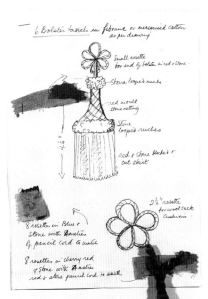

28

An early decorator's showroom

27. A room in the London premises of Essex & Co., *c.*1897. The furnishings on display are in an Arts and Crafts style. There are large samples of various wallpapers pinned up for examination, whilst open on the table lies a pattern book. On the walls, in the frieze and in the soffit of the archway to the right can be seen further examples and, most intriguingly, the ceiling has been divided into panels showing a variety of relief finishes. *Royal Commission on the Historical Monuments of England*

Decorative detail

28. Design for a tassel by Imogen Taylor of Colefax & Fowler, 1986. *Victoria & Albert Museum, London*

between this new breed, many of whom were for the first time career women, and their visually and socially aware clientele which lies at the heart of decoration as we now understand it.

From the beginning of our period, and more than ever today, the concept of decoration as a branch of fashion is a key one. The idea of a powerful avant-garde who formulate attitudes, create styles and rule upon taste is as important in the sphere of decoration as in couture, and just as in the world of fashion a look appears, is accepted, admired, disseminated and finally devalued by a host of imitators, so too ideas in decoration move down-market after their initial success.

From a little before the turn of the century, when photographers began to be able to cope more easily with the technical problems of recording rooms, photography has played a major role in influencing the development of room treatments and decorative schemes of all kinds. By the 1930s some rooms, such as Syrie Maugham's, were clearly decorated to look good when photographed for publication, and magazines devoted to the subject have steadily gained in both popularity and real influence since that date. Today we have reached the point where it is hardly too much to say that the major 'glossy' journals have become the true arena in which many of the aesthetic battles of our generation are fought.

Style will perhaps always remain very difficult to define and to attribute because it is so seldom the unequivocal creation of a single figure: witness the seemingly simultaneous 'invention' of all-white schemes by Syrie Maugham and Elsie de Wolfe in the early 30s. Style develops out of the constant interchange of ideas between influential groups of friends, colleagues, acquaintances and, indeed, rivals – artists and craftsmen, scholars, collectors and dealers, fashion designers and architects. The decorator is a vital part of this group and it is he or she who, at the crucial stage, identifies a style and retails it to a fashion-conscious public. In the last few years the level of interest in the decoration of houses has risen to a phenomenal level and the decorator's position has finally been established, not just as the purveyor of chic, but as the arbiter of taste in what has become, in the twentieth century, the only art to be practised universally: the arrangement and adornment of the spaces in which we live.

1. Edith Wharton and Ogden Codman Jr, *The Decoration of Houses*, New York, 1897. Reprinted with introductory notes by John Barrington Bayley and William A. Coles, New York, 1978
2. Quoted in J. Cornforth, *The Inspiration of the Past*, London, 1985
3. W. Pater, *Studies in the History of the Renaissance*, London, 1873
4. J.-K. Huysmans, *A Rebours*, Paris, 1884. *A Rebours* appeared in English first in 1922 as *Against the Grain*, but the best translation is that by Robert Baldick, *Against Nature*, Penguin Classics, 1959 and later editions.
5. P. Thornton, *Authentic Decor: The Domestic Interior 1620–1920*, London, 1984
6. J. Laver, *Style in Costume*, London, 1947
7. O. Lancaster, *Pillar to Post*, London, 1938
8. O. Lancaster, *Homes Sweet Homes*, London, 1939
9. M.E. Haweis, *The Art of Decoration*, London, 1881. Mrs Haweis's other publications included *The Art of Beauty*, 1878, *The Art of Dress*, 1879 and *Beautiful Houses*, 1882.
10. C. Eastlake, *Hints on Household Taste*, London, 1868
11. O. Wilde, 'Pen, Pencil and Poison' in *Intentions*, London, 1891
12. C. Beaton, *The Glass of Fashion*, London, 1954
13. The original title of 'The Firm' was Morris, Marshall, Faulkner & Co., Fine Art Workmen in Painting, Carving, Furniture and the Metals. In later years this was shortened to Morris & Co.

Before 1900
THE LEGACIES OF THE PAST

In the years around 1900 throughout Europe and in America it is fair to say that the great majority of really interesting rooms were the creation of artists and collectors; most other rooms which reached any serious level of ordered elegance and distinction came into being as the result of architects taking an interest in the work of fitting out and decoration, or at times fighting for their ideas after the structural work had been completed. Artists, by creating their own environments in their studios almost as extensions of their pictorial preoccupations with spatial and colour arrangements, not only made novel or suggestive groupings of quirky objects, but also introduced an important element of stage-set fantasy into the decoration of everyday rooms.

The classic artist's studio, filled with such 'studio props' as pieces of armour, old carvings and scraps of rich textile, has a long history stretching back to the days of Rubens and indirectly to the princely 'cabinets of curiosities' of the late sixteenth and early seventeenth centuries. For nineteenth-century painters whose work was concerned with the re-creation of the past in the form of elaborate costume pieces this sort of treasure house setting was entirely appropriate. Those of which contemporary records survive, such as Olana (pl. 30) on the Hudson River in upstate New York, or the house and studio of Lord Leighton, the 'Prince of Aesthetes', in Holland Park, London, reveal just how rich and successful such interiors could be. As late as the turn of the century this deliberately overblown style was still considered fashionable. The artist Alphonse Mucha, who furnished his Paris studio (pl. 45) in rue Val de Grâce the moment his posters for Sarah Bernhardt brought him sudden prosperity, did so in an opulent manner remarkably similar to that of the rich and successful painters of the previous generation, such as Rudolf von Alt and Hans Makart in Vienna, where he had worked as a theatrical painter from 1879 to 1884.

It is in the circles of the more self-consciously aesthetic painters that a distinct new spirit in the creation of room settings begins to become apparent. A key figure is the American painter James McNeill Whistler, whose friendships (and, almost equally important, whose animosities) link the Pre-Raphaelite worlds of Ruskin and Rossetti to those of the Impressionists in Paris and to the *fin-de-siècle* London of Aubrey Beardsley and Oscar Wilde. Whistler's own London studio-house in Tite Street, designed by E.W. Godwin in 1877, was a landmark in the development of a new domestic architecture, and we know from contemporary descriptions that the interiors of that house and others with which Whistler was associated, including his 'Peacock Room' for the London mansion of the collector Frederick Leyland earlier in the decade, created a considerable sensation. The English aesthete and illustrator Charles Ricketts, who took over the lease of Whistler's other house in The Vale, Chelsea, recalled how 'the Master' had carried the subtle and sometimes surprising harmonies of his 'arrangements in colour' into his decorative schemes, distempering the walls in interesting greens and the brilliant yellow which so impressed Oscar Wilde on a later visit, and which he enthusiastically described to Ricketts as 'the colour of joy'.[1]

The influence of Huysmans's novel, *A Rebours*, the 'breviary of decadence' as it was called by its devotees, brought about a number of interiors in France and England from which the colours of joy were conspicuously absent. Characteristic of these rooms was Beardsley's drawing room (which was also the room in which he did his drawings) in his house in Pimlico. Intended to be seen only at night and lit by candles in a pair of massive Empire ormolu candlesticks, the walls were painted orange and the woodwork enamelled in a deep indigo blue; a scheme taken directly from Huysmans's description of a room in des Esseintes's retreat. Beardsley hung the walls with his rare

Mantegna engravings and with some of the more beautiful Japanese erotic prints from his collection of *curiosa*, thus creating a scheme which was intriguing for its deliberate perversity and intention to shock the casual visitor, but more especially for its completeness as an expression of highly individualistic taste and its evocation of 'mood'. Although no image of this room is known to survive, something of the studied preciousness of Beardsley's concern for rooms can be seen in the photograph of him in the room in the hotel in Menton which he 'decorated' and in which he died in 1898 (pl. 34).

On a more accessible level, the fashionable and 'artistic' rather than bourgeois interiors of the period tend to reflect the current preoccupations of architects and designers with the various national forms of Art Nouveau. In England the influence of Morris continued to dominate the world of the Arts and Crafts, leading even those who were well aware of Continental developments to adopt a rather gentle, low-key version of Art Nouveau. Extreme or exaggerated forms tended to be avoided, and in this context it is highly significant that a powerful lobby of designers and art-educationalists succeeded, shortly after the turn of the century, in having a major group of pieces of Continental decorative furniture effectively removed from public exhibition at the South Kensington Museum (now the Victoria & Albert) as a 'pernicious' influence.

In France the scene was dominated by the taste of the entrepreneur Samuel Bing who, by appropriating the name 'L'Art Nouveau' for his shop at the very moment when it was becoming more widely used as a convenient tag for the style, assured himself of both a reputation as a new Maecenas and a considerable fortune, much of which he laid out in commissions to promising young artists, decorators and furniture designers. In Bing's lavish galleries, which opened in 1895, each of the rooms was arranged as a complete setting by an individual designer or displayed items brought together with a sure eye by the proprietor. Artists of real versatility such as Georges de Feure sprang to prominence through the encouragement of Bing, and it is clear that his attitudes did much to promote the notion that designers of interiors should give their attention to doorhandles and even knives and forks as well as to cornices and curtains. Such ideas were not exactly unknown to the French, who needed only to look to the perfection of *dix-huitième* room settings to see the virtue of such an approach, but a note was struck which found sympathetic echoes in the English Arts and Crafts and in the nascent design movements not only in Germany and

Austria but also in the United States.

In stark contrast to the florid, 'whiplash', curvilinear excesses of French Art Nouveau, German and Austrian designers cultivated a more austere and essentially recti-linear aesthetic, balancing smaller areas of rich or intricate patterns with larger areas of plain surface. There remains, however, in spite of these national characteristics, an extraordinary similarity in feel to the designs of artists and architects working throughout Europe, from Barcelona to Brussels, from Glasgow to Munich, and as far away as Hungary or the Balkans. Comparisons of the work of designers with backgrounds and training as disparate as Antonio Gaudí, Victor Horta and the Munich architect August Endell reveal an astonishing degree of sympathy in aims, and a noticeably parallel development in the rejection of accepted forms for building and decoration and in the substitution of a new order of un-historical ornament applied to novel structures which often utilized new materials (pls 47–9).

It is a characteristic of the Art Nouveau style (known in Germany as Jugendstil and in Italy as Stile Liberty, reflecting the famous London store Liberty & Co.'s position of influence which was similar to that of Bing's), that whilst it was the most written about, illustrated and discussed style, in its pure form it was to be found in only a small proportion of the houses of those who could afford to indulge their tastes in new decorative schemes or in the commissioning of *objets d'art*. In Europe the great majority of households of the well-to-do, the comfortable established bourgeoisie or the *nouveaux riches* were furnished in a dense, dark and, for the most part, unappealing style based heavily on badly digested historical prototypes, which had been adapted to the mechanical manufacturing processes developed in the nineteenth century and disseminated through an unenlightened trade.

In England, the nature of society dictated that the old family house, which had naturally been furnished in the past in then up-to-date styles, was the smartest thing. Society hostesses held court in those great town houses which survived and, in the country, in rooms which contained the fruits of perhaps a century and a half of acquisition. The gradual process whereby movement in such rooms came to be impeded by ever increasing numbers of chairs and plump ottomans arranged 'for conversation' in part merely reflected social conventions, but it was closely paralleled by the accumulation of more and more bibelots: often worthless things or sentimental trinkets which came in due course to cover every available surface and to fill glass-fronted cabinets provided to protect them from dust (and perhaps from dusting). The private apartments of the Prince and Princess of Wales (later King Edward VII and Queen Alexandra) represented the high point of this eclectic, or rather accretive, style of decoration and had a wide influence not only in the royal couple's immediate circle, the 'Marlborough House Set', but throughout upper and middle-class life in England (pl. 29).

In France, where similarly crowded rooms became the norm among the bourgeoisie, it has been convincingly argued that the appearance of such rooms reflected not just a desire for density but also a new social phenomenon: the emergence during the second half of the nineteenth century of women as a distinct 'consumer group', with the leisure time to visit the great Parisian shopping arcades and stores and the means to indulge their whims in purchases. The consequent craze for objects which were considered to make the home not only 'beautiful' but also 'artistic' was aptly called by contemporaries 'Bric-à-brac-o-mania'.

At a more exalted level, the nineteenth century as the age of revivals brought with it new attitudes to the past and to the art objects and artefacts which remained as testimonies of past styles. The collecting of what began more generally to be called 'antiques', which had previously been the preserve of the scholarly antiquarian, became increasingly widespread, and we begin to recognize in England, and especially in America towards the end of the century, the origins of many of our own attitudes to historic houses and their furnishing. Already by this date the great tide in the movement of art objects, which had eddied from Italy across France and to England in the eighteenth and earlier nineteenth centuries, was beginning to flow strongly towards the United States, with the result that the placing of major works in new domestic contexts began seriously to affect the arrangement and the decoration of all sorts of houses. The very rich industrialist-collectors of America, men such as J. Pierpont Morgan, were seen, according to

the standpoint of the observer, either as great merchant princes on the Renaissance pattern or as robber barons. They were, by and large, uninhibited by social anxieties about the opulent appearance of their new palaces (pl. 81), and were happy to build on a vast scale, utilizing the finest available materials. They developed a particular love for first-rate European pictures and furniture, the panelling of whole rooms and objects of known and distinguished provenance.

On a scale far removed from the great Newport mansions, which the designer and theorist T.H. Robsjohn-Gibbings would later satirize as resembling 'Grand Central Station with tapestries', many of those who considered themselves visually aware were looking with a new understanding at old European houses and to American houses which survived from the Colonial or Federal periods. Such houses with their furnishings, where they too survived, were published in some of the earliest photographic surveys. In their simplicity they began to influence designers and decorators towards a clearer, more rational and above all a more architectural approach to the arrangement and decoration of houses. Echoes of this can be seen in the interiors of architects such as Richard Norman Shaw, Edwin Lutyens and others working in England in what has been called the 'Wrenaissance' style: a freely adapted classicism based on the ideals of Palladio but with the injection from time to time of a dash of bolder (but still basically English) baroque feeling in the handling of space and ornamental detail. On the Continent, where simplification would eventually be taken to its logical conclusion in the reductive architecture of Adolf Loos, there are nevertheless parallels. It is in this new architectural ideal that the origins of the finest twentieth-century decoration lie.

1. For Wilde's visit to The Vale see W. Rothenstein, *Men and Memories, Recollections of W.R., 1872–1900*, London, 1931, and S. Calloway, '*Tout pour l'Art*, Ricketts and Shannon and the arranging of a collection' in *Journal of the Decorative Arts Society*, 8, 1984

29

Royal opulence and clutter c.1890

The Prince of Wales's study, Marlborough House, London

The increasing richness and rather overpowering splendour of the principal entertaining rooms of the grander English houses was a phenomenon felt in both town and country. For many the beau idéal for the decoration of a great London house as a setting for the social season was Marlborough House, as it had been arranged and decorated for the Prince of Wales, later Edward VII, and his consort Alexandra. In general walls were hung with rich silks and paintwork was picked out with gilding. Lighting was supplied by a profusion of shaded candles, often in multi-branched candelabra or the very popular vases with gilded flowers and foliage containing sconces. Even these elaborate forms of fitting were frequently converted to electricity, which began to be a factor in the night-time appearance of rooms at this time. Lavishness of lighting may well have been associated in the minds of many with opulence, just as Sir Walter Scott had burned prodigious numbers of the then novel domestic gas lamps at Abbotsford in the 1820s and as Norman Hartnell would do at Lovel Dene in the 1950s, electrifying Regency chandeliers and keeping them blazing with light even during the day. At Belvoir Castle, where the dining and drawing rooms were among the first in an English country house to be lit by electricity, it was said that the Duchess of Rutland experienced increasing difficulty in finding guests who were willing to subject themselves to the tiring, and worse, unflattering glare. Other characteristic elements of the Marlborough House style were the extraordinarily muddled groupings of often unmatching chairs and other pieces in gilt, painted or polished wood and, as can be seen in this photograph, lavish displays of lilies, orchids, camellias and other hothouse-cultivated blooms. In this photograph of the Prince of Wales's study his desk can be seen cluttered, as his mother Queen Victoria's had been, with a multitude of silver-framed photographs.

Reproduced by gracious permission of H.M. The Queen

29

30

31

West Coast grandeur mid-1890s

Back parlour of the George Gray house, Stockton, California

The tendency towards a heavy and stifling opulence in the decoration of American rooms had been viewed with misgiving by observers and writers such as Edgar Allan Poe as early as the 1840s, but the trend continued with some regional variations as the century progressed. This parlour in a West Coast provincial house of some pretension to grandeur reveals the way in which the rooms of the 1880s and 90s continued to reflect the styles popular at the time of the Civil War. The draperies of such schemes had continued to increase in luxuriousness and complexity however,and, whilst the furniture may be simpler than the celebrated excesses of carving carried out by the mid-nineteenth-century manufacturer John Henry Belter, the individual pieces are still elaborately ornamented. They are grouped in dense and usually unmatching arrangements, supported by a great many decorative and ornamental objects, which might include, as here, pieces of sculpture in niches or on pedestals and groups of vases and other china.

The Haggin Museum, Stockton, California

30

An aesthete's palace on the Hudson River 1880s

The court hall at Olana, New York State

Olana, built by the painter Frederick Church, remains one of the most celebrated 'palaces of art' created during the Aesthetic period, and makes a fascinating parallel with the London house of Lord Leighton, the 'Prince of Aesthetes' – although sadly no direct link has yet been established between the two painters. Church, as a luminary of the Hudson River School, chose a fine setting for his house and commissioned the architects Calvert Vaux and F.C. Withers, who began work in 1870. He amassed a rich collection of objects, which included eastern and oriental pieces, and it is this profusion of pretty and desirable things as much as the inherent opulence of the architecture which gives the house its distinctive character and appeal.

New York State Office of Parks, Recreation and Historic Preservation, Olana State Historic Site, Taconic Region

31

32

32

All for Art c.1888

Charles Shannon in his studio at Edith Terrace, Chelsea; photograph from the artist's own albums

Charles Ricketts and Charles Shannon, artists, collectors and celebrated aesthetes, met as students of wood engraving in the 1880s and lived together for nearly fifty years, arranging their extraordinary collection of paintings, drawings and antiquities with fastidious care in a sequence of self-consciously 'artistic' rooms. The studio they took in 1887 marked a turning-point in their awareness of the way in which objects of all dates and styles could be grouped together; the unifying factor being that each had been chosen with a view to its intrinsic merit, its beauty of form or simply its colour. In the Edith Terrace studio there is still a strong feeling of the Aesthetic movement. The walls are covered with an embossed paper imitating stamped leather, much favoured in schemes of the kind that the movement referred to by the generic name of 'Art Furnishing', and on this background are grouped Japanese prints and a number of pieces of richly worked textile. The furnishings are still very modest and, with the exception of what appears to be a pretty lacquer cabinet standing on a small eighteenth-century table, would all have been considered at the time to be merely second-hand rather than antique. The total effect, however, is charming, 'Bohemian' and clearly intended to reflect as far as possible the grand and opulent style of the studios of successful artists such as Lord Leighton in England or the Viennese painters Rudolf von Alt and Hans Makart.

33

Against Nature 1880s–90s

Les Recherches de M. Huysmans; *drawing by Philippe Jullian, from* Les Styles, *Paris, 1962*

Huysmans's novel *A Rebours*, published in the year 1884, finally severed his connections with Zola and the realists. Widely hailed as a masterpiece, *A Rebours* came to be known as 'The Breviary of Decadence', and the perverse tastes of the anti-heroical central character des Esseintes were much emulated by would-be decadents. In this pastiche Philippe Jullian has drawn together a number of the elements in the descriptions of the decoration of the fictional Château de Lourps, concentrating on the room

33

bizarrely decorated with church furnishings, which comes across to the imaginative reader as a cross between the rooms of Alexandre du Sommerard, whose collection of medieval and Renaissance objects formed the nucleus of the Musée de Cluny in Paris, and an opium den. The des Esseintes pose of langour and extreme artificiality affected the whole generation of the 1890s in France and in England, where Oscar Wilde, Aubrey Beardsley and others were influenced in their personal style and, in the case of Beardsley, in the actual decoration of his rooms. Huysmans himself lived in comparatively modest and unexceptional surroundings and died bearing the agony of a cancer of the throat with great fortitude.

Courtesy of Comte Ghislain de Diesbach and Editions Plon, Paris

34
Fin de siècle 1898

Aubrey Beardsley in the hotel room in which he died in 1898, Menton, France; photograph by M. Abel from Under the Hill and other Essays in Prose and Verse *by Aubrey Beardsley, London, 1904*

This room in which Beardsley, the most brilliant illustrator of the 90s, and the 'Fra Angelico of Satanism', died in Menton on the Riviera, where he had retired in order to try to fight the consumption which he knew was killing him, represents his last attempt to impose his studied decadence upon the comfortably complacent taste of the day. In a room decorated with the nightmare-inducing relish of all French hotel-keepers for pattern-on-pattern, Beardsley created a corner haven in which he could read and, at the ever-diminishing times when he felt strong enough, draw. Here on the little writing table were placed his crucifix and the pair of Empire ormolu candlesticks by the light of which he had become accustomed to write or draw. To the right stood a bookcase containing his books: for the most part editions of eighteenth-century French novels, together with a few devotional works given to him by his Catholic convert friends such as André Raffalovich. The wall above was decorated with Beardsley's collection of engravings by Mantegna and his circle. The prints, which even at that time were beginning to become quite highly prized, were pinned up with a border of black ribbon, a method of display which can also be seen in the photograph of Charles Shannon's studio. Beardsley's ideas

34

about decoration were always original. His schemes were influenced by his reading of French books and by his love of Japanese art. Sadly no image survives of his rooms in Cambridge Street, Pimlico, London, but it is recorded that he based the decoration of the drawing room, which had indigo woodwork and erotic Japanese prints hanging against sharp orange walls, on the description by Huysmans of the fictional apartments of his anti-hero, the decadent des Esseintes, in his novel *A Rebours*.

Private collection

35

35
Mrs Wharton's mother's parlour c.1885

The Jones House, West 25th Street, New York

This view shows the interconnecting sitting and drawing rooms in the house of Edith Wharton's mother, Mrs George Frederic Jones, at West 25th Street in New York, an address which would have been considered a very good one a generation previously, but which by 1885 was somewhat less than smart. Mrs Jones's decoration was none the less in a reasonably up-to-the-minute version of the opulent 'French look' popular in the city. With its co-ordinated wall covering, draperies, heavily fringed armchairs and banquettes it remains a quintessential example of upholsterers' decoration. Yet in the absence of too many discordant notes or too great a clutter of small objects – the two besetting problems of most arrangements of the day – we can perhaps discern a gentle influence towards that more 'comely sobriety' in furnishings of which the future novelist was to become so eloquent an advocate. In this room the elaborate draping of the opening is very typical of the commercialized Aesthetic taste of the period in its lavish swags and tails edged with bobble-fringing. Above the opening, however, is an interesting narrow panel which seems to have as its central motif, visible to the left of the handsome French chandelier, a little cartouche with the Bourbon fleur-de-lis. Also noteworthy are the vase-shaped oil lamp with an elaborate pleated shade, of the kind which in later years was to be used as the model for early electric table lamps, and, on the polished wood floor, a mounted fur rug. It is recorded that Edith Wharton was married in this room.

Beinecke Library, Yale University (Edith Wharton Papers)

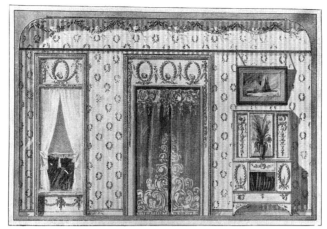

36

36
An early Empire revival wallpaper treatment 1893

Scheme for decoration by Christian P. Roos, from
The Decorator and Furnisher, *New York, November 1893*

The American periodical *The Decorator and Furnisher*, like many of the decoration magazines of the day, was slightly down-market, being aimed at the decoration trades and at middle-class house owners who might not be in a position to consult a fashionable firm when considering the style in which to do over their property. The appearance of a smart suggestion for an Empire-style treatment therefore leads us to suppose that such schemes were already chic by this date in America as well as in France. Roos's design uses a striped paper with a superimposed Empire wreath, manufactured by the firm of Robert Graves & Co., but beyond this there is little else to give a true Empire feel. The draperies in particular are very disappointing, with a highly conventional pair of *portières* and an equally unexciting treatment of the muslin draperies at the window to the left. In the accompanying text, however, another much more intriguing scheme is described: 'A choice combination of artistic and natural beauty is the Empire onyx wall-paper, in which all the colours of marble are produced, each separate slab representing marble [and] having a pattern that produces the effect of an Empire olive wreath in gold bronze.' Even in Europe there would be little that could rival this until the 1920s and 30s.

37
Ancien régime revival 1893

The Marie Antoinette room, executed by L. Alavoine of Paris for the Columbian Exposition, Chicago; from The Decorator and Furnisher, *New York, November 1893*

A number of the grander European firms exhibited room sets at the Columbian Exposition of 1893, and most of these were in an historic style of some kind. Alavoine of Paris, noted for the theatrical flamboyance with which they approached schemes of decoration intended to evoke a particular period, scored the greatest success with this rather heavy-handed attempt to recreate the quintessentially light and understated look of Marie Antoinette's style. Enough people must have liked the effect, for from about this time Alavoine maintained a studio and office in New York.

37

38
Pattern-on-pattern in France *c.1900*

Interior with Women; *oil painting by Edouard Vuillard*

The French love of laying layer upon layer of co-ordinated (or even, at times, less well co-ordinated) pattern has been a formative influence in the development of what may be identified as a national style; one which is equally often to be met with in the grandest town house or the smallest room in a provincial hotel. Vuillard, whose finest work is to be found in the exquisitely judged views of figures in interiors and painted screens which engaged his artistic activities at the turn of the century, is the painter who best captures the special quality of this kind of decoration, delighting in the subtle interplay between colourful wallpapers, bright chintzes and the more sombre richness of oriental rugs.

The Carnegie Museum of Art, Pittsburgh; acquired through the generosity of Mrs Alan M. Scaife, 1962

39
The Morris tradition *c.1900*

May Morris working a piece of embroidery; from an old photograph probably taken at Kelmscott, Oxfordshire

The Arts and Crafts movement in England had its origins in the highly idealistic productions of William Morris and his band of 'art workmen' in the 1860s. By the turn of the century, although influenced visually by Continental Art Nouveau design, the movement had really changed very little and remained centred in the Cotswold region of Oxfordshire and Gloucestershire. One of the great emotional centres of the movement was Morris's house, Kelmscott Manor, which he built into the mythology of Utopian craftsmanship in his ideological novel *News from Nowhere* of 1890. After Morris's death in 1896 his daughter May assumed an increasingly important

39

position in the movement. She carried on at Kelmscott, living there in her latter years with a companion, still acting as hostess to socialist events and continuing with the sort of needlework she had carried out with her mother Janey for more than thirty years. In this recently discovered photograph, probably taken at Kelmscott, she can be seen seated in a good, sound eighteenth-century nailed armchair of the kind Morris fully approved for its sturdy fitness for its purpose. She is working a panel of embroidery in a design reminiscent of crewelwork and deemed suitable for the hangings and covers of beds. The scene reflects the tremendously important part hand-worked textiles played in the Arts and Crafts interior.

Private collection

40

Munstead Wood is above all a house in which vast timbers create an atmosphere of ancient but rustic dignity. The massive baulks of oak are handled with elegance and a certain concealed sophistication. In the intervening spaces elegant fitted shelves and cupboards make the house comfortable and, for its day, efficient. If there was an inherent danger of lapsing into tweeness it was avoided, for in furnishing and fitting out the house Lutyens and Miss Jekyll chose with rare discrimination pieces of solid and simply handsome old English furniture.

Country Life

41
A new order   c.1890

Drawing room at Clouds, Wiltshire, by Philip Webb

The Hon. Percy Wyndham built Clouds in 1888–90, choosing Philip Webb as his architect. The house is a remarkable essay in the reformed taste advocated by the group of English aristocratic intellectuals known as 'The Souls', and fully reflects their ideal of a house as a setting for civilized life and a collection of beautiful objects. In Webb's architecture and in the decorations by Morris & Co. there is a wholly new and refreshing restraint. As in other late Webb houses much of the architectural enrichment is painted white, and pictures and other objects are arranged without cluttering the spaces. The furniture is an eclectic mix of good old pieces along with some simple new pieces of comfortable seating, which are intended to be conducive to good conversation. They are chosen, it seems, without any pretence of grandeur. The only self-consciously clever feature of the room at this time was the chimneypiece, which is a play on the Italian hood-style mantels of the Renaissance. In some ways it seems almost out of place in a room in every other way so rational and understated, and it is a curious sidelight on the progress of taste that subsequent owners of the house in the 1920s chose to remove it and to substitute a smaller and more conventional Adamesque neo-classical grate and chimneypiece.

Country Life

40
The English vernacular genius   1896

The Gallery, Munstead Wood, Surrey, by Edwin Lutyens

Lutyens trained in the stimulating environment of the office of the fashionable architects George & Peto, but the most formative influence of his early years was his association with the remarkable gardener Gertrude Jekyll. It was the commission to build Munstead Wood for Miss Jekyll which guided the young Lutyens to the fruitful exploration of the English vernacular tradition, and it was her satisfaction with the house which, in no small degree, set her protégé on the path to the success of his later years.

42

Life in the cathedral close c.1900

Canon Valpy's house, 3 The Close, Winchester;
watercolours by B.O. Corfe

42

The study

43

The drawing room

Canon Valpy, a cultivated married clergyman of considerable private means, lived in the provincial backwater of Winchester a life of what might best be described as inconspicuous luxury. His rooms were furnished without any overt regard for fashion; and yet in their eclectic mix of good eighteenth-century furniture, modern chintz-covered comfortable chairs and uncluttered arrangements of well-chosen books, objects and pictures, they are remarkably similar to the more consciously avant-garde room arrangements of London artists and intellectuals such as Ricketts and Shannon (pl. 32). The Canon's study, a room with dark-stained panelling in the most traditional manner, perhaps reflects his character more fully than the light and pretty dining and drawing room, which may be the creation of his wife's more delicate taste. Clearly the Valpys were collectors of pictures in a modest way. In the drawing room gilt-framed watercolours and prints seem to predominate, whereas in the study, true to type, the Canon hung the 'improving' prints, after the great religious paintings of the Italian Renaissance, issued by the Arundel Society, which had been founded earlier in the century, under the influence of Ruskin and Prince Albert, to promote an improved taste in pictures among the public. These inexpensive, pioneering colour reproductions formed a crucial element in the decoration of many enlightened middle-class homes during the period and their popularity persisted well into the new century.

Victoria & Albert Museum, London

43

44

An Art Nouveau pattern book 1902

Design for a dining room by Alphonse Mucha;
from Documents Décoratifs, *Paris, 1902*

Mucha's designs for furnishings, room settings and individual objects, collected in book form by the publisher Lévy, reveal an artist and master of the creation of pattern and surface ornament striving to relate the curvilinear motifs of Art Nouveau to three-dimensional forms. The fact that the basis of all the pieces suggested in these plates lies in Mucha's graphic mannerisms does impart a certain unity to the designs, and this consistency within a room setting, embracing not only the wall treatment and major pieces of furniture, but also the table linen, cutlery and glasses, is typical of the ideals of domestic interior design at the turn of the century.

Private collection

44

45

45

An opulent artist's studio, Paris c.1900

Writing corner of the studio of Alphonse Mucha,
rue Val de Grâce, Paris

Alphonse Mucha, a struggling Czech artist working in Paris, achieved recognition overnight for a poster for Sarah Bernhardt, became her court painter and with new-found riches set about the creation of an extraordinarily opulent studio in the classic mould. His son Jiri Mucha, in his 1971 monograph *Alphonse Mucha, Posters and Photographs*, has described the scene at the time of the painter's greatest celebrity: 'the bizarre luxury with which the studio was furnished became famous. The small forest of articles which he had accumulated ... had become a veritable jungle. All year round there were fresh flowers and palms; baroque furniture, brocades, costumes, draperies, stuffed animals and countless *objets de vertu* jostled for space in an atmosphere which was described by one visitor as a "profane chapel", and which some critics have seen as an effort to re-create the settings of the Moravian churches of his childhood.'

Private collection

46

46

Le Pavillon de l'Art Nouveau 1900

Boudoir designed by Georges de Feure for Samuel Bing

Like Arthur Lasenby Liberty in England, Samuel Bing in France had established himself in the world of decoration as an expert on oriental art and decorative traditions. As his interests widened to include the work of contemporary furniture designers, metalworkers and ceramicists, his shop became a recognized centre for the avant-garde, and its name, La Maison de l'Art Nouveau, grew increasingly synonymous with the style. For the great Paris Exhibition of 1900 Bing created an entire pavilion as a showcase for the work of a few of his favourite and most successful designers, among whom were Eugène Gaillard and Georges de Feure. De Feure's work is characterized by a light and elegant, almost feminine charm. It avoids the aggressive 'whiplash' motifs of many of his Parisian *confrères,* and seems to translate into modern terms the shapes, forms and colours of the furniture and decoration of the period of Louis xv.

Editions d'Art Albert Skira S.A.

47

Three masterpieces of curvilinear Art Nouveau

47

Staircase hall of the Atelier Elvira, Munich, by August Endell   1896

48

Staircase of no. 6 rue Paul-Emile Janson, Brussels, by Victor Horta   1892–3

49

Staircase of the Casa Batlló, Barcelona, by Antonio Gaudí   1904–6

The essential similarity between these staircases, each by a highly individual genius of the art Nouveau-Jugendstil movement, lies in the ability of their three designers to dispense entirely with any historic architectural point of reference, to build with total conviction in a novel manner and to match this boldness with a new architectural language containing a highly imaginative vocabulary of decorative motifs. In Endell's Atelier Elvira the richness of effect derives from elaborate relief decoration in coloured stucco, which echoes the extravagant decoration of the famous façade of the building, unfortunately destroyed in 1944. By contrast Horta, in the Brussels house, plays elaborate games with flat decoration in paint and mosaic to create an ambiguity between the wall surface and the wildly contorted, but still basically structural, ironwork of the stair. Gaudí, who must rank as the greatest innovative architect of the three, worked in effect as a sculptor in each of the materials he employed (stone, brick, wood, metal or even broken ceramics), modelling his buildings in flowing, three-dimensional forms as though all were clay.

47   *Bildarchiv Foto Marburg*
48   *Musée Horta, Brussels; copyright A.C.L. Bruxelles*
49   *Fisa industrias gráficas, Barcelona*

The Empire revival in a large hotel, London c.1896

The ladies' drawing room of the Hotel Cecil, decorated by Maples & Co.

There is a fairly close connection between fashions in the decoration of large hotels and in that of grander houses at the turn of the century. There were many in society who did not find it extraordinary that their entertaining rooms should have a slightly impersonal air of grandeur; and of course hotels, then as now, sought to attract clients by the combination of comfort and chic which the decor promised. In the Hotel Cecil's public rooms the old-established furnishers Maples pulled out all the stops in an attempt to put together a fashionable Empire look. It is perhaps not at all surprising that in so doing they created rooms which have about them very little of the feel of 1810, but which resemble very strongly the redecorations carried out at Malmaison for the Empress Eugénie, redolent of the *grand luxe* of the Second Empire. As always, light fittings and the detail of the ornament give the game away, whilst the profusion of palms proclaims the date most loudly.

Royal Commission on the Historical Monuments of England

51

German neo-classicism 1897

Entrance hall of the Villa Stuck, Munich

The German response to Roman and Greek antiquity has always been a special one: a complicated, earnest and scholarly approach very different from that of the English dilettante of the eighteenth century or his latter-day successors. German artists espoused a cool, analytical attitude to classical architecture and developed an extraordinary fondness for plaster casts after the antique. Both these elements can be discerned in the entrance hall of the villa created by the once highly regarded painter Franz von Stuck in Munich. Stuck's own classicist canvases, which include strong elements of heavy-handed humour as well as being laden with obscure imagery, are today not so easily appreciated, and it is somewhat difficult to understand the enthusiasm felt for them by the worthy burghers of Munich, which enabled the artist to realize his architectural fantasies in concrete form. It is particularly interesting to see that the casts of antique reliefs have been picked out in colours, not merely in order to create a decorative effect, but in response to the theories of the day concerning the extent to which the originals had been painted: an artistic debate of surprising longevity.

Photograph A.F. Kersting

52

Couturiers' chic, London 1896

The Hat Shop; *oil painting by Henry Tonks*

Tonks's delightful *Hat Shop*, apart from being a superb piece of painting with clever *contre-jour* passages, is also an intriguing document of fashions in late Victorian millinery, and tells us a great deal about the relationship between couture and chic in interior decoration. In England at the turn of the century most fashionably dressed women looked for their lead, like the rest of the civilized world, to Paris. In this prevailing climate to be English was to be second-rate, and most of the major establishments found it necessary to maintain at least the polite fiction that they were French in origin or had close connections with their Parisian *confrères*. In this, the decoration of the main salons and often of the small private fitting rooms, in which assignations were not unknown, could play an important part. The most popular look seems always to have been a watered-down Louis Quinze or Louis Seize in pinks, creams or, more sophisticatedly, pale greys. Little French chairs and tiny tables were dotted about and a great many looking-glasses helped to build up an image of *grand luxe*. When done well the result was reminiscent of a Helleu etching (pl. 53), but the look fossilized and moved down-market between the wars and has remained ever since the quintessential style of thousands of provincial hairdressers ('Coiffeurs') and superior dry-cleaning establishments.

Birmingham City Art Gallery

53

The 'Old French look' 1896

Madame Helleu debout, devant le buste de Marie Antoinette; *drypoint etching by Paul-César Helleu*

Helleu is justly celebrated for the exquisite series of drypoint etchings which he made in the 1890s depicting his wife and her elegant companions in the rooms of the house which he had arranged in homage to the eighteenth century. This print shows the chimneypiece of the drawing room, which had a large looking-glass in the simplest of frames flanked by tiny ormolu candle sconces, while on the severely architectural mantel stood a terracotta bust of Marie Antoinette. All the colours of the room, from *boiseries* and other woodwork through to the covers of the delicate Louis Quinze and Louis Seize furniture, were

53

pale and soft. The total effect, in complete contrast to the overblown exoticism of the clichéd bohemian interiors of artists' studios of the Second Empire period and the *belle époque*, clearly foreshadows the 'Old French look' as propounded by Elsie de Wolfe. Edith Wharton and Ogden Codman, whose book *The Decoration of Houses* appeared in the year after this print was made, would have approved not only the way in which such fine French things were chosen, but also their austere and architecturally correct arrangement.

Courtesy of Lumley Cazalet Ltd, London

Clearing away clutter, Maryland late 1890s

Photographs from Newton Elwell, The Architecture, Furniture and Interiors of Maryland and Virginia during the 18th Century, *Boston, 1897*

54,55

Two views of the parlour in the house of Dr Crim, Baltimore, Maryland

56

The dining room, Brooklynwood, Maryland

56

These views illustrate two distinct phases in the American attitude to the furnishing of historic houses. The house of Dr Crim of Baltimore is that of an avid collector and is filled with an overwhelming assemblage of objects, most of which seem to date from the late Colonial or Federal periods. However they are massed in a profusion

and density entirely of the late nineteenth century and in a sense, therefore, the decoration of the house has been brought up to date. This is confirmed by the detail view in which, behind the splendid American Empire period couch, the chimneypiece with its fashionable Aesthetic tiles is decked with vases of peacock feathers. The dining room of Brooklynwood presents a contrast, for it is an early example of an historic house in which some conscious attempt had been made to remove the accretions of clutter, unearthing the much barer bones of the eighteenth- and early nineteenth-century appearance of the house.

57

create interior architecture and grandiose decoration of a serious and scholarly nature, however, placed him in the forefront of the 'American Renaissance'. This position was recognized as early as 1885 when Mrs Schuyler van Rensselaer, writing in the *Century Magazine*, described the interiors of the Villard houses in New York City, by the partnership of McKim, Mead & White, as the very best in the country. Fortunately some of these have survived, restored to their original grandeur as part of the Helmsley Palace Hotel.

Courtesy of the New-York Historical Society,
New York City

58

The house of an
art-lover   late 1890s

The music room of 152 Beacon Street, Boston,
the home of Isabella Stewart Gardner; oil painting by
Martin Mower

A certain informal quality of comfort seems to have humanized the opulence of Isabella Stewart Gardner's rooms, in spite of the extent and splendour of her celebrated collections. This may well be a result of her particular devotion to the more accessible charm of the Venetian decorative tradition, of which she was so early and so notable a devotee. This aspect of the way in which she used her works of art to create rooms of great charm is already visible in this early view of her music room at Beacon Street, destroyed around the turn of the century, where gilt furniture was grouped informally against a very rich background of silks and brocades. The confidence with which fine Renaissance carvings and architectural features, such as the hood chimneypiece visible to the left in this room, are mixed with eighteenth-century chairs and other objects is highly successful. It is still one of the delightful characteristics of the room arrangements in the Isabella Stewart Gardner Museum, which now houses her collections.

Courtesy of the Trustees of the Isabella Stewart Gardner
Museum, Boston

57

Opulence and eclecticism in
New York   1890s

First-floor reception room of Stamford White's own
house, 121 East 21st Street, New York

A s an essay in the opulent eclectism of the 1890s Stamford White's own house on East 21st Street is an important clue to the understanding of his flamboyant personality and architectural style. This first-floor reception room, which contained a number of the architect's more prized objects including a fine Venetian gondola seat, was intended to some degree as a showpiece; yet it seems deliberately to suggest the studio of an artist or the rich informality of the dilettante collector. White's ability to

1900–1920
THE AVANT-GARDE AND
THE REVIVAL OF PERIOD STYLES

It is a characteristic of the books and journals of the turn of the century that they devote far more space to architects' decorative schemes than to any other kind of interior. With titles such as *The House Beautiful*, still redolent of the self-consciously 'sensitive' poses of the Aesthetic movement, they perpetuated an artistic hierarchy which placed the work of architects at its head and descended, not to that of the more mundane upholsterer-decorators but, through the earnest creations of the Arts and Crafts movement, to the sort of 'artistic' work, such as embroidery or the decoration of china, that the lady of the house might expect to undertake herself. Many of these magazines and early house manuals chose specifically to promote the Art Nouveau style, but did so in such eccentric ways, or in combination with other elements that were so unlikely (including 'Olde English' quaintness, Tudor or early Dutch nautical imagery or Middle Eastern richness of patterning) that a decorative style came about that was so hybrid as to be quite without precedent.

More high-minded publications such as *The Studio*, which enjoyed a wide circulation not only in England but in cultivated circles throughout Europe, could afford to take a more purist but also more international stance, and chose to champion only those designers and architects working in the style of which the editors approved, whether they were from Chelsea or Czechoslovakia, Hampstead or Hungary. *The Studio* had consistently interested its readers in work from the Celtic fringes and had in particular done much to bring the buildings and artefacts of the Glasgow School to a wider Continental audience. And so, by the early years of the century, the ironical situation had arisen whereby a number of designers working in an essentially regional or even folk-inspired version or adaptation of the Art Nouveau style had not merely achieved some degree of local acclaim but had come to represent the European avant-garde ideal. The most significant individual designer to gain such an international reputation was the acknowledged leader of the 'Glasgow Boys', Charles Rennie Mackintosh.

Mackintosh and the Manx architect M.H. Baillie Scott were the two prize-winners in a German competition for the design and decoration of a 'house for an art-lover' (pls 59, 62). Both had their schemes published in Darmstadt by the powerful architectural writer and publisher Alexander Koch, and as a result they came to exert an extraordinarily high level of influence on Continental interiors for a generation. In both Germany and Austria their following became immense and manifested itself in diverse ways, such as the more obvious Anglophile tendencies in the work of the Viennese designer and theorist Adolf Loos; in the rejection of curvilinear Art Nouveau by Josef Hoffmann, the founder of the Wiener Werkstätte; and, perhaps more subtly, in the fascination for English architecture, design and domestic arrangements which underlay so much Germanic thinking of the period, and which found its most characteristic expression in Hermann Muthesius's monumental study of the English house, *Das Englische Haus* (Berlin, 1904).

In England a number of architects of some calibre, such as C.F.A. Voysey, combined the careful detailing and attention to craftsmanship of the Arts and Crafts movement with stylistic traits more readily associated with Art Nouveau, but in general it was in the more commercial areas of design that the style found most popularity. By the early years of the century the household furnishing trade had grafted many of the mannerisms of Art Nouveau on to otherwise conventional and undistinguished forms. Firms such as Oetzmann of Hampstead Road were mass-producing cheap versions of the kind of Art Nouveau pieces, made originally in fine woods and mounted with hand-beaten hinges and lock-plates, which belonged to the later Morris tradition in the crafts. The most successful commercial version of the style, and certainly the most consistent stylistically, was the wide range of goods, including furniture, textiles and domestic wares in silver, pewter and ceramic, offered by the celebrated London store Liberty & Co. Arthur Lasenby Liberty had opened his first shop in 1875, at the height of the Aesthetic craze for *japonisme*, as an oriental bazaar, but by this time had moved towards the position from which, with a stable of designers whose names were for the most part not revealed to the public, the Liberty store was able to offer a complete look which was to a considerable degree exclusive and readily associated with the name.

Although it lingered longer in France than almost anywhere else, Art Nouveau had effectively ceased to be seriously considered chic by about 1905 and by 1910 was all but dead, replaced by a multiplicity of stylistic possibilities, only some of which reflected the increasingly volatile contemporary movements in the other arts. Perhaps in reaction to the deliberate and often tiresome novelty of the previous decade, period furniture was discovered to have charm, and old pieces of good form and pleasing patination began to be much sought after. A number of highly distinguished rooms were created which, whilst not seeking exactly to re-create the appearance of interiors of an earlier age – mixing in for example modern pictures – tried specifically to capture some essence of the past and to distil something of the ordered calm which many prized as the real *Stimmung*, or feeling, to be found in the simple groupings of furniture and the subdued or faded colours of old houses.

The painters and art collectors Charles Ricketts and Charles Shannon were early, and notably successful, exponents of this look, both in their own houses and when they advised friends (pls 98, 99). For the house of the two lady poets who wrote together under the name of 'Michael Field' Ricketts had ordained a drawing room of silvery grey paper, which they later had the temerity to change to a more 'obvious' Regency stripe. The painter Sir William Rothenstein recalled the impression which the house gave:

> The Paragon, the Michael Fields' house at Richmond, was an eighteenth-century house with a garden running down to the river. In the living-rooms the furniture was of satinwood, chosen by Ricketts, and on the walls hung Shannon's lithographs, and prints by Ricketts ... exquisitely mounted. Ricketts and Shannon gave to mounting and framing the care which only Eastern artists give as a rule.[1]

Finally, in characterizing this fine interior, Rothenstein recalled: 'There were always choice flowers, lovingly arranged.'[2]

The essence of these rooms was reticence and refinement of taste. The meaningless clutter of indifferent objects began to give way to more telling groupings of well chosen pieces of furniture, and works of art of real quality replaced bric-à-brac. Morris's most perfect but most demanding dictum – 'have nothing in your home which you do not know to be useful or believe to be beautiful' – had struck a note which now found a new resonance and which chimed in with more recent ideas on the importance of respecting the architecture of a room and reflecting it in the choice and arrangement of the furniture, pictures and other objects. The elements which came together in these new attitudes include not only the Arts and Crafts desire for simplicity coupled with quality of workmanship and materials, but also, among those who cared for the past and were interested in the adaptation of historic styles to modern needs, a novel interest in the sort of plain rooms of the later eighteenth century that had always previously been ignored in favour of the more decorated and superficially showy.

Through the publication of his books *Ett Hem* ('A Home') in 1899, and *Larssons* ('At the Larssons') in 1902, the interiors of the summer cottage created by the Swedish painter Carl Larsson and his wife Karin became among the best known and most influential in Europe. They successfully mingled the influences of Art Nouveau, which the Larssons had seen at first hand during student days in Paris, the ideas of the English Arts and Crafts movement, and a strong feeling for the light, pretty and unaffected folk art and decoration of Sweden. The resulting rooms were cheerful, comfortable and, as the reader could readily appreciate from the painters' watercolour illustrations, colourful. Several of the interiors contained pieces of Swedish antique furniture of the Gustavian and Biedermeier styles, many of which had been painted in either white or strong clear colours – perhaps one of the earlier manifestations of the craze for re-finishing old furniture that was to sweep Europe and America. By the end of the decade the house had developed even further, with more rooms containing specially built painted woodwork and a richer array of textiles, including curtains and bed-hangings, worked by Karin Larsson in much the same spirit as those created by Jane Morris and her daughter May for the decoration of the rooms of Kelmscott.

With the appearance of a German edition of plates from the earlier books, called *Das Haus in der Sonne* ('A House in the Sun') in 1910, which sold 10,000 copies in two years, the Larssons were in effect promoting not just a decorative style but a way of life. *Åt Solsiden* ('On the Sunny Side'), published in 1910, was clearly intended to be what we now recognize as a 'lifestyle manual'. It also came out in Germany as *Lasst Licht Hinein* ('Let in the Light') in 1911, and carried the very modern-sounding subtitle: 'A book about rooms to live in, about children, about you, about flowers, about everything.'

All across Europe parallel movements in both period revivals and the creation of new styles can be discerned, with, everywhere, a new emphasis on architectural sobriety. The still calm of the almost empty interiors in paintings by the Danes Peter Ilsted and Vilhelm Hammershoi of their own austere rooms (pls 107,152) seems to share a quality of refinement not just with English artists' houses of the immediate pre-war years, but also with those subtle experiments in the Empire revival style carried out first in Paris and later in London by Edward Knoblock, and ultimately with the understated chic of the early phase of the Vogue Regency style. Ada Leverson, the friend of Oscar Wilde and an often acute observer of interiors in her novels, captures the precise moment at which this new taste began to spread:

'What a charming little room this is. It suits you. There's hardly a thing in it but everything is right.'

'I don't like to have too many things in a room', said Edith, holding out her delicate hands to the fire. 'It makes me nervous. I have gradually accustomed Bruce to my idea by removing one thing at a time – photographs, pictures, horrid old wedding presents, all the little things people have. They suggest too many different trains of thought. They worry me. He's getting used to it now. He says, soon there'll be nothing but a couple of chairs and a bookcase!'[3]

It was as early as 1897 and in America, however, that, as the result of the publication by the as yet unknown novelist Edith Wharton of her first important piece of writing, interior decoration as we know it became the subject for serious aesthetic debate. *The Decoration of Houses* was the result of the fruitful collaboration between the future writer and her protégé, the smart young New England architect Ogden Codman. Together they had begun, whilst engaged on alterations, additions and decorations for the Wharton houses, to formulate some more general theories of the ways in which domestic architecture and furnishings might be improved by the study of the best examples of the past.

Such an approach was hardly very novel (for nearly half a century it had been after all the guiding principle of the South Kensington Museum in London and of all the great decorative art museums throughout Europe which in any way followed its model), and yet in the fresh and intelligent ways in which the book outlined its simple and forceful argument, it became the most persuasive statement of a new way of looking at the creation of interiors. Together Mrs Wharton and Codman proposed a rational approach to rooms based entirely on sound architectural principles, upon the 'correctness' of the disposition of such elements as door and window openings, cornices and floors, and upon the appropriateness and quality of the furnishings selected, whether old or new.

The extraordinary success of *The Decoration of Houses*, and its appeal which remains even to this day, lies in the authors' combination of temperament and character, and the sympathy of ideas and tension between them. Mrs Wharton's mastery of subtle observation and nuance, coupled with her very precise understanding of society in New York (qualities which she shared perhaps only with Henry James, who was no decorator, although he appreciated the quality of rooms), allowed her to pitch the book with great exactitude, whilst Codman's superb architectural sense and knowledge of historic detail underpinned it with precision, ensuring that each point was made with a well-chosen and telling illustration. Although the book contains many Italian examples, *The Decoration of Houses* recommended especially a return to the inspiration of the best French classic models for building, for decorative schemes and above all for furnishings. In this the book is a crucial landmark in the long story of America's love affair with French art and life.

The book is insistent that good decoration can result only from getting the bones of a scheme right. It is concerned with the fundamental things, not with veneers of style, the 'superficial application or ornament totally independent of structure' or historical pastiche, but with 'house decoration as a branch of architecture'. Only in their search for excellence did the authors pay more serious attention to the very grand rather than the more modest houses of the past, and they were insistent that the benefits to be derived from their approach to the construction and ornamentation of rooms would in due course be felt universally:

If it be granted that a reform in house decoration, if not necessary, is at least desirable, it must be admitted that such reform can originate only with those whose means permit of any experiment which their taste may suggest. When the rich man demands good architecture his neighbours will get it too. Every good moulding, every carefully studied detail, exacted by those who can afford to indulge their taste, will in time find its way to the carpenter-built cottage.

If Wharton and Codman stated their case with elegance and a degree of reticence, it was in marked contrast to the self-confident assertiveness of Elsie de Wolfe who, having rapidly assimilated the ideas of *The Decoration of Houses*, turned them around into a way of life for herself, promulgated her 'Old French look' in the form of a bouncily written lifestyle manual, and thereby launched herself as a decorator, perhaps truly the first on the pattern which we recognize by the term today. The differences between the *Decoration of Houses* and Elsie's *The House in Good Taste* (1913) are immediately apparent even from their respective titles. *The House in Good Taste* is unashamedly personal and self-promotional, charting Elsie's path towards aesthetic enlightenment, even though it was largely ghostwritten by a bright young journalist called Ruby Ross Goodnow, who later, as Ruby Ross Wood, became a doyenne of the decorating world. The opening words strike a note of optimism and were clearly intended as both a rather knowing clarion call to America and as a professional testimonial: 'I know', said Elsie in Ruby's ringing words, 'of nothing more significant than the awakening of men and women throughout the country to the desire to improve their houses. Call it what you will – awakening, development, American Renaissance – it is a most startling and promising condition of affairs.'

It was indeed promising and Elsie de Wolfe rapidly established herself as a decorator, securing in fairly quick succession a number of key commissions which enabled her to develop her at first small business on new lines. Her work at the prestigious Colony Club established the all-important social status of the operation. She regularized the notion of buying furniture and other items on commission for her clients, with the result that, as she recalled in later years, when the industrialist and philanthropist Henry Clay Frick engaged her to arrange the family rooms of his house (which he later bequeathed to New York City to establish the Frick Collection) and then paid her a commission on the purchases from the Parisian residue of Sir Richard Wallace's collection which she negotiated for him, she became a rich woman overnight. In an unforgettable, but sadly unattributed, line she was said to have 'introduced New American money to Old French furniture'.

In England and France the pattern of the emergence of the new decorators becomes a recognizable one, based usually on the formal promotion by an individual or one small firm of a taste that can be identified as belonging to a group of friends, often including figures from both society and the world of art. The interrelationships between such cliques and the styles they favoured, the degree to which they also reflected developments in painting and the other arts, and the extent to which such tastes were taken up by a wider public, are all complex questions perhaps best elucidated by a few examples.

The quirky, Italianate, neo-baroque taste best exemplified by the Sitwells seems, for example, to have been formed almost entirely within the circles of the expatriate community in Florence, which centred around Harold Acton, the Sitwells and the architects Cecil Pinsent and Geoffrey Scott, who worked in most of the villas in the area over a number of years. Scott was also close to a number of Englishmen of aesthetic tastes in the British Embassy in Rome at different times, including both Lord Gerald Wellesley, architect, connoisseur and collector, and Lord Berners, composer, novelist and painter. His friendships later drew together such diverse figures as Vita Sackville-West, the decorator and gallery owner Dorothy Warren, and the Haslams, who owned a superb bed designed by him which formed a notable feature of their idiosyncratically decorated seventeenth-century house, Great Hundridge Manor.

A second, somewhat interlocking circle formed the taste in England for Regency and Empire furnishings. Lord Gerald Wellesley again is a key figure. Edward Knoblock, the collector of the celebrated Regency neo-classical furniture of Thomas Hope, was drawn in by his association with William Nicholson, who had painted a decorative scheme for his Parisian apartment,[4] whilst Nicholson's friend Mrs 'Dolly' Mann was the decorator whose shop brought painted furniture and Regency decoration to a wider public.

Another example of this kind, concerning the use of colour, suggests something too of the movement of international fashion in the arts. With the instant and astounding success of Diaghilev's Russian Ballet, a taste for rich and exotic decoration was rapidly disseminated in the wake of the company's European tours. Osbert Lancaster noted that the influence of the designs of Léon Bakst was so great that it was possible to speak in terms of a 'Russian Ballet style' in interiors around the time of the First World War, and it is certainly possible to see much of the use of brilliant colour – so noticeable a factor in the arts at this time – as a direct reflection of this.

In Paris Paul Poiret fell under the spell, and in England too remarkable colour combinations began to appear. Baron de Meyer, the most stylish photographer of the day and a respected observer of fashion, wrote in *Vogue* in 1914:

> It is astonishing how during these last few years colour seems to have been used indiscriminately, almost felt as a necessity, perhaps to counterbalance in some way all the sadness and mourning that pervades Europe. Never have we heard more of a shortage of dyes, never were they more scarce and costly, and yet, never have we had such an orgy of glowing oranges, greens or reds as during these last months.[5]

The architect Edwin Lutyens was experimenting in his interiors at this time with startling colours, such as brilliant scarlet lacquer against stark white paintwork and glossy black walls, while his close friend Lady Sackville, who had opened her decorating shop Spealls in 1911, was gathering extraordinary furnishings in her new house in Brighton and putting together colour schemes such as this one for her daughter Vita's room:

> Her walls are of shiny emerald green paper, floor green; doors and furniture sapphire blue; ceiling apricot colour. Curtains blue and inside-curtains yellowish. The decoration of the furniture mainly beads of all colours painted on the blue ground; even the door plates are treated the same. I have 6 bright orange pots on her green marble mantelpiece and there are salmon and tomato-colour cushions and lampshades. Pictures by Bakst, George Plank [her neighbour in Ebury Street] and Rodin, and framed in passe-partout ribbons.[6]

Frank Brangwyn, who unlike many of the more insular British painters at the turn of the century had lived and studied on the Continent, painted in a bold and colourful manner that made his work ideally suited for large-scale decorative schemes. His subject-matter – gaily clad women harvesting grapes – became the starting point for riotous essays in bravura paintwork and vibrant colour. His paintings became increasingly filled with swirling figures, flowers and a profusion of fruit, elements which spilled over into his later designs for the decoration of furniture and vast patterned carpets.

Even in Germany, where the Junker version of pastiche

'baronial' remained the most popular style, in spite of the reforming zeal of professors of design such as Bruno Paul in Berlin, it is fascinating to see, both in the interiors publications of the time such as *Farbige Raumkunst* (1911) and in the pattern books, the all-pervading influence of Bakst's brilliant colour.

Two final examples in this section must serve to outline something of the working methods of the small firms typical of this period. Among the very first to associate his name with an individual style was Marcel Boulestin, an Anglophile man of letters who had worked in Paris with the novelist Colette and her husband and collaborator Willy, and who came to England in 1906 to pursue his literary career, a move in which he had been encouraged by friends such as Max Beerbohm. Once he was in London chance led him in other directions: he opened an interior decorating business and eventually became a restaurateur of genius. His shop, Décoration Moderne, opened in Elizabeth Street in November 1911, was one of the very first of the small avant-garde decorators' showrooms and to begin with was highly successful, numbering among its clients such leading social figures in London as Lady Curzon, the Baroness d'Erlanger and Mrs Syrie Wellcome, who later became Syrie Maugham.

To give London an idea of what he could do Boulestin decorated the whole house in the most exciting Parisian manner, drawing heavily on the designs of Poiret whose complete range he represented in England. Though the stock was not large it must have been of excellent quality and chosen with real flair. He wrote:

> The silks, the velvets, the linens, the knick-knacks and the wall-papers came from Martine [Poiret's studio], André Groult and Iribe. I had bought stuffs at Darmstadt, Munich and Vienna; Berlin and Florence supplied me with certain papers, Paris with new and amusing vases, pottery, porcelain, glass and a few fine pieces of Negro art.[7]

Boulestin's shop must have given many of his English customers their first glimpse of this almost Arabian Nights fantasy world and their first opportunity to buy the necessary fabrics and objects to create their own versions of the Russian Ballet style. Following the presentation of Poiret's glittering costume ballet at the Alhambra Theatre in London, the designer even sent over to Boulestin a version of his own Parisian room, filled with stepped mattress divans covered in silks and strewn with cushions of gold, silver and furs. However, such hothouse exoticism did not really survive the shock of the first modern war in 1914–18. When Décoration Moderne reopened in George Street after the war Boulestin found that much of the previous enthusiasm for his wares had fallen away.

In his memoirs he philosophically listed a number of reasons for the difficulties into which the business fell:

> Perhaps it was a little too advanced – also during those years many shops had started what they called modern decoration; several of the Society women who used to be my customers had themselves become decorators; there was the beginning of the slump, and in addition to all these adverse circumstances there were practically no stocks of any kinds. Sometimes when there was an important order it could not be executed, the material being out of print, or printed on a cheaper stuff.[8]

This marked the lowest ebb of Boulestin's fortunes, and he eked out an existence making candle shades of 'java paper' for the dining tables of his former customers.

Candle shades coincidentally formed a part of the stock-in-trade of the best-known attempt to bridge the gap between the fine and applied arts. Roger Fry, the most influential writer on art of his day and one of the pivotal figures of 'Bloomsbury', founded the Omega Workshop in 1913 in order to raise the, as he saw it, generally very low artistic level of taste in household furnishings in England, whilst providing encouragement and employment for the new young painters he admired and sought to promote. The other partners in the enterprise were his friends the painters Duncan Grant and Vanessa Bell, both luminaries of the Bloomsbury Post-Impressionist aesthetic. Other artists were encouraged to come to the workshop and showroom in the heart of Bohemian Fitzrovia in Fitzroy Square, where according to which projects or commissions were in hand, they were set to design or actually make and paint pieces of furniture, and paint or hand-print the bold and colourful fabrics for which the workshop quickly gained a reputation. They were paid the generous rate of ten shillings for half a day's work. The productions of the firm, which remained in business for about six or seven years, reflect the intense reforming zeal inherent in all Fry's attitudes to the arts, and indeed it seems that during the years of the Omega experiment his enthusiasm was directed towards the applied arts as much as painting. Many of the creations of the workshop were highly innovative in terms of colour and style, but the accusation of poor workmanship often levelled against them at the time was in many cases justified. Fry's own defence has something of the sound of crying in the wilderness: '[our artists] refuse to spoil the expressive quality of their work by sandpapering it down to a shop-finish, in the belief that the public has at last seen through the humbug of the machine-made imitation of works of art.'[9]

In spite of all the efforts of reformers such as Fry, of aesthetes and avant-garde painters with an eye for decoration, and of those dedicated to the creation of unusual interiors, it has to be remembered that throughout this entire period the greater part of the trade was constantly engaged in the manufacture and supply of period-style work. At every level, from the finest antique furniture supplied by firms such as Lenygon's from their grand town house in London, or Alavoine in Paris and New York, down to the humbler makers of reproductions for use in modest room sets, the spell cast by 'Olde English' furniture in particular was potent, long-lived and, seemingly, endlessly adaptable.

1. W. Rothenstein, *Men and Memories*, London, 1931
2. Ibid.
3. A. Leverson, *Tenterhooks*, London, 1912
4. S. Calloway, 'A Special Decoration' in *Journal of the Decorative Arts Society*, 10, 1986
5. *Vogue*, Early spring number, 1914
6. Lady Sackville's Diary for 1918, quoted in V. Glendenning, *Vita*, London, 1983
7. X.M. Boulestin, *Ease and Endurance*, London, 1948
8. Ibid.
9. R. Fry, *Omega Workshop Prospectus*, London, 1914

59

59

International recognition for the Arts and Crafts movement 1901

The music room, from Baillie Scott, London: Das Haus eines Kunstfreundes, *1901 (vol. 1 of Hermann Muthesius, ed.,* Meister der Innen-Kunst, *Darmstadt, 1902)*

The design of a 'house for an art-lover', in which the most important room was to be a music salon, was the set subject in an international design competition organized by Alexander Koch, the Darmstadt publisher of the influential magazine *Innen-Dekoration*. The first prize was awarded to the architect and designer Mackay Hugh Baillie Scott, who had already gained some notice for his work for the Grand Duke of Hesse in the palace at Darmstadt. This idealized essay is in his distinctive style, which unites elements of the Arts and Crafts aesthetic with other more obscure influences, such as the kind of colourful painted joinery which is to be found in the Scandinavian or middle European peasant work shown in the pages of *The Studio* magazine at the time. As a result of his success in the competition Baillie Scott received a number of important commissions and his work became known to a wider European audience of designers and theorists, who clearly associated his style with that of the Glasgow School of designers centred around Charles Rennie Mackintosh. Baillie Scott was not only an architect of some accomplishment but also a remarkable designer of furnishings and textiles; his interiors exemplify the Arts and Crafts ideal that a room and all that is in it should be conceived by one mind in order to achieve a totally unified decorative effect.

60

60

Voysey's modern cottage style 1900

The hall, The Orchard, Chorleywood, Hertfordshire

The rooms of C.F.A. Voysey always remain interior architecture and rarely seem at all decorated, even though he was a good pattern designer and took great delight in drawing the small details of door furniture and other minutiae of a large project. In the hall of one of his most famous houses, The Orchard at Chorleywood, his special genius for the handling of simple contrasting forms and the interplay of horizontal and vertical elements can be seen. In particular he plays on the cottage style, placing elaborate hinges on a low, broad door which is scaled to relate to the height of a large chimneypiece and a continuous wide, flat-sectioned picture rail. But it is in the handling of the stairs which rise from this hall that he makes his most important visual coup. In place of the usual

banisters rising to a sloping handrail Voysey has elongated the vertical members to full height, creating two intriguing open screens flanking the first five steps. Content with this stunning feature, he left all the wall surfaces plain and felt no need to introduce any further decorative elements into the scheme. As an architect Voysey's reputation rests on the highly innovative houses which he designed in a manner that attempts to unite certain elements of the Art Nouveau style with the best principles of the Arts and Crafts. His typical long low lines of windows, surmounted by large and often asymmetrical gabled bays, can be seen as the direct antecedents of the standard English ribbon-development semi-detached house.

British Architectural Library, Royal Institute of British Architects, London

61

A modern dining room, Hertfordshire 1901

The Leys, near Elstree, Hertfordshire, by George Walton

George Walton is, in a sense, the *other* Glasgow designer; for if C.R. Mackintosh is to be thought of as the genius of the Glasgow School, then Walton must be seen as an outsider, quieter and in some ways more quirky. As an architect Walton worked for the most part in the rectilinear manner of the Glasgow School, using many of its mannerisms, such as white-painted panelling reaching right up the wall to a deep frieze and an exaggerated verticality in many of the elements of the structure and decoration of rooms. However, it is for his furniture designs that he should be most admired: extraordinarily mannered essays in the style of Sheraton and clever plays on all sorts of pieces from the past. In the dining room of this Hertfordshire house, The Leys, he used not his usual dining chair, which seems to stand on tip-toe on tiny outward-turning legs, but a more substantial design based on an early eighteenth-century type which also evokes a favourite pattern of Chinese chair. Also typical of Walton's style are the inglenook with settles built-in around the chimneypiece, and the serving table or sideboard at the far end of the room, which has an upper section of cupboards glazed with small panes of glass in a rectilinear pattern.

British Architectural Library, Royal Institute of British Architects, London

61

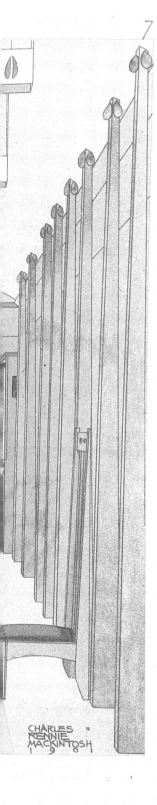

62

The Glasgow style 1901

The music room, from Charles Rennie Mackintosh, Glasgow: Das Haus eines Kunstfreundes, *1901 (vol. II of* Meister der Innen-Kunst*)*

The second prize in the Darmstadt competition for the design of a 'house for an art-lover' went to Charles Rennie Mackintosh, the acknowledged leader of the 'Glasgow Boys' and foremost exponent of their rectilinear genre of Art Nouveau, which was to have so profound an influence on the development of European design for an entire generation. Like the winning entry by Baillie Scott (pl. 59), Mackintosh's designs were published by the Prussian art educationalist Hermann Muthesius, who in his influential series *Meister der Innen-Kunst* (Masters of the art of the interior) championed both English domestic architecture and the intellectual link between the ideals of the Arts and Crafts movement in Britain and the emerging industrial aesthetic of the German design schools. In Mackintosh's competition scheme we can identify many of his most characteristic mannerisms: an emphasis on exaggerated verticals, especially in the high backs of the chairs and his favourite elongated window forms; the use of white-enamelled paintwork adorned with stylized floral motifs; and the balance of plain areas of wall or woodwork against more intricate decorative panels. In this instance these are identified as the work of Margaret MacDonald Mackintosh, the architect's wife, one of the pair of talented sisters (the other being Frances McNair) who contributed greatly to the formation of the Glasgow School look.

63

63

An all-white room, near Glasgow 1903–4

Bedroom, Hill House, Helensburgh, by Charles Rennie Mackintosh

Mackintosh's startling originality as an architect in the handling of form, and the extravagant novelty of his designs for individual pieces of furniture have tended to overwhelm his impact as a decorator of interior spaces. He had, nevertheless, a rare feeling for the importance of surface quality and finish to a successful room. His attention to the lacquering of his furniture is at least as important a factor as its form in the way it works in context, and the architect took almost a painter's delight in the use of colour. Instead of the obvious black he would often use a very dark blue or dull purple stain and then heighten the effect with one tiny note of brighter colour. In the bedroom at Hill House, a house in which all the prevailing tonalities are very light, he reaches the logical conclusion of playing with light on various surfaces: an all-white room.

Photograph T. & R. Annan & Sons

64

Sezession furniture design, Vienna c.1903

Breakfast room by Kolo Moser; from Dekorative Kunst, *vol. XII, 1903–4*

Through his involvement with the Sezession and his contributions to the movement's journal, *Ver Sacrum*, Kolo Moser came to occupy an important position in the artistic life of Vienna. In 1900 his appointment as director of the *Kunstgewerbschule* (Applied Art School) of the Österreichisches Museum für Kunst und Industrie brought him into closer contact with Josef Hoffmann, and together they reformed the teaching of applied art, thereby stimulating the emergence of a whole generation of talented designers working in a distinctive Viennese style. In 1903 he was one of the founders of the Wiener Werkstätte, but he broke off his association with the organization after only four years, criticizing the quality of its productions. Much of his own furniture was made by commercial firms, including Caspar Hrazdil and Portois & Fix, even though many of the pieces were unusual in form and highly complex in their decoration. Typical of the subtle geometrical forms he favoured is a breakfast room suite carried out in light and dark inlays, illustrated in a room setting which also contains an eccentric stove in geometrically patterned metal with a polished metal hearth-plate.

65

65

A designer's study, Darmstadt 1903

Study by Peter Behrens for his own house, Mathildenhöhe, Darmstadt

This library in the designer's own house is remarkably similar to that which he designed for the publisher Alexander Koch. Because of his position as the most influential publisher of his day in Germany of works on design, Koch's choice of the architect Peter Behrens for the design of his study is an interesting one. Koch was aware of what was being done as far afield as Glasgow and Budapest, and knew personally both leading academics and practitioners of architecture and decoration. The study in Koch's house was completed in 1901, the year in which he published the seminal sets of drawings submitted for the *Haus eines Kunstfreundes* competition, which brought the work of Mackintosh and Baillie Scott to a wider European audience. Clearly at this date his preference was for a heavy and visually concentrated scheme in the Continental Jugendstil or Art Nouveau manner, seen here in Behrens's own study, in which the young architect continued to practise until about 1904.

Bildarchiv Foto Marburg

64

66

The masterpiece of rectilinear Art Nouveau 1905

Dining room of the Palais Stoclet, Brussels, designed by Josef Hoffmann, mosaics by Gustav Klimt

Josef Hoffmann, Otto Wagner's finest pupil, was a founder member of the Vienna Sezession and, in 1903, co-founder of the Wiener Werkstätte (literally 'Vienna Workshops'), an important institution which combined educational and exhibiting roles in order to provide good modern design through an emphasis on craftsmanship. It set the pattern for much of the thinking about domestic product design in Germany and Austria in this period. Hoffmann's early work in a florid Art Nouveau manner had, by about 1901, developed under the influence of Mackintosh towards a more severely rectilinear style,

which can be seen fully realized in his designs of 1903 for a Convalescent Home at Purkersdorf and in the Palais Stoclet in Brussels of 1905. The Stoclet house is one of the major achievements of the Viennese designers. It remains Hoffmann's masterpiece, and is an enduring example of the possibility of harmonious and successful co-operation between an architect and an artist working in a decorative context. In the dining room Hoffmann created the perfect setting for Klimt's mural panels in mosaic, judging their placing and the relationship between them and the surrounding marble of the walls exactly both in terms of line and colour. In so doing he made one of the major discoveries of the emergent Modernism: that in seeking a modern style stripped of elaborate ornament it was essential to use fine materials in order to create an acceptable alternative luxury.

Österreichische Nationalbibliothek, Vienna

67

The Vienna Sezession style c.1908

Project for an entrance hall by Josef Hoffmann; from C.H. Baer, Farbige Raumkunst, *Stuttgart, 1911*

Baer's influential book *Farbige Raumkunst* (decor in colour) also appeared in editions in Paris and London soon after its first publication in Stuttgart. It provided an important survey of the work of architects and designers from the major German cities together with some examples of projects by their Viennese and Scandinavian colleagues.

In much of this work the influence of Mackintosh and Baillie Scott is perhaps all too readily apparent, and many of the schemes are simply weak in both conception and drawing. Undoubtedly the work of Josef Hoffmann stands out from the rest. This project for a hallway or entrance contains a number of characteristic features of his mature style. In the divisions of the wall surface and in the fenestration there is a strong emphasis on vertical linear forms or grid patterns, and these are complemented by the all-over small pattern of the flooring. Very typical too of Hoffmann's style is the use of an exaggeratedly tall frieze, plain except for small square panels of semi-stylized figurative decoration.

68

Sezession Style in Düsseldorf c.1911

Dining room by Max Benirschke; from C.H. Baer, Farbige Raumkunst

The influence of the Viennese architects of the Sezession, Josef Hoffmann and J.M. Olbrich, spread rapidly. Their use of rectilinear forms and very controlled pattern and colour, best seen in the work of Kolo Moser, set a style which was imitated with varying degrees of success throughout Germany and elsewhere. In this project for a dining room, which seems almost too austere and impersonal to be intended for a private house, the square tub chairs are extremely typical.

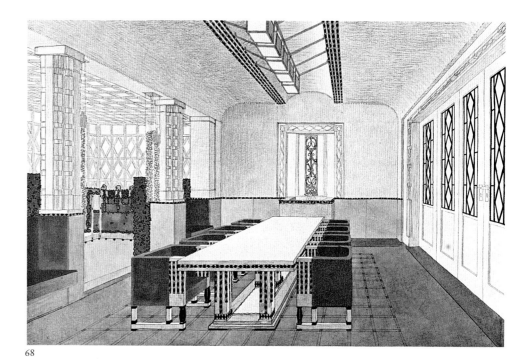

68

69

A white bedroom c.1910

Designed by Curjel & Moser, Karlsruhe; from C.H. Baer, Farbige Raumkunst

This at first glance uninspiring bedroom by the Karlsruhe partnership of Curjel & Moser in fact reveals some interesting points about the spread of the Mackintosh style in Germany. The debt to the master of elongated rectilinear forms is clear in every line of this design, and indeed there would seem to be direct parallels with Mackintosh's white bedroom at Hill House, Helensburgh (pl. 63). The two best things in this composition are the carefully worked-out bed carpet and the way in which the decorative motifs on the ceiling are carried down the frieze and related to the upright elements of the bedside cabinets.

69

70

Stripped classicism, Geneva 1904

Hall of the Villa Karma on Lake Geneva, by Adolf Loos

Adolf Loos, who had studied with Otto Wagner, the distinguished architect and professor of the Vienna Academy, became one of the most influential architectural theoreticians in Vienna at the turn of the century. Something of a dandy himself, he held that the reticent and correctly elegant dress and manners of the English gentleman could be taken as a model for architectural practice. Thus in about 1897 he turned away from the style of the Vienna Sezession and henceforth eschewed all ornament and decoration, which he held to be decadent. The 'well-mannered' but extraordinarily severe buildings and interiors which resulted from this 'road to Damascus' conversion pointed the way for the designers of the International Modern movement, but are also not wholly divorced from turn-of-the-century Austrian and German architecture. In a villa on the shores of Lake Geneva Loos created this hall in which all the forms are reduced to the simplest lines and the emphasis is entirely on the play of light from one plane to another. But in the paving of the floor even Loos has felt the need to hint in some degree at tradition, and to allow the colour of the materials to create if not ornament then at least some visually interesting pattern. Perhaps surprisingly, the total effect strongly suggests a connection with the more overtly decorative and historicizing work of other architects; for this hall has something of the feel of that German neo-classicism that gave rise to schemes such as the Pompeian hall by Richard Berndl of Munich (pl. 111).

Graphische Sammlung Albertina, Vienna

70

71

A modern kitchen 1906–7

Villa Hochstätter, Steinfeldgasse 7, Vienna, by Josef Hoffmann

The provision of new, modern-looking and, more importantly, functional kitchens and other service quarters in houses of all sizes became a matter of some concern to architects throughout Europe in the years immediately before the First World War. But it was in Vienna that the problem received the most serious attention, with architects of the stature of Hoffmann taking the time and trouble to rethink notions of how a working space of such complexity should be organized, and of what kind of decoration, if any, was appropriate. In the admirable kitchen of the Villa Hochstätter there is a tremendous step forward in terms of rational planning, and a new emphasis too on hygiene and efficient storage. Carefully planned and detailed storage areas, including open shelving and glazed cupboards, are treated in such a way as to be visually pleasing, and a black-and-white floor gives a crisp geometrical feel to the whole space. It is in fact the type of kitchen which would remain in favour for many years, until the advent of many more appliances and other gadgetry forced a further rethink in serious kitchen planning.

Österreichisches Museum für angewandte Kunst, Vienna

71

72

Design and industry in Germany 1914

Furniture by Josef Hoffmann at the Deutscher Werkbund Exhibition, Cologne

The Deutscher Werkbund was founded in 1907 and played a leading role in introducing the work of German architects, craftsmen and designers to the manufacturing industries. The association's annual exhibition and the yearbooks published from 1912 to 1915 showed important examples of mass-produced domestic products, including furniture by Richard Riemerschmid, Josef Hoffmann and other members of the Wiener Werkstätte. This group of pieces by Hoffmann shown in 1914 demonstrates his increasing use of large, undecorated rectilinear spaces and severely geometric forms for furniture: a style ultimately more influential in the decoration of public buildings such as cinemas than in a domestic context.

Private collection

72

73

The Liberty style c.1905

*Lithograph by A.E. Howarth, from Liberty & Co.,*Dress and Decoration, *London, n.d.*

Arthur Lasenby Liberty, who first opened his doors to an eager, artistically-minded public in 1875, did much to make interesting design and unusual objects more widely available. The early success of the store lay in two main areas: first the oriental bazaar and second, and ultimately more influentially, the promotion of commercially manufactured versions of the furnishings, textiles and objects of the English Arts and Crafts and Aesthetic movements. Liberty employed their own, for the most part anonymous, designers who copied and developed the styles of leading designers such as Voysey. One of the strengths of Liberty's lay in the fact that within one large shop it was possible to buy all the components necessary for a successfully artistic mode of life, and to be sure of their being acceptable to other aesthetically-minded people. Dress was as important as furnishings at this stage, with the effect that some of the early publications of the firm have the feel of being statements about lifestyle every bit as much as those of such great exponents of this approach in more recent years as Terence Conran, Laura Ashley or Ralph Lauren. Howarth's lithograph in colours from the booklet *Dress and Decoration*, of about 1905, shows a lady in a typically heavy commercialized Aesthetic costume deriving from late Pre-Raphaelite sources. She stands among pieces of furniture, including an 'occasional table' and a highly characteristic screen, which are poised stylistically between the Arts and Crafts manner and the greater extravagance of Continental Art Nouveau. On the table stands a classic Liberty artefact, a vase of eccentric form designed for Liberty's 'Tudric' range of domestic pewter wares by Archibald Knox.

74

74
'A chamber of horrors' 1903

Pen and ink drawing for a cartoon by R. C. Carter, signed and dated '03

A particularly well-observed parody of the furnishing styles of its day, this drawing by Carter makes a number of palpable hits on the worst excesses of the work of Baillie Scott and Voysey, and especially ridicules the absurdity of the middle-class home tricked out completely in a commercial version of it. It recalls the waggish line of that time: 'Liberty! Liberty! What crimes are committed in thy name!'

BBC Hulton Picture Library

75
The Arts and Crafts commercialized 1902

The Athelstan range of furniture made for Liberty & Co., and illustrated in Liberty's catalogue, Furniture for Town and Country Houses, *London, 1902*

This shows a group of the commercially produced versions of Arts and Crafts pieces in oak which the firm popularized for a widening public. Every piece can be related to a hand-crafted prototype, but each is simplified for manufacture and there is an increased emphasis on pretty or even twee details, such as heart-shaped cut-outs derived from the designs of C.F.A. Voysey. Liberty furniture was admired throughout Europe at this date and could be bought in Paris, Brussels, Berlin, Vienna and elsewhere. In Italy the international Art Nouveau or Jugendstil was known as Stile Liberty.

75

76

A Bugatti room for an Englishman c.1901

Bedroom designed for Lord Battersea's London home at Marble Arch

This quintessential example of the work of Carlo Bugatti reveals with tremendous clarity both the strengths and shortcomings of his work as a designer of furniture and decorator of rooms in a highly personal neo-baroque style. The designs of the many pieces included in this room are, according to taste, either endlessly inventive and entertaining or tiresome in their incessant striving after novelty. They cannot, however, be accused of dullness and the quality of workmanship is often quite high. Individual pieces were much collected in the late 1960s and 70s when they were 'rediscovered', mainly by pop stars furnishing their eccentrically grand houses, and it is easy to forget the importance of the ensemble in their original conception. This room is something of a rarity, being a complete scheme of decoration and furnishing by Bugatti for an Englishman, Cyril Flowers, first Lord Battersea.

Courtesy of Christopher Wood

77

Bugatti's fantasy furniture 1902

The Camera del Bovolo or Snail Room designed by Carlo Bugatti for the Turin International Exhibition

Carlo Bugatti was perhaps the most inventive of furniture makers during a period when a vein of extravagance and fantasy unparalleled before or since was running through Europe. Many of his pieces are near to purely sculptural forms, and the materials he used broke new ground. Rich woods were veneered and inlaid with pewter and other metals, and a remarkable effect was achieved by using sheets of vellum illuminated with colours and gilding, in patterns reminiscent of oriental calligraphy and formalized designs based on birds, flowers and insects. For the Turin International Exhibition of 1902 Bugatti created a suite of rooms, including the extraordinary 'snail room', which was the visual climax of the show, and more akin to recent 'installation' art than to true furnishing.

Bugatti Family Collection

77

78
Codman's crucial commission *c.1893*

Design by Ogden Codman for alterations and interior decoration at Land's End, Newport, Rhode Island; watercolour and pencil drawing for the library

The commission to make alterations at and to design interior decorations for the Whartons' Newport house was the turning point in this clever young architect's career. His work pleased the Whartons and they launched him into the almost inpenetrable society of turn of the century Rhode Island. But more than this, he discovered an extraordinary sympathy of ideas and taste existed between himself and Edith Wharton, the novelist-to-be, which led to their collaboration on *The Decoration of Houses*, the most seminal work on the subject of the whole period. Codman's treatment of the Whartons' originally modest house was a typical upgrading of the architectural features externally with pediments and stucco decoration, while inside he created a new and pleasing harmony based on a simple and rational disposition of the elements and the use of fine-quality materials and fittings brought over from France. In this design a new French chimneypiece is specified; it is surmounted by a classic French overmantel. Against Codman's favourite striped wallpaper stands a pair of rigidly ornamented bookcases.

The Metropolitan Museum of Art; gift of the Estate of Ogden Codman Jr, 1951 (51.644.75–1)

79
Harmony and proportion in a Newport palazzo 1895

Design for wall treatment in a room at The Breakers, the house of Cornelius Vanderbilt, at Newport, Rhode Island

Immediately before his major collaboration with Edith Wharton on *The Decoration of Houses*, Codman had been engaged on a project which had done much to enhance his reputation: the decoration of ten of the bedrooms in the vast palazzo built by Cornelius Vanderbilt which forms a central part of the smart summer house development at Newport. Although conceived on a far more modest scale than the entertaining or (one might almost say) public

78

79

rooms of the house, Codman's interiors already display that quiet assurance which derives from his sound knowledge of architectural and decorative precedents in eighteenth-century France and, equally, from his insistence that it was entirely appropriate to adapt these crucial models for the creation of fine and comfortable modern houses.

Society for the Preservation of New England Antiquities, Boston

80

Edith Wharton's parlour   c.1903

Decoration by Ogden Codman at 884 Park Avenue, New York

Codman collaborated with Mrs Wharton to transform her New York apartment according to the principles in which they both believed, and the result was a look which has never entirely passed out of fashion and which has its enthusiastic exponents to this day. The parlour, a small sitting room used by the novelist, illustrates just how radically their decoration differed from the fussy and overblown styles popular in New York at that time. A boldly striped wallpaper holds together the simple elements of a basically rectilinear scheme. The large glazed bookcase in the Louis Seize manner is in polished wood, but all the other furniture, including pieces from a suite of chairs with carved swans' heads in the Directoire style, is painted. The oil lamp has a very stylish and advanced shade of parchment decorated with neo-classical swags and roundels, entirely suitable to the clarity of the arrangement. Such rooms exerted a powerful influence on a new generation, not least on the emerging principal protagonist of the 'Old French look', Elsie de Wolfe.

The Metropolitan Museum of Art; gift of the Estate of Ogden Codman Jr, 1951

80

81

81
A New York treasure house 1906

The East Room of J. Pierpont Morgan's library; McKim, Mead & White, architects

The great American industrialist J. Pierpont Morgan cast himself in the role of a modern Maecenas, or of a Renaissance prince, scholar and patron of the arts, and in this light set about the creation of a palace worthy to receive the treasures he had amassed with a discerning eye and the expertise and flair of the most successful dealers of the day. His choice of architects fell on the highly regarded partnership of McKim, Mead & White, who conceived for him a mansion rich in decoration and built of the finest and rarest materials. The East Room, the main room of the library and the visual climax of the house, is a stunning Renaissance hall in which triple-storied bookcases rise to a high ceiling, vaulted and with painted panels in the quattrocento manner. Elsewhere in the house, in smaller rooms such as the study, sumptuous silks and brocades form the perfect setting for the discreet gleam of fine early bronzes and a seemingly endless array of important medieval and Renaissance objects.

Courtesy of the New-York Historical Society, New York City

82
A perfect French library in Massachusetts 1905

Mrs Wharton's library at The Mount, Lenox, Mass.

By the time that Mrs Wharton began work on what was to become her principal American residence, The Mount at Lenox, she declared that Ogden Codman had become too expensive, and instead engaged as architect Col. Francis Hoppen, the designer of the old New York Police Headquarters building. The interiors of the house, which was completed between 1901 and 1903, were nevertheless, as might be expected, nothing less than a perfect statement of the Wharton/Codman ideal. In the library the walls of books were framed in well-detailed panelling in the Louis Quinze style, the floor beneath the rich oriental carpet was of fine polished parquet, and the furnishings and other objects were of excellent quality and placed with respect for the architectural forms.

Beinecke Library, Yale University (Edith Wharton Papers)

83

A palace of art 1913–14

Living hall, the Frick Mansion, East 70th Street and
Fifth Avenue, New York, photographed in the 20s

83

Six years after the Colony Club decorations had launched Elsie de Wolfe's career, a major commission to do parts of the mansion of Henry Clay Frick established her at the top of the profession and in many ways redefined the role of the interior decorator. With the death of Pierpont Morgan in 1913 Frick was recognized as the most important of the very rich and very grand New York art collectors, and he began to think about rehousing his treasures, which up to that time had been arranged in the hectic, eclectic and over-decorated rooms of the old Vanderbilt Mansion at 640 Fifth Avenue. Frick had seen the Wallace Collection in Hertford House, London, and very much with the desire to emulate that example he commissioned a new and elegantly Italianate town palace from the architects Carrère & Hastings. Elsie de Wolfe managed

at this point, in spite of Lady Sackville's rivalry, to gain access for Frick to the residue of the Wallace pieces, then in Sir Richard Wallace's mansion in Paris. She bought for him on commission and, as she later put it, became both rich and famous overnight. Frick had until then relied heavily on the advice of experts in the formation of his collection, in particular that of Joseph Duveen, one of the grandest of all the dealers and one who also, with the help of the firm of William Allom and Francis Lenygon, would advise upon and carry out the installation of the works of art which he encouraged his predominantly American customers to buy. Elsie de Wolfe's more personal approach seems to have appealed to Frick, who enjoyed 'shopping' with his decorator and allowed her increasing influence over the way the mansion looked.

Frick Collection, New York

84

Elsie de Wolfe's 'effective use of colour' and choice of objects 1900s

Plates from E. de Wolfe, The House in Good Taste, *New York, 1913*

84

'Furniture painted with chintz designs'

85

'Mauve chintz in a dull-green room'

86

'The writing corner of a chintz bedroom'

It is from the rather curious colour plates with which *The House in Good Taste* was illustrated that we gain the best idea of the actual effect of the 'Old French look' advocated by Elsie de Wolfe. These plates were intended to show her particular use of colour in the creation of an atmosphere; at this stage in her career she seems to have preferred slightly off-beat combinations of dull or pale sage greens and pale mauves, which she considered wistful and suggestive of a vanished past. She was no coward in the use of the occasional brilliant touch of colour, however, and her schemes are lifted from the dismalness of much pastel-hued decoration of the Edwardian era by pieces such as a chest of drawers painted with flower garlands to echo a chintz, by picking out the metalwork of a sconce in red, or by the use of a startling black-background chintz. She always favoured French furniture and happily mixed good antique and reproduction pieces in order to create rooms that were comfortable and practical. She set great store by the rational notions that sitting rooms needed comfortable chairs, and bedrooms needed a quiet writing table placed in the correct relation to the light from the window and with lamps placed to allow writing at night. These groups became one of Elsie's hallmarks as a decorator and arranger of rooms, and have been influential ever since she first showed them in her book.

88

87

87

'Simplicity, suitability and proportion ... observed'

c.1898–1900

A hall designed by Elsie de Wolfe; from
The House in Good Taste, New York, 1913

The appearance of this dignified hall and the description of it, 'in this hall, simplicity, suitability and proportion are observed', are a perfect expression of Elsie de Wolfe's ideal 'Old French look'. She had learned a great deal from Ogden Codman and Edith Wharton's book *The Decoration of Houses* about the simple and uncluttered use of furnishings and objects, and was among the very first to understand and profit from their observations on correctness in architecture and the architectural placing of the decorative elements in an interior. Thus in a hall the following rules are observed: the floor is uncluttered to allow easy passage and is formed from durable materials in a strong and traditional pattern; the walls are divided into 'correctly' proportioned panels, plain in colour and without fussy pictures. Finally the decorative 'effect' is made by just a couple of suitable objects of sufficient scale: a practical writing table and a handsome piece of sculpture on an architecturally 'correct' pedestal.

88
Elsie de Wolfe starts her career 1906

Trellis room of the Colony Club, New York;
from The House in Good Taste

It was the legendary and larger-than-life figure Stanford White, of McKim Mead & White, who gave Elsie de Wolfe the first break that was to initiate her extraordinarily fortunate career as a decorator. Through his patronage Elsie secured the commission to carry out schemes of decoration in a number of the rooms of the Colony Club, the first club in New York, or indeed anywhere in the United States, for women. It may well be that the idea of employing a woman to design the decor was considered appropriate to the nature of the organization, but any doubts about her abilities must have been quickly dispelled when the schemes were revealed. Elsie's triumph was the Trellis Room, a delightful visual play on French garden *treillage* themes brought indoors and given an architectural grandeur. The room was furnished with chairs and tables which continued the garden motif, and the whole was widely imitated for many years thereafter.

89
High style in Boston 1905–6

Terrace entrance, the Anderson House, Brookline, Boston;
Little & Brown, architects

In this hall a rich design is further enhanced by the use of expensive materials. The trellis motif, which may well have been intended to evoke a Roman, or more precisely Pompeian, feel, is given an added dimension by the lavish use of mirror glass. As a decorative motif it also offers an intriguing parallel with the contemporary trellis scheme created for the Colony Club in New York by Elsie de Wolfe.

Society for the Preservation of New England Antiquities, Boston

90
Fake Louis in Paris   c.1905

Design for the salon of a Parisian apartment,
by Mewes & Davis

These pretty little drawings come from the series of sketchbooks used by the firm from about 1900 to 1910, which contain schemes for a large number of private houses and apartments in Paris, together with others clearly intended for hotels and other grand public buildings. All are in historic styles, mainly Louis Quinze and Louis Seize, and display a good working knowledge of the spirit as well as the details of the period looks which they copy. In this *petit salon Louis Seize* in blues and yellows all the elements, including every piece of furniture, would be faked up to create that feeling of *grand luxe* so much desired by rich clients for their own houses, and which came to be expected throughout Europe and America by patrons of the most expensive hotels.

Victoria & Albert Museum, London

91
Commercial historicism, France   c.1905

Design for a wall treatment by L. Alavoine & Co., Paris

In Paris, as in London or indeed New York, much of the expensive and up-market decoration was carried out by the few main large and old-established firms working in historic styles. These firms, the descendants of the great nineteenth-century upholsterers, relied on their traditions of good craftsmanship and worked from patterns long established and in many cases jealously guarded. They could supply tasteful decoration in each of the period styles thought appropriate for the various kinds of houses in which they were called to work, and would normally send well-prepared schemes to the client, often with quite beautifully rendered drawings. The houses of Jansen and Alavoine were both celebrated for their Louis revival interiors; this design, a typical watercolour produced in the studios of the latter, shows a proposal for the treatment of a wall with newly carved and daintily picked-out *boiseries*.

Stephanie Hoppen Ltd, London

92

92

Codman's ultimate grandeur c.1910

The Grand Salon, La Léopolda, near Villefranche-sur-Mer

The ultimate realization of his dreams of grandeur came for Ogden Codman in the creation of the sumptuous interiors of his vast house on the Riviera, La Léopolda. Here the quest for perfection in the architectural setting and the pursuit of the finest possible objects and furnishings combined for a while to fashion the quintessential statement of the 'Old French look', but finally ruined their creator. An anecdote records that when in later years Codman was forced to seek a tenant to ease the financial burden of the house, he 'interviewed' the Duke and Duchess of Windsor. They refused to pay what they thought was an extortionate deposit against breakages and damages to the important contents of the house, only to find themselves dismissed by the owner with the memorable phrase: 'I fear that the house of Codman finds itself unable to do business with the House of Windsor.'

Society for the Preservation of New England Antiquities, Boston

93

93

New England chic 1906

Circular hall, Sunset Rock, Beverley, Mass.;
Little & Brown, architects

This entrance hall by the Boston architectural partnership of Little & Brown reveals a remarkable degree of sophistication in the creation of a telling arrangement of furniture and other objects, and a feeling for the tension between bold and over-scaled pieces that is rare at so early a date.

Society for the Preservation of New England Antiquities, Boston

94

The 'Old French look', New York 1912

Dining room of Ogden Codman's own house,
7 East 96th Street, New York

The dining room of Codman's town house in New York is so much the perfect expression of his ideals that it must be described in detail. The room has that sense of elegance and poise that comes, as Codman would have it, only from a correct disposition of the architectural features, in particular the 'openings': the doors, windows and chimney. The actual detail of the room was based on an enlarged version of a small oval panelled room which Codman obtained from an eighteenth-century *hôtel particulier* in Bordeaux, and which is now installed in the Metropolitan Museum of Art, New York. The furnishings and all the other elements in the room, including silverware, glasses and even table linen, were collected by Codman during his annual extended trips to France and were, interestingly, a mixture of antique or original pieces and good modern reproductions. Codman's fanatical interest in the history of French architecture, decoration and culture of the eighteenth century was quite breathtaking in its scope and depth: it led him to compile a unique index with illustrations and details of all 36,000 known French châteaux. Digested, this knowledge and enthusiasm was to have a far-reaching effect on American decoration.

Society for the Preservation of New England Antiquities, Boston

94

95

White-painted furniture in Sweden 1909

*Living room of the artist's house; from Carl Larsson,
Åt Solsiden, Stockholm, 1910*

This is the ideal of unaffected comfort proposed by Larsson in his books, as depicted in the summer house created by the painter and his wife Karin, who may well have been responsible for much of the decoration. The furniture and woodwork in this living room reflect the mixture of influences which combined to give the house its particular flavour. There is a certain amount of constructed woodwork with a slightly Art Nouveau feel, the table seems to be a piece of commercial Art Nouveau, and the chair, like many throughout the house, is an elegant neo-classically inspired Biedermeier piece. All these diverse elements, however, have been linked together by painting. The fabrics are in simple peasant style, mostly striped, like the Swedish country flat-weave rugs and runners used on the floors of several rooms.

96
Biedermeier revival in Sweden 1909

Drawing room of the artist's house; from Carl Larsson,
Åt Solsiden

The painter's daughter is seen preparing for her marriage in the most formal and elegant room in the house. There is far less emphasis here on the colourful paint treatments seen throughout the rest of the house, and the fine pieces of Biedermeier furniture retain their original polish. The sofa and sofa table even have ormolu mounts, which marks them clearly as pieces for the drawing room, while the other chairs of a well-known Swedish pattern are equally elegant. Furniture in this comfortable, neo-classical manner became increasingly popular in Scandinavia and Germany at this time, and before long manufacturers were creating very high-quality reproduction pieces to satisfy the demands of decorators, much of which still circulates in the antique trade today as genuine early nineteenth-century.

96

97
A fresh, clean bathroom 1909

The painter's daughter Lisbeth bathing; from Carl
Larsson, Åt Solsiden

The clean, efficient and no-nonsense bathroom in the Larssons' summer house was an essential part of their self-consciously joyful and healthy life. The room was clearly fitted with sophisticated modern plumbing, and other convenient arrangements such as a soap rack on the wall near the tub and an interesting leather strap which formed a headrest for the bather. The most interesting feature of the room, however, was a wooden slatted floor which looks as if it may have been hygienic but rather uncomfortable to stand on.

97

98

98
Ricketts and Shannon discover 'comely sobriety' c.1899

Little drawing room at Spring Terrace, Richmond, London; photograph from the artists' own albums

The house in Richmond to which Charles Ricketts and Charles Shannon moved in 1898 was a Georgian one with a superb wooden porch, panelled rooms and other surviving details. They enhanced the period feel by painting in uniform pale colours and choosing mahogany and satinwood furniture of the later eighteenth century. These pieces were plain and very elegant, yet still at that date not highly regarded. The effect was in many ways very similar to 'comely sobriety', that spare and architecturally correct look propounded in America by Edith Wharton and Ogden Codman. Particularly worth noting are a large lacquer cabinet already in an advanced state of 'pleasing decay' and a very good long, lean English Regency pier glass of about 1810, painted white at this stage. By 1904 they had had it re-gilded, thereby completing a full revolution in taste long before the mania for painting or 'pickling' antiques. It is perhaps difficult to appreciate how remarkable this house was, for we have grown so used to this understated approach to the period interior, which became universally imitated between the wars and is still very much with us today.

Fitzwilliam Museum, Cambridge

99
A modern setting for art and antiques 1902

Drawing room of Ricketts and Shannon's studio apartment, Lansdowne House, Holland Park, London; photograph from the artists' collection as reproduced in H. Muthesius, Das Englische Haus, *Berlin, 1904*

Lansdowne House, a block of artists' studio apartments in a somewhat aggressive Viennese style, was built in 1901–2 by Sir Edmund Davis, South African millionaire art collector and a patron of Ricketts and Shannon. The drawing room of their new home quickly became something of a set piece; a room which was gradually used less and less but which was considered by those, such as the Prussian architectural theoretician Hermann Muthesius, who were fortunate enough to be admitted, to be the very epitome of advanced English taste. If the Richmond house was to some degree an essay in the creation of a 'period look', this room at Lansdowne House was distinctly 'modern' in feel and utterly free of any attempt to be 'artistic'. Nor, indeed, did any taint of commercial upholsterers' tricks mar the fresh and original appearance. The room had an elegant neo-Georgian chimneypiece lined with white tiles and an inset 'swan's nest' grate of the kind later to become such a decorator's cliché. The overall lightness of effect results in part from the extreme simplicity of the curtains, which were unlined and in a Morris-pattern chintz specially printed without the background colour. This customized fabric was also used for co-ordinated cushions and seat covers. Attenuated satinwood tables and an 'Adam' sofa were dotted about on polished parquet with a few choice Persian rugs. Most extraordinarily, and in contrast to any of the artists' previous rooms, lighting was from the start by electricity, with naked bulbs in 'plain sixpenny shades'.

Private collection

100

A private museum   c. 1920

*Photograph of the drawing room, Lansdowne House,
Holland Park, by Charles Ricketts*

In later photographs of the drawing room at Lansdowne
House the effects of twenty years of almost manic
collecting can be clearly seen. The room has quite simply
been filled with Ricketts and Shannon's accumulated
treasures bought from dealers and in sales in London and
on trips to Italy, Greece and Egypt. The display of so many
antiquities necessitated glass cases, and it is these more than
anything else which give the now little-used room its
characteristic feel of a small private museum. However,
Ricketts always maintained the more personal atmosphere
the room once had by placing flowers and bowls of water
containing shells on many of the tables.

Private collection

100

99

101

Early Regency revival, London 1907

A Bloomsbury Family; *oil painting by William Orpen*

This latter-day conversation piece shows the painter William Nicholson, his wife Mabel and their children in the dining room of their house in Mecklenburgh Square, in Fitzrovia-Bloomsbury. Both Mabel and William Nicholson had individual tastes in decoration. Mabel created what must have been, for the time, an extraordinary scheme in the handsome, high-ceilinged drawing room on the first floor, which included a Chinese dragon pattern carpet in bright colours and a sofa covered in black satin. William's taste was more for the Regency, a passion shared with his friends the influential dealer-decorator Mrs Harrington ('Dolly') Mann and Edward Knoblock, the celebrated collector. The dining room seen in Orpen's painting, done in lieu of rent for a studio, was entirely Nicholson's creation, with 'meerschaum-coloured' walls forming an almost club-like background for a classic Regency circular mirror and the painter's beloved collection of portraits of the Regency dandies by Richard Dighton. Nicholson affected an early nineteenth-century look, wearing high collars and a stock, and this stylish pose did almost as much as his painting and decoration to popularize the neo-Regency style, both in England and in France where his work was also known.

Scottish National Gallery of Modern Art, Edinburgh

102

An artistic house c.1914

Eric Gill and his wife; *oil painting by Sir William Rothenstein*

In this beautiful conversation piece Rothenstein, a keen observer of the subtleties of room settings, portrays an artistic house of the kind much favoured by the more intellectual English artists of the day. There seems to be very little overt decoration, but rather a delight in the charm of the simple marble fire surround and other plain surfaces and flat areas of colour. Gill certainly espoused a

102

philosophy based on the honest use of materials such as wood, stone and hand-made paper. Rothenstein recalled in his autobiography *Men and Memories* (1931) a telling remark he made: 'while God doesn't particularly approve of luxury, at least he wants it in good taste....'

Courtesy of Sir John and Michael Rothenstein (photograph Sotheby's)

103

'A polished period in decoration' 1912

Henry James's country retreat at Lamb House, Rye, Sussex

103

View from the hall into the 'Telephone Room'
Photograph by Alvin Langdon Coburn

104

The Oak Parlour (drawing room)

Henry James was perhaps the most famous expatriate American in London at the turn of the century. As one of the most admired writers of the day he was lionized by artistic and literary society, and his feats of endurance as a diner-out became something of a legend. Feeling the need to escape the continual pressure of London life, he went in the summer of 1896 to Rye, and discovered that 'the bliss of the rural solitude and peace and beauty are a balm to my spirit'. There he found Lamb House, a pretty, panelled, early Georgian house, with good details which had led James's friend, the architect Edward Warren, to draw it the year before. James took the long lease that was available and began to fill the rooms with his books and pictures and papers. Although a fastidious observer of rooms he seems, like many literary men, to have cared more for the associative than for the visual aspects of his possessions. He arranged his furniture for comfort and his favourite prints such as sets of 'Vertue's Heads' almost at random. Fortunately some rare informal photographs of Lamb House in 1912 survive. They give a delightful glimpse of the way in which many people who cared little for the precious dictates of fashion in decoration must have lived.

103 *International Museum of Photography at George Eastman House, Rochester, New York*
104 *The National Trust*

104

105

'A special decoration' by William Nicholson c.1912

The Anteroom, Beach House, Worthing, photographed in 1921

Edward Knoblock, an American expatriate and the now almost-forgotten author of *Kismet*, describes in his autobiography, *Round the Room* (1939), how in 1912 he took an apartment in the 'decayed and antiquated' Palais Royal in Paris. 'Apart from its beautiful architecture it is a haven of quiet, at the same time being in the very centre of Paris. It always surprises me that Parisians did not find this out sooner. The prejudice of fashion makes people blind.' He explained that the success of *Kismet* had allowed him at last to give full rein to his 'passion for collecting really good antiques', and, 'as all the world was collecting the earlier eighteenth-century furniture . . . ,' he continued, 'and as my taste lay in the direction of the Empire I gathered together things of the late Directoire – then still considered a bastard style – and furniture of the early days of Napoleon known

to the connoisseur as the "*retour de l'Egypte*". I engaged decorators to paint my little sitting room and bedroom in appropriate style and for the dining room I asked William Nicholson to design a special decoration.' Nicholson carried out the set of architectural and theatrical capriccios on glass panels set in a framework like a window, painting from the back so that he was obliged 'to put in his last touches first'. The panels, which are now on loan to the Victoria & Albert Museum from the National Trust, are technically a tremendous *tour de force*, boldly painted in a manner close to the simplified forms of Nicholson's woodcuts and brightly coloured in rich siennas against a turquoise-blue sky. Knoblock was clearly immensely proud of this imaginative commission, and when war broke out in 1914 he took the panels with him to London. In 1921 he acquired Beach House as a setting for his celebrated collection of Thomas Hope furniture and installed the Nicholson 'decoration' in the anteroom (this time fixing up the panels with studs in the manner of old French looking-glass panelling), thus reaffirming the confident modernity of his taste in 1912.

Country Life

106

A chic picture-hang, Denmark c.1910

An interior; oil painting by Peter Ilsted

From the days of Caspar David Friedrich and George Friedrich Kersting onwards the painters of northern Europe have been obsessed with the fall of light through windows. In Scandinavia it is an easily understandable preoccupation: Carl Larsson even made the phrase *Lasst Licht Hinein* (Let in the Light) the title of one of his books about how to live (pls 95–7). This study of the light from two windows reveals an intriguing room in an advanced neo-classical revival taste. The furnishings are sparse but good: a commode between the windows flanked by an elegant Directoire-style elbow chair. But it is against the far wall that the most interesting group of objects is arranged. Above an extremely stylish scroll-ended sofa pictures are hung in a single long, low line. This, it would seem, is based on a type of arrangement to be seen in pictures of early nineteenth-century rooms in Russia and Scandinavia, and its revival here is chic and effective, curiously suggestive of the clean, long, low lines of Scandinavian modern design later in the century.

Bury Street Gallery, London

107

Period charm in Denmark c.1910

The stove in the dining room at Liselund; oil painting by Peter Ilsted

The quiet grace and dignity of this almost monochromatic room in a fairly grand house in Liselund are typical of the atmosphere caught in the paintings of interiors by the group of artists which included Ilsted and his brother-in-law, Vilhelm Hammershoi. Their depictions of rooms have something of that enclosed stillness of seventeenth-century Dutch interiors, and there is a similar fascination with the play of light across floors and the mellow surfaces of furnishings. The rooms chosen are almost always furnished in the austere but delightful manner of the late eighteenth century. This marks them as the Danish equivalent of the Swedish revival of interest in the furnishings of the 'Gustavian' era (late eighteenth and

107

early nineteenth century,) and links the artists to enthusiasts for that period elsewhere, such as Professor Richardson at Ampthill in England or the restorers of Federal period architecture in the United States. In this canvas by Ilsted the central feature is the niche containing a large stove surmounted by a bust in white glazed ceramic: an arrangement typical of houses throughout northern Europe.

Bury Street Gallery, London

108

available in the early years of the century. Marmottan had a genuine love of the Napoleonic era in all its literary, political and military aspects and therefore was happy to create room sets in which the atmosphere worked for him alone. He believed that a good copy was an acceptable substitute for a genuine piece and that plain or uninspired pieces, such as his own Directoire bed by the furniture maker Georges Jacob, could be improved by the addition of elaborate ormolu mounts in a richer and later Empire taste. Ironically, after his death the house became a museum, and the first curator, the expert Henri Lefuel, himself a descendant of Jacob, stripped the rooms of clutter and certain of these later embellishments in an attempt to get nearer to the more austere taste of the early Directoire period. This photograph of one of the principal rooms shows the arrangement during Marmottan's lifetime.

Rizzoli Libri, Milan

108

An Empire collector, France c.1910

Salle de Psyche *at 2 rue Louis-Boilly, Paris, the house of Paul Marmottan*

Paul Marmottan, man of letters and an ardent Napoleonist, formed one of the earliest collections of Directoire and Empire furnishings and relics of the period, arranging his rooms in a large house in a spacious quarter near the Parc Monceau in Paris almost as a museum, even in his lifetime. He acquired major pieces at a time when such things were on the market at prices below those of the far more ordinary examples of the eighteenth century; but Mario Praz, who visited the house and knew Marmottan, has described in *On Neo-Classicism* (London, 1969, 2nd edn 1972; originally published as *Il gusto neoclassico*, Milan, 1969) the rather gloomy and lifeless feel of many of the rooms, criticizing the collector for not having bought the more interesting and personal items that were still

109

109

A French bedroom 1911

Bedroom of Lady Duff Gordon

To be really successful as a couturier it was important to either sound French or look it. Lady Duff Gordon, sister to the notorious novelist Elinor Glyn, did both. Assuming the highly appropriate name Lucile, she surrounded herself with a remarkably well-put-together 'Old French look'. Both her salon and her own house were done over in this way, and both became celebrated as paragons of good taste. The salon was painted throughout in subtle greys and had old French chairs with pleasingly rubbed paintwork. Photographs that survive of the house show that she lived in some style. Her own bedroom was decorated in a highly feminine version of the Louis Seize manner, with a good French bed beneath a prettily draped canopy garlanded with silk flowers. A small door led from the bedroom into an *en suite* bathroom, while close to the bed stood an elaborately flounced dressing table with a huge oval toilet mirror lit by double candle sconces. On the dressing table stood framed photographs and an array of dainty silver and other toilet articles.

Private collection

110

A Directoire dining room 1911

Dining room of Lady Duff Gordon

Even more than her 'Old French look' bedroom, which reveals its Edwardian date at once, Lucile's dining room is an extraordinarily convincing realization of a period look. The room is simple and uncluttered and contains a perfectly chosen group of late Directoire and early Empire pieces. The early French colour-printed wallpaper that forms the main feature of the decoration is a set of that same Psyche *papier peint* by Joseph Dufour after which Paul Marmottan named a room in his house. It would be tremendously hard to date this assemblage from the visual evidence alone, and it may well be that only the desk placed diagonally across the far corner of the room and the electrification of the period chandelier would give the game away.

Private collection

111

111

Pompeii in Munich c.1910

Hall by Richard Berndl; from C.H. Baer, Farbige
Raumkunst, *Stuttgart, 1911*

The German love affair with the classical world began in the eighteenth century with the writings of Winckelmann. Goethe and a great many other German writers, artists and travellers continued the tradition of forming their visual tastes in Italy, and by the late nineteenth century Renaissance decoration and a more archaeologically based repertoire of ancient ornament were two of the most popular styles in German interiors with any pretence towards being 'artistic'. Surviving examples of wall painting and other decoration which had been unearthed at Pompeii exerted a strong and long-lasting influence. Many felt that Pompeii gave the closest possible idea of the true nature of Roman decoration, and even though the best-preserved remains are for the most part the private houses of rich merchant-class Romans, the style was adopted with equal enthusiasm for artists' studios, grand houses and many public buildings.

112

Directoire revival, France c.1910

*A daybed in a painted alcove; watercolour
by Claude Boussin*, décorateur, *Paris*

This design for the painted treatment of an alcove by Claude Boussin, who described himself as a '*décorateur*' but about whom little is known otherwise, is in a very chic Directoire manner and reflects the growing fashion for a colourful version of that generally austere style. There can be no doubt here about the influence of the Napoleonic period decoration at Malmaison (pls 17–24), and certainly the style appealed to those, such as Edward Knoblock, who were beginning to collect the hitherto-neglected furniture of the period as well as more personal relics. In this case the painted wooden daybed with its immaculate striped silk cover and co-ordinated tasselled bolsters may well be reproduction. It may be this sort of painting to which Edward Knoblock refers in his autobiography *Round the Room* (1939) when he describes having had painters to trick out his Palais Royal apartment in the Directoire style in 1912.

Stephanie Hoppen Ltd, London

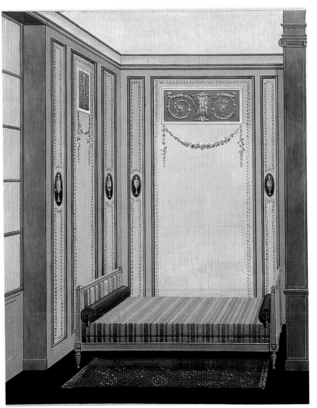

113

A lady's bedchamber, France c.1910

Chambre à coucher de Mme Guillet; *watercolour by Claude Boussin*, décorateur, *Paris*

Another design for an entire scheme of decoration in an historic style, this proposal for a pretty Louis Quinze bedroom for an unknown lady is superficially less chic than the Directoire scheme, but there are elements which set it apart from straightforward Louis revival. The drawing itself has a degree of charm from its resemblance to an old watercolour of an interior, and yet the furnishings seem grander than would fit the slightly provincial air suggested by the artist. More important, however, is the use of Chinese carpets laid on a black floor. These seem to be intended to find an echo in the splendid black and gold lacquer, ormolu-mounted commode, and they recall the descriptions that survive of the rather smart scheme contrived by Mabel, wife of the painter William Nicholson, for their drawing room in London's Bohemian Fitzrovia (pl. 101).

Stephanie Hoppen Ltd, London

113

114
'Russian Ballet Decadent', Paris c.1910

Drawing by Philippe Jullian, from Les Styles, *Paris, 1962*

Philippe Jullian's *Les Styles*, a brilliant book full of precise observation, was dedicated to Sir Osbert Lancaster, whose own essay in the genre, *Homes Sweet Homes* was its inspiration. Jullian's version of the Russian Ballet style brings out more of its decadent and exotic aspects and neatly points to the connection between the Russian costume designers and Paul Poiret's rich and evocative fashions.

Courtesy of Comte Ghislain de Diesbach and Editions Plon, Paris

114

115

115
'First Russian Ballet Period' c.1913

Illustration by Sir Osbert Lancaster from Homes Sweet Homes, *London, 1939*

In the characteristically incisive text accompanying his witty drawing Osbert Lancaster was among the first to notice that many of the fads and fashions commonly associated with the 'Bright Young Things' of the 1920s in fact had their origins in the years immediately prior to the outbreak of the First World War. The immense success of the Russian Ballet, not only artistically but also socially, meant that its influence in the worlds of *haute couture* and decoration was very far-reaching. The tendency towards the creation of 'stage-set' domestic interiors increased and people began, as Osbert Lancaster put it, 'to regard a room not so much as a place to live in, but as a setting for a party'. Richness and exoticism were the keynotes of rooms in this style, and under the influence of the designs of Léon Bakst and Alexandre Benois, colours became vivid and barbaric, with mixtures of heavily saturated greens, purples, reds and oranges. Eclectic arrangements of objects were made, as African carvings and theatrical masks were juxtaposed with Middle Eastern and oriental things. This striving to avoid the ordinary met with success only if carried out completely uncompromisingly.

John Murray Ltd, London

116

An African fantasy, Paris c.1919

Room setting by Paul Poiret's Atelier Martine

In a highly eclectic and perhaps not entirely serious room setting by the Atelier Martine a number of tastes of the period are drawn together. On the one hand, there are characteristic Poiret touches such as the piles of deep, soft cushions upholstered in rich stuffs and a colourful and hectic rug on the floor, whilst on the other a degree of novelty is introduced by the mural decoration with African motifs. This interest in African things centred on the Parisian art world, where a number of artists such as the Cubists, Picasso and Braque, gathered examples of tribal artefacts in their studios from about 1905 onwards. The popularity of these objects spread; in England they fascinated the Sitwell brothers and others such as the sculptor Jacob Epstein and by the 1920s a taste for African culture was widespread, contributing to the immense success in Paris of the *chanteuse* Josephine Baker and the famous entertainments of Le Bal Nègre. A further interesting detail in this Poiret room is the use of an African-looking woven grass or rattan wall covering, a type of natural-fibre fabric not generally popular until considerably later, but typical of the inventive and unconventional approach to the creation of successful interiors evident in Poiret's work.

Photo Lipnitzki-Viollet, Paris

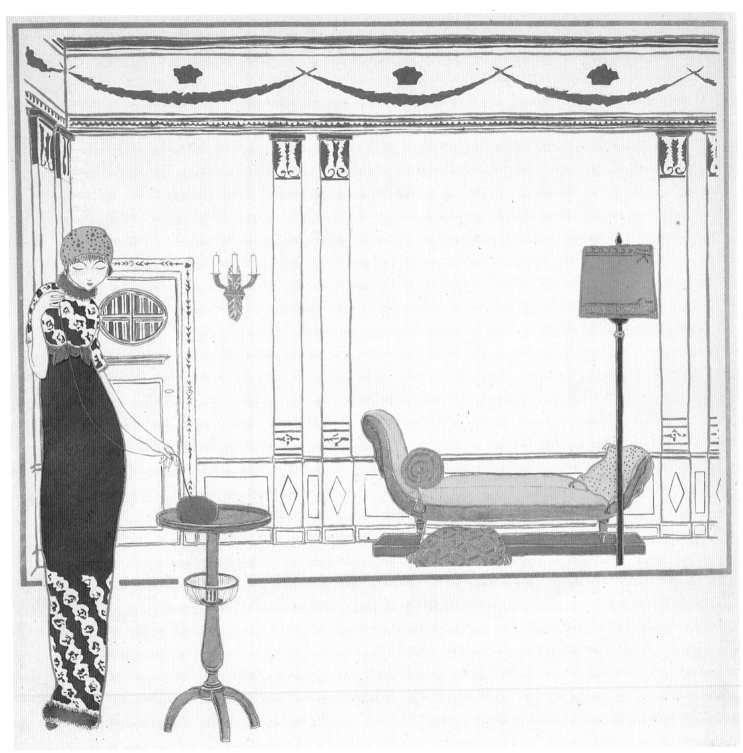

117

The Empire revival, Paris 1911

Plate by Georges Lepape, from
Les Choses de Paul Poiret, *Paris, 1911*

At a time when Paris remained the undisputed centre of the world of fashion Paul Poiret, director of one of the most famous houses, exerted a powerful influence in all matters of visual taste. His rich and exotic creations made the Russian Ballet look available to a wealthy and very chic clientele. His excursions into the field of interior decoration were equally important and stylish, culminating in the establishment of his Atelier Martine in 1911. Cecil Beaton wrote of the 'Arabian Nights', dream-like quality of the Martine interiors, strewn with cushions. Their richness and subtle beauty of colour is well brought out in these colour plates by Lepape, illustrating robes and accessories in interiors in a highly stylized Empire manner suggesting Léon Bakst at Malmaison. This combination of clothes and settings was a potent one, and reveals Poiret as among the first to realize the intimate and often symbiotic connection between the worlds of *haute couture* and *haut décor*.

118

118

A decorator's shop 1911

Marcel Boulestin in his shop in Elizabeth Street, London

Apart from the views of the premises of the very grand decorating firms such as Keeble's or Lenygon & Morant, we have almost no surviving images of the interiors of shops or showrooms of the period. This early photograph, however, shows the first-floor room of the house in Elizabeth Street occupied by Boulestin's Décoration Moderne between 1911 and 1914, and gives something of the flavour of the smaller individual decorators' businesses which emerged in London, Paris and New York at this time. Perhaps significantly, Boulestin himself is seen in the shop, showing a sample of Poiret fabric to a rather fashionably dressed young woman. Also visible are a modern table lamp with a shade of Poiret silk and a number of examples of the 'new and amusing vases' which Boulestin found in Paris and for which the shop was to become famous.

Michael Parkin Fine Art Ltd, London

119

Marcel Boulestin's trade card c.1918

Design by Jean-Emile Laboureur for Décoration Moderne

Boulestin's great friend and constant collaborator Laboureur made this design for use in the decorator's second shop, which opened in George Street in 1918 and closed when the business was forced into liquidation in 1921. The amusing little drawing is recognizably a portrait of Boulestin, surrounded by the 'knick-knacks' of which he kept such an interesting stock, showing fabric samples to an elegantly dressed customer.

Michael Parkin Fine Art Ltd, London

DECORATION MODERNE = X. M. BOULESTIN,
102, GEORGE STREET, PORTMAN SQUARE, W.1.
SOLE AGENT FOR MARTINE (PAUL POIRET).

119

120

A new theatricality 1906–12

The hall, Folly Farm, Sulhampstead, Berkshire, by Edwin Lutyens; photographed in 1922

This stunning achievement by the young Lutyens breaks much new ground as both architecture and decoration, in which he had become equally interested. The handling of the architectural forms here is suave and confident. Lutyens is able to marshall his 'Wrenaissance' forms with such ease that the play between inside and outside forms in the balconied window high above the room seems witty, effortless and inevitable. The decoration is no less innovative, with crisp white enamelled paintwork defining areas of wall finished in glossy black. Against this stands a cabinet of scarlet lacquer, echoing the red fretted balcony and placed with the dash and assurance which led the decorator Ronald Fleming to describe Lutyens's rooms admiringly as 'produced with a personal distinction and a new economy of means'. There is more than a hint in this new-found delight in playing with colour of the influence of his very close friendship with Lady Sackville, another devotee of red lacquer and a fearless innovator in her decorative schemes.

Country Life

121

A Renaissance bedchamber 1917

121

Bedroom of Mrs William K. Vanderbilt; from Vogue, *1917*

During Ruskin's sojourn in Venice he became particularly intrigued by the painting known as *The Dream of St Ursula*, one of the masterpieces of that strange and compelling artist Carpaccio. The scene of the painting is set in the saint's bedchamber, which the artist depicts in the height of the fashion of his day, with Ursula lying in a bedstead of distinctive Renaissance form. Following Ruskin's praise a number of designers seem independently to have realized the potential of the picture as an inspiration for the creation of a bed on a lavish scale for a modern bedroom. The architect Edwin Lutyens used several elements of the design on a more modest scale, but it was Geoffrey Scott, the author of the seminal book *The Architecture of Humanism*, 1914, and a great student of Italian Renaissance culture, who designed the most interesting version. This was executed in Florence for his friend William Haslam who later installed it in his English house, Great Hundridge Manor (pls 259, 260, 261). It still survives and may be seen in the Victoria & Albert Museum. The third version of the piece, and the grandest in scale and conception, was the one created for the Vanderbilt mansion, which appears in the *Vogue* decoration pages for 1917. Here the bed has been scaled up to fill a large apartment and, according to the description of the room, everything was chosen to have a richness evocative of the early Italian 'palazzo' style. In fact from the *Vogue* identification of the colours used, which included violet and other bright shades, the whole feel of the room must have owed as much to the influence of Paul Poiret as to that of Carpaccio.

Condé Nast Publications Ltd, London

122

122

An actress's room c.1910

Intérieur de Mlle Sorel de la Comédie Française;
photograph by Eugène Atget

As a star Mlle Sorel could clearly afford to indulge her tastes in furnishings. Her *petit salon* on the avenue des Champs-Elysées had, it seems, rather good *boiseries*. Beneath a portrait flanked by *lampes d'applique* with electrified candles and silk shades stands an austerely elegant commode between a pair of lyre-back chairs, while a large floor-length looking-glass reflects a second room which may well be decorated *en suite*. Everything here speaks of quality and refinement, and there is none of the flashy or meretriciously over-decorated furniture usually associated with the theatrical world.

Private collection

COMTESSE MATHIEU DE NOAILLES

123

123
Exoticism in Paris c.1913

*The Comtesse Anna de Noailles in her boudoir, from an
early autochrome photograph*

Anna de Noailles, Romanian by birth and a spirited
poet, occupied an important position in Parisian
social and artistic circles in the years before the Great War.
Her personal magnetism and original exoticism gained her
a reputation as a hostess, and her verses were also held in
some esteem. Her love of the striking and exotic costumes
of the Middle East, which she contrived to wear in the
Poiret manner, encouraged her liking for colour and rich
fabrics, and this taste also spread into her rooms. Like her
friend Robert de Montesquiou she created settings of a self-
conscious preciousness, rooms filled with exquisite flowers,
prettily bound books and a mixture of fine Louis Quinze
furniture and some indifferent pieces chosen merely for
their shape and colour. In her boudoir a tiny marquetry-
work table stands beside a silk-upholstered *lit de repos*
upon a Chinese rug, and the whole group is enclosed by a
low screen. There is a shaded lamp and a characteristic
profusion of books and flowers.

Jean-Loup Charmet, Paris

124
Transatlantic chic 1906

Consuelo, Duchess of Marlborough; *oil painting by
Giovanni Boldini*

In this picture Boldini, one of the greatest stylists among
society portrait painters, fixes for all time the glamorous
image of one of the great taste-makers. Consuelo Vanderbilt was the most brilliant, the most beautiful and perhaps
also the richest of the American women who married into
the English aristocracy, and whose lifestyles and ideas did
so much to change the English way of life in town and
country at the turn of the century. It is a studio portrait and
therefore generalized, but it does convey a precise sense of
the luxury without vulgarity that was the hallmark of
Consuelo Vanderbilt's style.

*Metropolitan Museum of Art, New York;
gift of Consuelo Vanderbilt Balsan, 1946*

124

125

Biedermeier revival in Berlin c.1919

Reception and work room in the artist's house, by Professor Bruno Paul; from A. Koch, Handbuch neuzeitlicher Wohnungskultur, *Darmstadt, 1919*

This is one of the classic statements of the Biedermeier ideal, carried out with extraordinary subtlety by a leading exponent of the style in Berlin, a practising architect and professor, Bruno Paul. (The title of this book means 'handbook of contemporary domestic culture'.) In the time-honoured tradition of grouping furniture in the German parlour or grander reception room, Paul has placed paired elbow chairs and a low circular table with curly supports in front of a remarkable sofa of his own design. This sofa is a play on the characteristic form of the Biedermeier sofa with scrolled ends and tasselled bolsters, but elongated to twice the usual length. With a pair of small side tables flanking it and framed architectural prints, including a Piranesi view of the Pantheon, hanging above, Paul creates a symmetrical composition filling the entire length of the end wall of the room. The centrally placed window embrasure provides the space for a pretty Biedermeier clock, and there are formal draperies of dark but transparent muslin with a valance and tiebacks suggesting but not copying the style of 1820. The floor treatments seem equally intended to evoke the early nineteenth century in a playful manner, with a square carpet of geometrical design laid over a huge check pattern: like the sofa a scaled-up version of the 1820s.

125

126
Biedermeier revival in Vienna 1912

A lady's boudoir by Professor Otto Prutscher; from A. Koch, Handbuch neuzeitlicher Wohnungskultur

This pretty and very feminine version of the Biedermeier revival style is unusual for a Viennese scheme of its date, being very much influenced by Parisian ideas. However if some elements, such as the curtain treatment and above all the pair of silk-shaded standard lamps, are close in feel to things that Paul Poiret was doing, there is no mistaking the essentially Austrian character of the dressing or work table and the tall cabinet at the back of the room. Both derive from the quirky forms of Viennese pieces of the 1820s and 30s and are made in the much-loved blond wood that is so typical of the furniture of that period.

126

127
A student's room 'à la Malmaison' c.1919

Bedroom study by H.E. Linder, Basle; from A. Koch, Handbuch neuzeitlicher Wohnungskultur

Alexander Koch chose to print two views of this clever and extremely stylish forerunner of the modern multi-purpose room. Linder's design for the study and sleeping quarters of a student seems to have been conceived with a mind to the very essence of the problem of living in a small space. The solution, which allows a far greater degree of civilization than in many other such attempts to reconcile a variety of needs and functions, was based on reducing the number of pieces to a minimum, making each as elegant as possible and, most importantly, enclosing the bed within a movable set of hangings on free-standing poles. Cleverly Linder made the poles in the form of spears and so imparted to the whole room a suggestion of the splendours of Malmaison (pls 17–24), while retaining the spare and utilitarian atmosphere of military campaign furnishings. This is a well-chosen model both in aesthetic and associative terms, and is equally effective as a practical working environment for the visually aware student.

127

128

In the far north c.1910

Smoking room by Gesellius, Lindgren & Saarinen, Helsinki; from C.H. Baer, Farbige Raumkunst, Stuttgart, 1911

Throughout northern Europe around the turn of the century the influence of the English Arts and Crafts movement and that of Continental Art Nouveau blended with a revival of interest in rustic or folk-art decoration to produce a hybrid style, suitable for the hall of a mountain king or an aesthetically-minded troll. This oddly appealing look gained tremendous impetus from the publication of articles on folk art in *The Studio* magazine, and above all from the appearance in print of M.H. Baillie Scott's designs for the residence of the Grand Duke of Hesse at Darmstadt and Le Nid, the more modest but delightful retreat of Crown Princess Marie. The leading Finnish architects Gesellius, Lindgren & Saarinen carried a number of schemes in this style, one of which was published by Baer. It is a sophisticated essay in the interplay of forms, and uses colour and pattern to good effect. In particular, the way in which the banquette seating relates to the almost free-standing hooded hearth is worth noticing, as is the integration of the clock with the panelling and the book-cases. Eliel Saarinen became one of the most widely admired of all Scandinavian architects and designers, especially in Germany where he secured a number of commissions for houses.

129

Munich neo-classicism c.1910

Dining room by P.L. Troost; from C.H. Baer, Farbige Raumkunst

It has been pointed out that this design for the decoration and furnishing of a dining room owes much to the inspiration of the style of Thomas Sheraton and, perhaps more specifically, his German imitators in the early years of the nineteenth century. What seems to be equally fascinating about Troost's work is the way in which he succeeds in integrating a number of characteristic Sheraton forms, such as the basic chair type and the elongated urns surmounting the china cabinets, into a fundamentally rectilinear aesthetic which is in fact that of the Viennese Sezession architects. The light fittings and other objects such as the grid-pattern candlesticks displayed on the sideboard are more thoroughly 'modern' in feel; but, in spite of the bold geometric patterning of both the ceiling and the floor, the room still evokes the elegance of the late eighteenth century through its linear clarity and lightness of effect.

129

130

Comfortable modernity, Darmstadt 1909

Drawing room by Robert Hommes; from C.H. Baer, Farbige Raumkunst

Darmstadt's emergence as an important centre for architecture, design and decoration was in no small part due to its openness to foreign influence, and specifically to that of the Glasgow designers, the most important of whom was Charles Rennie Mackintosh. Among the Darmstadt architects a very wide spectrum of taste is discernible, from the ultra-modernistic through to comfortable and unadventurous domesticity. This salon by Hommes represents the middle ground, in which elegant and basically traditional furniture forms are integrated into a setting in which the rectilinear panelling and deep frieze reflect more advanced spatial experiments in the domestic interior. There is also a very good example of the exciting and stylish use of electric light bulbs and their flex to dictate a novel form for the main light fitting.

130

131

Neo-baroque in Mitteleuropa 1919

Chimneypiece by Ludwig Kozma, Budapest; from A. Koch, Handbuch neuzeitlicher Wohnungskultur, *Darmstadt, 1919*

The extent to which English or American designers thought about the great decorative traditions of Middle Europe can perhaps best be judged by the stylish but usually ludicrous settings of the early Dracula films. In Germany, however, there seems to have been some real appreciation of the splendid native baroque and other exuberant styles of the cultural area defined before 1914 as the Austro-Hungarian Empire. Koch included in his pages a number of examples of the interesting new work carried out in a baroque manner by architects and designers such as Kozma in Budapest. In this particularly striking and successful room for a collector, Kozma combined seventeenth-century chairs and other early carved objects with a highly sculptural chimneypiece reminiscent of the wild Mannerist compositions by the late sixteenth-century theoretical architect and print-maker Wendel Dietterlin.

131

132

Muslin drapery in Berlin c.1919

An anteroom by Professor Bruno Paul; from A. Koch, Handbuch neuzeitlicher Wohnungskultur

In this 'antechamber to a gentleman's room', as it is described by Koch, Bruno Paul makes use of a typically pretty muslin drapery in the Biedermeier manner, with a valance and bobble fringing echoed in the inner curtains of the closet on the far wall. The doors of this curiously constructed feature of the room have elaborately fretted panels, but apart from this touch of exotic pattern all is cool and rather neo-classical in feel. The simple form of both bookcase and chairs, the white hanging lamp and the narrow-striped wallpaper indeed suggest a certain affinity with those parallel movements in taste which found expression in England as Regency revival and in France and the United States as the Louis Seize style.

132

133

133

Refined baronial taste in Germany c.1919

A 'hunting room' by Paul Würzler-Klopsch, Leipzig; from A. Koch, Handbuch neuzeitlicher Wohnungskultur

This corridor room in a substantial house functions, in the traditional manner of the trophy room, as a small personal museum, but it is at the same time a light and witty restatement of the theme. Instead of the usual oppressive dark panelling all is bright, white-lacquered woodwork. The showcase doors have small panes of blown bull's-eye glass which reflect a sparkling light from the windows to the left, and the shape of the antler trophies seems to be echoed in the attenuated forms of the line of chairs. All this is typical of the taste of the cultivated minor aristocracy in Germany before the war. Many chose to break with the dark and heavy traditional forms of decoration which had been widely adopted by the bourgeoisie, who associated heaviness with substance. These enlightened patrons had their portraits painted by and commissioned other works from contemporary artists, had bookplates designed for their libraries of well-bound books, and in many cases engaged in elaborate building projects, such as the private chapel created by the Graf von Heil near Worms.

134

134
Light and colour in Bremen 1907

Garden room by Runge & Scotland; from C.H. Baer,
Farbige Raumkunst, *Stuttgart, 1911*

With its brilliant hues of strong yellow and sharp green, this is clearly a summer room. Described by Baer as a garden room, with its huge and uncurtained windows it would be uninhabitable at any other time of the year. It is obviously designed with little regard for the climate of northern Germany, and intended to evoke the grand garden rooms and orangeries of the palaces of France and Germany. There is very little detail shown in the room, and apart from the boldness of the colour most of its effect derives from the suggestion of grandeur through the use of huge pier-glasses with divided panes hanging above paired commodes. The only other fittings visible are a candle sconce (and no other light fittings), a rather dull rug, and a commonplace upholstered chair; all of which imply that we are seeing the room at a moment when it is not entirely functional.

135

A smoking room in Berlin c.1910

*Design by Professor Bruno Paul; watercolour
R. Boehland; from C.H. Baer*, Farbige Raumkunst

While all too many of the plates in Baer's *Farbige Raumkunst* (other than those shown here) have an unpleasant quality, this example by Boehland showing a smoking room by Paul has much of the delightful feel of the watercolours of the 1820s and 1830s. Without the use of any very precise historical details the *Stimmung*, or atmosphere, of early nineteenth-century German rooms is suggested both in the choice and grouping of the furniture, and especially by the colour and striped pattern of the wallpaper. As was thought appropriate for a smoking room, the chairs are 'masculine' in feel, and at that date the massive sofas of the Chesterfield pattern had about them an aura of the gentleman's club rather than of the domestic interior.

135

136

Native baroque in Dresden c.1911

A scheme of decorative painting by Richard Guhr; from C.H. Baer, Farbige Raumkunst

The German native baroque and 'artisan mannerist' traditions belong in the main to the south, and so this exuberant scheme of painted decoration seems somewhat unusual in the context of a beamed hall in Dresden. The professor of painting Richard Guhr created an entirely convincing arrangement of broadly treated undulating 'Salomonic' columns in *trompe l'oeil*, however, dividing figurative panels depicting the kind of dubious and sexually menacing scenes so greatly favoured by the German Symbolist painters and their respectable patrons.

136

137

Old English grandeur c.1920

*Lady Ancaster's bedroom, Grimsthorpe Castle,
Lincolnshire, photographed in 1924*

The restoration and redecoration of the grander rooms in important country houses in England had long been the prerogative of the great upholsterers such as Keebles. These old-established firms commanded armies of craftsmen and could carry out elaborate schemes in all the 'correct' historic styles, drawing only the vaguest of lines between repairing the old and creating a new. Thus in a room such as the grand bedchamber used by Lady Ancaster at Grimsthorpe the feeling of a fine old room untouched – filled by a gradual accretive process with fine pieces of old English furniture – is in fact a self-conscious creation, redolent of a particular attitude to the English country house, and an image which tells us far more about 1920 than about 1720.

Country Life

A Palladian showroom c.1919

31 Old Burlington Street, London; from F. Lenygon,
Decoration in England, *London, n.d.*

138

First State Room

139

Second State Room

These photographs show the rooms of the grand Palladian house acquired by the furniture dealer and decorator Francis Lenygon in 1909 in order to display his desirable stock of early English furniture. By 1915 he had entered into partnership with the old-fashioned upholsterer Morant and had secured the services of the first serious furniture expert, Margaret Jourdain, who prepared the texts of the books on the history of furniture and decoration that appeared under Lenygon's name. The sheer quality and historical importance of the pieces offered for sale by Lenygon & Morant is astonishing, and many items, such as the pair of Kentian stands flanking the chimney-piece in the First State Room, ended up in the Victoria & Albert Museum or other principal collections. The concentration on English furniture alone in the early days of the

138

139

firm is significant, and in the periods covered there is a further reflection of the magisterial but narrow taste of the time. One room was devoted to Elizabethan and Jacobean pieces and distinguished by the name 'English Renaissance Room'. There were important groups of late seventeenth-century 'Wrenaissance', and nothing else was later than the early years of the eighteenth century, with a heavy bias towards the then most highly regarded of all styles, the baroque Palladianism of William Kent and Lord Burlington, the house gods.

Georgian partly revived 1909

Designs by H. Pringuer Benn from H.P. Shapland, Style Schemes in Antique Furnishing, *London, 1909*

140

A 'New Georgian' hall

Shapland's handbook of 'interiors and their treatment' typifies the heavy-handed Edwardian approach to the creation of rooms intended to evoke the past. A great many firms specializing in the manufacture of good quality reproduction furniture and most of the old-fashioned upholsterers were capable of carrying out such schemes; they nearly all fell into the trap of making their so-called Georgian interiors pastiches of the late Victorian drawing room or parlour disguised with a thin veneer of eighteenth-century ornament and detail. In this scheme for an entrance hall the proportions of the room, with its three-quarter-height panelling and deep frieze, are unmistakably turn-of-the-century, as is the complicated white-painted woodwork, with the doorway framed by colonnettes and flanked by symmetrical seats with squab cushions. The free-standing furniture includes favourite reproduction items such as a wing armchair and a circular gate-leg table, both of which are just credible as 'Georgian', and a large cupboard which in its eccentricity of form most certainly is not. The red-figured wall covering and deep-green brocaded hangings again suggest the late nineteenth century rather than the eighteenth, and this is underlined in the choice and positioning of a number of pieces of 'art pottery', which must be a hangover from the period when furnishing catalogues included such pieces to convey the idea that their effects were 'artistic'.

140

141

A 'New Georgian' dining room

This scheme for a 'late eighteenth-century' dining room reveals the most serious mistake of the Edwardian manufacturers of reproduction furniture, which was to thicken the lines of all the furniture. This has the result of making copies of early Georgian pieces in the Kent manner even more splendidly robust, but it is disastrous for the lighter lines of the increasingly popular Sheraton and Hepplewhite period. This dining room, lit by an Edwardian skirted lamp that can be adjusted up and down by the flex which runs over pulleys, like the earlier 'Georgian' hall is unmistakably of its period, but it does have some good features, such as the imitation neo-classical carpet instead of the almost ubiquitous Turkey. Also interesting is the colour scheme. It plays on the off-beat relationship between a dull purple, terracotta and green and although it lacks the eighteenth century's confidence in strong, clear colour it does at least suggest something of the quirkiness of much original paint and upholstery. As the author points out in his introductory remarks, 'definite colour-schemes are suggested ... [for] no room can be successful which does not represent an orchestrated scheme of colour, in which every tone plays its part in the general harmony.'

142

Edwardian Chinese Chippendale

Shapland states with some degree of self-applauding virtue that his remarks are addressed to 'the ever-increasing section of the public who wish their surroundings to be characterised by individuality and good taste', by which of course he means his taste. He makes a particular point of the fact that the schemes are not for 'mansion or castle', but are such as 'might be carried out in any middle-class home', and further explains that 'the right appreciation of tradition will prevent making a living-room a species of modern museum, or a mere heterogeneous collection of furniture and bric-à-brac, thrown together in a haphazard way.' It is surely ironic that making a living museum and gathering eclectic groups of furniture and objects were two of the most intriguing approaches to the creation of original interiors with which the real avant-garde were playing at this very time. Despite his well-intentioned text, the actual schemes proposed in the book are all rather watered-down commercial furnishings in a sub-Art Nouveau manner but tricked out with feeble historicizing detail: High Street furnishings looking ill at ease in their fancy dress.

A·CHINESE·CHIPPENDALE·DINING·ROOM·SCHEME·

142

143

144

Lady Sackville's grand manner 1918

Photographs of 40 Sussex Square, Brighton

143

The Regency bedroom

Lady Sackville took a profound interest in decoration after her marriage when she became mistress of Knole, one of the most delectable houses in England. In the subsequent unhappy years of her marriage she amused herself with a small decorating business, Spealls. In 1918, with the Spealls enterprise behind her and her position at Knole now untenable, Lady Sackville moved to Brighton, taking 40 Sussex Square and the two adjoining houses. Her new friend and confidant, the architect Edwin Lutyens, helped with the elaborate works necessary for a vast house with a grand salon and a totally unnecessary number, as Vita Sackville-West thought, of bedrooms(twenty-four). As a result of the collaboration the house had some startlingly original features, including a columbarium in the area, with arches and niches containing vases. Lady Sackville filled the place with her usual idiosyncratic mixture of highly decorative furniture, seven vanloads of which came from Knole. 'I don't want to spoil Knole and take too many of my things away; I love Knole too much for that,' she wrote.

The Regency room, one of the two principal bed-chambers, was fitted with a remarkable carpet woven to a design, probably by Lutyens, of *faux-marbre* paving squares in red and white. (One piece of this extraordinary carpeting survives at West Dean in West Sussex; Edward James presumably bought it for its surreal quality.) Other features of the room included a so-called state bedstead which Lady Sackville seems to have concocted from various carved Prince of Wales feathers, and some good mirrors and pieces of early nineteenth-century furniture, as well as an early example of a tented washing alcove, here topped with a baldachin matching the tester of the bed.

Country Life

144

Lady Sackville's Chinese bibelots

Lady Sackville's love of pretty, exotic and costly objects and her curious mania for artificial flowers came together in her remarkable collection of Chinese jade and amber flowers. As a naturally gifted arranger of objects and a devotee of colour, she was among the first to place amber, jade and coloured glass against windows and to have display cases fitted with electric light bulbs. Her collection of Chinese ambers helped to form a taste for such things and was admired by that great royal connoisseur of the costly bibelot, Queen Mary. The Queen's own copy of the Sackville sale catalogue survives in the London Library and is annotated at Lot 114, a Queen Anne period ivory and gold miniature cabinet: 'I bought this small cabinet.' This perfect little piece in many ways epitomizes the patrician taste of the day, and links the names of two of its most celebrated collectors and protagonists.

145

The drawing room of a 'Soul' c.1900

Violet, Duchess of Rutland's drawing room,
16 Arlington Street, London

The town house of the Dukes of Rutland was a magnificent early eighteenth-century mansion by William Kent which stood in Arlington Street at the heart of social London. It retained in the principal rooms all its panelling and rich plasterwork, and was presided over by Violet, Duchess of Rutland, mother of Lady Diana Cooper and one of the most talented of the group of intellectual and artistically-minded young aristocrats who came to be known as 'The Souls'. Generally the Souls thought themselves above fashion and, coming from old families of

145

property, they were not the creators of many new interiors. Nevertheless their way of life and their attitudes to the place of art in the house make them a crucial link between the high ideals of the Pre-Raphaelites and William Morris, whom they revered, and the socially based world of decoration that centred for many years on Mayfair. The Duchess of Rutland had a talent well beyond the average for drawing and was a very fine sculptress. She tended to use a great many of the rooms at Arlington Street as studios: thus her many friends and loyal staff were used to finding half-finished masterpieces and unlikely props all over the house. In this early photograph of a corner of the drawing room a number of portrait busts and other pieces can be seen to have infiltrated into the otherwise grand but rather untidy space.

Royal Commission on the Historical Monuments of England

'A land fit for heroes' 1919–20

Designs by Shirley B. Wainwright, from 'The Studio' *Year-Book of Decorative Art, London, 1920*

146

Group of dining room furniture

In an important section devoted to the reconstruction of the furnishing and decorating industries in relation to modest homes, *The Studio Year-Book* of 1920 raised some interesting points. It was useless, it was suggested, merely to attempt to mass-produce poor imitations of pre-war goods for a world in which needs and values had changed so greatly. New furnishings loosely based on the simpler vernacular models were advocated, and a number of examples illustrated. Having recommended reproduction Windsor pattern chairs, the article went on to offer this group of dining room furniture. The chair, it proposed 'might have a rush or wood seat, with a loose cushion which it would be within the capacity of the lady of the house to provide. Such cushions would be useful for introducing valuable colour notes, and, incidentally, need not all be covered with the same material.'

147

146

148

149

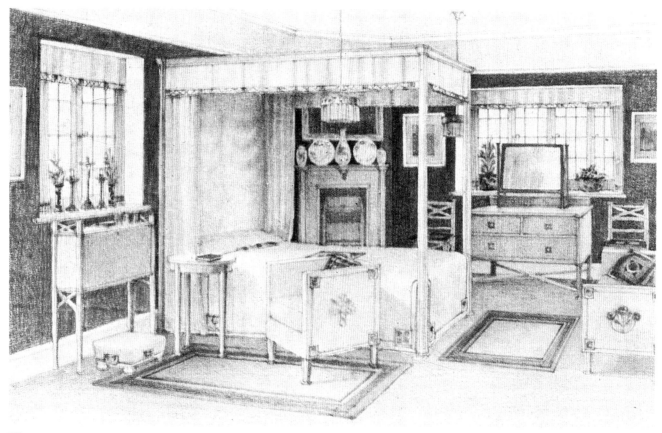

150

147

Side of a sitting room with recessed book or china cupboards

148, 149

Corner chimneypieces

These designs for the modest house reach a certain quiet level of distinction. In the arrangement of a chest of drawers flanked by glazed cupboard doors there is a suggestion of the rational approach to proportion and symmetry advocated by Wharton and Codman and taken up in England by the neo-Georgians. The corner fireplaces are more aggressively innovative and their decoration points the way to the more unfortunate excesses of 'Jazz Modern', the name given in later years to the angular and stridently coloured abstract decorative style which emerged in the 20s at the same time as and parallel to the more widespread Art Deco style.

150

Modern eclecticism, England 1920

Design for a bedroom by Frederick Towndrow, from 'The Studio' Year-Book of Decorative Art, London, 1921

A confused eclecticism was by no means the preserve only of those who confected interiors in period style. This suggestion for a bedroom by the architect Towndrow seems to stand uncomfortably at the crossroads between vernacular tradition, historic pastiche and ill-digested modernism. There are hints of an incipient mock-Tudor manner creeping in, with small-paned windows and an allusion to 'olde English' cottage interiors in the low proportions of wall and window, but the actual pieces of furniture clearly derive from the style of Mackintosh, whose elegance they lack; perhaps there is also a reference to the work of Viennese designers such as Moser.

151

151

Ghastly good taste, England   c.1914

'*A country chair in beech and a half-circle table of mid-eighteenth-century date*'; *from John Gloag*, Simple Furnishing and Arrangement, *London, 1921*

The many books written by John Gloag extolling the virtues of simple, undecorated provincial or country-made English furniture of the eighteenth century are a fascinating expression of a very particular aspect of puritan or rational taste in England in the early part of the century. Gloag for the most part used examples from his own modest collection to make his points, deliberately photographing them against austere backgrounds and in rooms of astonishing plainness. His desire to exclude all ornament seems less fanatical than the extreme attitudes of Adolf Loos in Vienna, however, because of his evident feeling for the qualities of colour and patina to be found in early pieces, and because of his humanizing touches, such as books and simple bowls and vases of country flowers. In a sense this is the very antithesis of real decoration, and so appealed to many who might have considered the idea of designing and beautifying an interior as unmanly, or even in an obscure way un-English. Certainly the suggestions for arrangements in *Simple Furnishing* must be among the dullest ever made in any book on the subject, and they are entirely suited to that worst aspect of the 'Englishman's home is his castle' mentality.

152

Plain furniture in Denmark   c.1910

The Music Room, *oil painting by Vilhelm Hammershoi*

Hammershoi's delight in the simple elegance of Danish provincial furnishings of the late eighteenth and early nineteenth centuries is curiously reminiscent of that of Gloag for English pieces of the same date.

Bury Street Gallery, London

153
The beginnings of Swedish Modern 1917

Living room by Gunnar Asplund

In such rooms as this, with simplicity of form, neutral colour, absence of ornament and emphasis instead on the quality of materials, are to be found the beginnings of the Modern movement in Swedish design. As in the contemporary room by Malmsten there is in this example of the work of Asplund a considerable debt to the traditional Swedish country style of the Gustavian period. There are distinct references in the pitch-pine boarded ceiling and the woven striped rugs to simple farmhouse furnishings; but in the light, based on a playful reference to the bags in which chandeliers were preserved, and in the over-scaled clock above the straight-backed sofa, there would seem to be some rather more knowing games being played with tradition.

Nationalmuseum, Stockholm

153

154

154
The Gustavian revival, Sweden c.1920

Furniture designed and made by Carl Malmsten; from 'The Studio' Year-Book of Decorative Art, London, 1921

The enormous popularity of Carl Larsson's books depicting his own house and lifestyle, which had appeared between 1899 and 1910, gave a strong impetus to the tendency among Swedish designers and craftsmen in the early years of the century to look to their own traditions for inspiration. Just as Larsson had treasured the simpler late eighteenth- and early nineteenth-century country furniture of the Gustavian period, so a new generation learned to play variations on the well-loved forms and decorative elements of the late eighteenth century, and also experimented with the paint finishes so characteristic of the style. A room setting by the designer-furniture maker Malmsten shows a typical adherence to the Gustavian forms for chairs, wooden sofa and small table; but the total effect of the austere room, almost without enrichment, also points undoubtedly towards the clear, cool qualities of what was to become in due course Swedish modern design.

155

155

'The colour of joy' c.1910

A Richmond Interior; oil painting by Spencer Frederick Gore

Spencer Gore's *Richmond Interior* is a characteristically well-observed study of the effects of light and colour in a modest room: the kind of subject matter drawn from everyday life that had appealed to the Impressionists and which was espoused in turn by the distinctly English band of their admirers known as the Camden Town Group. The room depicted, the back parlour of the ground floor overlooking the garden, is furnished as an informal sitting room or study with a small writing table and a rather more impressive late eighteenth-century glazed bureau-bookcase. These are pieces of, at that time, inexpensive antique furniture chosen for their elegance of form and, no doubt, for the beauty of their patina, which is so delight-fully suggested by Gore in his handling of the reflections of the light that filters through from the conservatory. These things are reminiscent of Sir William Rothenstein's description of the elegantly artistic choice of furniture of the Sheraton period made by Charles Ricketts for his friends the writers Edith Cooper and Catherine Bradley, whose pretty little house was in The Paragon, an early Georgian row in Richmond. As in the painting by Gore they had walls with stripes as a background for some modern prints and drawings, and they too loved the colour yellow. It recalls Oscar Wilde's enthusiastic praise of Ricketts and Shannon's house in The Vale in Chelsea: 'You have yellow walls – so have I; yellow is the colour of joy.'

Present whereabouts unknown

156, 157

Cottage style in England   c. 1920

Two interiors for a cottage by M. H. Baillie Scott,
from 'The Studio' Year-Book of Decorative Art,
London, 1921

156

As one of the pioneers of Celtic Art Nouveau Baillie Scott had enormous influence at the turn of the century. His prize-winning designs for the Darmstadt competition (pl. 59) brought his work to the attention of architects and decorators throughout Europe, and helped to establish the international Jugendstil-based 'troll style' all over northern Europe. Baillie Scott's own development, however, lay towards a simpler, much less contrived or ornamental style of building strongly grounded in native vernacular traditions. Many of his later buildings are modest in scale: simply pleasing, small houses for people to live in unpretentiously. In these two designs for the living room and the bedroom of a cottage there is so strong a feel of the traditional country cottage interior that it is almost hard to see where the designer of the Grand Duke of Hesse's palace has been at work at all. Closer inspection will, however, reveal a number of distinctly personal touches. For example, in the living room the mannered form of the settle beside the window is typical and the dresser to the right has a familiar Baillie Scott motif in the edging of the drawers and on the central support; and in the bedroom an unmistakably Baillie Scott chair stands by the fire.

157

158

The beginnings of a celebrated collection c.1910

Professor A.E. Richardson's drawing room, Cavendish House, St Albans, Hertfordshire

Albert Richardson, professor of architecture in London and later President of the Royal Academy, first trained as an architect in the tradition of the Arts and Crafts movement in the office of the ecclesiastical architect Verity. He rapidly developed a feel for the architecture of the eighteenth century and the Regency period, however, upon which subject he became an acknowledged expert, writing and lecturing with tremendous energy and enthusiasm. He began his collection 'in order to develop his knowledge of the life and culture of the eighteenth century' (quoted in a prospectus of Avenue House, Ampthill, c.1968), and so gathered not only fine furniture and pictures but also the everyday objects of 1800, such as kitchen equipment and old light fitments. Between 1909 and 1919 he lived in Cavendish House, St Albans, which he set about furnishing

159

with late eighteenth-century pieces, not at that period highly regarded, and simple Regency furniture that would have been considered merely second-hand. Although there are in the photograph of the drawing room a number of quite good pieces, such as the pretty ormolu chandelier, hung suitably low in the room, and a fine Regency Grecian sofa placed historically 'correctly' at right-angles to the chimneypiece, there is not much attempt at a scholarly re-creation of an earlier period, and the ambience is unmistakably that of a late Victorian or Edwardian parlour.

Courtesy of Simon Houfe

158

159

Professor Richardson discovers the 'cadence of form' c.1919

Drawing room, Avenue House, Ampthill, Bedfordshire;
from Our Homes and Gardens, *London, 1921*

Although the professor had begun to collect late eighteenth- and early nineteenth-century furniture in earnest during the early years of the century, when he lived at St Albans, it seems that it was only with the discovery of Avenue House at Ampthill, into which he moved in 1919, that he really became aware of the way in which such a collection could be arranged to give an accurate and evocative 'period feel'. His earliest arrangements of furniture were spare, bringing out the full elegance of the rooms – especially the drawing room and principal bedroom, both of which are in the grander Regency wing of the house. At this stage there were almost no pictures, the walls were plain, hung with period light fittings, and the curtains and carpets were also unpatterned. Ornamentation in the drawing room was confined to a broad frieze beneath the cornice and painted in the same shade, in a manner rather reminiscent of the white-painted decoration favoured by Philip Webb and seen at Clouds (pl. 41). As one of the principal protagonists of the Regency revival in England, Richardson's taste was highly influential. He organized the construction of an 'Empire Room' for the great British Empire Exhibition at Wembley in 1924, which gave a wider public a chance to see pieces gathered from the collections of a number of his friends and fellow (or rival) collectors, including Lord Gerald Wellesley and Edward Knoblock. From his own collection he lent an important black and gold lacquered music stand of about 1790, which normally formed part of the group of early musical instruments and related pieces of furniture from the drawing room at Avenue House, one of the Professor's first 'set pieces' to be photographed.

160

160

'Unconventional and comfortable', London c.1920

'A small London House', Edwardes Square;
from Our Homes and Gardens, *London, 1921*

The drawing room of this house, described as 'unconventional and comfortable', has been chosen to exemplify in its furnishings the abolition of the 'bogey of period'. In its arrangement it bears a striking resemblance to Professor Richardson's drawing room at Cavendish House, St Albans, and it seems to mark a similar stage in the assimilation into a contemporary scheme of a number of pieces of antique furniture, mirrors and light fitments. Of particular interest are the way in which mirrors have been placed in the recesses that flank the chimneypiece, and the rather eclectic group of upholstered seat furniture. Lighting is from two interesting conversions: an oil lamp turned into an electric table lamp, and a large lantern, of the kind usual in the halls or dining rooms of grand houses, with a shaded light bulb hanging inside it. Throughout the house, we are told, great emphasis was placed on the adventurous use of colour: in the drawing room the walls are distempered in lemon yellow, Oscar Wilde's 'colour of joy'.

The Omega Workshop experiment 1913 and later

The Omega Workshop, founded in 1913 by the artist and critic Roger Fry with the assistance of his Bloomsbury friends the painters Duncan Grant and Vanessa Bell, was the most serious attempt in England to reflect avant-garde artistic developments on the Continent, and to apply the visually exciting ideas of the Post-Impressionists to the decoration of rooms and individual pieces of furniture.

161

161

The Omega Workshop signboard 1913

The firm's signboard was painted by Duncan Grant to hang outside the workshop and shop premises in Fitzroy Square. The boldly painted design includes the Greek letter omega set in an arrangement of panels of exuberant and freely drawn marbling, typical of the kind of near-abstract decorative painting which the group favoured at this time. The board itself is a stout panel of wood, chosen with some thought for its durability and thus, sadly, in marked contrast to the materials of many of the workshop's subsequent productions.

Victoria & Albert Museum, London

162

Painted screen of 1913 by Duncan Grant, incorporated in the decoration of Charleston

This screen, with a bold figurative design by Duncan Grant, was among the group of painted furnishings and other decorative objects shown at the first Omega Workshop show in July 1913. It can be seen in several of the photographs that appeared in the press at the time of the exhibition, which received a somewhat mixed reception. It was presumably unsold since it was later taken by Duncan Grant and Vanessa Bell to Charleston. This old manor or yeoman farmer's house, which stands in the rolling countryside of Sussex on the estate of Firle Park, became a sort of country retreat for the Bloomsbury Group and their friends, and over the years during which it was occupied by them the decoration gradually grew in elaboration. Amid the clutter of books and papers which finally overwhelmed every room of the house can be seen, to the right of the screen, one jamb of the drawing room chimneypiece with a bold caryatid figure painted by Grant in his more mature style.

Photograph Howard Grey

163

Decorative painting at Charleston c. 1918–20

A corner of Duncan Grant's bedroom at Charleston reveals the delight which he and Vanessa Bell took in creating colourful arrangements of wall paintings, boldly printed fabrics and pieces of old furniture refinished with colour and pattern to fit the setting. The mural decoration here is characteristic in its use of abstracted forms, which are none the less suggestive of architectural features, as a framework for more spontaneously grouped floral or geometric motifs.

Photograph Lucinda Lambton, Arcaid

162

163

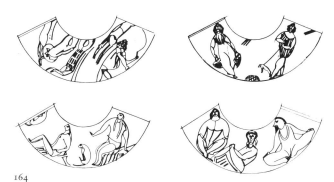

164

164

Candle shade designs by Wyndham Lewis 1913

Process engravings on card

Wyndham Lewis, the bellicose leader of the Vorticists and a painter and writer of major international importance, found himself for a short while a niche within the Bloomsbury Group and, along with Duncan Grant and Vanessa Bell, supplied work for Fry's Omega Workshops. By 1914, however, he had broken away and formed, with Edward Wadsworth, Frederick Etchells and later William Roberts, the Rebel Art Centre. For the Omega he made a number of designs, including these candle or lamp shades intended to be cut out and coloured by hand by the more modest talents working for the firm. The subjects of the drawings are humorous and somewhat 'advanced' in a typically Bloomsbury manner, including such scenes as 'stages in the bargaining between a roué and a procuress for the purchase of a young woman'. The shades when cut and made up were suitable for use on ordinary candles or on the popular patent candle fittings such as Green's Arctic Lights. Similar examples can be seen on table lamps in the photographs of the 'decorated lounge' at the 1914 Allied Artists' Exhibition at Holland Park Hall in London. Such accessories were one of the mainstays of the smaller independent decorators such as Lady Sackville's Spealls, and it is recorded that when Marcel Boulestin was at his lowest ebb financially he eked out an existence by painting silk candle shades. According to the Omega prospectus the shades retailed at from 4s.6d for hand-painted on silk and on card from 2s. These examples were given by Duncan Grant to Maynard Keynes.

With kind permission of the Provost and Fellows of King's College, Cambridge

165

'Haute Bohème' in Oxfordshire c.1919

The Red Room, Garsington Manor

When Lady Ottoline Morrell, the celebrated socialite, literary hostess and eccentric figure in Bohemian London, came to Garsington (the original inspiration of Aldous Huxley's *Crome Yellow*) she immediately began to transform the sleeping and monochromatic Jacobean house into a vibrant and literally colourful centre for her house parties – at which, in Horace Walpole's famous phrase, 'the Nobility met the Mobility'. In stark contrast to the reticent approach to the way in which old woodwork should be treated of a figure like John Gloag, Lady Ottoline boldly lacquered the ancient panelling in many of the rooms to form a striking background to a rich and varied collection of decorative furniture and objects. In the drawing room she used red as a foil to a black and gold Chinese cabinet on a gilt stand, and grouped Chinese bowls and vases containing peacock feathers (not shown in this later photograph) on the two-tiered mantelshelf in the manner of the Aesthetic movement. The so-called Green Room was lacquered in a blue-green reputedly chosen to match Lady Ottoline's eyes.

Country Life

166

An urban Arts and Crafts room c.1920

'A Living-Room in a Small House in the Suburbs',
Robert Atkinson, architect; from R. R. Phillips, ed.,
The Modern English Interior, *London, 1929*

This room, described as a dual-purpose dining room and sitting room – an increasingly necessary solution to pressures on housing space after the First World War – is evidence both of the lively continuity of the Arts and Crafts ideal and of the possibility of its adaptation to a new and more sophisticated urban milieu. The furniture, which includes a gate-leg table and a set of Voyseyesque chairs in unpolished wood, is arranged with elegance and clarity. There are a few 'artistic' objects and the plain walls are decorated with good modern pictures.

166

167

A classic English room c.1920

Interior in Lady Colefax's Argyll House, King's Road,
Chelsea

Cecil Beaton, writing in *The Glass of Fashion* (London, 1954), has left the best description of that singular adornment of London society in the period between the wars, Sybil Colefax. He characterized her as a 'collector of interesting and imaginative people' and recalled how at Argyll House 'she entertained ceaselessly, peopling the delightful rooms that were decorated with all the restraint of an eighteenth-century intellectual'. Drawing an important distinction between the rooms of her own houses and those which she decorated in later years, when she was the proprietor of the celebrated Colefax & Co., Beaton mentioned both her use of 'off-colours – pale almond greens, greys and opaque yellows' and the way in which she eschewed grandeur in the choice of furnishings, preferring to create her effects by attention to details, such as glass vases of jasmine 'freshly filled with water that was still full of oxygen bubbles'.

Victoria & Albert Museum, London

167

1920–1930
THE LURE OF ANTIQUES AND THE MODERN STYLE

The 20s, almost more than any other decade of this century, have been subjected to a myth-making process that has tended to obscure its richness, and especially its variety, with a generalized image of 'Art Deco'. Books such as Evelyn Waugh's *Vile Bodies* (1930) capture with all the incisiveness of the best caricature the brittle, artificial elegance of society at the time, fixing for us the picture of the 'bright young things' – the first generation for whom fast motor cars, wireless sets, exquisitely decorated flats and ocean liners had become the playthings. Yet it is crucial to remember that by the early 20s a pattern of revivalism in decoration was also well established wholly suited to the rather hectic, post-war frivolity which prevailed in smart circles in both Europe and America.

Among fashionable groups in London a taste for grandeur lingered and in the drawing rooms of the last surviving great London town houses a sense of *grand luxe* and chic was maintained. Michael Arlen, the author of ornate and mannered novels of fashionable London life, perhaps evokes most exactly the languid elegance of this world:

> In the drawing room of a house midway on the entailed side of [Berkeley] Square sat a lady and a gentleman silently. Or rather, the lady lay, while the gentleman sat, and the sofa on which she lay was far from the arm-chair on which he sat. The room was spacious; four shaded candles in candlesticks of ancient brass gave calm colour to its dimness; and four open windows, from which the curtains were withdrawn in slack folds of shining silver, gave out to the leaves of the trees, which murmured among themselves just a little.[1]

It was in this period that the 'Decorator', in particular the 'Lady Decorator', established such a powerful position in society. Those who had 'Taste', defined variously as a good eye for colour or grouping or perhaps a knowledge of furniture or ceramics, found themselves courted to 'help' with their friends' decorations. (Only commercial firms 'did' interiors and thereby a neat distinction was subtly maintained.) The most successful figures, such as Lady Islington, who was universally admired for her discrimination in furnishings and for her ability to direct the painting of colour with an unrivalled understanding of the final effect of one element upon another in a room, began to drift in a rather haphazard way into business. The Hon. Mrs Guy Bethell was one of the first to put her operations on anything like a sound commercial footing, and her firm Elden set the pattern for a host of more or less successful similar enterprises, of which, at a slightly later date, Sybil Colefax's and Syrie Maugham's would become the most famous.

In America too a similar pattern emerges, though the rather different social patterns there led to a somewhat more realistic appraisal of the followers of Elsie de Wolfe. A not uncommon attitude was neatly satirized in Eleanor Gizycka's classic novel of 1926, *Glass Houses*, in an episode where the society lady Judith leaves Newport to look in on the progress of her ballroom in New York: '. . . the hangings have come and they're all yards too short, and they've got the wrong grey on the walls . . . silly fool women decorators. . . . They should be limited by law to sofa cushions and lamp shades.' The problem, she continues, is that: 'All lady decorators are recruited from the ranks of the great misunderstood. You know what we say in America about them? Is she happily married or an interior decorator?'[2]

Interior decoration came increasingly to be considered as a branch of fashion in the 20s, and began noticeably to be written up as such in the pages of magazines like *Vogue*, which did much in this period to promote the idea that decoration should change more rapidly, that it should often be frivolous and, most importantly, that it should be an essential part of an attitude which has come to be denoted by that disagreeable word 'lifestyle'. Elsie de Wolfe's instructions on how to dine elegantly, rather than merely how to decorate the dining room, express this perfectly. From this time the journalism of decoration, at the upper end of the scale at least, effectively ceased to be concerned with practicalities and concentrated on style, exclusivity and chic. In this milieu, not surprisingly, approaches to the creation of what was called 'the smart look' became immensely varied, ranging from versions of grand historical styles adapted to the smaller scale but faster pace of modern life, to the more self-consciously modernistic styles which echoed avant-garde movements in the arts.

In modest schemes for decoration a mixture of old and new furnishings was often thought to be both comfortable and safely tasteful. In America, influenced by the theories of Frank Alvah Parsons, President of the New York School of Fine and Applied Art, a large number of books appeared which sought to combine a certain amount about the history of furniture and decoration, style by style, with chapters on the more practical aspects of putting a room together. By contrast, the more interesting English and French publications, such as the highly important books by the English decorator and theorist Basil Ionides or the French stylist Léon Deshairs, tended to concentrate on particular aspects of the craft, such as the use of colour – which is revealed as far and away the most obsessive theme of the decade. Most books of the period tended to underline the desirability of creating 'modern interpretations' of past styles. This idea, which seems such a good one, often however amounted to little more than the uneasy mixing of a number of slightly unsympathetically finished reproduction pieces with the more unavoidable trappings of modern life. A classic example of this attitude is Ethel Davis Seal's manual *Furnishing the Little House*, published in New York in 1924. In one of the illustrations we see 'a modern interpretation of the Elizabethan style', including a table with heavy baluster legs which is described as 'one of the few Elizabethan types suitable for use in the living-room of the modern home' (pl. 178). In fact several such well-known types and classic pieces, for example the candle-stand lengthened to form a standard lamp, or the famous 'Knole sofa', which was copied in a thousand versions, were adapted, tamed and cosmeticized by the furniture trade for the smaller house or apartment.

At the grandest level fine antique furniture and period style decoration of the highest quality in workmanship and materials remained the ideal. In England firms such as Trollope's, White Allom and Keebles vied with Lenygon &

Morant, the leaders in this field, to create room settings in Tudor, Carolean or early eighteenth-century styles in which meticulous detailing was matched by carefully restored pieces of furniture, often of museum quality. Lenygon's reputation was by this time international. The firm's scholarly head, Francis Lenygon, who sponsored the pioneering researches in furnishing history by Margaret Jourdain, established an important association with the celebrated art dealer Joseph Duveen, supplying to the grandest of his American clients 'authentic' settings for the masterpieces of English, French and Italian art which crossed the Atlantic in these years. Looking back at this period in later life, when he had become a grandee of taste and an undisputed arbiter of historic styles, Ogden Codman singled out Lenygon's work for praise and recalled that Freeman Smith, who had overseen much of what the firm did in the United States, had, of all decorators, 'the finest command of eighteenth-century work'. In France a similar position was occupied by the House of Jansen.

The essentially ponderous quality of much of this kind of decoration was relieved by some essays in the more light-hearted styles of the past. At this date it was still possible to find examples of the more bizarre furnishings of the seventeenth and eighteenth centuries, such as scarlet lacquer work, *verre églomisé* and, perhaps most popular of all, early Chinoiserie. As a result quirky schemes enjoyed a considerable vogue, for as an anonymous writer in *House & Garden* observed in 1920: 'The enthusiastic collector of the amusing does not pursue wardrobes.'

The fashion for Chinoiserie is highly interesting because of the way in which it spread through all levels of the decorating profession, and one element in particular, Chinese wallpaper, illuminates the workings of the trade and changing attitudes to antiques. As a background to the furniture of the eighteenth century, grand firms often supplied panels of original Chinese wallpaper, much of which had come to England during the 1750s, and a fair amount of which remained. At first such paper was merely removed from existing walls and carefully cleaned, restored and remounted. As the demand for good early pieces began to outstrip the supply the firms, who had at first tentatively repainted small missing areas of original paper, began to supply larger and larger missing pieces to complete rooms, and in due course entire sets of panels. The main firm which undertook such work was Thornton Smith (and it was in their painting-studio at their premises in Soho Square in London that the young John Fowler was first employed) but many others were involved in what, in the absence of a sufficient supply of the genuine article, became ever more rapidly the business of reproduction. Much the same story is true of other categories of furniture and objects in the preferred styles, with the result that the more inventive and imaginative decorators, and certainly those working within more modest budgets, were forced to try something different. The alternatives were either to find new areas of antiques, such as Continental baroque, Regency or even, for the very adventurous and confident, Victorian pieces, or, instead, to abandon antiques altogether and explore other possibilities, such as the use of colour and the commissioning of new furniture in novel materials.

In England experimental or modernistic interiors of any quality were almost all the creation of painters who also had an interest in working in the applied or decorative arts. The Bloomsbury painters, most notably Duncan Grant and Vanessa Bell who under the banner of the Omega Workshops had been the most consistently involved with earlier experiments in this field, continued to carry out interesting schemes of decorative painting. They also applied their bright, colourful and dashingly painted patterns and panels depicting pots of flowers and Post-Impressionist figure groups to the surfaces of furniture, to chimneypieces and, with considerable success, to a variety of tiles and other ceramics. The majority of their commissions came from their Bloomsbury friends and acquaintances, but gradually, towards the end of the decade, the circles both of patrons and of artists employed began to widen. This was due in part perhaps to Raymond Mortimer and Dorothy Todd's championing of this kind of decoration in *The New Interior Decoration* (1929), one of the most thoughtful and well-received books on this subject of its time.

Among the circles of avant-garde writers, artists, architects and decorators who chose to play with the more amusing aspects of antique furnishings, the two cult styles which had arisen before the First World War, Vogue Regency and the neo-baroque, grew in popularity. For many they overlapped to some degree: a figure such as Lord Gerald Wellesley, who at this date was a successfully practising architect, can certainly be said to have been a central figure in both camps. The Regency revival is closely associated with neo-Georgian architects such as Professor Albert Richardson and Clough Williams-Ellis, of whose school Osbert Lancaster wrote: 'Today, the more sensible of modern architects realize that the desperate attempt to find a contemporary style can only succeed if the search starts at the point at which Soane left off.'[3]

Even more inventive than the rooms created by the collectors of Regency things were those assembled in his London house by the writer Arnold Bennett. Bennett, who often mentions furniture and objects in his *Journals*, gathered not only some good French Empire pieces but also modern pictures and a collection, most extraordinarily for the time, of Victoriana: Parian china, wax fruit under glass domes and other curiosities of that age which seems to have both baffled and fascinated the intellectuals of the 20s. Visitors to Arnold Bennett's house apparently had difficulty in understanding whether it was to be taken seriously as a scheme of modern decoration or enjoyed as an amusing joke about style. Lady Ashton, who went to see it at this time intending to write it up as a feature for *Vogue*, recalled that the powers at the magazine would not at first use the photographs, fearing that the piece would be too far in advance of public taste and would result in ridicule.

Curiously no such problems assailed the Sitwells in their quest to bring themselves and their works before the widest possible public. The virtual invention of the new baroque by the Sitwell triumvirate, Osbert, Sacheverell and Edith, in the early 20s was one of the first instances of a decorative style or 'look' being associated in the public eye with the way of life and artistic and literary achievements of a self-consciously famous, and indeed self-promoting, group of personalities. 'They put the "cult" in "culture",' quipped the poet and historian Peter Quennell.

The Sitwells' espousal of the 'cult of the obscure' and their love of the grandiose stemmed from their extraordinary father Sir George, and the strong visual influence of the Sitwell family houses: Renishaw in Derbyshire and the baroque and romantic Castello di Montegufoni near Florence which Sir George had bought in 1909. Steeped in the work of little-known painters and architects of the seventeenth and early eighteenth centuries, Osbert and Sacheverell began to forge a new aesthetic which also embraced happily the extreme avant-garde in painting and decorative effects, and by imaginative patronage of young artists they formed an intriguing collection and at the same time enhanced their own image. The Carlyle Square house shared by the brothers became a showpiece of the Sitwellian baroque, in which lugubrious Neapolitan paintings and works by the Vorticists William Roberts and Wyndham Lewis hung together in rooms furnished with eighteenth-century silvered grotto chairs and elaborate Regency pieces, such as a massive console table on dolphin supports (pl. 255). In the light refracted by Poiret's Atelier Martine wire and silk lampshades, Murano glass and other 'Sitwellian' *trouvés* glinted. Arnold Bennett noted: 'a house with much better pictures and bric-à-brac than furniture ... bright walls and bright cloths, and bright glass everywhere....'

The Sitwellian ideal was a complex and obscure form of Modernism and, as such, was poles apart from the mainstream of development towards a style of decoration based on new forms and new materials, as was emerging at this time on the Continent. The centre of this development, in terms of innovative styling and the creation of luxury goods, was Paris, where the Exposition des Arts Décoratifs, held in 1925, marked a high point in French achievement.

The Exposition drew together the very best work being produced in the modern manner, and all the great names in the decorative arts, including jewellery, ceramics and textiles as well as furniture and decorative painting, were represented in the various national pavilions. In comparison with the French exhibits the other nations, and notably Britain, cut a very poor figure, for the wares shown by the hosts were of a degree of sophistication in design, materials and craftsmanship that was unrivalled. In general the Exposition, in both its strengths and weaknesses, supplied a touchstone by which the arts of furnishing and decoration in the new bold and colourful modernistic style could be measured – and in addition it provided that useful, if at times rather vaguely applied, term Art Deco.

Official recognition of the quality of the French contributions came in the form of the lavish government-sponsored folios of designs and illustrations which proliferated during the course of the show. They record in the beautiful and expensive colour printing of the day the schemes of French designers such as Jacques-Emile Ruhlmann, whose Hôtel du Collectionneur formed a celebrated attraction of the French section. Among other notable exhibits, Paul Poiret contributed a room set on a barge moored in the Seine (pl. 183), which attracted considerable interest and vied for attention with the work of designers such as André Groult and Paul Iribe in the main pavilion.

It was in their approach to the use of strong colour that the designers of 1925 set themselves apart from their predecessors. Writing in one of the official folios, *Intérieurs en Couleur, France* (Paris, 1925) the editor Léon Deshairs neatly characterized the modern spirit: the charm of the 'songs in grey' so dear to their elders between 1890 and 1900, the hazy contrasts of worn-out shades, seemed to them outmoded. The most subtle of them in their search for harmonies in colour arrangement, Groult, Ruhlmann, Louis Sognot, never confused delicacy with the insipid.

It is a commonplace in modern design history to place in opposition the school of 'decorating with antiques' and 'modern' French design as represented in the 1925 show, yet in truth they are often very close in spirit, sharing a delight in the quality of materials and workmanship and concern for exclusivity in matters of taste. The true dichotomy lay between the French who cared for luxury and a new northern European tradition of austerity which sought to democratize design, making it the province of the artist and designer in the service of a new design-conscious working society.

The beginnings of Swedish modern design lie in such theories, which had found expression as early as 1917 at the 'Home Exhibition' staged at the Liljevalch Gallery in Stockholm. There the designers of the newly formed Svenska Slöjdforeningen (Swedish Society of Industrial Design), directed by Gregor Paulsson, had made their first statement. Of particular interest was a room by Gunnar Asplund with simple spruce furniture against a blue and white paper (pl. 153). The next decade saw considerable advances and culminated in the reasonably strong Swedish showing at the Paris Exposition, dominated by the figure of Carl Malmsten, and the successful exhibition of Swedish industrial and domestic art in Stockholm five years later.

It is to the Bauhaus, and to the vigour of its teaching and the essential simplicity of its vision, that design historians have looked most frequently when attempting to lay bare the roots of International Modernism. Individual pieces by Marcel Breuer, Josef Albers and Laszlo Moholy-Nagy without doubt represented perfection of a kind, yet it remains unclear to what extent it is possible to speak of a Bauhaus interior at this date. Not until the next decade can we speak with any seriousness of the International Modern movement or ideal, and for many at this time 'modern' was just another style to be utilized like Chinoiserie.

1. Michael Arlen, *These Charming People*, London, 1923
2. Eleanor Gizycka, *Glass Houses*, New York, 1926
3. Osbert Lancaster, *Homes Sweet Homes*, London, 1939

168

A novel use of concrete   1924

Living room, the Ennis House, Los Angeles,
by Frank Lloyd Wright

The Ennis house is one of four major domestic projects realized by Frank Lloyd Wright in the area around Los Angeles in the mid-20s. All the houses are placed with a considerable feeling for the landscape which he so admired (whilst loathing the city itself), but their crucial importance lies in the novel construction method, using hollow concrete blocks, which Wright developed at this time. The structures are conceived both externally and internally entirely in terms of arrangements of these plain, moulded and pierced blocks, and the formal patterns which derive from this 'building block' principle dictate a new and exciting architectural language. The patterns moulded into the blocks, which Wright had made to order locally, seem to derive in part from the carvings of the ancient Aztec and Mayan civilizations of Central America, but there is little about these houses, other than their slightly mysterious spatial grandeur, to suggest an archaeological approach inspired by the great temples. They mark the high point of the architect's interest in surface pattern and of his involvement in the design of complex furnishings related to his architectural projects.

Ezra Stoller, © *Esto*

169

170

Omega-painted decoration 1921–6

169, 170

Panels for cupboard doors

Designs by Duncan Grant and Vanessa Bell for Maynard Keynes's house, 46 Gordon Square, London, c. 1921

171

Decoration for a library (see pl. 173)

Watercolour by Duncan Grant for Mrs St John Hutchinson's house, 3 Albert Gate, Regent's Park, London, c. 1926

Towards the end of the First World War Maynard Keynes, the great economic theoretician and a central figure in the Bloomsbury Group, commissioned his friends Duncan Grant and Vanessa Bell to decorate his rooms in Gordon Square. The project involved a considerable amount of purely decorative painting, but also a number of panels with figurative scenes, such as these cupboard doors from about 1921, representing breakfast being taken in various manners associated with different countries. English and Italian breakfast are both by Duncan Grant, while the French and Italian panels are the work, almost indistinguishable at that time, of Vanessa Bell. The depiction of an essentially mundane or even ludicrous subject – such as a pair of fried eggs – in the manner of high art decoration is a characteristic example of the intellectual humour enjoyed by members of the circle, and much favoured by them for the adornment of the rooms in which they lived and worked.

169, 170 With kind permission of the Provost and Fellows of King's College, Cambridge
171 Victoria & Albert Museum, London

171

Bloomsbury taste 1920s

Decorations by Duncan Grant and Vanessa Bell, 1926–8

172

Clive Bell's library at 50 Gordon Square, London

From D. Todd and R. Mortimer, The New Interior Decoration, *London, 1929*

173

Mrs St John Hutchinson's library at 3 Albert Gate, Regent's Park, London

From Architectural Review, *March, 1930*

173

Raymond Mortimer drew heavily on the work of his friends to illustrate what he saw as the best trends in English decoration in his survey of the European scene, *The New Interior Decoration*, published in 1929. A recurrent and crucial theme in the book was that, while interesting architectural work was going on both in Britain and on the Continent, most decoration was inevitably carried out in existing spaces in old houses and for people who generally wanted interiors with historical references. Mortimer and his collaborator Dorothy Todd chose rooms in their friends' eighteenth- and early nineteenth-century London houses decorated in the 'Bloomsbury' style as the quintessence of civilized life. They stressed how much a good scheme of painted decoration could do for a room and advocated the idea that in an era of far greater mobility artists should paint on canvas panels which could be taken on to the patron's next house if necessary. They suggested, too, that such decorative painting should take into account all the existing architectural features of the room, such as the chimneypiece, door panels and the natural divisions of walls. Duncan Grant and Vanessa Bell had carried on working together in just this way long after the demise of Fry's original Omega Workshop project during the war, and by the 1920s their schemes, although composed from elements painted in their bold and colourful post-Cubist manner, had begun to achieve an almost eighteenth-century architectural dignity and poise.

172

174

A Bloomsbury joke 1920s

Raymond Mortimer's dining room in Bloomsbury, London; from D. Todd and R. Mortimer, The New Interior Decoration

The line between Bloomsbury innovation and Bloomsbury humour is often a very difficult one to draw. The idea of adapting rather than rejecting traditional forms and simultaneously ridiculing them was characteristic of a number of the members of the circle. In this room a totally conventional arrangement of pictures and rather fine period furniture is stood on its head as a formal scheme of decoration by the outrageous use of 'newspapers of all nations' as the wallpaper. The decorative treatment becomes at once a confident statement of avant-garde taste and a delightful visual and literary joke.

175

A mosaic hall 1920s

Executed by Boris Anrep in the house of Miss Ethel Sands, Vale Avenue, Chelsea; from D. Todd and R. Mortimer, The New Interior Decoration

The Chelsea house of the American artist Ethel Sands was a favourite meeting place for the more consciously avant-garde writers and painters of London's Bohemia. At her celebrated parties members of many of the artistic factions and camps met on neutral territory, and several unlikely friendships were made with this remarkable hostess as sponsor. In particular she favoured the Bloomsbury circle and its allies and protégés, such as the young Boris Anrep, one of the very few artists at that time interested in the medium of mosaic, then largely forgotten outside church decoration. It is perhaps typical of the clever and knowing attitudes of Bloomsbury to regard in a new light the material of which Victorian hallways were made, and to see its potential as an effective element in a total decorative scheme. And so Miss Sands commissioned a hallway from Anrep. It was to have floor and walls covered with figure subjects, which gave him the chance to carry out an amusing iconographic programme incorporating light-hearted portraits of distinctive figures such as Lytton Strachey, whose head appears at a window. Anrep also carried out a large commission to decorate areas of the floor of the entrance hall of the National Gallery in London, and these have not so far been removed.

174

175

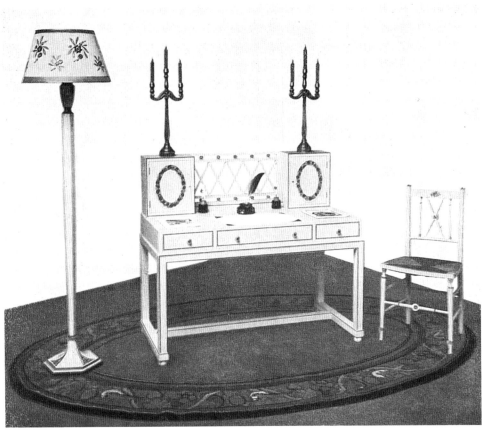

176

176
The Arts and Crafts tries for chic 1921

Painted furniture designed by Ambrose Heal; from 'The Studio' Year-Book of Decorative Art, London, 1921

Ambrose Heal was throughout his career a staunch supporter of the ideals of the Arts and Crafts movement, and an influential figure in the early days of scholarly research into the history of furniture making and other crafts. His own designs for furniture, executed in the workshops of the family firm and sold in the celebrated Tottenham Court Road store, did much to prove that design, craftsmanship and business could coexist happily. Heal's most famous range of furniture was in pale, untreated oak, but he was not unaware of fashion and from time to time responded to its stimulus and produced groups of pieces in the popular taste of the day. This curiously hybrid set of desk, chair and lamp standard seems to be inspired by the then current interest in painted finishes, and in its forms must reflect the 'Old French look' of Elsie de Wolfe, for both chair and desk hint strongly at Louis Seize originals. The lamp, the least successful of the pieces, attempts a free modern style, unfettered by the historical models to which most contemporary light fittings paid unnecessary lip service.

177
The table lamp 1924

Drawing by Marion Dismant; from Ethel Davis Seal, Furnishing the Little House, New York, 1924

This is one of the earliest suggestions for decoration in which the classic electric table lamp is incorporated into a grouping of objects and account is taken of the effect of the shade in the arrangement of pictures. There is no indication of the flex but there are some words of warning about shades in the text: 'Avoid lamp-shades that look like party-hats or enlarged boudoir-caps, or as though they had been made by a fussy dressmaker. Parchment shades should be plain in preference to the deteriorated naturalistic ornament that is so often seen.' The electric light certainly did not sweep away candles entirely, and they remained chic not only on dining tables but also in the grander drawing rooms for many years. Lamps and lampshades, however, became a mainstay of the trade for many modest decorating establishments.

177

178

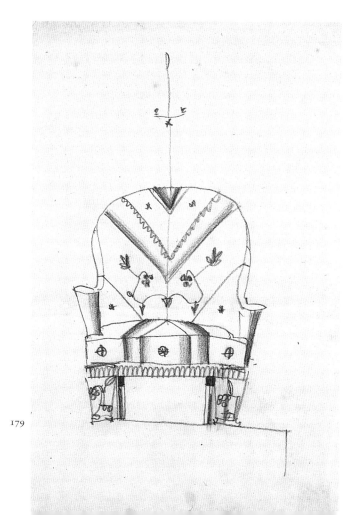

179

178

'A modern interpretation'   1924

Drawing by Marion Dismant; from Ethel Davis Seal,
Furnishing the Little House, *New York, 1924*

In modest schemes for furnishing, a mixture of old and new was often thought to be both comfortable and safely tasteful. Influenced by Frank A. Parsons (whose ideas informed a whole generation of designers in America) a number of books on decoration appeared which, like his, sought to combine a certain amount of the history of furniture and decoration, style by style, with chapters on the more practical aspects of putting a room together. The idea of making 'modern interpretations' of the past, which seems such a good one, often amounted to little more than the use of obviously reproduction pieces mixed uneasily with the more unavoidable trappings of modern life. In this illustration by Marion Dismant, 'a modern interpretation of the Elizabethan style is to be seen in this table, which is one of the few Elizabethan types suitable for use in the living-room of the modern home'. In fact several such well-known early classic pieces, including the famous Knole sofa, were adopted and tamed by the furniture trade.

179

Amusing upholstery, Vienna   c.1923–5

Design for an armchair by Bertha Sander

Bertha Sander was a promising young German designer, the daughter of the editor of an influential journal concerned with the upbringing of children. Some of her earliest designs were for children's beds and other nursery things, and these were published in the pages of her mother's magazine in the early 1920s. Unfortunately she contracted tuberculosis and was forced to spend several years in a Swiss sanatorium, but she recovered and was able to take up her design career. In about 1923–5 she worked at the Wiener Werkstätte, where she produced designs in the freer and jollier style that had succeeded the severe rectilinear manner of the institution's first years. At this time Bertha Sander designed complete schemes of furnishing, as well as the delightful individual pieces of which this chair is a typical example. She was also a good flat-pattern designer and a number of her drawings for textiles, wallpapers and decorative printed papers are extant.

Victoria & Albert Museum, London

180

180

A Cambridge undergraduate aesthete 1922–3

Self-portrait taken by Cecil Beaton

Cecil Beaton went up to Cambridge in October 1922 and, finding that he had not been allocated rooms in his college, St John's, took lodgings in nearby Bridge Street above a shop. They proved '... charming, with sloping floors and ceilings, white walls and black beams'. It was his first chance to decorate according to his own rapidly developing tastes and he was soon hanging pictures – especially black-framed prints by Pamela Bianco – and

filling the place with expensive flowers. One of his first purchases was a pair of twisted wooden candlesticks of the kind he had seen in the rooms of other Cambridge undergraduate aesthetes. They were proudly displayed as the main table decoration for many of Beaton's tea parties until they were eventually discarded as being too cottagey in feel for his ever-increasing sophistication. The total effect of the rooms must have been typical of those of the more visually aware students of moderate means, but clearly could not compare with the dramatic creations of the richer undergraduates, who went to tremendous lengths to impress with the lavishness of their surroundings and hospitality.

Cecil Beaton Photograph; Courtesy of Sotheby's, London

181

Lacquered exoticism 1919–22

Mme Mathieu Lévy in her apartment, decorated by Eileen Gray, in the rue de Lota, Paris

Eileen Gray is most celebrated for her severely elegant furniture of the 1930s in chrome, glass and lacquer, many classic pieces of which are still in production in Paris by Andrée Putnam's firm Écart. Her earlier work, however, was in a more exotic vein and is best seen in the apartment she decorated and furnished between 1919 and 1922 for her patron, Mme Mathieu Lévy who, under the name of Suzanne Talbot, was one of the most successful modistes in Paris. Mme Lévy is pictured here in a characteristically decorative pose in a remarkable 'gondola' daybed in rough-textured lacquer. This extravagant and decadent piece represents the culmination of the first phase of Eileen Gray's career, which had begun in 1907 when she went alone to Paris to set up as a designer. Her early experiments with lacquer techniques before the war brought her to the notice of the influential connoisseur Jacques Doucet, and she created her first major piece for him, the screen called *Le Destin*, in 1914. By the time of the commission for the Lévy apartment she was already experimenting with a more simplified modernistic aesthetic based on the surface qualities of flat planes and angular forms, and her design for a bedroom-boudoir shown at the 1923 *Salon des Artistes-Décorateurs* was criticized in the press for being too severe.

Courtesy of Philippe and Lucilla Garner

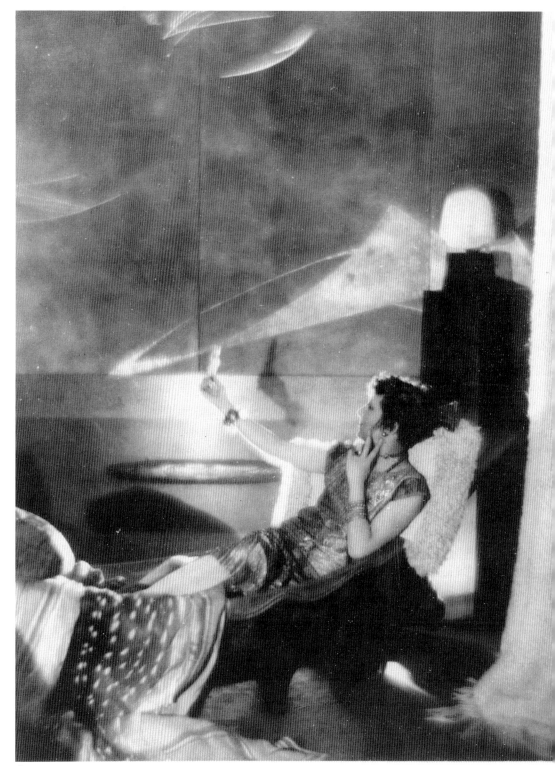

181

182

L'Art Déco and the Paris Exposition des Arts Décoratifs 1925

Four plates from Léon Déshairs, Intérieurs en Couleurs, *France, Paris, 1925*

182

Neo-Empire boudoir with a *bonheur du jour*

Design by Jacques-Emile Ruhlmann

183

Dining room on the barge *Amours*

Design by Poiret's Atelier Martine; from a watercolour by Boris Grosser

184

Dining room for the Galeries Lafayette

Design by Maurice Dufrène; from a painting by the collaborateur-dessinateur Englinger

185

Smoking room in yellow

From a design by Francis Jourdain

183

184

The view that the French decorative arts, and in particular French modern furniture designs, were infinitely more sophisticated than any of their rivals seemed to many to be all too readily demonstrated by the various nations' displays at the great Paris Exposition of 1925. The relatively poor showing made, for example, by British firms only served to enhance the lustre of the French manufacturers' offerings, and to point up the richness and variety of the work of the French designers and the high quality of workmanship that went into the manufacture of some of the more extravagant pieces. Several official and many semi- or unofficial publications recorded individual pieces and some of the more important designs for complete schemes of decoration. *Intérieurs en Couleurs* remains one of the most important documents for its plates, many of which reproduce drawings by the designers themselves or by artists connected with their studios, who were employed as '*collaborateurs-dessinateurs*' to create seductive images of proposed schemes.

185

PUb-H-382

186

A costume designer's studio 1925

Erté in the studio room of his apartment in Paris

The extravagant designer of costumes and stage-sets for revues Erté (Romain de Tertoff) created for his own Parisian apartment a curious decor which mixed influences of the Poiret and Russian Ballet style, which one would expect, with elements more reminiscent of the Viennese designers of the Sezession. In his studio the ceiling is a high curved vault from which, at each end, suspended tassels form a kind of frieze. The walls are lined with a great many of the artist's own distinctive and highly decorative drawings, and the floor and cushions are in boldly contrasting geometric designs. The desk and a chest of drawers, or plan chest, are of very simple form, but in its rigid stylization the chair shaped like a box with eight legs in which Erté sat to work might almost be by Kolo Moser or Josef Hoffmann.

Michael Parkin Fine Art Ltd, London

187

A Dada interior 1926

Hall of the house of Tristan Tzara in Paris, by Adolf Loos

Tristan Tzara, the eccentric poet and major protagonist of the Dada movement, chose Adolf Loos to create a house which accorded with his aesthetic ideals and which was clearly intended to underline his pose at the cutting edge of the European avant-garde. The hall, which is a classic of Loos's reductive principle, is fascinating for the way in which it eschews not only conventional notions of decorative detail but also even the plainest of architectural details such as architrave and door mouldings. Lighting is from uncompromising strip light fitments and the effect, reminiscent of a Dadaist gesture, is completed by the seemingly contradictory or inexplicable inclusion of several arresting African masks and some idiosyncratic but quite good seventeenth-century polished wood chairs.

Graphische Sammlung Albertina, Vienna

187

The Bauhaus aesthetic, Weimar 1920s

The Bauhaus, one of the great centres of the International Modern movement, came into being when the architect and theorist Walter Gropius succeeded Henry van de Velde as director of the Weimar art and architecture schools. The introduction of a new machine aesthetic was central to the philosophy of the school, and all notions of the design of interiors were therefore based on the concept of an interior architecture rather than of decoration. But the teachers of the Bauhaus, including Gropius himself, the painters Paul Klee and Wassily Kandinsky and others such as László Moholy-Nagy, did not entirely abandon the use of colour and pattern, and so continued in a sense to teach within a framework that admitted the concept of the decorative arts. Indeed it can be argued that the Bauhaus aesthetic is in fact a self-conscious 'manner' as well as a philosophical proposition, and now that we view the Modern movement more historically and in the light of a greater range of alternatives which now flourish, we may well come to see *Modernismus* to some degree as just another historic style.

188

Director's office in the Bauhaus, Weimar, with armchair by Walter Gropius   1923

189

Dining room in Moholy-Nagy's house   1925–6

Furniture by Marcel Breuer, colour scheme and painting by Moholy-Nagy, and lighting fixture by Gropius

190

A 'bed-sit' in Berlin by Lilly Reich   1931

191

Children's furniture by Marcel Breuer and nursery carpet by Benita Otte   1923

192

Display cabinet in chrome, opaque glass and mirror, by Josef Albers   1923

189, 192 Bauhaus Archiv, Berlin
190 Archiv Dr Sonja Gunther

189

190

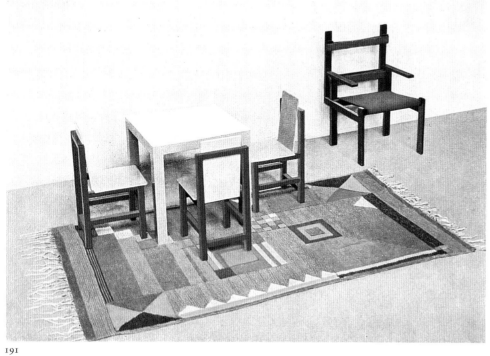

191

192

193

193
Trying to be modern late 1920s

A bedroom; from R.R. Phillips, The Modern English Interior, *London, 1929*

This unidentified room illustrates in its rather charming naivety the way in which ideas in decoration began to filter down to the more modest home with increasing rapidity in the 1920s. It has a Chinese carpet laid over plain matting in the newly fashionable manner, and the walls are painted in one flat, light colour. The bed, with a satin fitted cover and a heap of cushions including round gathered ones and bolster shapes, shows an awareness of the style popularized by Paul Poiret and his Atelier Martine designs. Sadly, however, any chic which might have been created is just as quickly dispelled by the good, sound writing table on twisted legs and the stout, no-nonsense Georgian chair, both of which belong to an aesthetic very remote from the self-conscious exoticism of the Poiret style.

194
A modern Empire look in France 1922

Gentleman's bedroom by Atelier Primavera for Au Printemps, Paris

This curiously hybrid set piece of Parisian commercial furnishing for the department store Au Printemps mixes Empire revival motifs with what seem to be several varieties of modernistic elements. The basic ambience of the room, with the classic arrangement of the bed in a draped niche, is presumably meant to evoke an Empire bedchamber. This theme is followed through in the use of the bold, broad-striped wall covering, but begins to break down in the choice of the rest of the furnishings. The square, upright upholstered armchair may well be intended to suggest the lines of a Directoire piece, but the small table and the dressing table, contrived from two low cabinets and a full-length looking-glass, are in a proto-Art Deco manner which is echoed in the geometric pattern of the carpet. The light fitting is equally modern but the pictures, hung like washing on a line, are disastrous.

Private collection

195

The modern style in Paris 1925

*Salon of the Maison Martine, by Paul Poiret, in the
faubourg St-Honoré*

The extent to which architecture and decoration were
integrated in Parisian schemes of this period is a major
factor in the very strong showing of the French compared
with any other competitors at the great Paris Exposition of
1925. The salon at the Maison Martine is typical of this
sophisticated interplay between the elements of an interior,
and here it is possible to see in the carefully sculptured
forms of the furniture the beginnings of trends which would
develop in the 1930s. At this stage, however, there remains
a strong feeling of Poiret's Russian Ballet-inspired period,
with sumptuous cushions covered in seductively rich
fabrics and laden with heavy tassels.

Lipnitzi-Viollet, Paris

196, 197, 198

A modern French Maecenas c.1925–30

Three views of the villa of Jacques Doucet at Neuilly

One of the great taste-makers in French decoration, Jacques Doucet deliberately set out to make his villa at Neuilly a statement of what he considered to be the best in contemporary design and the finest of recent craftsmanship. Until about 1912 he had devoted his considerable energies and powers of discrimination to the collecting of fine early furniture and other works of art, but after that date his interests became more or less exclusively modern. He commissioned Paul Iribe before 1914 to decorate and furnish a house in Paris in his gently Empire-inspired proto-Art Deco-Empire manner. Doucet's taste, however, was moving on rapidly and already embraced such avant-garde elements as tribal sculpture, as well as the works of many young and promising artists. In 1926 he began to furnish the villa at Neuilly and used a great many of the leading designers of the day. The main schemes were by Pierre Legrain, who had worked with him since 1917, but in

196

197

198

addition there were contributions from Eileen Gray, André Groult and the makers of bizarre furniture Clément Rousseau and Rose Adler. Certainly it was a remarkable assemblage: writing in *L'Illustration* in 1930, in appreciation of the rare combination of intellectual curiosity, quality of connoisseurship and independence of thought which had brought it all together, André Jouvin declared Doucet to be one of the '*plus illustres amateurs de notre temps*'.

196 Jean-Loup Charmet
197, 198 Courtesy of Philippe and Lucilla Garner

199

Garden suburb modernity mid-1920s

Decorative objects designed by Claude Flight in the drawing room at 8 Wellgarth Road, Hampstead Garden Suburb, London

Claude Flight is remembered today chiefly for his championing of the linocut as a legitimate and wholly independent art form, a distinct method of making colour prints and an aesthetically influential form of expression. He was a central figure at the independent Grosvenor School of Modern Art, which first opened its doors to students in 1925. Through his teaching at the school he met Edith Lawrence, who became his lifelong companion and with him formed a small interior design and decoration company. Their productions were of a modest nature, quite adventurous in taste and in many ways reminiscent of those of the Omega Workshop. This photograph shows the drawing room in the house of Flight's sister, Mrs Friede Slater, in Hampstead Garden Suburb. Visible are a screen, cushions and a pouffe, all designed by Flight, the last being executed in cross-stitch by his mother, which probably gives some indication of the actual scale of the business.

Courtesy of the artist's family and the Redfern Gallery, London

199

200

Boulestin in the bathroom 1920s

Decorative scheme for a bathroom, by Marcel Boulestin

The great glories of Victorian and Edwardian plumbing often made the bathrooms of those eras splendid. In a spacious room brass, tile and mahogany combined in clouds of steam to suggest an opulence that was partly Roman and partly of the age of Brunel. The more modest and confined bathroom of the post-war period often lacked any serious attempt to provide an aesthetic as well as a cleansing experience. This simple scheme by Boulestin shows him at his most inventive for, in a narrow space and with no interesting features with which to play, he contrived a look which was at once fresh and amusing. The use of marine imagery for the decoration of bathrooms has a long and distinguished history, and this form of decoration was to remain popular well into the 1950s.

Private collection

201

200

DIY Chinese bathroom 1920

Lady Diana Cooper's bathroom, Gower Street, London; from R.R. Phillips, The Modern English Interior, *London, 1929*

In 1920, needing more space than they could find in Arlington Street, Duff and Diana Cooper took a fifty-year lease on a late eighteenth-century house in the rather unfashionable Gower Street in Bloomsbury. To this they quickly added the first floor of the house next door and in due course that of the third house in the terrace. The first annexe provided a large bedroom and a splendid drawing-room-sized bathroom, appropriate to Lady Diana's status as emerging star of stage and screen and one of the most glittering ornaments of London society. For the new bathroom she conceived a scheme of decoration based on an original Chinese wallpaper in her family house, Belvoir Castle in Leicestershire. She and her mother, the Duchess of Rutland, a talented amateur painter and a very good sculptor, carried out the copying of the paper, and the room was completed with carpet and other luxurious fittings and furnishings. Because it was widely photographed at the time, this room and the glamour of its owner's way of life did much to popularize the warm, furnished and civilized bathroom in England.

202

Empire néo-grec in America 1920s

Master bathroom at Vizcaya, Miami, by F. Burrall Hoffman Jr, architect, and Paul Chalfin, decorator

Vizcaya is an extraordinarily successful essay in a complex Empire revival or néo-grec idiom, built originally for James Deering, but since 1953 open as a museum of the decorative arts. It is the result of a happy collaboration between the architect F. Burrall Hoffman Jr, who was responsible for the structure, plan and basic disposition of the architectural elements, and Paul Chalfin, who as decorator contrived the visual effects which make the rooms so intriguing. Much of the decor is a series of plays on Empire versions of neo-classical Greek and Egyptian decoration. The lavish use of fine materials played an important part in the creation of settings of great opulence and refinement. The marble-lined bathroom typifies many of these points, with its luxurious use of extravagantly veined marble, silver and gold-plated ornaments reflecting the Greek and Egyptian cross-currents in the scheme, and the ceiling suggestive of Malmaison with its sensuously billowy tenting.

Courtesy of Villa Vizcaya Museum and Gardens, Miami, Florida

202

203

Pattern and colour in Dresden 1920s

Plate by Paul Knothe from Dekorative Raumkunst, Malereien von Atelier Stenzel, *Dresden, n.d.*

These colourful and exotic designs for stencilled wall decoration by Paul Knothe of the Atelier Stenzel in Dresden draw together a number of influences. In their colouring they have something of the richly saturated hues and intriguing contrasts, such as purples and oranges, of the Russian Ballet. The forms of the decorative elements suggest the highly popular Chinoiserie of the day, but interpreted in the very free manner of the Brighton Pavilion rather than with the accuracy of the nineteenth-century encyclopedist Owen Jones, whose *Grammar of Ornament* (London, 1856) was a central monument of the age of revivals. In their lightness and prettiness they have a similar feel to many of the designs of the mid-1920s by artists associated with the latter days of the Wiener Werkstätte.

203

204
204

Laboureur paints a restaurant 1927

Decorative panel of a circus sharpshooter, surrounding a door, Restaurant Boulestin, Covent Garden, London

Of the decorative panels on a circus theme in the Restaurant Boulestin William Gaunt wrote:

The first room is a brilliant *hors d'oeuvre*. The faculties become awake and vivid at the sight of M. Laboureur's panels with their cunning notes of black and red and buff, their suggestion of an active gaiety, of the laughter and entertainment, of clowns and strong men. Then over the door is an *entrée*, fair and fleeting, rich and elusive, a tenderness of blue and rose, by Marie Laurencin.

Michael Parkin Fine Art Ltd, London

French chic in London 1927

Restaurant Boulestin, Covent Garden

The curious progression of Marcel Boulestin's career, from man of letters to decorator and thence, after the failure of the business, via writing cookery books to owning two successful restaurants, accounts in part for the remarkable visual as well as culinary standards that he maintained. His close friendship with a number of leading artists of the day, including Jean-Emile Laboureur, Marie Laurencin and Raoul Dufy, also played an important part in the creation of that special ambience for which the Restaurant Français, Leicester Square, and later the Restaurant Boulestin were celebrated. Boulestin always seems to have taken a mainly entrepreneurial role, and in the execution of the Restaurant Français schemes in 1925 he combined the skills of a leading architect of the younger generation, Clough Williams-Ellis, with the more purely decorative expertise of Allan Walton, then about to take up an important post as head of the decoration department of Fortnum & Mason (which like other big stores at the time began to offer a full interior design service as well as retailing furnishings). With their use of a light and spacious neo-Georgian idiom and simple furnishings, some modernistic decorative panels and a subtle element of *faux-marbre*, Williams-Ellis and Walton broke entirely new ground in the Restaurant Français interiors, and certainly played a major part in attracting a fashionable crowd who came as much for the style of the surroundings as for the delicious food.

Boulestin's second restaurant was an even greater success than his first, both in social terms and as a celebrated scheme of decoration. He brought together a number of his artist friends in order to create a special and distinctly French atmosphere. His old collaborator André Groult oversaw the entire project, sending over from Paris panels enlarged from designs by Marie Laurencin and Jean-Emile Laboureur. These panels were on a circus theme and gave the first room a degree of jollity (pl. 204). The second room was painted in a rich, deep yellow, which as it further deepened with age gave rise to the legend that the paint had been mixed with Guinness. The main element of the decor of this room was a magnificent set of curtains in a yellow silk by Dufy, to be seen in this contemporary photograph which also shows the restaurant's famous totem, an enormous bottle of 1869 liqueur brandy. Writing in *The Studio* in 1928, William Gaunt described the decoration of the restaurant in the most enthusiastic tones:

205

It is too little understood in England that the preparation of food is an art in itself: still less that its degustation may be rendered wittier and more pleasant by the secondary attraction of other arts. At Boulestin's new premises in Southampton Street enlightenment prevails. The *table d'hôte* is reinforced by the *tableau d'hôte* ... in place of the sounding brass of a huge orchestra, that marble and dull crimson, which in common restaurants are the direct cause of indigestion, the jaded diner-out will find his senses soothed by pure colour and elegant form, by mural paintings that convey a sharper savour to the delicious morsels on his plate, and curtains that are strictly eupeptic. *L'appétit vient en regardant.*

Michael Parkin Fine Art Ltd, London

206

Principles of decoration, America 1923

Illustrations from Frank A. Parsons, Interior Decoration, Its Principles and Practice, *New York and London, 1923*

206

'Man's living-room'

207

Papered bedroom

In the earliest years of the century most decorators had come from the upholstery or antique furniture trades or, like Lady Sackville in England and Edith Wharton and Elsie de Wolfe in America, from other walks of life entirely. Those who had any relevant formal training tended to have studied either architecture or painting. It was therefore something of a landmark when the Parsons School was established in New York upon the premise that decoration, which previously had been held to be the exercise of inherent taste and flair, could in fact be taught as a system of principles. In his teaching, writing and the schemes which he carried out, Frank Alvah Parsons subscribed to most of the current ideas derived from Wharton and Codman and Elsie de Wolfe, but his work represents the increasing widening of the market for decoration, and consequent shifting of the emphasis from the precious and the exquisite to the comfortable, the economic and the efficient. Where Codman had advocated a 'rationality' based on proportion and visual clarity, Parsons propounded one of practicality. The modest papered bedroom, reminiscent of the upper servants' quarters of an English house of 1840, was illustrated to show the way in which wallpapers can be chosen as a background for hanging pictures and prints 'without destroying the effect [of] either …' In rooms such as the 'man's living-room' Parsons represented the ideal balance between 'period feel' and modern convenience that most people who consulted a decorator were seeking. Parsons described it thus: 'There is a "comfort quality" essential in the thought of every room. In this man's living-room comfort is apparent, while decoration has in no case been sacrificed. See placing of lamps for use.'

207

208

208

The 'Old French look' in France early 1920s

The sitting room of Edith Wharton's house, Pavillon Colombe, near Paris

For each of the three great figures in American decoration – Edith Wharton and Ogden Codman, advocates of the 'Old French look', and Elsie de Wolfe, the popularizer of their ideas the logical outcome of their enthusiasm for architecture and their obsession with the arrangement of interiors was the purchase of a house in France. The three chose eighteenth-century houses, of course, but each on a different scale. Codman was eventually ruined by *folie de grandeur*, but both Mrs Wharton and

Elsie de Wolfe created houses of a manageable size which became havens of quiet and stylish distinction. Mrs Wharton's Pavillon Colombe, just to the north of Paris, decorated immediately after the First World War, was the perfect mature expression of the ideal way of life of which she had written with Codman in 1897 in *The Decoration of Houses*. Her personal taste, unlike Elsie de Wolfe's, seems always to have remained for the understated. Her simple but exquisite sitting room exemplifies her desire to be surrounded by fine but unostentatious pieces.

Beinecke Library, Yale University (Edith Wharton Papers)

209

Elsie de Wolfe's Villa Trianon 1920s

Redecorated after the First World War and photographed in 1949 shortly before Elsie de Wolfe's death

209, 210

The Long Gallery

211

The Salon

Elsie de Wolfe and Elizabeth Marbury found the decayed and abandoned Villa Trianon at Versailles in 1903, and it became theirs after protracted negotiations. Elsie worked at the refurbishment and decoration with increasing enthusiasm with the help of the rapidly improving finances that her work at the Colony Club brought. From the rich American Minna Anglesey, who had been one of the first to discover the delights of living near Versailles, but who had fallen for the charm of Art Nouveau decoration, she bought good eighteenth-century *boiseries* for the principal salon, while for the long gallery she secured a parquet floor which had come originally from the nearby palace. It has been said that at this time, just before and immediately after the war, fine and important furnishings could still be had relatively cheaply from the smart dealers in Paris, and even the little junk shops of the Left Bank contained many an unconsidered trifle. Elsie

210

bought well and assembled some distinguished pieces with which to re-create the interiors of the villa according to her own influential precepts. During the war parts of the house were used by troops, the gallery serving as a hospital ward. After the war Elsie embarked on new and stylish schemes of redecoration. These included a set of mural paintings by Drian and the rather daring use of leopard skin for the upholstery of seats and stools in a much more dramatic 1920s manner. Elsie continued, with ever-increasing grandeur, to hold court in her splendid rooms at Versailles, and it was here that the young Paul Channon, taken by his father Sir Henry to meet the awe-inspiring Miss de Wolfe, asked her, in some confusion, if she had known Louis xv.

Photographs Jerome Zerbe

212

211

212

'Successful dining'   1920s–30s

'At Villa Trianon, Versailles. Buffet table for small informal lunches'; illustration from Elsie de Wolfe, Recipes for Successful Dining, *London, 1934*

Elsie de Wolfe's recipe book was in effect, just like *The House in Good Taste*, a manual proposing a whole style of living, an attitude to life and the enjoyment of material luxury. The illustrations are all from photographs taken in her own houses and represent with perhaps a little embellishment the carefully contrived daily life which she lived in Paris and at the Villa Trianon. While in some ways the table arrangements seem pretentious and intended to impress, there can be no doubt that one of Elsie's firmest beliefs was that one honoured one's guests by taking endless pains to present everything beautifully.

213

'A dining room decorated in an unusual manner' late 1920s

Dining room of Basil Ionides's own London house; from R.R. Phillips, The Modern English Interior, *London, 1929*

In addition to his skills as a colourist (see p. 190) Ionides was also one of the most consistently innovative designers of interior effects. In his London dining room, which had been plain until about 1926, he carried out this delightful *jeu d'esprit* of 'paste-pot architecture'. Of this room Randal Phillips wrote: 'Coloured landscape papers are here seen framed by cut-out geranium-patterned paper, on which is a gold trellis, giving an arbour-like effect.' Other elements in the room are kept simple, with light 'Chinese Chippendale' chairs, rush matting and an unusual

213

214

but unfussy window treatment in a thin, unlined striped fabric from which the skirt of the hanging light is also made. The chimneypiece contains an early 'Georgian revival' electric fire and on the mantel are a group of obelisks, later to become one of the classic decorators' clichés.

214
Twenties Chinoiserie   late 1920s

Music room in Sir Albert Levy's flat in Devonshire House, London, designed by Oliver Hill and decorated by George Sheringham

George Sheringham, because he was quite a good painter – a colourist who worked in a highly decorative manner, made quite an interesting decorator too. This rather successful essay in Chinoiserie is typical of his idiosyncratic approach and has something of the atmosphere of 1920s fairy-tale book illustrations. The painting of the wall panels sets the theme and contrives at once to hint both at early nineteenth-century panoramic wallpapers and oriental screens. Ronald Fleming, writing of this scheme in 'Fifty Years of Rooms' in *The Saturday Book* (19, 1959), contrasted it with a room of his own done in a conventional eighteenth-century English country-house Chinoiserie style and criticized the 'curious self-conscious effort at originality in the fire-place and settee'. These elements seem to be well in keeping with the slightly whimsical effect, however, and give the room a strong and pleasing character, even though the only genuine oriental pieces are a few ceramics which are confined to the mantelshelf and one small shelved recess.

Country Life

215
Ultra-chic Chinoiserie   mid-1920s

Doorway to the terrace of Condé Nast's residence, 1040 Park Lane, New York, designed by Elsie de Wolfe; photographed by Hewitt & Smith, 1927

The commission to work for the arbiter of taste and fashion, Condé Nast, at his New York residence on Park Avenue was, even at this date, a major coup for Elsie de Wolfe, who pulled out all the stops in order to create a memorable interior scheme for lavish entertainments. A principal feature of the house was an enclosed terrace which could be used as a dining area. For this space Elsie played up the association with the orangeries of grand European houses, and further enhanced the feel of a magical garden by suggesting its presence from inside by the use of a Chinoiserie-style *trompe-l'oeil* garden wall. This she pierced with an exquisitely draped opening capped with a gilt pagoda-crested pelmet. Finished at the height of the vogue for Chinoiserie decorations, this arrangement was without doubt one of the most complete and successful expressions of the style.

Courtesy of the New-York Historical Society, New York City

215

A famous eighteenth-century house decorated c.1922–4

Carlisle House, Soho, decorated by Keebles

216

Main staircase

217

The Chinese room, styled by Ronald Fleming of Keebles

Not to be outdone by its rivals Lenygon & Morant, which had set up in tremendous grandeur in Old Burlington Street (pls 138, 139), Keebles, which could trace its origins in the upholsterers' trade to the London of the 1690s, established showrooms in the splendid and once notorious town house of the Earls of Carlisle in Soho Square. The house had been the setting for the brilliant

216

soirées given by Mrs Cornelys, who made the promenade rooms famous as the smartest meeting place for fashionable and aristocratic society. In later years her clientele changed and Carlisle House became no less celebrated as a place of assignation. Much of the original structure survived and in various parts of the house, such as the great staircase, Keebles' team of craftsmen were able to restore to its original splendour the rich eighteenth-century plasterwork and decorations carried out for Lord Delaval. Other rooms were decorated in a traditional manner appropriate to the period of the house or in versions of the historic styles which the firm could offer, but from surviving photographs it seems that the rooms never quite achieved the magisterial grandeur of Lenygon's, either in the quality of the stock or in the decorative effects. The Chinese room on the ground floor was one of the invented room sets. Styled by Ronald Fleming, then head of Keebles' design team, it was typical of the firm's work at this time, and unmistakably a room of the 1920s in spite of the use of many good antique pieces. Once decorated the rooms were kept, and only the furniture changed as pieces were sold and new stock acquired. These photographs were taken in 1938 and record the appearance of the staircase and Chinese room more or less unchanged since the 20s. Sadly, Carlisle House was destroyed by bombing during the war.

Royal Commission on the Historical Monuments of England

217

218

Coco Chanel's grand luxe late 1920s

Salon at 29 faubourg St-Honoré, Paris

Throughout a long career as one of the formative taste-makers in the Parisian fashion world and, to many, the very quintessence of chic, Coco Chanel lived and worked in a series of rooms renowned for their stylishness and sense of total luxury. Following the successful launch of her Chanel No. 5, perhaps even today the most famous of scents, she moved to a palatial suite of rooms on the principal floor of the Hôtel Pillet-Will, a classic Parisian *hôtel particulier* of 1719. Chanel affected to dislike the superb *boiseries* which survived and the historic colour in which they were painted, dismissing it all as 'split-pea green'. Encouraged by her friends José-Maria and Misia Sert she had Jansen carry out an extraordinary scheme that covered all the panelling with mirror glass, which gave the rooms an ambiguous spatial quality, but at the same time an undeniable grandeur and richness. Much of the furniture supplied by the decorators was superb and of early eighteenth-century date, and to this Chanel added those objects that became so closely associated with her 'look': beautiful flowers, Chinese ceramics, finely bound books, and especially the exquisite Coromandel screens for which she claimed to have had a passion 'from the age of eighteen' and of which she came to own dozens. The strong influence of the taste and skill of the painter José-Maria Sert can also be felt in the many glittering chandeliers and candelabra which he found for her or made up from old rock-crystal drops, glass pyramids and prisms, and from pieces of amethyst and other semi-precious minerals. The essentials of the Chanel style hardly changed over the years, and she remained remarkably faithful to a favourite colour scheme featuring biege and black, best seen in the famous rooms of her rue Cambon premises. Even at the age of eighty she retained a great interest in the beauty of her interiors, although by then she would vehemently insist that the style was all her own, uninfluenced by the work and ideas of Sert or other friends of the early days such as Jean Cocteau.

Private collection

218

219

Graphic clarity in New York late 1920s

An early disciple of the teachings of Elsie de Wolfe was Mrs Archibald Brown, the founder of the decorating firm McMillen Inc. Mrs Brown had a distinctive look: it was crisp and clear, often based on French Empire period pieces but always at the same time 'modern'. She favoured above all the use of a strong, clear yellow for walls, accenting it with thin mouldings and highlights of gilt in the wall sconces and other small decorative objects. Chairs were usually French, either gilt or painted off-white, and invariably placed symmetrically. Her own apartment, decorated to this formula and still extant, has remained almost unchanged since she conceived it. Of this style Derek Patmore, the English decorator and popular writer of design manuals in the 30s and 40s, who admired her work, wrote that it illustrated 'the tendency towards a return to ornamental features in the modern interior, whilst preserving the effect of simplicity'.

219

Entrance hall

220

Drawing room

Two rooms for Mrs Millicent Rogers, New York, by Mrs Archibald Brown of McMillen Inc.

Mrs Brown was engaged in the late 20s by a Mrs Rogers to create a series of rooms which would display to advantage her collection of eighteenth- and, more unusually for the period, nineteenth-century American furniture and decorative objects. In the entrance hall Mrs Brown juxtaposed eighteenth-century paired painted chairs and a baroque mid-nineteenth-century sofa, lavishly upholstered in satin, against a background of *trompe-l'oeil* walls and crisp chequerboard floor. A similar eclectic mix can be seen in the drawing room, which was draped in crimson silk swagged from gilt cloak-pins in the French Empire manner. Here the simple forms of the modern sofas and plain drum-shaped shades on the electrified oil lamps are contrasted with the richness of a floral carpet, the more intricate forms and decorative finish of eighteenth-century tables, and some rather good mid-nineteenth-century black and gold side chairs.

Courtesy of McMillen Inc., New York

221

222

221

The dining room in Mrs Brown's own apartment, Sutton Place, New York, decorated 1928

Drawing by Pierre Brissaud, 1934

For her own apartment Mrs Brown contrived a stylish circular dining room in which she combined elegant Directoire and English Regency furnishings with modern sculpture adorning the four niches that concealed the heating. The French mantel was echoed by a marble buffet on which stood a fine pair of French bronze and ormolu candelabra. The floor, inlaid in green and creamy white, set the colour scheme, and all other surfaces and decoration, including the simple gathered curtain without fussy swags, were kept very plain.

Courtesy of McMillen Inc., New York

222

Drawing room of Mrs Brown's apartment

Drawing by Pierre Brissaud, 1934

Brissaud's watercolour drawing of the drawing room, made in 1934, is interesting because it shows Mrs Brown's original colour scheme, in which pinkish walls and a grey frieze were articulated with very simple cream pilasters. Shortly after this date the room was recast in a more cheerful vein, using the decorator's favourite yellow as the background to the rigidly symmetrical groups of French chairs and tables. Subtle highlights of gold on the old pieces of furniture and other objects are played off against the simple, plain forms of the modern sofas and comfortably capacious armchairs.

Courtesy of McMillen Inc., New York

223

The colours of nature 1920

Colour treatment for a Georgian room; from
Edward J. Duveen, Colour in the Home, *London, n.d.*

Two seemingly unconnected factors gave rise to the enormous degree of interest which colour treatment began to attract in the 1920s. Most obvious was the influence of avant-garde movements in the arts, for much new painting was essentially concerned for the first time with the values or effects of colour, rather than with form and its representation by the traditional methods of drawing or the conventions of chiaroscuro. However, there can be little doubt that at about the same time the grander decorating firms began to experience increasing difficulty in finding the right sort of very high-quality antique furniture and objects required for their most important projects. The

result was that the middle-range firms or individual decorators were forced to explore hitherto unfashionable areas of the antique market or to try to find new ways of creating effects. Many turned to the use of colour, and a large number of publications appeared on the subject, several advocating the use of natural objects such as flowers or minerals as the starting point for colour schemes for decoration. Duveen seems to have been among the very first to notice that the complex and subtle colour combinations in the wings of butterflies were especially suitable for this kind of approach, and he realized too, as some others did not, that the relative proportions of the colours were important. His use of greys and taupes for a Georgian panelled room is very pleasing, but other plates in the book, such as a dark-brown panelled room with touches of creamy yellow and violet, are less successful.

223

224

224
A Thomas Hope collector c.1920

Edward Knoblock's inner hall at the Beach House, Worthing

Edward Knoblock had arrived in England from Paris at the outbreak of war in 1914 with his tastes for Directoire and Empire decoration already fully formed, and to a great extent it was he who opened the eyes of his English friends to French *papiers peints*, the *style Retour d' Egypte* and the robust beauties of the later Empire and Regency periods. He first installed himself in some grandeur in a set in Albany, London, with marbled walls, deep purple Lyons silk curtains with a palmette border and furniture which he described as 'solemn Regency'. Following his great success at the sale of Thomas Hope's furniture from his house, The Deepdene, in 1917, when, outbidding friends and rivals such as Gerald Wellesley and Professor Richardson, he secured many of the finest pieces, he found the Beach House at Worthing, which he restored and decorated between 1918 and 1921 as a worthy setting for his collection. The architect Maxwell Ayrton carried out the serious work of bringing the grand seaside villa back to its correct period appearance, and Knoblock laid out his pieces with characteristic flair. From this simple and uncluttered hall with its trophies of ancient musical instruments there is a view through to the anteroom, in which Knoblock reused the painted glass panels which he had commissioned from William Nicholson in 1912 for his Palais Royal apartment.

Country Life

225
A modern Regency drawing room c.1930

17 Park Square East, London, by Lord Gerald Wellesley, for H.J. Venning Esq.

Lord Gerald Wellesley and his partner Trenwith Wells did much to promote the interesting style based on what their friend Christopher Hussey called 'this kinship between Regency and modern taste'. The notion that Regency architectural ideals and motifs could be restated in a new classical idiom was proved in this drawing room overlooking Regent's Park. Here Lord Gerald's marbled paper 'paste-pot architecture' is used to give an early nineteenth-century-looking articulation to modern painted panels, which themselves have something of the feeling of early *papiers peints*. The furnishings are elegant black-painted Regency pieces, and the chandelier with its rather smart shades is modern Venetian glass, which works well with the mirrored chimneypiece and with the large panels of mirror bordered with coloured glass at each end of the room.

Country Life

226

225

226

New-Georgian grace mid-1920s

'A modern room furnished with old pieces'; the drawing room at Chester House, Clarendon Place, London, by Sir Giles Gilbert Scott

In a large and grand room of which one end is entirely taken up by five great floor-length windows, Giles Gilbert Scott, the architect of Battersea Power Station, displays his usual magisterial touch. The architectural forms are simple, in a 'stripped neo-classical' manner, and form the perfect setting for some good early nineteenth-century furniture, including an elegant scroll-ended sofa and a set of Regency painted and lacquered chairs. Writing about this room in *The Modern English Interior* (1929) Randal Phillips was particularly impressed with the neat way in which the curtains and their headings or pelmets were fitted inside the window embrasures, and with the novel method of heating by means of hot-water pipes covered by tall, narrow bronze grilles, which were set into the panelling and echoed the graceful verticality of the design.

Country Life

227

227

Vogue Regency   late 1920s – early 1930s

Drawing by Osbert Lancaster, from Homes Sweet Homes, *London, 1939*

The version of the Regency revival that Osbert Lancaster chose to portray was the one which he felt was chic and forward-looking. It was also the kind of decoration which he had at that time chosen to live with himself and which, while others such as Norman Hartnell may have thought it just a glamorous fashion, Lancaster seriously considered to be the style of the future. In his text he makes a genuine case for the revival of Regency furniture because it will harmonize with new things too – 'A Récamier sofa is in no way embarrassed by the close proximity of a rug by Marion Dorn' – but his main thesis is that,

> … today the more sensible of modern architects realize that the desperate attempt to find a modern style can only succeed if the search starts at the point where Soane left off.… So long therefore as no attempt is made to follow the fatal will-o'-the-wisp of period accuracy, Vogue Regency remains as suitable a style as any for a period in describing which the phrase Transitional, it is now apparent, is the grossest of understatements.

John Murray Ltd, London

228

229

Edward Knoblock's London house   mid-1920s

Back drawing room, 11 Montagu Place, London

Although much of his best furniture and a great deal of effort went into the reconstruction and arranging of the Beach House, Knoblock also took a house in London near those of his friends Gerald Wellesley and H.L. Goodhart-Rendel. Here he installed a number of his important pieces by Thomas Hope. His interconnecting drawing rooms in Montagu Place became something of a showpiece of the Regency revival style and were discussed at length by Christopher Hussey in his article 'Four Regency Houses', published in *Country Life* in 1931, which did so much to identify and promote as a movement what had been, until that point, merely the obsessive enthusiasm of a small band of collectors, artists, architects and decorators.

Country Life

228

Empire in the nursery   1924

Design for a bed alcove by J.B. Platt; from Vogue, *1924*

In a spread in *Vogue* devoted to recent examples of mural decoration the most delightful was this suggestion for 'an amusing room for a young boy with history and adventure motifs', by the American designer J.B. Platt. The bed, which stood in a grey-blue niche, had a 'vermilion and gold painted motif of carved wood' above it, the colourful Empire-striped bed cover was in cream and vermilion and the dado was blue. The painted scenes were each enclosed within a wreath of laurel against a dull-cream ground, and below in the dado were lozenge-shaped panels of ornament. These last details especially underline the references to the decoration of Malmaison (pl. 21), with which Platt seems to be playing, and the star pattern of the drapery on the walls of the niche became a favourite and easily understood allusion to the Empire period, used by many decorators in the late 1920s and 30s.

Condé Nast Publications Ltd, London

230

The Regency revival late 1920s

Lord Gerald Wellesley's house,
11 Titchfield Terrace, London

230

Drawing room

As both a good architect practising in an interesting modern style and a respected scholar of the decorative arts of the Regency period, Lord Gerald Wellesley arranged rooms in a manner which veered between the avant-garde and the antiquarian. In his own house in London he created one of the cleverest evocations in its day of the period of his ancestor the Duke of Wellington. The success of these greatly admired rooms derived as much from his ability to place objects with clarity and a firm sense of design as from the inherent quality of the furniture and objects, for which he had an unerring eye. The drawing room was decorated with tremendous verve, using a reprinted 'satin' paper of the Regency period of acid yellow with moiré stripes, divided architecturally with a border composed of a red key pattern, also printed from old blocks, figures cut from a period frieze paper and panels of sphinxes drawn by the architect himself. The centre of each floor area was lit by electric bulbs concealed in a pair of hanging colza-oil lanterns of the 1830s used as reflectors. These and many other good decorative objects would have come from the family house, Stratfield Saye. Throughout his life Lord Gerald remained fascinated by his illustrious forebear and was fond of Wellington memorabilia, such as the iron plaque of the Iron Duke which is visible lying in the grate of the rear room.

Country Life

231

Dining room

This rich and highly successful scheme is almost a showcase for the inventiveness of Lord Gerald Wellesley as a designer and arranger of interiors. As a setting for a group of very fine quality Regency dining furniture the architect contrived a sumptuous essay in what he described as 'paste-pot architecture'. The walls are covered with individual sheets of Sienna marbled paper arranged as blocks and divided by pilasters of a contrasting marble with *trompe-l'oeil* shadowing. Other elements, such as the door-cases and skirtings, are finished in painted *verde antico* marble, and a richly variegated floor of marbled linoleums echoes the cross-banding around the circular table. Lighting is again from a colza lantern used as a reflector, and there are a number of choice objects appropriate to a late neo-classical dining room, including some pieces of the distinctive Herculaneum ware china.

Country Life

232

A neo-Regency drawing room c.1930

H.L. Goodhart-Rendel's own house,
13 Crawford Street, London

Of all the rooms designed by his friends that Christopher Hussey featured in his 1931 *Country Life* article 'Four Regency Houses', the room by the architect Goodhart-Rendel in his own Crawford Street house had the most feeling of 1930 and the least of 1815. The walls, divided by attenuated pilasters, were finished with panels of *trompe-l'oeil* drapery in a very modern coffee colour relieved with Wedgwood-blue above: a scheme used by Edward Knoblock in 1920 for the Beach House library. By comparison with the richness of Lord Gerald Wellesley's arrangements, however, or the bold scale and forms of Knoblock's, the design seems thin and unconvincing. But there are interesting and innovative features in the room, including a pair of extraordinary architectural columns and bases made into very Art Deco lamps and, between the windows, a shallow, faceted, mirrored niche with the head painted in coffering. It contains a marble bowl on a stand that lights up.

Country Life

231

232

233

'Lovely white and gold Empire'   1924

Drawing room of Miss Dorothy Warren's house, London; from Vogue, *1924*

Dorothy Warren was an elusive figure in the world of decoration of whom we catch only the odd fleeting glimpse. She was the daughter of the President of Magdalen College, Oxford and moved in artistic circles. At first a bluestocking among the English and American colony in Florence, she fell, like many, under the spell of the dashing architect and writer Geoffrey Scott. Back in England she had a small shop near St James's Street for a while, selling antique furniture to decorators, and at one time she ran a tiny London art gallery with some degree of success. In 1924 *Vogue* showed a view of her drawing room furnished with 'some . . . lovely white and gold Empire chairs, covered in pale blue silk embroidered with flower motifs'. The rest of the scheme was colourful in the emerging Vogue Regency manner with 'walls . . . painted a clear lettuce green and the curtains . . . of faded rose, yellow and green striped satin'. Miss Warren eventually married the American decorator and designer Waymer Mills.

Condé Nast Publications Ltd, London

234, 235

A French Empire scheme   1924

Villa Corne d'Or, Cannes; decoration by Jansen of Paris

The Villa Corne d'Or at Cannes was decorated throughout in the Empire manner for the owner, Mrs Sedan Henry, by the House of Jansen, the most celebrated Parisian decoration house. The decorative schemes were historically 'correct' and tended towards a rather surprising and very pleasing understatement. The quality of the furniture was high and this clearly made the more traditional arrangements of the rooms successful, although the actual effects of colour and texture were by no means

234

233

235

dull. The bedroom, which was one of the rooms in the house which first sparked off the imagination of the important English decorator Ronald Fleming, was hung with a rough silk in a strong, sharp yellow, 'bound with a plum coloured braid which colour is taken up in [the] carpet and chairs'. Even though there is a considerable number of desirable pieces in the room the effect is still one of relatively austere elegance, influenced no doubt by the increasing accuracy of period reconstruction at Malmaison (pls 17–24) and in other French historic houses. There is also, perhaps, a certain similarity of feel with the interiors of the Francophile Edward Knoblock at the Beach House, Worthing (pl. 224).

Victoria & Albert Museum, London

236

340). The dining room was perhaps a less successful scheme and many felt that the boldly stylized frieze of Egyptian, Assyrian or even Minoan figures by Philpot, working in his newly adopted Jazz manner, was too assertively modernistic for Tilden's Renaissance-feeling room. The total effect was certainly somewhat mixed, and a contemporary photograph shows the curious combination of the architecture and decorative painting with the rather splendid furnishings, which included stylish console tables in a neo-Regency taste by Tilden and a magnificent set of twelve Russian Empire period chairs.

Country Life

237

A brilliant-yellow dining room 1920

Duff and Lady Diana Cooper's dining room, Gower Street, London

For the decoration of the main rooms of their Gower Street house, the Coopers enlisted the help and advice of the decorator Basil Ionides. As usual he treated the rooms as a series of essays in colour, and his solution to what at that time seemed a problematic dining room became particularly well known. The room at the front of the ground floor was in fact a handsome one with a good late eighteenth-century chimneypiece, curved back walls flanking double doors and pretty mouldings. But as R.R. Phillips wrote, clearly prompted by Ionides, in *The Modern English Interior* (London, 1929), '... facing east, this room ... is seldom used before lunch, after which time the sun does not shine on its windows: yellow of a golden hue is therefore the ideal colour here. The walls are glossy as the colour is strong enough to glow through the glaze in spite of contrary reflections.' Ionides loved to play with light, and one further interesting detail was the way in which he placed mirror glass in a decorative lunette resembling a fanlight over the double doors. However by the time this photograph was taken, at a slightly later date, this had been replaced by glass in order to let in more light. Over the chimneypiece hangs Ambrose McEvoy's celebrated portrait of Lady Diana Cooper, which the family always referred to by the nickname of 'the invitation to orgy'.

Millar & Harris Ltd, London

236

A modern country house late 1920s

Dining room, Port Lympne, Kent, by Philip Tilden, murals by Glyn Philpot

Port Lympne was begun before the First World War by the great establishment architect Sir Herbert Baker for Sir Philip Sassoon, and became in the words of Osbert Sitwell 'one of those houses filled always with politicians, painters, writers, professional golfers and airmen'. After the war the house was extensively remodelled for Sir Philip by the talented architect Philip Tilden and a number of major projects of decoration were carried out. These included mural paintings by Glyn Philpot and José Maria Sert and, a little later, a splendid room by Rex Whistler (pl.

238

A frankly modern scheme 1924

Showpiece dining room by Lord Gerald Wellesley and Trenwith Wills; from R.R. Phillips, The Modern English Interior, *London, 1929*

This prize-winning and elegant design was much publicized in England in 1924 as a good example of a modern room, and five years later Randal Phillips was still sufficiently enthusiastic to illustrate it in *The Modern English Interior* and write: '... this dining room breaks away from traditional treatments, and finds a fresh expression in terms of today. Colour enters largely into its effect, the walls being a lively yellow, and the furniture and decorations painted gaily.' The whole architectural effect of the end wall depended on *trompe-l'oeil* painting, and the vases in niches between the windows were carried out in the same style. In fact the entire scheme, looked at objectively, is an exercise in historical pastiche, and can hardly compare for inventiveness with anything being done in Paris at the

238

same date; and yet it does have a sophisticated elegance all of its own, and its awareness of traditional forms links it with the most interesting and ultimately most fruitful aspects of English design in the 1930s.

237

Colour and decoration 1926

Illustrations by W.B.E. Ranken, from Basil Ionides,
Colour and Interior Decoration, *London, 1926*

239

Pink drawing room by Basil Ionides

Basil Ionides was without doubt the most interesting colour theorist among the decorators of his generation, and it is fortunate that the appearance of so many of his own schemes is preserved in the series of illustrations by his friend, the watercolourist W.B.E. Ranken, prepared for the two books he wrote. Ionides had the gift of being a great natural arranger of objects: he grouped things sometimes thematically, but more often for their colour effect or in order to enjoy the play of light and colour, which he loved to observe and which he was certainly the first to analyse systematically. His choice of furniture was often idiosyncratic. He was quite capable of designing pieces for a specific purpose, but in general appears to have preferred older pieces, often using what would have been considered dowdy late nineteenth-century tables or chairs if they suited his purpose. In this room Ionides nods towards the great

240

vogue for Chinese things, but his scheme makes no attempt to suggest the Orient with any exactitude. Rather, it is concerned with the contrasting effects of the blush of soft pinks on the walls and the stronger deep-pink notes of the upholstery. Typically, the furniture consists of almost entirely undistinguished pieces of the 1880s.

240

Basil Ionides's dining room

This remarkable room is the most fully resolved expression of Ionides's colour theories. The room itself is a handsome one, with good eighteenth-century panelling and other details and furniture of appropriate quality, but it is the colour treatment which sets it apart from a thousand other 'period' rooms of its day. The walls were painted in a strong blue created by stippling with two different blues over a ground of pink. This, Ionides explained, gave the room its extraordinary vivacity, which

239

is so rarely achieved in blue schemes. The effect was further enhanced by the rosy hue imparted to the light by crimson silk sun curtains at the windows or by crimson candle shades at night-time. The contrast between warm light and cool shadow is to be seen in the play of colour across the ceiling and cornices, echoed in the niche containing early Leeds creamware china and on the white porcelain figurines placed on the chimneypiece.

241

Basil Ionides's country sitting room

In the parlour or informal sitting room of his house Ionides used simple limewash on the bare plaster as a sympathetic background to the soft and varied tones of wood and old textiles. The furniture is an interesting mixture of mainly seventeenth-century pieces, some sophisticated, such as the high-backed William and Mary chair and the cabinet on a stand, others with a more rustic feel, which is echoed by the rush matting. The effects of light falling on the plaster wall are observed and there is a glimpse through the open door to the more colourful staircase hall and the blue dining room (pl. 240) beyond.

241

242

242

Empire and Victoriana 1924

The house of Arnold Bennett, London, from Vogue, *1924*

The *Vogue* article on the house of the popular novelist Arnold Bennett is a classic case study in the history of taste, shedding some interesting light on the movement of fashion in revivals of historic styles. As early as 1921 or 1922 the *Vogue* staff had become aware that Bennett not only had an intriguing collection of old furniture and modern pictures, but also that it was arranged in an amusing way. Bennett was a close friend of Edward Knoblock, with whom he collaborated from time to time, and like Knoblock an ardent Francophile. He too had good Empire pieces in two major groups, an important bedroom suite and more furniture in a stylish drawing room, and these *Vogue* admired. However, the novelist had also formed an idiosyncratic collection of mid-Victorian furniture and objects, such as items under glass domes and pole-screens with Berlin woolwork panels, which he had

gathered together in the dining room as a sort of homage to an era for which he had a curious, if ironic, affection. The design pundits at *Vogue* felt that this was going too far (or coming too near), and would not publish the photographs for fear of ridicule. Two years passed and in 1924 Bennett's taste was beginning to look just avant-garde. *Vogue* showed the house, still concentrating on the Empire rooms and on clever features such as in the hall a Modigliani picture hung above 'some pieces of deal furniture that Mr Bennett has had lacquered in scarlet'. Of the dining room they remarked that it was 'furnished with Victorian furniture, which has merit and is amusing'. One piece, a chiffonier, was described as 'buoyant' and a final note of exclamation informed the amused reader that 'there are even lustres on the mantelpiece'.

Condé Nast Publications Ltd, London

A modern baroque house early 1920s

Clough Williams-Ellis's own house,
22 South Eaton Place, London; from R.R. Phillips,
The Modern English Interior, London, *1929*

243, 244

Sitting room

Clough Williams-Ellis, who became best known for his quixotic stance as the eccentric creator of Portmeirion, an extensive Italianate architectural fantasy in north Wales, was in the 1920s a leading protagonist of the neo-Georgian school and the designer of some interesting interior schemes. In the remarkable double sitting room the architect gave full rein to a love of colour and baroque exuberance. The walls were 'mottled a bright lapis-lazuli blue' and this was further enhanced by woodwork and mouldings stippled in two shades of purple. Against this stunning background he arranged some magnificent and theatrical pieces, such as the ornate gilt-framed looking-glass over one of the twin chimneypieces. A carpet of a modernistic conventionalized marble pattern struck an interesting note of contemporaneity, but it was in the fitting up of the Regency breakfast table, served by a dumb waiter connected to the kitchen below, that Clough took the most pride. Describing the very great convenience of his arrangements, he pointed out the way in which up-to-the-minute gadgetry, including a house telephone and an electric

243

toaster with the toast rack logically but unusually placed above the source of heat, could be incorporated into even the most stylish of rooms.

245

A marbled hall

In the entrance hall, where space was restricted, he adopted a Soanian manner, based on thin, crisp mouldings and shallow recesses, to suggest a greater degree of grandeur than the hall really commanded, and further enhanced the effect by the use of Italianate decorative features. The walls here were 'stippled and marbled in bright colours', reflecting a revival of interest in these paint effects, to which a number of magazines refer at the time. The gilt-framed looking-glass of baroque form and the tiny crystal glass electric light fitting, not at that date considered to be kitsch, are typical, if slightly hesitant, expressions of Sitwellian taste.

244

245

Three rooms with colour themes by Basil Ionides 1926

Watercolours by W.B.E. Ranken, from Ionides, Colour and Interior Decoration, *London, 1926*

246

Sitting room in violet-grey

247

London room in tones of red

248

Little yellow sitting room

Each of these successful rooms is given its distinct feel by the dominant use of one colour, around which Ionides builds up a scheme of carefully related minor elements. In the yellow room, with its bold opposition of near-primary colours in the pinkish-red lampshades and cushions and the blue-and-white china, there is also a classic sub-theme for yellow rooms in the use of black and gold furniture. In the more subdued grey-violet room the foil is again gold, this time in the Chinese screen and touches such as the mirror frame and the spines of leather-bound books in the cases. The red room uses one of the increasingly popular *toile de Jouy* fabrics to enhance the crisply urban chic of white paintwork, and the combination is echoed in the red-and-white striped sun awnings. The great resurgence of interest

246

in eighteenth- and early nineteenth-century plate-printed cottons, produced first by J. Oberkampf at the village of Jouy near Versailles, is in itself an interesting aspect of the Regency (or Empire) revival in the 1920s and 30s. Many of the most delightful patterns were reprinted and enjoyed popularity well into the 1950s, when new designs drawn in imitation of the originals were added to the range. The red-on-white and blue-on-white colourways seem to have been most favoured, even though some of the more unusual purples and greens were available to decorators.

247

248

249

'Curzon Street baroque' 1920s

Drawing by Osbert Lancaster, from Homes Sweet Homes, *London, 1939*

Writing in 1939 when the neo-baroque was still very much in evidence in the world of smart decoration, Osbert Lancaster correctly traced its popular origins to the immediate post-war years when the Edwardian taste for French decorative arts of the eighteenth century began to lose ground to a feeling that the earlier rococo and even baroque of Venice and southern Italy, south Germany and Spain offered tremendous potential for the decorator. As he wrote,

> Gone were the Louis Seize chairs and Largillière portraits, and their place was taken by innumerable pieces of hand-painted furniture from Venice and a surprisingly abundant supply of suspicious Canalettos. At the same time a markedly ecclesiastical note is struck by the forests of twisted baroque candlesticks ... old leather bound hymn-books cunningly hollowed out to receive cigarettes, and exuberant gilt *prie-dieux* ingeniously transformed into receptacles for gramophone records.

In the drawing Osbert Lancaster also identifies several other clichés of the style: the reproduction 'Knole' sofa, the elaborate shades on the chandelier and wall sconces, and the use of wrought iron as a decorative feature.

John Murray Ltd, London

250

Rococo revival in Paris c. 1922–4

Lady Rothermere's flat, decorated by Ronald Fleming

Ronald Fleming was in Paris looking at French decoration when he came to the notice of Lady Rothermere, who asked him to help with the decoration and arrangement of her apartment. Pleased with the results, she encouraged his studies at the New York School of Architecture and Decoration. Fleming created an interesting look for his first patron, mixing fine rococo and Chinoiserie pieces with some more obviously theatrical elements such as the elaborate pair of candelabra with shell-shaped shades. The project was publicized at the time and proved an excellent start to a distinguished career.

Victoria & Albert Museum, London

250

251

Country baroque   late 1920s

'A long sitting room in a country house, Robert Lowry, architect'; from R. R. Phillips The Modern English Interior, *London, 1929*

This highly sophisticated room in a country house, 'with an end window opening into a garden room', shows the integration of the chic neo-baroque taste into the comfortable informality of traditional English decoration. There is the usual eclectic mixture of good old pieces of furniture, but among them are several of seventeenth-century date chosen for their newly fashionable robust and decorative forms. Above a very severe and plain chimney-piece, with long, low lines echoing the proportion of the room, is a handsome pair of massive gilt wood sconces flanking an elaborate baroque-framed looking-glass. The effects of colour and the use of materials are unusually clever for a modest house in the country, for the room is described as having apricot-painted walls, a ceiling covered with silvered paper and a floor made of wood blocks stained in various shades of blue as a background for Persian rugs. It must have looked stunning.

252

'Solemn Regency' colours c.1930

An Interior; *oil painting by Francis Campbell Boileau Cadell, RSA, RWS*

In one of the most beautiful paintings of an interior of the period Cadell records the sombre but richly evocative colour scheme of an unknown room. It is a double drawing room furnished with eighteenth- and early nineteenth-century pieces, including a fine pair of black-lacquered Regency elbow chairs and a magnificent pair of crystal chimney-lights. The scheme of decoration is unusual, and in its combination of deep blue walls, black curtains trimmed with gold, and black and apple-green paintwork it is reminiscent of the confident handling of colour by Basil Ionides. His influence is very much suggested as well by the use of a bright red translucent sun curtain, which imparts a purplish cast to the blue walls.

The Fine Art Society Ltd, London

252

'Bringing sunshine into a north room' 1921

Lady Katharine Somerset's house in Regent's Park, London

253

Dining room

Oil painting by H. Davis Richter

254

View showing window treatment and a 'modern' arrangement of branches in a vase

Illustration from Our Homes and Gardens, *1921*

The magazine *Our Homes and Gardens* chose this room to illustrate the way in which the new attitudes to colour in decoration could overcome the perennial problem of aspect. Too many north-facing rooms, it was suggested, were painted and upholstered in red in order to give a feeling of warmth and only ended up by being oppressive. Here the scheme was based on a light and stylish use of white walls and woodwork, a black-and-white painted floor and a sunny golden yellow for the curtains, all the seat coverings and a simple screen. This golden yellow was further echoed by the dull gilt of the chandelier and the wall sconces, and in the picture and looking-glass frames. As the writer explained,

> ... the use of bright colour in our rooms is widely advocated today, but not infrequently with this colour has come a vividness which is disturbing, so that rooms so treated, however arresting, are not restful to live with. The exact opposite is seen in this Regent's Park dining-room. Clean colour is there, but it does not shout out at you, and its use in conjunction with old furniture of refined character produces a most harmonious result.

253 Royal Borough of Kensington and Chelsea Libraries

253

254

Sitwellian baroque mid-1920s

The house of Osbert and Sacheverell Sitwell,
Carlyle Square, London

255

The drawing room

256

The back drawing room

The Carlyle Square house which the brothers took in 1919 quickly became a celebrated showpiece of the Sitwellian neo-baroque aesthetic, and the theatrical backdrop for their many-faceted activities in the avant-garde art world of the 1920s in London. Writing of the house in 1924, *Vogue* observed that 'there are two ways of decorating a room: the grimly historical and the purely whimsical'. In the utterly serious pursuit of the whimsical Osbert and Sacheverell drew together an extraordinary collection of old and new things, confidently mixing them with the notion that all good and interesting things go together if the *mélange* is the product of a fastidious taste. This idea of 'unity in diversity' became their artistic standpoint and led Osbert in particular to create rooms in which Venetian and southern Italian silvered grotto furniture, amusing pieces of Victoriana and ethnic sculptures were displayed against brilliant-coloured walls. In the dining room, with its marble-topped table and Venetian consoles and mirrors, a William Roberts painting hung next to works by Magnasco, Salvator Rosa and Carlo Dolci against a background of turquoise-silver lamé. More dolphin pieces were gathered in the little back drawing room where a splendid Regency console supported favourite pieces of Murano glass. Here and in the front half of the room hung a

255

256

Chilham Castle, which they used as a weekend retreat, they assembled a stage-set Italianate baronial interior, tricking out the roughcast walls and rustic panelling with an array of ancient armour, swords, pikes and other weaponry. Large and gloomy oils complete the scene and the whole effect unmistakably points the way to that sophisticated urban version of the style which Osbert Lancaster so perfectly characterized as Curzon Street baroque (pl. 249), but which may be paralleled most closely by the complex Italianate ideas of the Geoffrey Scott circle in Florence.

Fitzwilliam Museum, Cambridge

large number of pictures and drawings by the Sitwells' friends such as Lord Berners and his protégés Gino Severini and Pavel Tchelitchew. As Alan Pryce-Jones recalled in later years, 'The whole house was a temple of a now forgotten style called "the Amusing" … it was all most dashing' (quoted in Lawrence Mynott: 'Unity in Diversity' in the *Journal of the Decorative Arts Society*, no. 8, 1984).

255 *Architectural Press, London*
256 *Condé Nast Publications Ltd*

257

Italian baronial style in Kent c.1925

Dining chamber in The Keep, Chilham Castle; photograph from Ricketts and Shannon's own collection

The last development in Ricketts and Shannon's taste in decoration was towards a grander, more patrician Italianate style. In their final house in London, Townshend House, Regent's Park, huge gilt console tables with marble slabs of red and green lined the walls beneath important paintings in heavy frames, and the aesthetes dined at a table made from lapis lazuli. In The Keep in the grounds of

257

258

258

A neo-baroque bedroom 1920s

Lord Gerald Wellesley's house, 11 Titchfield Terrace, London

Lord Gerald Wellesley was, along with the Sitwells, a founder of the Magnasco Society in 1924, the year in which Sacheverell Sitwell's seminal book *Southern Baroque Art* first appeared in print. The society, in which grandees and aesthetes mingled, had been founded both as a convivial dining society and for the purpose of bringing to wider attention the glories of the largely obscure and despised art and architecture of the late seventeenth and early eighteenth centuries. This other important aspect of

Lord Gerald Wellesley's taste can be seen in the principal bedroom of his otherwise neo-classically inspired house (pls 230, 231). The bed itself is another fine piece of the late Regency period, but its spirited form and carved decoration of massive scrolls and vigorous dolphins are full of baroque feeling. This is echoed by the use of several different boldly figured fabrics including *toile de Jouy* curtains and a rich brocade on the walls. Against this is displayed an interesting group of objects, among which can be seen a *cassone* (Italian chest), upon which stands a lively sculptor's model for a monument to a pope, a number of sombre baroque pictures and a bronze relief.

Country Life

259

Italianate baroque in Buckinghamshire late 1920s

Great Hundridge Manor, Chesham

259

The Painted Parlour by Firelight; oil painting by John Hookham

William Heywood Haslam bought the exquisite William and Mary house at Great Hundridge in 1927, and with the help of a number of his friends transformed it into the most interesting expression of the complex Italianate ideals of his circle. Clough Williams-Ellis carried out sympathetic restoration and alterations, but in many ways it was the influence of Geoffrey Scott, the architect and author of *The Architecture of Humanism*, that gave the house its special atmosphere. Emphasizing the splendid panelling and introducing highly individual pieces of furniture, the Haslams created interiors which suggested the feel of an old Italian palazzo and, while very different from those of the Sitwells, were equally rich and baroque in effect. This painting shows the sombre splendour of the panelling of the Painted Parlour illuminated by firelight and electrified gilt ecclesiastical candlesticks.

Private collection

260

The Blue Room

This photograph clearly shows the then very finely preserved marbling and graining of the seventeenth-century panelling, since, alas, barbarously stripped by subsequent owners of the house. The furnishings are a fascinatingly quirky mixture of the kind of pieces which became decorators' favourites in the 1930s. There is a classic urn-shaped firebasket in the open grate; by the fireside stands a Victorian coal-scuttle or purdonium. The carpet worked in needlepoint is also mid-nineteenth-century, and the centrepiece of the room is a slightly earlier and very unusual bed decorated in penwork.

Country Life

260

261

William Haslam's bedroom

Haslam's own bedchamber was the finest room in the house, with panelling painted to simulate marbling and incorporating grotesque landscapes. This very rare scheme, which survives to this day, was carried out in shades of umber, burnt sienna, ochres and Indian red; it formed the perfect setting for the turquoise and gilt bed which Geoffrey Scott had designed for Haslam some time before his marriage and purchase of Great Hundridge. The bed, which must have been made by Florentine craftsmen, was said to be based on the one depicted by Carpaccio in the famous painting of St Ursula in Venice, but in fact it would seem to be modelled more closely in both proportions and detail on an illustration of a very similar bed in the Renaissance woodcut book, the *Hypnerotomachia* (battle between sleep and love) of Poliphilus, printed by Aldus in Venice in 1499. In its assured mixing of the best of the old and the best of the new this room must be accounted one of the most successful in all twentieth-century decoration.

Country Life

262

262

True Spanish baroque
taste   c.1930

*The bedroom of the Duchess of Lerma; drawing by Cecil
Beaton from* The Glass of Fashion, *London, 1954*

Writing in 1954, with his love of French 'drawing-room
ormolu' as he put it 'considerably abated', Cecil
Beaton reflected on the possibility of a simpler style based
on a 'combination of the "modern" point of view with that
of Jacobean English or Spanish taste'. Recalling the
vulgarities of the Spanish style as it was interpreted in
America by Randolph Hearst (pls 267–9) and other rich
collectors, he went on to describe the palace of the elderly
Duchess of Lerma at Toledo. 'Among the fine homes I have
been privileged to see throughout my travels in Italy,
France, Spain, India, China, Germany and America,' he
wrote, 'none is in nobler taste.' He described how the
Duchess, who lived in one wing of the palace, 'accustomed
to every luxury riches can provide, has eliminated everything that is superfluous from her life'.

> Her bedroom is of a monumental simplicity, decorated
> only by the sunlight . . . filtering through the shutters on
> to the tall white walls. . . . The bed, a giant four-poster, is
> upholstered in the darkest green Genoese velvet. A
> writing table is covered with a cloth of the same material,
> and there is no ornament upon it except a massive inkpot
> of gold, innocent of all chasing or decoration. There are
> one or two stout, high-backed chairs of dark polished
> wood, a few rugs of superb quality on the stone floor, and
> possibly a Greco to be admired upon an easel.

263

The baroque image   1927

Edith Sitwell receiving breakfast in bed at Renishaw

The self-conscious image-making of the Sitwells, which
had already made them important figures in the avant-
garde of taste in the early 1920s, was tremendously
enhanced by the introduction into their orbit of Cecil
Beaton. Together he and Edith Sitwell created a theatrical
pose of patrician eccentricity to which the splendours of the
Sitwell houses, Renishaw in Derbyshire and the castle of
Montegufoni near Florence were the perfect background,
but which also found a natural expression in the most

263

modern painting, music and writing. Cecil Beaton's ability
to stage photographic portraits with the pomp, grandeur
and something of the inherent humour of baroque paintings resulted in a number of highly original images of Edith.
In this portrait she sits in her bed at Renishaw, turbaned
and bejewelled, receiving her morning cup of chocolate
from a black servant: a scene like a picture by Longhi.
Beyond the artifice and pose is revealed the extent to which
the Sitwells used decoration and the creation of interesting
interiors as an integral part of their artistic activities.

Cecil Beaton Photograph; Courtesy of Sotheby's, London

264

264
Comfortable commercialized early Georgian   late 1920s

Drawing room design by William Henry Haynes & Co.; pencil and watercolour drawing for a prospectus

Here the once grandiose vision of early Georgian England purveyed by the grander firms such as Lenygon & Morant is reduced to a comfortable and economically priced formula. The panelling is of reasonably correct proportions and detailing, with an elaborate chimneypiece flanked by pilasters echoing an elegant doorcase with an enriched head, but is shown stripped according to the unhistorical preference of the day. This mania for uncovering the surface of woods never intended to be seen unpainted has never left us, and indeed in the 1960s and 70s resulted in the destruction of many interesting examples of old paintwork and innumerable fine pieces of furniture. This room setting by Haynes & Co., who operated as antiques dealers as well as decorators, is typical in its use of rather undistinguished genuine furniture of the earlier eighteenth century alongside reproduction pieces such as the 'Knole sofa', here tamed and domesticated in scale and decoration from the rather barbaric splendour of the original. Note also the use of modern pottery lamp bases and shades, one of which rests on a candlestand beside the armchair while the other is placed much lower on a small wine table. Pictures and other ornaments are small and sparsely arranged to suggest the austerity of early Georgian taste as it was popularly conceived at the time.

Victoria & Albert Museum, London

265
Period upholstery late 1920s

A corner of a drawing room by William Henry Haynes & Co.; pencil and watercolour drawing for a prospectus

Another design, showing the use of rich upholstery on a quirky reproduction sofa, suggests something of the Olde England mentality of much furnishing of the period. Here at least both shapes and colour are bold and carry some conviction, but the effect of the lacquer cabinet on a stand and the shaped pelmet and draperies surrounding the sofa is a very long way from the theatricality and graphic clarity that Lutyens or Lady Sackville had brought to such things.

Victoria & Albert Museum, London

266
Breakfast in the loggia, Germany late 1920s

Design for a loggia or garden room by Paul Groscher

Illustrations of rooms and representations of furniture in use are much rarer than illustrations of fashionable and formal room arrangements. This charming exception shows a columned loggia, shaded by a striped awning and opening directly on to an extensive park. All the furniture is of cane or rattan and fitted with upholstered squabs and cushions *en suite* with the curtains. It is a scene redolent of the comfortable country life of the inter-war years, and could just as well be in France or England or even somewhere in New England.

Stephanie Hoppen Ltd, London

265

266

A newspaper baron's baroque palace 1920s

The Hearst Castle, San Simeon, California

267

A group of treasures

268

The cinema

269

A bedroom

268

267

William Randolph Hearst, who acquired an enormously powerful and valuable newspaper empire, established himself in what came to be called Hearst Castle in California. Here the man who was the inspiration for Orson Welles's classic film *Citizen Kane* gathered an extraordinary collection, rich in Renaissance and baroque furniture, carvings and textiles. Those who had the good fortune to be invited to visit the house were generally intimidated by the host's overwhelming personality, but the effect of the decorations was clearly a factor which contributed to the awe in which Hearst was held by all who came into contact with him. Cecil Beaton was of the party that saw in the new decade at the castle and recorded in his diary (31 December 1929):

> I was speechless at the place ... my room was enormous with carved gilt ceiling, huge carved Jacobean beds with gold brocade covers [*sic*] and on the wall hung old tinselled velvets and gosh the view from the window!

In every part of the house there were arrangements of exquisite objects, but the most extraordinary room of all was the private cinema conceived as a little theatre of the Louis Quatorze period. It had a screen within a proscenium arch and flanking walls with over-life-size caryatids bearing torchères in both hands. The seating was contrived, with engaging wit, out of rows of velvet-covered, brass-studded banquettes which resembled a sort of continuous Knole sofa.

Courtesy Hearst San Simeon State Historical Monument, California

269

270

270
Stockbroker's Tudor   1920s

Drawing by Osbert Lancaster, from Homes Sweet Homes, *London, 1939*

One of Sir Osbert Lancaster's most palpable hits, this is a style to which his brilliantly descriptive name will always stick. His drawing brings out the tenuous connection between the Tudor revival and the Arts and Crafts movement, apparent in small details such as the rustic door-latch. In fact very little in the furnishing of the mock-Tudor house was hand-made, for the style was essentially one favoured in the more expensive suburbs and created in the main by high street shops rather than the major decorating firms. Osbert Lancaster also made the important observation that many things of other later periods, such as early nineteenth-century samplers, Georgian four-posters and pretty Victorian chintzes, 'came to be regarded as Tudor by adoption'.

John Murray Ltd, London

271

271
An obsessive collector   1920s

The 'Zenith' room at Snowshill Manor, Gloucestershire

Charles Paget Wade, an obsessive collector from childhood, was serving as a sapper during the First World War when he saw an advertisement in *Country Life* for the sale of Snowshill. Immediately after the war, having inherited the family West Indies sugar fortune, he bought the decayed but delightfully unspoiled property and began a sensitive programme of restoration. He took down plaster ceilings to reveal the timbers and restored as closely as possible the original fenestration and internal divisions of the typical Cotswold house. It was for Wade's remarkable collections, however, and the way in which he arranged them in a series of thematic rooms that Snowshill became celebrated, and a favourite haunt in the 1920s and 30s for other collectors such as Professor Albert Richardson. Each of the rooms had a name expressing, albeit obliquely, the theme of the objects grouped in it: 'Seraphim' and 'Salamander', 'Zenith' and 'Nadir', and a nautical sequence including 'Admiral', 'Top Gallant' and 'Mizzen'. Wade wrote of his decorative principles in his delightful *Haphazard Notes*, which he set down in about 1945:

> I set out to find furnishings that would make an attractive series of rooms pictorially, not to form a museum. I have not bought things just because they were rare and valuable, there are many things of everyday use in the past, of small value, but of interest as records of various vanished handicrafts. My guiding essentials have been *design, colour* and *workmanship*. I am often tempted to let colour come first, though it cannot retrieve bad design. Many of the pieces were bought for the particular place they now occupy.

H.P. Molesworth, the celebrated Keeper of Furniture at the Victoria & Albert Museum, wrote that Wade's collection was 'the perfect expression of the nostalgic but strangely limited taste of its period'; and yet there is a fascinating range of objects, from the ancient bicycles in the 'Hundred Wheels' room, through beautiful seventeenth- and eighteenth-century lacquer cabinets to the important group of Japanese armour and oriental and Middle Eastern ceramics.

The National Trust, London

272

272

American historicism mid-1920s

American Wing at the Metropolitan Museum of Art, New York, photographed in the 30s

In the early years of the century nearly all the grandest and most sophisticated American decoration was carried out in period style. The French and English tastes predominated, even as settings for Italian art, and much of the work was done by firms from London or Paris, who maintained offices in New York and imported not only grand furnishings but also entire rooms from Europe. However there was a growing awareness of the nation's identity, shared by many Americans and perhaps fostered by the decisive role played by the USA in the First World War in 1917–18. A major expression of this feeling was the creation at the Metropolitan Museum, in the context of the greatest collection of art in the New World, of a section devoted to the decorative arts of the original colonial states. The American Wing drew together and gave status for the first time to these specifically American antiques. New types of furniture were thus drawn into the canon of good taste, and in particular the simpler rustic styles began to be admired by collectors and decorators with the sort of enthusiasm previously reserved for early English pieces or the work of the French *ébénistes*. The central space of the new wing was a great beamed hall in which were shown old weapons, Windsor, bobbin-turned and ladder-back chairs, plank tables and examples of traditional textiles and other native decorative objects, as well as the more sophisticated productions of the early indigenous furniture makers and silversmiths.

The Metropolitan Museum of Art, New York

1930–1945
PLEASING DECAY AND
THE ALL-WHITE ROOM

The 1930s have the distinction of being the first decade in the century in which it was unquestionably smarter to have rooms decorated in a modernistic manner than in one of the grand historic styles. A new aesthetic which for the first time was based on long, low horizontal elements affected every part of the room, from the shape of the windows and their curtain treatments to the upholstery of sofas and the lines of new furniture types, such as the coffee table. Colour, which had coruscated in the brilliant rooms of the 20s, was almost banished, and natural or neutral materials were reflected in the discreet gleam of dark mirror glass and the sleek surface of chrome. The classic statement of this new look, and perhaps one of the most famous and successful rooms of the century, was the 'All-White Room' (c.1929–30) created by the decorator Mrs Syrie Maugham in her own house in the King's Road in Chelsea (pl. 362).

Syrie's rooms, which were closely paralleled by the work of others, – notably Elsie de Wolfe who was working along very similar lines at exactly this date – mark a crucial development in decoration towards an abstracted notion of chic. Influenced by the ideals of the emerging Modern movement in architecture and to a degree reflecting movements away from traditional forms in the other arts, her effects were based on an ideal of *luxe* that for the first time did not depend on historical precedent, on the inherent quality or price of the materials or on the richness and intricacy of decoration and ornament.

Where good pieces of furniture were included in such schemes, they would often be stripped of their original polish and painted in a pale, rubbed finish, limed to give that much-favoured silvery hue, or lightly waxed. This fashion for what was colloquially called 'pickling' became something of a mania with decorators, and was widely criticized as a barbaric practice by those who lamented the loss of the patination of centuries on fine pieces of furniture, sacrificed to the creation of an 'amusing' effect. In his delightful 'Child's Guide to Interior Decoration', published in *For Adults Only* in 1932, Beverley Nichols, who was a close friend of Syrie Maugham, neatly satirized the lady decorators who indulged in the practice through the fictitious character of the Countess of Westbourne. He describes the scene thus:

A small furniture shop not far from Berkeley Square. In the window is a piece of incredibly expensive and astonishingly dirty brocade, hanging over a 'pickled' chair. A Provençal dix-huitième commode, also pickled, looms forbiddingly in the background. There is little else save a few cushions and a Sheraton writing desk.[1]

The Countess is undergoing a 'particularly ferocious cross-examination' from her small daughter who repeats criticisms to her such as, 'why did Lady Swooning say she would rather live in a cow-shed than in any house you'd had anything to do with?' The little drama concludes with the damning remark: 'why did she say that you'd pickle the Mona Lisa if you got the chance?'

The fashion for stripped wood extended, too, to the panelling of whole rooms. This fashion was set by the handsome carved pine classical drawing room of a house in South Street, Mayfair, built shortly after the First World War by the architects Wimperis & Simpson, with the assistance of Harold Peto, for the Hon. Henry McLaren (later Lord Aberconway). As the decorator and writer Ronald Fleming later recalled in his unpublished memoirs of the period:

'cigar-box' rooms as they were called became extremely popular with the rich, and many a fine old painted panel room was stripped of its original coats of paint and laid bare with all the imperfections of notches etc.[2]

The idea was, he continued, 'copied until the 1939 war almost *ad nauseam*'.

With the widening dissemination of the teachings of the Bauhaus and a new internationalism in design, the 30s saw the popularization across a broad spectrum of the ideals of Modernism. For many, however, the mental leap from the pure, beautiful and rational architecture of Palladio's villas to the rational, proportional, machine aesthetic of Le Corbusier proved too great, and a distinction set in between tradition and innovation which divided decoration from what we might most aptly term interior architecture. It is a distinction as much to do with attitude as with aesthetics and it has continued to divide thinking right up till the present day, being maintained in the notional opposition of interior decoration, the work of decorators, and interior design, which is held to be the province of 'serious' designers and architects.

The great figures of the so-called heroic phase of Modernism seem in retrospect to have had a greater influence on the appearance of public or commercial spaces than on the way most people chose to live in their own domestic environments. They produced individual 'classic' pieces of furniture, such as Mies van der Rohe's Barcelona chair of 1929, but, ironically, an overt stylist such as Serge Chermayeff, designer of smart kitchens and radio cabinets, is more easily placed in the story of the development of the modernistic interior than more obviously important figures such as Mies or Walter Gropius.

The point at which the new aesthetic really impinged on the everyday interior tended to be on a more comfortable and less uncompromising level. In England the versions of Modernism which were more widely accepted were the simplified, rather puritan style favoured by intellectuals such as Herbert Read and neatly captured by Osbert Lancaster in his drawing 'Functional' (pl. 288), and a rather more luxurious style in which upholstery softened the beautifully veneered forms of built-in-furniture, best exemplified in the work of Gordon Russell or in the mirrored chic of the Hartnell salon (pl. 361). More individual and intriguing essays in the application of the modern aesthetic to the comfortable interior are to be found in the rooms of Oliver Hill and in the theoretical schemes as well as the actual creations of Paul Nash. Both sought to make the modern room more interesting and to enliven it both with some elements of colour and with a greater variety of form.

Dissatisfaction with the pattern of rooms established in the sub-Syrie manner is expressed in the recollections of Charles Wade, the eccentric collector of Snowshill Manor, Gloucestershire:

A room with a multitude of objects in it can have, and usually has, a most restless and disquieting atmosphere, as the Victorian period very clearly showed. At the other extreme there has been of late years the completely bare room with nothing but two vast armchairs and a vast settee, an ashtray and a distorted lifeless electric clock above a mock fire-place which is set with a lifeless tube of electric heat in a wire cage. Just a world of washy porridge beige colour and utter blankness; nothing whatever to stimulate the imagination. There are thousands of such cells of depression to be found. I am miserable in such surroundings and want a room to be full of interesting things.[3]

Among those searching within the modern aesthetic for a renewal of interest and amusement we may cite Frank Lloyd Wright. Wright's great early phase of achievement, his Prairie houses, was already well known in Europe from the publication in Germany of the Wasmuth Portfolio (1910 and 1911). By this period he has been described as entering into his 'second maturity' with major projects such as the house called Falling Water, in which natural forms play a striking part in enlivening the interior spaces (pl. 284).

Edward James, poet and patron of the Surrealists, is a key figure who, by his imaginative use of a large inheritance, formed a remarkable collection of works by young painters of his day. He also stimulated new developments in the ballet and stage design, and created for himself a remarkable series of rooms in his grand London house in Wimpole Street and at Monkton, the Lutyens house which his parents had added to their large estates at West Dean, Sussex. James's taste for the bizarre led to the creation, especially at Monkton, of extraordinary and highly theatrical room sets in which major works by Salvador Dali and Picasso, Pavel Tchelitchew and Rex Whistler were complemented by strange pieces of furniture such as the famous 'Mae West's Lips' sofa (pl. 357). A rich array of rare and delightful objects was displayed with eccentric brilliance in a setting which made use of strange techniques, such as quilting on the walls and carpets specially woven to look like the footprints of James's dog or his soon-to-depart wife, the beautiful actress Tilly Losch (pl. 356).

Both in England and in France the influence of Surrealism on avant-garde decoration was considerable. In France the classic example of the genre was the apartment created by the millionaire socialite and patron, Charles de Beistegui, a Maecenas of his day whose tastes, decorative flair and exotic whims lie at the very heart of the emergence of that grandiose chic which we distinguish by the name of *haut décor*. Beistegui's first celebrated apartment high above the Champs-Elysées was a 'machine for living' by Le Corbusier. Almost as soon as it was finished, however, Beistegui tired of Modernism and, with the complicity of his friend the learned gentleman-architect Emilio Terry, set about its transformation into a Surrealist fantasy. The main room, rather like Monkton, was quilted, and madly rococo commodes and Second Empire stuffed seats were imported. The walls were filled with grand-looking mirrors and a plethora of crystal chandeliers and girandoles lit the space with fantastic flickering light. On the roof terrace even more Surrealist effects were contrived with an artificial lawn, garden chairs and a cement 'commode' surrounding a 'chimneypiece' above which, as though it were a looking-glass, an oculus offered a Magritte-like view down the avenue towards the Arc de Triomphe. Beistegui's own explanation of this extraordinary confection was '*il faut rompre avec les habitudes*'; Paul Nash later wrote, 'I know of no other such authentic example of a completely Surrealist interior.'[4]

Among French avant-garde circles the other great patrons were the de Noailles, who employed Jean-Michel Frank to create interiors of great richness in their modern house at Hyères. Their circle included such luminaries of chic as Christian Bérard, but also provided a link with the English fringes of the Surrealists and with the neo-Romantics Rex Whistler and Cecil Beaton. The houses which Beaton and his close friend Stephen Tennant created at Ashcombe and Wilsford Manor in Wiltshire stand as twin monuments to the English baroque whimsy of the inter-war years. Paul Nash, talking about such fantasy interiors, had warned: 'once the introduction into the home of what the French describe as *objets trouvés* has begun, anything may happen. All the ornaments and bric-à-brac of the Victorian past were never such a threat to man's sanity as *les objets trouvés*.' And yet there can be no doubt that in the tastes of Beaton and his friends such as Whistler, in their attitudes to decoration, and especially in their love of a romanticized image of English country house life, we may discern the origins of one of the most potent influences on the decoration of houses in England, and indeed in America, for the next forty or fifty years.

It is true of both America and England, though perhaps to a lesser degree of the rest of Europe, that traditional and modern decoration came to coexist more comfortably in these years. Figures such as Derek Patmore, who was

celebrated in the press as 'an English decorator in New York', began to work in a variety of styles, from a tame Modernism through to Regency revival or neo-Georgian. The large stores in New York and London which established decorating departments at around this time were certainly an influence towards catholicity of taste, and several, such as Fortnum & Mason in London, who employed Alan Walton as their expert, produced room settings that were both fashionable and stylish. In particular the stores seem to have encouraged the vogue for 'theme' rooms, perhaps in part to try to win custom from the more established small firms which each had an individual image. Themes which enjoyed a perennial popularity included 'Olde English' (sometimes meaning Tudor, but sometimes anything between the mid or late seventeenth century and Late Georgian), and of course Chinoiserie, whilst one-off imaginative leaps produced such curiosities as Derek Patmore's 'Wedgwood cameo room' (pl. 312).

According to Ronald Fleming, a significant figure who was associated at various times with many of the leading firms and whose own work mixed the old and the new, the *annus mirabilis* for the modern style in England was 1933: the year of Edward James's *Ballets* and the founding of MARS (the Modern Architectural Research Group, which introduced Continental theories of Rationalism to Britain). Amongst other avant-garde experiments Fleming staged the influential 1933 exhibition of modern decorative arts at Dorland Hall, the well known Bayswater venue for applied arts displays. In it he introduced the work of a number of young painters who were interested in carrying out work for interiors, such as Geoffrey Houghton-Brown, who had already painted Edward James's bathroom, Nicolas de Molas and the better-known muralists Eric Ravilious and Rex Whistler. Most of the work on show was of the kind which interpreted historical forms and styles in a vaguely modernistic manner, and in feel it was close to much of the sort of work which French decorative artists were producing at this time.

The 30s in America saw the emergence of a number of the major decorators whose work has been given the name 'High Style'. Basing their styles on English and French period detailing and relying heavily on the use of high-quality antique pieces, the rooms which resulted were of a degree of richness and grandeur rare outside the most exalted circles in Europe. The background to this world of acceptability was intensely social and operated within strict bounds with regard to both residential areas of New York and the location of country houses and summer retreats. Billy Baldwin, who began work in 1935 'with that *doyenne* of the New York scene Ruby Ross Wood', described in his reminiscences how he had invited his all-powerful employer to view his first tiny apartment and then waited with trepidation for the verdict. The decorative scheme passed Miss Wood's severe scrutiny with only a small criticism of some over-emphatic piping on the shaped pelmet boards (which was of course removed the next day). He had, he realized, made the grade and was admitted into that charmed circle which was presided over by the magisterial eye of Parsons, and which came to include such figures as 'Sister' Parish, Elsie Cobb Wilson, Nancy McClelland and Mrs Archibald Brown, formerly Eleanor McMillen of McMillen Inc. Baldwin eventually became the most respected figure on the New York scene, but always remained ready to acknowledge those who had influenced him in developing his style. He cited in particular the young Baron Niki de Gunzburg, who had set himself up with a great degree of chic in New York, decorating a memorable library with hundreds of tiny pictures hung against green baize walls, and two other great influences who shared his love of rich dark greens: Elsie de Wolfe, whose green-leaf chintz he liked to use for garden rooms, and Van Day Truex, a great if shadowy stylist who taught Baldwin the use of lacquered colour on walls, and whose green taffeta room with Biedermeier furniture was, Baldwin recalled, one of the most revered rooms in New York. Billy Baldwin came to be called the 'Dean of American Decorators', and his own joke about the nature of his business recalls the old line about Elsie de Wolfe. Baldwin claimed that what really interested him was bringing together two things: FFF and FFV – Fine French Furniture and the First Families of Virginia.

By 1937 *Decoration*, a short-lived but in its time excellent magazine which reflected modernistic attitudes to interior decoration in the 30s, was surveying the scene and suggested that, like everywhere else, 'London is waiting for a certain gaiety ... something more subtle and cultivated must be achieved to do away with the present tendency towards insipid decoration'. The answer for many it seems lay in the richness of historic decoration and in the clever adaptation of historic styles to modern needs. Whether this took the form of the almost morbid romanticism of obsessive collecting, as exemplified in Rome by Mario Praz,

or in the more light-hearted revivalism of the later Vogue Regency collector-decorators, the results were always to some degree concerned with the evocation of the magic of the rooms of the past; with the poetic quality of the reflection of candle-light in darkened mirror; and with the feeling of lost grandeur.

Lady Lancaster (who as Anne Scott James was one of the sharpest observers of the period as a journalist and later broadcaster), recalls that there seemed to be a precise moment when modernistic decoration in the Syrie style ceased to feel chic or to reflect the spirit of the times. At that moment a new and crucial figure had appeared on the stage who was to dominate the decoration world in England for a generation: John Fowler.

John Fowler had begun work in the studio of Thornton Smith, painting Chinese wallpaper and creating pastiche architectural *capricci* in the manner of Pannini, which in the mid-20s were in tremendous demand. Shortly after, he had gone to the decorative furniture department of the Peter Jones department store, whence, after a disagreement with the management, he had taken the best elements of the workforce and set up in business in the King's Road in Chelsea, just along the road from where both Lady Colefax and Syrie Maugham lived. Already he was recognized as an original and influential figure and the two leading ladies courted him to join their firms. Reputedly he went to Colefax & Co. because he found Sybil less domineering than Syrie. In truth there can have been very little in it. Even at this early stage of his career friends recall that Fowler's knowledge of the history and mastery of the practicalities of decoration were formidable and his grasp of the appropriate atmosphere or 'feel' of a room quite unique. Somehow, even in the pre-war period, at a time when lavish schemes such as Sir Alfred Beit's neo-baroque library (pl. 331) or Sir Henry ('Chips') Channon's Amalienburg dining room (pl. 332) were the most celebrated society rooms, Fowler had caught the new mood and made 'humble elegance' and 'pleasing decay' his ideals.

1. Beverley Nichols, *For Adults Only*, London, 1932
2. Ronald Fleming, 'Memoirs of English inter-war period decorators', MS in the Archive of Art and Design, Victoria & Albert Museum, London
3. Charles Wade, *Haphazard Notes*, London, 1979
4. Paul Nash, 'Surrealist Interiors' in *Decoration*, June, 1936

273

273

Good commercial neo-Georgian mid-1930s

Dining room by Ronald Fleming, for Kelso

Ronald Fleming's work as senior designer for the old-established decorating firm of Kelso was mainly in an historical vein. He chose to use good antique furniture for the most part, but would not hesitate to have individual pieces such as an extra pair of chairs made up when necessary. Here, in an architecturally unpromising room,

he has run a boldly moulded cornice and installed a fine early eighteenth-century chimneypiece. The curtain treatment is interesting, and typical of the elaborate shaped and braided pelmets that remained fashionable until John Fowler revived the heavy swagged and draped treatments of the early nineteenth century. Most of the other pieces in this scheme are of the late eighteenth century, arranged with simple elegance against plain walls. Unpatterned wall-to-wall carpets, often in strong clear colours, were also a characteristic element of schemes of this period.

Victoria & Albert Museum, London

furnishings and decoration as well as in all architectural matters. The resulting house was a classic of its period, with Crittall metal-framed windows and a severe functionalism in the interiors which the architects admitted they had derived from a close study of Le Corbusier's Villa Savoye at Poissy, Gropius's work at Dessau and the works of J.J.P. Oud in Holland. The living room at Lobden was photographed and published in a number of contemporary journals as an important example of a room in which the architects had full control of the entire design process, including not only fixed and fitted furniture but even the moveable chairs and occasional tables. All these pieces were made by the family firm, Gordon Russell Ltd. Noel Carrington, writing in appreciation in *Country Life* in February 1933, just after the scheme was completed, enthused that 'rectangle and sphere, plane and circle of machine production are cleverly woven into harmony'.

Courtesy of Gordon Russell plc, Broadway, Worcs.

274

Modernity in the Malvern Hills 1932

Living room, Lobden, near Malvern, Worcestershire; designed by R.D. Russell and Marian Pepler

Lobden was built for a Mr and Mrs Hartley, for whom Marian Pepler and R.D. (Dick) Russell, the brother of Gordon Russell, had only three years previously built Folifoot, the much more conservative house near Harrogate in Yorkshire. At Lobden the Hartleys allowed their chosen architects *carte blanche* in the design of the

275

Fitted furniture 1935

Flat at 42 Upper Brook Street, London, by Serge Chermayeff

This remodelled flat, with furnishings and decoration in the 'stripped' or minimalist aesthetic of the mid-1930s, is a good example of the way in which designers grasped the possibilities of 'building-in' much of a room's furnishing thus saving space and creating a more harmonious effect than would otherwise have been possible in the new smaller flats, where several functions had to be combined in one room. In this smart scheme in Upper Brook Street Chermayeff has dispensed entirely with architectural detail, and confined all the colour and pattern to the two different carpets in the distinct halves of the room. The furniture, which follows the walls, includes glass-fronted cabinets and a desk area with a section of 'pigeonholes'. In the nearer part of the space there is a modular table which can be divided or used as one large dining table.

Architectural Press, London

Two versions of the 'machine for living in' late 1920s

276

Living room by Mart Stam, Rotterdam

From D. Todd and R. Mortimer, The New Interior Decoration, *London and New York, 1929*

277

Dining area in a house by Ludwig Hilberseimer, with furniture by Thonet

Designed for Die Weissenhofsiedlung in Stuttgart, 1927

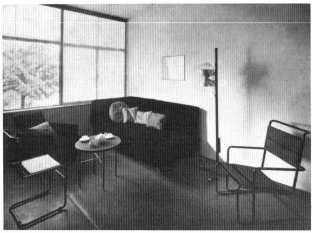

276

These two rooms are typical versions of the extreme, stripped functionalism of the late 1920s, characterized by Le Corbusier's theory that a house should be a 'machine for living in'. Both take the rational ideal to its limits in eliminating all ornamentation, as Loos had advocated, but the appeal of such rigorously austere schemes was not wide. Mart Stam, the Dutch architect of the functionalist school, was a contemporary of Gerrit Rietveld and an associate of the 'De Stijl' group. He claimed to have designed the first tubular steel chair on the cantilever principle as early as 1926, before similar ideas were developed by the Bauhaus designers. Todd and Mortimer, in describing the Mart Stam living room, managed to raise sufficient enthusiasm to praise 'this agreeable room arrangement' and to suggest that it 'conveys an atmosphere of repose and comfort in spite of what might generally be considered the austerity of its main elements'. The architect Hilberseimer's 'dining niche', furnished with the slightly more human bentwood furniture manufactured in huge quantities by the Thonet company, was also reproduced in Todd and Mortimer's book; they were clearly more wary of this room, expressing in their remarks the unvoiced but utterly Bloomsbury question as to whether civilized life is possible at all without a proper dining room.

277   *The Art Institute of Chicago*

277

278

The UAM style   1931

*Salon de M. Lacrois at Croix, designed by
Robert Mallet-Stevens*

The Union des Artistes Modernes was founded in Paris
in 1930, with Hélène Henry, René Herbst, Francis
Jourdain, Raymond Templier and Robert Mallet-Stevens
as its principal protagonists and first committee members.
Other important figures associated with the Modern
movement in France, such as Eileen Gray, were encouraged
by this inner group to exhibit with them at the regular
UAM shows. The emphasis was to a great extent on form
and structure rather than decoration, but the 1925 Paris
Exposition had had its influence on many of the group, and
certainly led to a feeling for the use of richer materials than
the Bauhaus designers had considered appropriate to the
modern house. This dining room by the architect Mallet-
Stevens, who designed an important house for the de
Noailles (pls 349, 350), gives a precise idea of the 'look'
created by the group in its crisply chic emphasis on line,
geometric pattern and new fittings.

Collection Musée des Arts Décoratifs, Paris

Practical modern 1933

279

The 'Weekend House'

Designed by Serge Chermayeff and exhibited at Dorland Hall, London

280

A practical modern kitchen

Designed by Serge Chermayeff and Erich Mendelsohn

The extreme simplification of these interiors by Chermayeff conforms to contemporary notions of the desirability of rationalization in every part of the home, be it apartment, town house or country cottage. The intriguing consequence of this as a design rationale is that town kitchen and 'cottage' drawing room are both created with exactly the same minimalist aesthetic, and even use some of the same design detailing, such as the adjustable lamp. Chermayeff's modernistic cottage was shown at the exhibition of architecture and decoration held at Dorland Hall in 1933, and prefigured the similar idealized scheme by

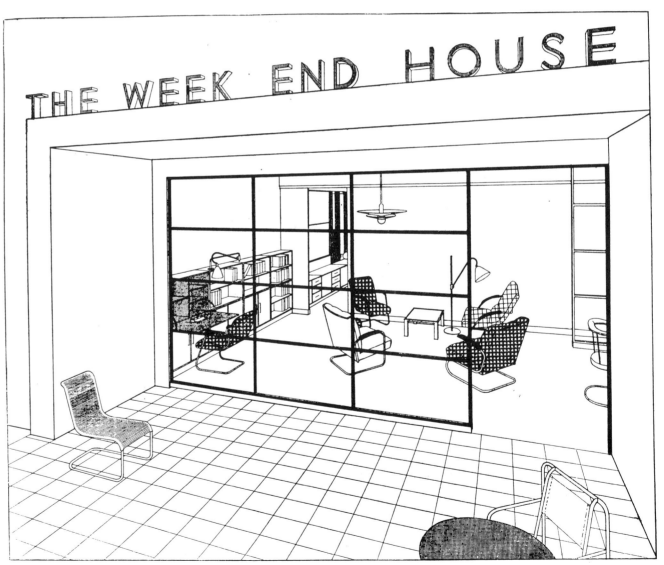

279

Gordon Russell and others, which formed the centrepiece of the British pavilion at the 1937 Paris Exposition.

279 *Architectural Press, London*
280 *Private Collection*

281

An up-to-date kitchen, London 1937

Kitchen of the house of Jack Payne Esq., Highgate; from Decoration, 1937

280

The introduction of design into the previously utilitarian domain of the kitchens and sculleries of ordinary houses came a little later than the movement to unite aesthetics and ergonomics in the bathroom. However, by the 1930s several factors had combined to throw a new emphasis on these areas which has grown steadily ever since, reaching the point where the quality of kitchens and bathrooms is now said to be the most determining factor in the way people judge a house or flat. Changes in social patterns made it essential that kitchens should become more pleasing spaces in which to work. The general tendency was for the old notion of the basement kitchen to be abandoned, and many chose to adopt the homely ideals of the Arts and Crafts movement, at the same time introducing some modern gadgetry and other improvements. As the writer in *Decoration* suggests in the article from which this illustration is taken, 'So many practical things are made for the kitchen nowadays that everyone should be able to have a workmanlike room which is easy to keep clean, and where they can move about and find things easily without groping at awkward levels and banging against projecting corners.' This example in a house in the newly fashionable suburb of Highgate seems typical of the more compact and rationally laid-out kitchens of the period, and is fitted with the classic Ascot Multipoint Gas Water Heater.

281

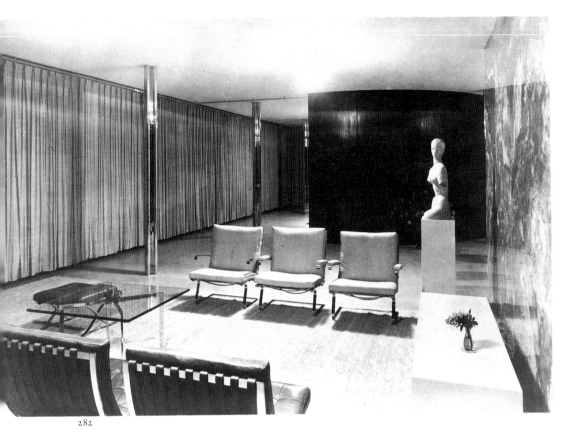

282

283

'New house, new world'   1932

Corner shelf by Erich Mendelsohn from Neues Haus, neue Welt, *Berlin, 1932*

Erich Mendelsohn's *Neues Haus, neue Welt*, which appeared in 1932, documented in the minutest detail the design and construction of a house intended to break existing moulds, and to set a pattern for a rational and beautiful style of building related to modern needs and new constructional methods. In reality the house was, like most ideal visions of the future, not a little influenced by the fashions of the day. This shelved corner area in metal and glass is certainly stripped and functional, but even in its minimal detail and rather chic degree of polish it seems to belong to an Art Deco aesthetic. Mendelsohn left Berlin for Holland in 1933 and subsequently moved to London, where he went into practice with Serge Chermayeff, completing the celebrated Modernist De La Warr Pavilion at Bexhill-on-Sea, Sussex, in 1936.

A domestic room by Mies   1930

Sitting area of the Tugendhat House, Brno, by Mies van der Rohe

The later work of each of the major figures of the Bauhaus experiment developed the basic aesthetic in different ways. Mies van der Rohe's interiors for the German pavilion at the Barcelona International Exhibition of 1929 marked an important step in the humanizing of those original austere ideals, and his chair in steel and hide produced at that time became one of the great classics of modern furniture design. He used the 'Barcelona' chair and another design, the 'Brno' chair, in the interiors of the celebrated Tugendhat House at Brno which he designed in 1930. In its free-flowing spaces a new richness of materials contributed to the total effect, and elsewhere in the house Persian carpets added a note of more luxurious pattern and vibrant colour.

Courtesy of Mies van der Rohe Archive, the Museum of Modern Art, New York

283

284

284

An 'open-plan' house 1936

Falling Water, Bear Run, Pennsylvania, by Frank Lloyd Wright

Frank Lloyd Wright is the architect who did most to abolish the artificial distinctions between architecture and decoration. His ideal of the interior and exterior of the building as interpenetrative elements led to a new emphasis on the flow of all the design motifs throughout the structure. Influenced by the work of the architect H.H. Richardson, Wright developed a distinctive feel for the 'open plan'. In his earlier work he used a great deal of ornament, especially as architectural decoration in relief (pl. 168), but gradually considerations of form, structure and materials became more important. In the 'prairie houses' built around Chicago there is a growing sense that the house should be a formal development of the natural surroundings, and this is clearly visible as one of the major themes of Edgar J. Kaufmann's house, Falling Water, at Bear Run in Pennsylvania. Here the chimneypiece and stone walls are developed from the forms of the living rock, and in the face of nature all other decoration is relegated to a minor role.

Photograph Wayne Andrews

285

285

Comfortable Modernism in Germany 1930

Boudoir by W. Gutmann of Frankfurt;
from Modern Interiors in Colour, 1930

This room in a colourful and 'easy to live with' modernistic style is in many ways advanced for its time and prophetic of things to come. It has an uncontrived and relaxed feel, based on simple functional considerations in the design and arrangement of the furnishings, that would hardly be out of place in the 1950s or early 60s. The picture window and generally exaggerated horizontality of the design are characteristically international features of decoration of the period; while the woven textiles, and in particular the striped rugs, give a more specifically Scandinavian feel to the room, being based on the typically brightly coloured Swedish weaves that were popular for many years after Carl Larsson's revival of country-style furnishing.

286

Commercial Modernism c.1935

Design for a room with furniture in light woods,
by Gordon Russell Ltd

Among those who managed to reconcile modernity of form with modern and economic manufacturing methods, Gorden Russell stands out as one who shows that the designer's integrity need not always be the first casualty in any engagement between the worlds of art and commerce. The pieces of Russell furniture suggested in this drawing are typical in the generally low, straight lines of the fitted units that his firm Gordon Russell Ltd did much to make more widely available, while the armchairs have the ample and simplified rounded shapes which in the 1930s implied comfort to the conservatively-modern observer. The pale tones and un-glossy finish of Russell furniture went well with the prevalent plain walls and stripped architectural detailing of the day, and these undemanding pieces allowed many people to live comfortably while maintaining their illusion of having avant-garde taste. The drawing is characteristic of the 'excitingly progressive' way in which Gordon Russell's image was projected; indeed he may well have been the specific target of a lampoon in the pages of *Decoration* in 1936, which sent up the sort of young designer who would use an axonometric drawing just to illustrate an armchair.

Victoria & Albert Museum, London

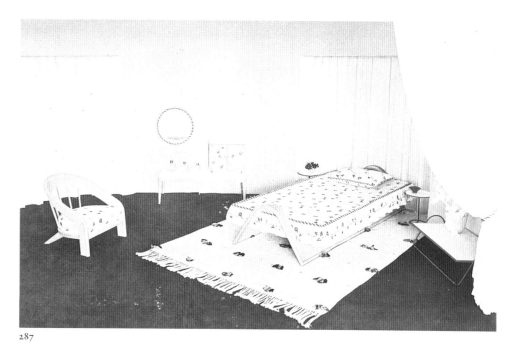

287

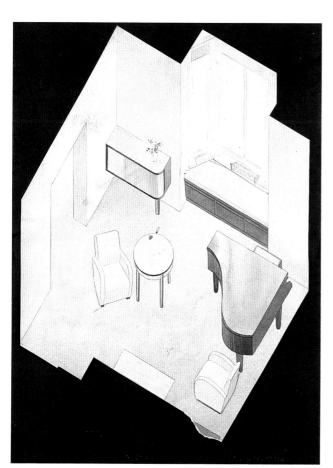

286

287

'A bedroom for a débutante' 1937

Bedroom setting designed by Jean Royère for Maison Gouffé; from Le Décor d'aujourd'hui, *Paris, 1937*

This design for a young lady's bedroom was described as an example of suitability of design for purpose in the 'freshness of the colour scheme' and in the 'virgin simplicity of the chief characteristics of [the] room'. In fact it is the bold asymmetry of the arrangement and the deliberately novel forms of the bed and other pieces which are most noticeable. The 'original and unusual design' is hailed as a 'welcome departure from the conventional', but it does echo very clearly the long, low lines that were so prevalent in the design of furniture at the time, and which often lent a degree of elegance to this kind of quirky, diagonal placing, which would be disastrous with more formal and conventional pieces. The group formed by the circular mirror and the low dressing table, upon which stand a small cabinet and three very large scent bottles, is also an interesting composition, and one that seems distinctly to look forward to the 1950s.

288

288

'Functional' 1930s

*Parody of the English intellectual modern style
by Osbert Lancaster, from* Homes Sweet Homes,
London, 1939

As always, Osbert Lancaster strikes to the heart of a style, deliberately emphasizing what he saw as the utter cheerlessness of the intellectual Modernists. Rain slants down on the tubular furniture outside a 'picture window' while the heavily bespectacled, pipe-smoking thinker huddles in hairy tweeds beside a wall-mounted electric fire. The furniture includes a table and stool by Alvar Aalto, and there are a few decorative objects, which Lancaster describes as 'a grim collection' but which nevertheless fulfil the seemingly ineradicable human need to have at least a few things about a room, even if they 'compromise' the strictest puritan design ethos. As Osbert Lancaster put it, 'The vast majority, even including many readers of the *New Statesman*, crave their knick-knacks.' On the wireless cabinet 'grimaces' a Benin bronze. There is an excessively ugly cactus plant on the ziggurat bookcase, while above the fire, lit by a strip lamp, hangs a modernistic picture, which may well be a serious lapse of taste not unlike Graham Sutherland's painting *A Sick Duck*.

John Murray Ltd, London

289

'Modernistic' 1930s

Drawing by Osbert Lancaster from Homes Sweet Homes,
London, 1939

This is perhaps the cruellest of all the brilliantly observed illustrations that Osbert Lancaster made for his great survey of the history of the decoration of the English interior. It represents that hideously debased modernistic style which all too many manufacturers of furnishings and objects adopted in the late 1920s and 30s and foisted upon a growing middle-class and predominantly suburban public for well over a decade. As Osbert Lancaster observed, the 'style' was an unhappy amalgam of the worst elements of several of the design fashions of the day such as 'Jazz Modern', itself the result of the 'fearful' union of the ill-digested influences of the Ballets Russes and a hopelessly vulgarized Cubism. The flashier elements of the design aesthetic of the Paris Exposition of 1925 were also copied, and this accounted for a love of what Lancaster described as the 'all too generous use of the obscure and more hideous woods'. All these factors were combined, he says, with a 'half-hearted simplicity that derived from a complete misunderstanding of the ideals of the Corbusier-Gropius school of architects and found uneasy expression in unvarnished wood and chromium plate, relentlessly mis-applied'. Curiously, this extraordinarily debased style is not peculiar to England: similar versions, with a degree of local colour, can be found in France and Germany, and indeed in the suburban houses of the great American cities.

John Murray Ltd, London

290

289

290

Intellectual modern styles 1930s

Herbert Read in the study of his London house

Herbert Read remains in many ways the epitome of the visually aware, intellectual Englishman of the 1930s, who sought to escape the snares of aestheticism and historicism in design. His influential views on the history and the ideal future of the fine and decorative arts were essentially austere and stressed the importance of functionalism rather than fashion, and of rational design over meaningless ornament or decoration. The arrangement of his own house became the perfect expression of this puritan visual ethic and lifestyle. In the study can be seen an entirely modern and functional chimneypiece with its clean, efficient electric fire requiring no servants and creating no mess. Books, as intellectual tools, are neatly ordered on plain shelves, and the sparse furnishings include a classic minimalist table in tubular chrome by Marcel Breuer for Pel Ltd, the Birmingham metal furniture manufacturers. On the floor is a khilim rug which Read would have admired for its honest workmanship, unpretentious design and fitness for purpose. These qualities are also to be read into the other objects visible, some early glass and ceramic wine flagons displayed on top of the bookshelves and on the mantelshelf. Above hangs a Cubist picture by Ben Nicholson, and beside his shoulder is a small sculpture by Barbara Hepworth, both examples of the kind of art which Read championed.

Architectural Press, London

291

A functional study c.1936

Library-study at Timber House, Sevenoaks, Kent; architect Walter Gropius, fittings and decoration by Duncan Miller

In an important house in Sevenoaks dating from early in his English period, Gropius, once director of the Bauhaus, collaborated with the respected designer Duncan Miller in the creation of this functional library-study. In fact Miller is usually credited with the actual design of the shelving and all the other built-in fitments, including the handsome and practical desk. On and near the desk are grouped a number of the design classics of the day: a square

291

glass ashtray and a Dunhill lighter, a pillar desk calendar, a very simple all-metal desk lamp and, of course, the perfect early GPO pyramidal telephone.

Architectural Press, London

Colour schemes and modern furnishing early 1930s

Plates from Derek Patmore, Colour Schemes for the Modern Home, *London, 1933*

292

Derek Patmore's books were influential both in England and in America, where he had found some success as a practising decorator as well as a design pundit. His book on the use of colour, reprinted after the war, contained a number of excellent examples of the work of his friends and contemporaries on the inter-war decorating scene. Patmore seems to have had a good eye for the work of others (perhaps better than for his own), and wrote well and generously about his professional rivals. Each of the schemes he chose to reproduce makes an interesting point

and most propose a rather restrained Modernism which takes as its starting point quite traditional forms.

292

Painted 'room divider' by Eric Ravilious in the flat of Sir Geoffrey Fry in Portman Square, London

The problem of how to make folding doors between two rooms interesting even when they are closed is solved here by the painter Ravilious, who has treated the individual panels as though they were windows and created a typically pleasing vista of a garden with a tennis court.

293

293

Dining room modernized from an earlier scheme in his own house by C. Maresco Pearce

Here a deep painted frieze of *trompe-l'oeil* swagged drapery adds interest to the old wall surface, and the designer has painted an overdoor appropriate to the room function. The paintings are by Pierre Bonnard and Walter Sickert, and a Paul Gauguin woodcut hangs nearest to the door.

294

Drawing room of Lady Leucha Warner, decorated by Ronald Fleming

Patmore admired the way in which this 'definitely period room' was 'treated in the modern manner'. The main design feature is the wall treatment in squares of gold-coloured straw paper placed alternate ways to create a pattern. This use of the material must derive from the example of rooms created in a similar vein by Jean-Michel Frank, which were widely discussed at this time and which Fleming may well have known at first hand.

295

Modern workroom or study by Rodney Thomas

Design for Ashley Havinden at Highpoint 1, Berthold Lubetkin's celebrated block of flats, 1933–5, in Highgate, London

This room is a good example of the way in which the functionalist ethic became watered down in England. For the well-known graphic designer Ashley Havinden Thomas created a room conducive to work which appears at first glance to be rational and economically put together; there is in fact some degree of luxury in the use of materials, and a strongly decorative feel is apparent in the detailing of elements such as the over-scaled clock.

294

295

296

Neo-classicism and 'Jazz Modern' *c. 1930*

Drawing room, Mulberry House, Smith Square, London

Mulberry House, the home of Lord and Lady Melchett, was originally designed by Edwin Lutyens for Mr Reginald McKenna before the First World War in a distinguished but hardly adventurous neo-Georgian style.

In the late 1920s this young and extremely social couple decided to undertake a major scheme of rebuilding and decoration in order to provide themselves with a suitably spacious and stunning set of rooms for entertaining. The result was one of the most interesting and successful blends of traditional and avant-garde decorative art of the whole period. The architect Darcy Braddell remodelled the rooms of the principal floor, retaining Lutyens's fenestration but entirely recasting the interiors. He used real stone and marble, bronze and fine woods to create an utterly modernistic framework for painted and carved decoration, suggesting both the simple grandeur of the architecture of Greek temples and the subtlety of the interior of the Regency London town house. In the main reception room there were two decorative elements, both by first-rate artists. The mural decorations, featuring scenes from the 'Lives and Loves of the Gods' were painted by Glyn Philpot in his recently developed 'Jazz Modern' manner on a silver-leafed surface. They incorporated erotic figure groups placed against starkly stylish backgrounds which could be primeval rocks or the skyscrapers of New York. Very much in keeping with Philpot's highly charged decorations, for the important space above the chimneypiece the sculptor Serjeant Jagger modelled a relief on the theme of 'Scandal'. Sadly Mulberry House, one of the finest achievements of the collaboration between interesting patrons, an adventurous architect and painters and sculptors of real worth, was destroyed by bombing during the Blitz. Only a portrait of the exquisite young Lady Melchett by Philpot survives as testament to this stylish collaboration.

Country Life

297
An exhibition of decorative arts 1932

Furniture, painted hangings and other pieces from the Dorland Hall Exhibition, London

The Paris Exposition of 1925 did much to stimulate the interests of artists in the creation of decorative art objects, furniture and textiles, and there was in consequence a gradual rise in the quality of household furnishing. Decorators and their artistic collaborators sought to bring their work to the notice of a wider public – who might otherwise have seen only what could be bought from the big stores or from their own high streets – by means of temporary exhibitions. Such shows were popular and received considerable notice in Paris, London and other major centres of taste and fashion. In London Dorland Hall in Bayswater was a favourite venue, and this photograph shows a group of pieces arranged by Ronald Fleming, the organizer of the most important of the shows staged there in 1932. Fleming was working at that time for the firm of Kelso, for which he produced mainly period schemes, but his own tastes ran from the historical through to a colourful and personal mixture of the old and the very new. In this

297

group can be seen pieces of furniture designed by him for the apartment of the actress Gertrude Lawrence (pl. 301), and behind them draperies painted with modernistic classical motifs by Fleming's friend, the painter Geoffrey Houghton-Brown, in a manner similar to his bathroom scheme of this period for Edward James (pl. 355).

Victoria & Albert Museum, London

298

298

Music room in the Omega Workshop style 1932

Room setting by Duncan Grant and Vanessa Bell, realized in the Lefevre Gallery (Alex Reid & Lefevre), London, 1932; from Derek Patmore, Colour Schemes for the Modern Home, *London, 1933*

In this music room all the main elements of an Omega interior can be found. There is a strong emphasis on the free, painterly use of pattern in the hanging panels, textiles and furniture, and this is echoed in the ornamentation of the frame of the looking-glass and in the painted ceramic tiles of the hearth. The carpets have large-scale abstract and asymmetrical patterns, but most of the other elements in the scheme are more typical of the Omega and Bloomsbury love of imposing clever new decorative ideas on basically conventional forms. The schemes carried out for the Omega Workshop were beyond doubt important as design, but were even more influential ideologically in their radical attitude to the relationship between the fine and applied arts. Years later, Derek Patmore could still illustrate this very room as an example of advanced taste in the post-war edition of his earlier books, *Colour Schemes and Modern Furnishing* (1945), describing it as a 'striking example of how modern artists are willing to co-operate with the interior decorator'.

Decorative painting in the interior early 1930s

Plates from Derek Patmore, Colour Schemes for the Modern Home

299

Dining room with wall decorations by John Armstrong

300

Entrance hall designed by Allan Walton for Fortnum & Mason

A wide range of artists became interested in working in the context of decorative painting in the inter-war years, and many adapted their styles with success to meet the demands of the decorators. Derek Patmore illustrated several examples, some of which worked better than

299

others. The hallway designed as a showpiece for Fortnum's decoration department was designed and executed by the head of the studio, Allan Walton. He introduced into the small space a jolly scene of a stretch of water seen as from a balcony, painted in his characteristic style, not in any serious attempt at *trompe-l'oeil*, but observing the basic conventions of perspective and light and shade. The furnishings are pleasing if unexceptional Regency pieces, and there is a novel and interesting floor made from particoloured rubber composition inlaid in a petal design in shades of beige and pink. On a supposedly more elevated level is a scheme for a dining room by an unrecorded designer, based round a set of panels by the excellent painter John Armstrong representing various ancient Roman themes. Sadly, they seem to lack harmony in either scale or colouring, and they and the eighteenth-century furniture have no real point of contact. The contrast between the pretensions and the degree of success of these two rooms points up the interesting fact that often it is not so much the quality of decorative painting that is crucial to the success or failure of a scheme, but rather the extent to which decorator and painter have understood each others' intentions.

300

301

'Modern austerity' 1930

*Drawing room of the apartment of Miss Gertrude
Lawrence, 73 Portland Place, London; decoration by
Ronald Fleming*

Ronald Fleming, writing many years later about the decoration of the period between the wars, used this scheme which he had created for the actress Gertrude Lawrence in 1930 as an example of the austerity of the period – which he attributed not to the rise of a modernistic aesthetic, but to the effects of the world slump of 1929–30. His own description of the scheme is telling: 'Mirror and white walls were relieved with a scarlet carpet and pale grey covers. It made a somewhat severe background for a vivid personality, and any furnishings of quality were sadly lacking.' Ronald Fleming showed some examples of the upholstered chairs at one of the regular Dorland Hall decorative art exhibitions the year after this flat was completed, and from publicity photographs for the exhibition the occasional tables made in the form of side-drums became well known and much imitated. Cecil Beaton, for example, seems to have picked up the idea as being appropriate for his 'Circus Bedroom' at Ashcombe (pl. 368), and had made not only tables but also chairs with drumsticks for the arms. One of these chairs is now in the Victoria & Albert Museum.

Victoria & Albert Museum, London

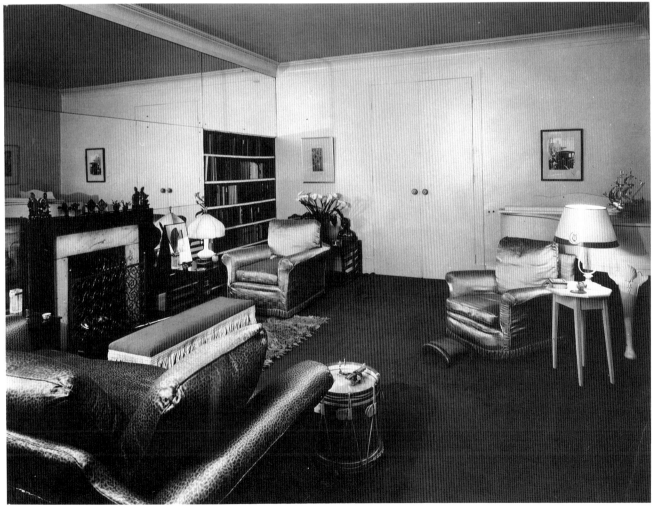

301

302

303

302

Design for a bedroom, Brussels 1934–5

Drawing for twin beds and other pieces, by Jules Leleu

Leleu was among the many fine craftsmen working in Paris in the 1920s and 30s whose work combines the influence of tradition and a concern for modern design. Lacking the genius for the *tout ensemble* of Ruhlmann, he is best remembered for individual pieces. This design for a bedroom and its furnishings is from a group of drawings relating to Leleu's commission to create a house for M. and Mme Grandchamps at 55 rue Mignot-Delstanche, Brussels, a project on which he was engaged from 1934 until work was halted by the outbreak of war in 1939. Even though the effect of austerity is heightened by the linear drawing style and lack of indication of colours, the scheme is none the less characterized by the very 'stripped' vocabulary of the architecture, such as the stylish, symmetrical curved doors, and decorative elements. There is here the subtlest suggestion of the neo-classical idiom, a theme taken up rather more positively in the design of several of the pieces of furniture. The pair of *lits en bateau* (boat-shaped or 'sleigh' beds) in particular makes direct allusion to that very popular form of bed during the Empire and Restoration periods in France. It is not known how much of the detailed planning of the project was ever realized, but invoices show that the dining room was certainly carried out.

Brighton Museum and Art Gallery

303

Comfortable Modernism in England 1936

Living room for a house in Esher, Surrey, designed by Hugh Casson

Hugh Casson, as a practising architect and, from 1953 to 1975, Professor of Interior Design at the Royal College of Art in London, did much to promote the idea of decoration as interior architecture – a professional discipline on an equal footing with architecture as one of the liberal arts, rather than a dilettante occupation. Many of his own early schemes were in a comfortable modernistic manner that is now very hard to appreciate because it exerted such a wide influence, and, in being so much imitated, inevitably moved down-market and finally lost all appeal in the post-war period. In this room of 1936 for a Mr and Mrs Notley in Esher, he used a fabric with a repeating star motif that enjoyed a brief popularity with the exponents of Vogue Regency. Here it was used in contrasting colourways of pale apricot with green stars for the curtains and the reverse for the covers of the large, square armchairs. The curtains have simple box pelmets, and the equally plain chimneypiece is made from very characteristic buff tiles with some simple black detailing. All the other surfaces are in plain colours: 'clear green' for the carpet and a pale vellum for the walls. In its day this scheme would have been thought to combine practicality with a certain degree of elegance.

Courtesy of Sir Hugh Casson

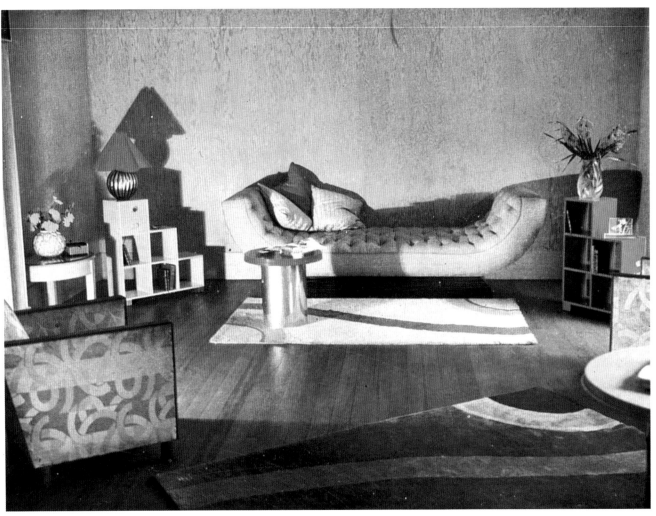

304

304

Modern panelling early 1930s

Room set with furnishings by Betty Joel; from Derek Patmore, Colour Schemes for the Modern Home, *London, 1933*

Betty Joel founded a firm making furniture to her designs shortly after the First World War, with works at Hayling Island and a showroom in Sloane Street, London. In a later showroom in Knightsbridge she sold not only furniture but fabrics woven in France and carpets which she commissioned from China. She is best remem-bered today for some inventive furniture designs of the 1930s in which interesting lines were combined with an unusual use of materials and finishes. The sofa and ziggurat bookcases in this group are typical pieces, and the use of veneered panels of Canadian pine with a grain 'resembling watered silk' is a typically clever and quirky touch. The other colours used are bright and confident: red on the shelves, table top and cushions and pale yellow enamel on the ceiling. Betty Joel seems always to have had the courage to carry out unlikely schemes, such as an all-silver lac-quered bedroom at Elveden Hall in Suffolk which defies all conventional wisdom about decorating in the country.

305

The brilliance of modern colouring early 1930s

Bed-sitting room designed by Herman Schrijver for Miss Gladys Burlton; from Derek Patmore, Colour Schemes for the Modern Home

Having arrived in England from his native Holland, Herman Schrijver quickly established himself as a versatile stylist and worked for short periods of time with a number of different firms, adopting varying looks to suit the house style or the particular requirements of the client. One area in which he excelled was in the confident handling of a rich palette of strong colours, creating rooms such as this bed-sitting room, a novel arrangement of the period, in which the colours are not only bold in themselves but exaggerated by the use of brilliant satins. The bed here is covered in pink percale and trimmed in green and kingfisher blue, which are the colours of the chairs, while the walls and (we are told) the ceiling are painted in another tone of pink. The pillows on the bed could easily be transformed with zip-fastened covers into 'scatter-cushions' during the day. This scheme is interesting not only for its exciting qualities as a colour exercise, but also as an illustration of the way in which more modest projects increasingly came to be undertaken by even quite well-known decorators, who by this time often found themselves called upon to do up a single room or provide a small number of decorative additions to an existing but insufficiently interesting room.

305

306
English style   mid-1930s

Bedroom by the Hon. Mrs Guy Bethell of Elden Ltd;
from Herman Schrijver, Decoration for the Home,
Leigh-on-Sea, Essex, 1939

The emergence of a stylish, simple and elegant version of the look of the classic eighteenth-century English country house was not due to the efforts of Colefax & Fowler alone. Among others who made a very important contribution to the new restrained look was the Hon. Mrs Guy Bethell, the influence of whose work through her small decorating firm, Elden Ltd, has been greatly underestimated. This bedroom was used for some time as the firm's advertisement, and is an excellent statement of her ideals. The bed is hung with a French percale in a bold floral pattern of wreaths, lined with another similar fabric with a small all-over pattern in the same colouring of red on a cream ground. The pelmet, edged in red braid, is formed of separate panels, each with an element of the pattern placed centrally, and the red is picked up by the plain-coloured carpet. The treatment of the walls is extremely simple, relying on the restrained good proportions of chimneypiece and panelling for its effect. All clutter and any suggestion of the hectic Victorian chintz bedroom have been swept away, and there is a delightful feeling of that calm correctness which characterizes so much of English eighteenth- and early nineteenth-century building and decoration.

307

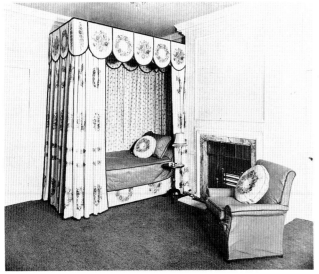

306

307
Mrs Tree's bedroom   c.1933

Bedroom at Kelmarsh Hall, Northamptonshire,
decorated for Mrs Ronald Tree by the Hon. Mrs Guy
Bethell of Elden Ltd

When Mrs Ronald Tree (afterwards Mrs Nancy Lancaster) took on the beautiful but decayed Kelmarsh Hall, she enlisted the help of Mrs Bethell whose ideals in decoration she already shared. Together they built on their common love of eighteenth-century order and restraint to create some of the most influential interiors of the whole period. They swept away all the confusion of the later nineteenth century, organized rooms and chose fabrics, carpets and furniture that were never uninteresting and yet never over-assertive. In the neat symmetry and elegant clarity of their arrangements of objects they forged an aesthetic which would influence not only work carried out by Mrs Tree's later partner, John Fowler, but also that of almost every decorator who has worked in the period style to this day. The bedrooms at Kelmarsh especially displayed Mrs Bethell's genius in the arrangement of old damasks, brocades and painted or embroidered stuffs as stylish bedhangings, and her particular skill in handling a narrow range of pale tones to create rooms which in their day were unusual for their sophisticated relationship with the past.

Country Life

308

'Homes of the Stars' 1936

Mae West's boudoir, reproduced in 'The Homes of the Stars' at the Ideal Home Exhibition, 1936, Olympia, London; from Decoration, *1936*

Although Mary Pickford and Douglas Fairbanks had already established at 'Pickfair' in the 1920s the main ingredients of the Hollywood style (extravagance and fantasy amid an insistent luxuriousness most often expressed in outrageously bogus period styles), by the early and mid-1930s a more sleekly modern form of *grand luxe* was becoming the ideal of the screen goddesses and their more astute publicists. Mae West's bed is almost as much an icon of its age as her lips became when immortalized as a sofa (pl. 357). The bed is padded, cushioned and draped in heavy folds of richly glossy satin, and there is a counterpane of the same material made up in the classic pattern of the day. It was the huge baroque-shaped panels of mirror glass at the head of the bed and on the ceiling above, however, that gained the scheme its notoriety. Mae West's famous talent for coining memorably risqué one-liners led her to explain the mirrored ceiling with the comment, 'I like to see how well I'm doing!'

309

309

Commercial version of the baroque revival late 1930s

'A modern adaptation of a William and Mary four-poster bed', design by Herman Schrijver of Elden Ltd; from Herman Schrijver, Decoration for the House, *Leigh-on-Sea, Essex, 1939*

The splendidly exaggerated proportions of this bed, designed as an exhibition set piece by Herman Schrijver, are reminiscent of Cecil Beaton's celebrated image of Edith Sitwell taking her breakfast chocolate at Renishaw (pl. 263). By the mid-1930s Schrijver, who was a stylish and idiosyncratic designer, had taken control of the design studio of the firm of Elden Ltd. Elden carried out distinguished work at this time, and under the direction of Schrijver became better known publicly than in the time of the rather more self-effacing Mrs Bethell, who had been content with the credit of having 'helped' her friends and clients with their schemes. This splendid bed was upholstered in white damask, and piled with luxurious heaps of cushions in velvets and other rich fabrics as well as the printed *toiles* of which Schrijver was so enthusiastic an advocate. The lion was said to be a piece of Spanish seventeenth-century ceramic work.

308

310

Old and new in two rooms by John Hill early 1930s

310

'Contemporary Living-room. Period Style.'

From Derek Patmore, I Decorate My Home, *London, 1936*

311

Drawing room in pink

From Derek Patmore, Colour Schemes for the Modern Home, *London, 1933*

It is interesting that Derek Patmore, himself an important decorator but better remembered as one of the more intelligent popular writers on the subject, consistently chose to illustrate the work of John Hill, of the firm of Green & Abbott, as representative of the successful blending of the traditional and the modern. In the pink drawing room he particularly drew attention to the 'cleverly draped pelmets', which so successfully allude to the past without recourse to any copying of actual historical examples, and to the use of the neat and simplified version of the famous Knole sofa. In the living room Patmore describes with approval the seemingly effortless mixture of old and new which lends to the room what he calls a 'definite Regency influence'. In this room a good Biedermeier secretaire stands on the newly fashionable flooring of squares of three-ply waxed birchwood, and the curvilinear forms of a Regency-inspired sofa find echoes in the swirling elements of the hand-made circular carpet. Both rooms have colour schemes which satisfy the 'modern desire for restful colour', and both epitomize the cool elegance and understated subtlety for which John Hill became celebrated.

312

An English decorator in New York 1935–6

'*Scheme for a Wedgwood dining room*'; *drawing by Derek Patmore from* I Decorate My Home, *London, 1936*

Derek Patmore went to New York in the summer of 1935 at the invitation of Altman's, one of the city's leading department stores, and created for them a sequence of twelve rooms. The styles chosen were a significant

311

Scheme for a Wedgwood dining-room

312

indication of the sort of clientele for whom decorators catered at this time, and *Decoration* noted that 'Mr Patmore had to remember the very considerable difference between English and American taste.' He found in New York, it was said, a prejudice against 'too severe modernity' and a strong preference among American women for the Georgian and eighteenth-century French styles. The room sets he designed for Altman's included four with colours and motifs derived from old Wedgwood, one of his favourite conceits; two grand set pieces, a baroque music room and a 'Renoir boudoir'; and a series of six more modernistic schemes which used bright colour, new furniture and a range of English fabrics not previously seen in America. The living room created with pieces in a simplified Chinese style was one of the most obviously thematic of the rooms, and introduced a new and luxurious kind of schematic Chinoiserie which remains remarkably popular in the United States even to this day.

313

Old furniture and the modern background 1936

Smoking room with Restauration furniture, by M. Imbert, Paris; from Decoration, *June 1936*

Ralph Edwards, the celebrated connoisseur and curator of furniture at the Victoria & Albert Museum, was among those who were already by the mid-1930s advocating that old furniture should be integrated into modern schemes of decoration. His article 'Old furniture and the

modern background', in the influential magazine *Decoration*, voiced a view widely held, especially in England, that there were few pieces of modern furniture of sufficient calibre in terms of design, quality of manufacture and scale to hold their own in an important room. It was suggested that in this the Modern movement had thus far failed to respond to the challenge of creating pieces to equal those of the past. To illustrate his argument Edwards used a room by M. Imbert 'of Paris' in which the architectural and the minimal decorative elements, in the international, anonymous stripped manner, contrast with and, we are told, complement a mixed suite of French furniture of the Restauration period. Light blue walls 'offset' the characteristic pale maple finish of the furniture, and vases of opaline glass in rose and green create a 'note of gay colour' in an otherwise slightly austere and light-toned scheme for a smoking room. It is easy to see in such a room the beginnings of a new taste for the more exuberant and colourful furnishings and objects of the mid-nineteenth century, especially for opaline glass, which became increasingly fashionable after the war in both London and Paris. In France it was Mme Madeleine Castaing who became the greatest exponent of this new style, while in England a number of fashionable writers, artists, photographers and fashion people, such as John French, Lady Ashton and Digby Morton, created a vogue for 'Victoriana'.

313

314

'Period influences' in America c.1938

Four rooms from Walter Rendell Storey, Period Influences in Interior Decoration, *London and New York, 1938*

Each of these rooms takes as its starting point a very specific stylistic source, and each obeys a set of self-imposed limitations by using only objects and furniture from the 'correct' historical period. Yet each room is stylish and successful in its own way, and a well-chosen example of the ways in which period styles can be restated endlessly in every succeeding era.

314

Sitting room with Spanish furnishings, designed by W.R. Storey

The Spanish look, using baroque or earlier pieces, was popular in America in the 1930s, where it was done with more seriousness than in England. Sadly, the more interesting and sensitive schemes carried out in this manner eventually led to the vulgar excesses of the Hollywood Hispanic style, favoured by film stars and moguls. Storey noted: 'somewhat austere but graceful and always ornamental are Spanish furnishings'.

315

Entrance hall in the rococo manner, designed by Nancy McClelland

One of the most respected and knowledgeable decorators of her generation, Nancy McClelland employed period styles in an easy and confident way. Here she makes a plain entrance hall both impressive and full of a welcoming lightheartedness by using a Venetian rococo theme, uniting elaborate furniture and light fittings with extravagant *faux-marbre* paint treatments on doorcases and dado.

315

316

316

Federal period dining room, designed by Elsie Cobb Wilson

In a very clever scheme, one of the most modernistic of those chosen by Storey, Miss Wilson managed at once to make an up-to-date statement and to give the feel of an historical room, in this instance of the Federal period. The furnishings are period but the main effect of the room comes from the bold use of mirror glass. The entire chimney-breast is mirrored in a way which has now become so much a decorators' cliché that it is hard to imagine the excitement it aroused as a novel feature. A typical Federal circular gilt-framed mirror is superimposed on the chimney-breast, and further mirror glass, backing two flanking panels, echoes the theme. These panels form a background for a display of vases, each arranged on a separate bracket to form an exciting visual pattern reminiscent of the similar grouping of the porcelain collection of her daughter, Mrs Paravicini, carried out by Syrie Maugham at about this date (pl. 364).

English Regency dining room, decorated by Thedlow Inc.

Although the dining table and chairs in this highly successful scheme are in the English Regency style, everything else about the room suggests that particular American Regency period interpretation of the French Empire taste. The general idea seems to be based, perhaps loosely, on the famous dining room scheme at Malmaison, but the more specifically American elements include the bold draperies in two contrasting colours and the splendid painted floorcloth imitating a complex inlaid marble floor.

317

318

Light in the morning room early 1930s

Morning room by John Hill; from Derek Patmore, Colour Schemes for the Modern Home, *London, 1933*

Morning rooms enjoyed tremendous popularity among those arranging their houses in the more spacious days of the 1920s and 30s. They were generally conceived as an informal or private part of the house, and decorative schemes for them tended to avoid too great a degree of elaboration or enrichment, with colour ideas that were usually light in tone. In the setting of a handsome period room with a good eighteenth-century chimneypiece John Hill, a decorator especially adept at combining 'the best of the old and the best of the new', used pieces of antique furniture cleverly co-ordinated in colour with the upholstery of a typically modern armchair and with the abstract pattern of the hand-made rug laid over plain close carpeting. The main feature of the room, however, was undoubtedly the three full-length windows and their curtains of white satin stencilled with a stylized feather motif in shades of blue, green and yellow, showing the influence of the

318

Omega Workshop (pls 161–3, 169–71). Leaving a blank area of the pale and neutral wall colour above the chimneypiece to create a sense of space is a trick tried by many decorators of the period, and employed here with tremendous assurance by John Hill. Another notable feature is the use of nineteenth-century turquoise glass lamp bases and other ornamental pieces. This was forward-looking at this date, one of the first manifestations of a tentative rediscovery of the decorative values of certain kinds of Victorian artefacts.

319

The cool colours of 'good taste' early 1930s

Double drawing room in his own house in London, designed by Allan Walton; from Derek Patmore, Colour Schemes for the Modern Home

I n a house with the typically restrained good proportions and elegant details of the 1820s and 30s, a type particularly common on the northern fringes of the City, Allan Walton created this subtle statement of his belief in underplayed design, in stark contrast to his theatrical work for Fortnum & Mason (pl. 300). In a scheme of gentle creams in the front room and greens at the rear, the only really bold or obviously decorator's touch is an apricot ceiling. Beyond this all is deliberately quiet and harmonious. On the simple white marble chimneypiece are three fashionable *blanc de chine* figurines and a tiny pair of English Regency candlesticks with lustres. The necessary notes of detail and colour are provided by an 'easy chair' upholstered in salmon, and a pretty French country elbow chair with a squab seat, of the kind favoured by Dante Gabriel Rossetti, who designed a version for manufacture by Morris & Co., and later by Monet, who had them in his house at Giverny. The two rooms are united by the use of a single stone-green-coloured carpet, and before the chimneypiece is a smaller rug which was made to Walton's design. The glass dome of shell or silk flowers is a curiosity at this early date, and points the way towards the more full-blown Victorian revival of the immediate post-war period.

319

320

320

A Vogue Regency dressing table 1930s

Bedroom designed by T. Hayes Marshall; from Marshall's Interior Decoration Today, *Leigh-on-Sea, Essex, 1938*

Among English designers of the 1930s it was T. Hayes Marshall who comes nearest to catching the special quality of American – particularly Hollywood-style – decoration and adapting it to suit an English audience. This design for a dressing area in a bedroom comes close to being a parody of the style that was popular with the more flamboyant exponents of the Regency revival, such as Norman Hartnell. Marshall uses here the favourite starred satin and gathers it into rich and generous folds for curtains and the draping of the dressing table. The stool is a nice Regency piece upholstered *en suite*, but the other elements are more outrageous: the carpet is shaped and its pile sculpted, and on the table stand an elaborately framed

toilet glass and a pair of flanking lamps created from old silver-plated candlesticks, electrified and tricked out with shades of lace net with ribbon bows in a taste distinctly verging on the camp. Marshall, who was Director of the Decorative Furniture Department at Fortnum & Mason in London, captioned this a 'perfectly simple and moderately low-priced scheme, but the choice and arrangement are right'.

321

Period grandeur in London c.1935

321

Drawing room

The house of Mr and Mrs Anthony Sewell, Rutland Gate, decorated by Elydr Williams; from Decoration, *June 1936*

This room, designed and decorated by the popular society decorator Elydr Williams, contrives to be both a classic white-and-gold Empire scheme and at the same time a highly sophisticated statement of the cool, chic aesthetic of the 1930s. In comparison with earlier versions of the Empire revival, such as those by Lord Gerald Wellesley (pls 231, 258), there is a far greater emphasis on flat planes of pale colour and a simplification in all the details. The plain curtains, hanging in perfect flutes, echo the 'stately' white-painted columns which stand in the windows and support a fine pair of Empire vases, and there are a number of other rather good pieces all in white and gold. Colour is kept very subtle and is found mainly in the delightfully playful painted pelmet boards, in the 'pale Samarkand rugs' and in crisp chair covers in white and pale green. The client was Mrs Anthony Sewell, already at this date becoming well known as a writer under her maiden name, Mary Lutyens. She was one of the two daughters of the architect Sir Edwin Lutyens.

322

'Combined entrance hall and occasional dining room'

Design by Waring & Gillow; from Herman Schrijver, Decoration for the Home, *Leigh-on-Sea, Essex, 1939*

This exercise in the acceptable and cheerfully stylish (rather than morbidly artistic) version of the neo-baroque, carried out by Waring & Gillow in a small modern service flat, has a number of good features – although the overall effect of cramming the appurtenances of the house of a Spanish grandee into the hall of a suburban apartment is not without a note of ludicrous comedy. In the scheme's favour are the very deep cornice, unusual in a commercial piece of architecture of the time, and the rather rich and pleasing appearance of the ironwork grilles. The table is a splendidly confident piece of pastiche baroque which must have looked very funny when laden with things like a bowler hat and briefcase.

322

323

Vita Sackville-West's writing room 1930s

The Tower Room, Sissinghurst Castle, Kent

Vita Sackville-West and Harold Nicolson acquired the ruins of Sissinghurst Castle in 1930. Four separate wings were restored, Vita reserving for her own virtually private use the tower, making her sitting and writing room on the first floor. From here she said that she could 'see without being seen' while enjoying unrivalled views of her justly celebrated gardens. Vita stamped her own particular blend of Italianate grandeur and almost rustic simplicity on the whole house. Her taste was certainly influenced by that of her mother Lady Sackville, and both drew their main inspiration from the furnishings of Knole; but where Lady Sackville saw richness and colour, Vita responded to the faded charms of old fabric and the mellow comfort of faded woodwork. Her writing room is the perfect expression of this taste for the feel of a decayed Tuscan palazzo set in rural England. As elsewhere in the house, where grand but shabby painted cabinets and other pieces of furniture are flanked by the simplest bookshelves knocked together by an estate carpenter, everything is entirely unpretentious. Vita wrote sitting in a simple Morris armchair at a desk made of planks of old timber, above which hung a beautiful fragment of a garden tapestry. There is a sort of Renaissance table with three lion's-paw feet standing on a well-worn carpet, and a few notes of intense colour from pieces of glass which, like her mother, Vita loved for their decorative quality.

The National Trust; photograph A. Pressi

324

Lawrence of Arabia's retreat before 1935

Study Room, Clouds Hill, near Dorchester, Dorset

The curiously contrived house to which T.E. Lawrence retreated in 1923, after his eccentrically heroic exploits in the Arabian desert theatre of the First World War, combines elements of both the Modern movement and a traditional eccentric Englishness related to his fascination with William Morris. Until his death in 1935 Lawrence lived a reclusive life devoted to reading and writing, but with the pleasing diversion of listening to music on an immense horn gramophone, including the many records given to him by Mrs George Bernard Shaw. The house had a number of bizarre features which fully reflect the self-assured idiosyncracies of Lawrence's character and tastes. He slept on a small bed perched above a fitted chest of drawers in a room lined with metal foil which was intended to be warm in the winter months and yet remain cool during the heat of summer. In the study there was a large divan covered with a leather squab cushion the size of a double mattress, on which he would lie to read, and beside this an armchair of conventional up-to-date box form, but again covered in leather, brass-studded and fitted with sheepskin cushions in a combination that seems to suggest an RAF fighter pilot's jacket. The almost fetishistic nature of these furnishings has not gone unnoticed.

Photograph Derry Moore

324

325
Swagged curtains at Kelmarsh c.1933

Salon at Kelmarsh Hall, Northamptonshire, decorated for Mrs Ronald Tree by the Hon. Mrs Guy Bethell of Elden Ltd

This view of the sparsely and elegantly arranged salon at Kelmarsh shows the successful window treatments, carried out for Mrs Tree by Elden Ltd in the style of the very early nineteenth century. John Fowler, who later went into partnership with Mrs Tree, greatly admired the work of Mrs Bethell, already a distinguished decorator when he was starting. As John Cornforth has pointed out in *The Inspiration of the Past* (London, 1985), Fowler seems to have learnt much from the example of her work at Kelmarsh.

Country Life

326
The early Colefax & Fowler style 1938

Room set at 24 Bruton Street, London

John Fowler's style is immediately recognizable in this room set, photographed in the Bruton Street showroom shortly after he joined Sybil Colefax. The blind is made from his favourite fabric and the curtains are richly draped, with a lavish particoloured fringed swag looped around the over-scaled pole. The elegant objects and slightly idiosyncratic late eighteenth-century furniture are in a taste shared by Lady Colefax and her new protégé, but the Victorian upholstered chair seems to be more in his style alone. It has an extraordinary valance which reveals Fowler's lifelong fascination with dressmaking and millinery details; a fascination that led him to perceive the analogy between *haute couture* and decoration which has proved such a fruitful way of looking at these symbolic worlds. The arrangement of flowers is very much in the manner of Constance Spry.

Millar & Harris, London

327

326

327

The Fowler Touch   c. 1934–6

Showrooms at 292 King's Road, London

When John Fowler left Peter Jones department store, where he had been responsible for specialist paint finishes in the furnishing department, and set up his own showroom in the King's Road, his style was already maturing. Although this scheme seems clumsy in its handling when judged by what he would do only a very little while later, it already reveals a number of recognizable features of his own. The not quite perfect swagged curtains, for example, are trimmed in an unusual way with a tartan ribbon edging, a quirky touch of the kind which would always amuse him, even in later years when he could afford to use the most expensive *passementerie*. Inside the dress curtains are blinds made from a fabric with a 'Venetian blind' pattern which remained one of his firm favourites, and other bold fabrics include the very wide-striped cover of the sofa and the shiny, deep-buttoned silk on the 'Victorian' chairs.

Courtesy of Stanley Falconer Esq. and Colefax & Fowler

328

328
A clever revival   1934

The 1834 Room created by Ronald Fleming for the Ideal Home Exhibition, 1934

This re-creation of a room of one hundred years before was one of the main attractions of the Ideal Home Exhibition of 1934, and now looks interestingly prophetic about the direction in which a great deal of contemporary English decoration would turn in reaction against the rigours and austerity of the International Modern movement. As a practising commercial decorator Ronald Fleming knew the history of his craft more intimately than almost anyone. He hit very precisely the look and feeling of the, then as now, little-known and undervalued 1830s, a period during which the true Regency taste almost imperceptibly took on the traits and mannerisms of the style which we recognize as early Victorian. Fleming is historically correct in the way in which he places his late Regency furniture against a background of emphatically bordered trellis-pattern paper, but ironically his scheme bears a very strong resemblance to many houses of the first half of the nineteenth century in America, where the so-called Empire style lingered on until the 1840s.

Victoria & Albert Museum, London

329
'A weakness for Empire'   late 1930s

Dining room of the apartment of Mario Praz, Palazzo Ricci, Via Giulia, Rome; from M. Praz, The House of Life, *London, 1964*

Professor Mario Praz was the most gifted literary scholar of his day. He was the acknowledged expert in his field of seventeenth-century iconography, and his study of the darker side of eighteenth- and nineteenth-century writing, *La Carne, La Morte e Il Diavolo nella Letteratura Romantica* (1930; published in England as *The Romantic Agony*, 1933), is one of the most penetrating works of all literary criticism. Mario Praz's lifelong enthusiasm for the Empire period and its decorative arts led him to study the history of the style in all its European variants, and his gloriously discursive writings on the subject of pictures, objects and furniture and what he called, following Edgar Allan Poe, 'the Philosophy of furnishing' are the finest in their genre. His own collection, acquired mainly from Roman dealers in the years before and after the war, was fascinating. It became a place of pilgrimage for all enthusiasts of the period, and the real subject of Praz's autobiographical *The House of Life* (*La Casa della Vita*, Milan, 1958). Praz had taken the first-floor, *piano nobile* apartment in the then run-down Palazzo Ricci in the ancient Via Giulia in 1934, and there found rooms of the scale and noble proportions required as the proper setting for the magnificent pieces which his 'weakness for Empire', as he called it, led him to acquire. He made few alterations to the old rooms: an 'ordinary baroque mantelpiece' was torn out of the drawing room to allow the substitution of a fine white marble Empire chimneypiece with herms, and over a period of time a variety of colourful Roman workmen painted the doorcases in a bright *faux marbre*. In the dining room this was in yellow sienna, in contrast with the pale terracotta of the walls, with a superb curtain swag of sharp golden-yellow and violet silk, for which the materials were found at an ecclesiastical supplier's, there being no demand for good, clear Empire colours at the usual decorators' suppliers. In this view a number of important pieces are visible, including an early nineteenth-century Tuscan log box and, on the fine Regency mahogany pedestal, a version of Canova's *Laura*.

Arnoldo Mondadori Editore, Milan

329

330

330

A Regency revival library   c.1935

The house of Sir Henry Channon, 5 Belgrave Square, London

Sir Henry ('Chips') Channon, a prominent social figure between the wars, made his Belgrave Square house the greatest of his many social assets and entertained there on a lavish scale. His great friend Mrs Mann carried out decorations in the Regency revival manner in much of the house, including the large double drawing room, supplying many good period pieces of furniture. Half of this handsome room was Chips's library, for which he had bookcases designed by Lord Gerald Wellesley. Above were panels painted with 'modern' neo-classical figure groups in heightened silhouette by Michael Gibbon.

Country Life

331

332
A rococo dining room c.1935

The house of Sir Henry Channon, 5 Belgrave Square, London

Sir Henry ('Chips') Channon left a remarkably interesting political diary which, in addition to valuable insights into contemporary events, reveals among other things a great deal about his love of architecture and decoration. From it we know that, pleased as he was with the effect of this room, he was undoubtedly most proud of his celebrated rococo dining room in blue and silver, copied from a Cuvilliés room at the Amalienburg hunting lodge in Munich. This stunning creation was the work of Stéphane Boudin of the House of Jansen in Paris, who supervised the execution of the decoration not in wood, as Channon thought, but in plaster. The silver side table was a genuine piece bought by Jansen from the Hotel Parr in Vienna, but the set of chairs was made up by Boudin from one original. The dining table had a mirrored top which, of course, reflected the decoration of the room and the light of the many candles in the chandelier and wall brackets. These remarkable rooms were all destroyed by bombing during the war.

Country Life

331
A baroque conceit after 1936

Library of Sir Alfred Beit at 15 Kensington Palace Gardens, London, designed by Lord Gerald Wellesley and Trenwith Wills

This architecturally remarkable room, unique in the history of the baroque revival, was created by the architects Lord Gerald Wellesley and Trenwith Wills, who usually worked in the Regency style. They took as their starting point the picture hanging over the chimneypiece, *A Cabinet of Curiosities* by Jacques de Lajoue, which Sir Alfred Beit added to his celebrated collection in 1936. The detailing of the bookcases was taken directly from the picture, as were the colours of the marbling, which was carried out in a pretty and very Continental scheme of pink, dove grey, *verde antico* and white. As a nice conceit, the floor of the room echoes the floor in the picture.

Country Life

The new art of flower arrangement 1930s

333

Illustration from Constance Spry, *Flower Decoration* London, 1934

334

Constance Spry's own bedroom 1936

The arrangement of flowers in the house and on the dining table was by tradition a polite accomplishment of the lady of the house, aided by the more or less artistic efforts of her staff. In the latter part of the nineteenth century in smart society almost the only flowers thought

333

334

suitable for grand occasions were hothouse blooms, while greenery in the form of palms heightened the exotic effect. Queen Alexandra, when still Princess of Wales, did much to make more ordinary flowers popular and favoured generous arrays of garden flowers, which she enlivened with huge boughs of 'common' beech, in the drawing room at Marlborough House. It was Constance Spry, however, who revitalized the art of arranging flowers by seeking inspiration in the flower paintings of the past. Taking as her starting point the works of the Dutch seventeenth-century masters of the genre, she gradually incorporated all kinds of other ideas until she had forged an entirely new aesthetic of arrangement, based on making both flowers and container integral parts of the composition. Her own rooms revealed a serious interest in modish decoration, and her style of decoration very quickly became established as the only chic way in which to decorate with flowers. Indeed it formed the basis of the art virtually to this day. The group in this illustration from her book *Flower Decoration*, is based very closely on a well-known flower piece by Caravaggio.

333 *Courtesy of Constance Spry and the Cordon Bleu Group, London*
334 *Millar & Harris, London*

335
New York chic late 1930s

A view in Ruby Ross Wood's New York office

This unusual photograph reveals a typical glimpse of the highly chic New York decoration scene of the immediate pre-war period. Having begun her association with the profession in its emergent days, working as Elsie de Wolfe's ghostwriter for *The House in Good Taste*, Ruby Ross Wood had herself become something of a doyenne of the world of society decoration. Her taste was greatly influenced by her mentor, and she in turn played no small part in forming the ideas and style of her most celebrated protégé, Billy Baldwin. Baldwin joined Miss Wood in 1935 and rapidly established his position as one of the great exponents of High Style. He is seen here in the reflection of a rather curious ceramic-framed looking-glass in her New York office, engaged in conversation with the influential *Harpers'* journalist Louise Macy.

Louise Dahl-Wolfe, courtesy of the Staley-Wise Gallery, New York

335

336

Couturier's Vogue Regency c.1935

Hall of Norman Hartnell's house, Lovel Dene, near Windsor, Berkshire; decorations by Norris Wakefield

The house which Hartnell created, and which he ensured received more than the usual publicity accorded to a country weekend retreat, was undoubtedly part of his self-consciously created image. The schemes were realized in an extravagant Vogue Regency manner by Norris Wakefield, who was the junior partner in Mrs Mann's firm, and who had already worked with Hartnell in the creation of his great salon in 1934 (pl. 361). At Lovel Dene, Hartnell used yet more crystal chandeliers and wall lights which, to the delight of the popular press, he burned with conspicuous extravagance throughout the day. The furnishings at Lovel Dene included some good Regency pieces supplied by Mrs Mann, the doyenne of the style, and there were rich silks and velvets and a great deal of gilding and coloured glass. Writing in *Decoration* for 1936, Ronald Fletcher enthused: 'Lovel Dene is the last word in reconstruction among the smaller houses in the English country. Its decoration is lustrous and colourful, in complete contrast to the all-white, matt-surfaced affectation popular in recent years ... conducive to monotony and dreariness.' Certainly there was nothing dreary about a house which included a hallway in turquoise blue and silver, with Regency chairs upholstered in velvet stamped with silver stars and a Venetian looking-glass hanging above a glass table, leading into a drawing room in lilac-mauve with Vaseline-yellow and leopard-skin carpets, ivory and gilt furniture and Venetian carved and gilded blackamoors. Swan motifs abounded throughout the house, and boldly swagged draperies in striped silks gave the rooms an entirely theatrical Regency flavour – which only became popular and more widely imitated after the war.

Millar & Harris, London

336

337

Couturier's baroque   c.1936

Living room of his own house, Bruton Street, London, designed by Victor Stiebel

In the 1930s the couturier Victor Stiebel was established in fashionable Bruton Street, only a few doors along from his great rival Norman Hartnell. Indeed, Hartnell confessed in his autobiography of these years, *Silver and Gold* (London, 1950), that it was not without a tinge of jealousy and with an eye to outshining Stiebel and Edward Molyneux that he determined to take on the larger and grander premises that became the famous Hartnell salon (pl. 361). Stiebel had at about this time decorated his own salon and the rooms in which he lived and entertained, but in comparison with the chic and stylish effects of Hartnell's establishment they look somewhat tawdry and slightly makeshift. There is a definite attempt to pick up some of the ideas popular among those who had seen and admired the creations of Cecil Beaton at Ashcombe or Stephen Tennant at Wilsford, but by comparison with those self-assured statements of the neo-baroque taste a room such as this looks hesitant and a little pretentious.

Millar & Harris, London

337

338

A baroque architect's house and office 1930

Studio, Romney House, Hampstead, London, converted for his own use by Clough Williams-Ellis

If Clough Williams-Ellis's house in the 1920s (pls 243–5) showed a certain tendency toward the love of baroque objects, his architectural taste at that date led him to deploy them within a more conventional neo-Regency context. His home for most of the 1930s, converted about 1929–30 from the idiosyncratic remains of a building beside Hampstead Heath that had once been the painter Romney's studio, allowed him ample scope to display a new-found mastery of baroque detail and organization of space. Within the dilapidated building Clough carved out grand, double-height and galleried spaces and formed an impressive enfilade leading from the entrance hall through a living area and culminating in what must have been the most spectacular architect's drawing office since John Nash built his Regent Street library and gallery. This room, called the Studio, had a giant order of pilasters, full-height windows on one side and on the other a row of oculi. The floor was 'paved' with huge squares of light and dark maple plywood, the walls had a gloss finish, and high in the centre of this vast space hung a grand eighteenth-century English baroque giltwood chandelier of twelve branches. The architect's desk faced into the room from one end where, behind his gilt chair, was a spectacular Italian baroque doorcase flanked by a pair of enormous hanging lanterns of lemon silk and gilding in a modernistic Venetian style. The impression on visitors and clients must have been that of being ushered into the presence chamber of a grandee of some ancient empire or, as Hugh Casson wrote in *Decoration* (June, 1935), 'the reception gallery of an eighteenth-century prelate'. Not only was the scale immense, but there were also staggering effects of colour: against the cream and parchment of the walls and ceiling the eight pilasters were sienna marble, their capitals gilded and their bases green to match the skirtings and doorcases. The windows were painted in scarlet and magenta and framed by blue-green curtains echoing the colour of the cornice.

Architectural Press, London

339
Neo-baroque in a modern shell 1938

The Great Hall at Charters, Berkshire, home of Mr and Mrs Frank Parkinson; architects George Adie and Frederick Button, interior design by George Webster Ltd

Charters was something of a rarity, a large-scale and really very grand country house new-built and in the modern style. Frank Parkinson, a self-made electric motor manufacturer, commissioned the architects Adie, Button & Partners to create for him a house of beautiful materials, conceived on thoroughly rational principles and equipped throughout with all the latest in domestic technology. The result was a house needing ten servants and built of modular facing blocks of Portland stone with window openings containing bronze panes designed on the same grid. It represented the *dernier cri* in house building on this scale and cost the patrons the then staggering sum of £140,000. Mrs Parkinson, it seems, did not care for the modern style and declared that she would have her way in the decoration of all the interiors. At this point the architects washed their hands of the project, leaving Geoffrey Webster to work with the mistress on some extraordinary neo-baroque schemes. In the Great Hall, a vast near-cube room of 35 × 32ft, and 32ft 10ins high (10.7 × 9.8m, and 10m high), furnished with reproduction baroque furniture, Martin Battersby carried out a vast programme of murals and designed a splendid chimney-

piece in black and white marble. All this has been swept away, but from surviving photographs it is clear that the painting was rather mannered, in the general style of Rex Whistler but influenced too by J.M. Sert, that it contained allusions to the Parkinsons' interest in gardens and that it included their initial borne aloft in a cartouche. Elsewhere in the house were a very conventional library-drawing room and an altogether much more interesting bathroom in extravagantly striped marble. Adie hated what became of his design, and would perhaps have been most at home in the immaculately planned boiler room.

Country Life

339

Decorative schemes by Rex Whistler c. 1930–44

Following the great success of his first cycle of murals *The Pursuit of Rare Meats*, 1924–5, in the restaurant of the Tate Gallery in London, Rex Whistler was almost constantly engaged in painting large-scale decorative schemes for society patrons until his untimely death in 1944. The sheer visual delight of these schemes is seldom well represented by photographs, for, in addition to the rich fantasy of his conceptions, Whistler also possessed a grasp of the practicalities of painting successful architectural *trompe-l'oeil* equal to that of the best masters of the past, and probably unchallenged to this day.

340

'The Painted Room'

Port Lympne, Kent, the seat of Sir Philip Sassoon, 1930–2

Port Lympne, a house rich in exotic and fantastical touches, was built for Sir Philip Sassoon by the talented and underrated architect Philip Tilden, who also designed much of the classically inspired furniture. Earlier schemes of decorative painting had been carried out in the dining room by Glyn Philpot and in the drawing room by J.M. Sert (pl. 236), but both were entirely outshone by the beautifully resolved treatment of walls and *trompe-l'oeil* tenting in Whistler's hall. The tassels are real.

Country Life

341

Gothick drawing room

Mottisfont Abbey, Hampshire, painted for Mrs Gilbert Russell, 1938–9

The Gothick Room at Mottisfont, commissioned by Mrs Gilbert Russell, wife of the celebrated theatrical producer, is a *tour de force* of painting in imitation stucco decoration. The work was carried out by Whistler with the assistance of two theatre scenery painters, and was the last major scheme which he completed before enlisting in the Welsh Guards at the outbreak of war. The handling of the deep cove to the ceiling is one of the most telling elements of the design, but there are many other delights in the room, including a brilliant piece of *trompe l'oeil* marbling on the chimneypiece and splendidly theatrical cut-out swags to the curtains, painted to imitate ermine-trimmed velvet and resembling vast peer's robes draped at the windows: a characteristically Whistlerian note of visual irony.

Country Life

342

His last room

Decorative painting in a room at 39 Preston Park Avenue, Brighton, 1944

In the days spent waiting in Brighton to embark for France, Rex Whistler diverted himself and his brother officers in the Welsh Guards Tank Regiment enhancing a

341

room in the house where they found themselves billeted with a scheme imitating Chinese wallpaper. On one wall he painted the now well-known comic scene *Allegory. HRH The Prince Regent awakening the Spirit of Brighton*, which shows the Regent as a grotesque and leering cherub with wings and the sash of the Garter uncovering the sleeping form of a sylph-like personification of the once-innocent village. Above the chimneypiece was this more elegant portrayal of George IV in profile silhouette surrounded by a crowned wreath. When the house was demolished after the war the large panel and this smaller oval section were preserved.

Private collection

342

343

Detail of mural decoration in the dining room

Painted by Rex Whistler for the Marquess of Anglesey, 1936–8, at Plas Newydd, Anglesey

John Cornforth, in *The Inspiration of the Past* (1985), has rightly described the great dining room scheme carried out by Whistler for the Marquess of Anglesey as one of the most perfect statements of that romantic feeling for architecture by the group of aristocratic patrons, writers and artists who did so much in the inter-war years to form the taste for grandeur and pleasing decay that is still a potent element in attitudes to country houses and conservation. This attitude has done much to inspire the tremendous nostalgia that is still felt for the architecture and decorative styles of the past expressed, for example, in the curious mania for country-style kitchens in cities and the desire to have Edwardian plumbing in bathrooms of the 1980s. Whistler's work at Plas Newydd is perhaps his most perfectly realized scheme, and in many ways represents a summation of his aesthetic ideas. The painting reflects all the many influences which formed his style, including the work of Canaletto and the *vedutisti* of Venice, English Palladian and Roman baroque architecture, and the romantic landscapes of Claude, Vernet and Salvator Rosa. This detail from a corner of the room shows a cleverly contrived arcade which seems to open through an archway in the end wall, and in which the tiny figure of a man sweeping is a self-portrait.

The National Trust; photograph John Bethell

344

A Neptune carpet   c.1932

Design for the carpet of the dining room of Edward James's house in Wimpole Street, London; oil on canvas by Rex Whistler

344

The principal feature of the grand dining room at Wimpole Street was an enormous carpet designed for the room by Rex Whistler and woven in the Axminster carpet works. Whistler conceived the carpet rather in the manner of a baroque tapestry laid on the floor, and all the other elements of the room were co-ordinated in colour and remained subservient to it. The dominant sea-green colour, with contrasting touches of coral, was echoed by a magnificent set of chairs in painted wood which were supplied by Mrs Mann, whose firm had a particular reputation for both original and reproduction pieces of Regency painted furniture. The central group of the design represents Neptune drawn in a shell-chariot by seahorses and attended by figures, one of whom supports a cartouche upon which appear Edward James's initials.

The Edward James Foundation, West Dean; photograph courtesy of Christie's, London

345

345

The Modern movement decorated c.1933–6

The 'movie room' in Charles de Beistegui's apartment on the Champs-Elysées, Paris; reproduced from Architectural Review, *April 1936*

At the beginning of the 1930s, fired with enthusiasm for all that was most avant-garde in art and architecture, the Mexican millionaire collector Charles de Beistegui asked Le Corbusier to design an apartment for him in Paris. 'Il faut rompre avec les habitudes,' he proclaimed; but, though initially delighted with the results, within only a year or so Beistegui was calling this 'machine for living in' an 'uninhabitable machine'. He then set about decorating the cool, clear spaces in the most incongruous manner imaginable. With the help of the Spanish dilettante and accomplished architect Emilio Terry, the walls of some rooms were quilted and walls and curtains trimmed with braid in elaborate Second Empire designs. Extravagantly baroque pieces of furniture were dotted about the apartment and a large number of gilt-framed panels of mirror

with candle sconces were introduced, complementing the vast chandeliers of which Beistegui was always inordinately fond. Le Corbusier's startlingly stylish spiral stair with a central glass newel post led from the movie room to an equally extraordinary roof terrace. This staircase alone of all the architect's original features retained the power to compete visually with the riot of glass and gilding, white and gold rock-work and life-size, ostrich-plumed Venetian figures with which it eventually became surrounded.

Architectural Press, London

346

Theatrical splendour, London 1937

Drawing room in the house of Lady Jean Bertie, Upper Belgrave Street, London, decorated by Felix Harbord; from Decoration, *May 1937*

Felix Harbord's remarkable mastery of the theatrical grand manner is seen to great advantage in the Belgravia drawing room which he contrived for Lady Jean Bertie, using Venetian blackamoor figures as uplighters and ornate gilt furniture to create an early version of the 'old palazzo style'. The Venetian theme was taken from two painted panels by Veronese, the colours of which were echoed in the red of the upholstery, in the red, peach and golden brown of the fine Savonnerie carpet, and in the pearl-coloured curtains. The central element of the room was a bizarre pair of chandeliers designed by Harbord as a bold statement to set the character of the other decorations. Carried out in white-painted carved wood, they incorporated baroque shells and rockwork from which 'dripped' crystal glass. Schemes like this, according to *Decoration*, showed Harbord's desire to get away from the average 'dull London interiors and exteriors'. It was his belief they reported, 'that London is shouting for a certain gaiety, which will be more than welcome after the drabness in which many are forced to live. Something more subtle and cultured must be achieved to do away with the present tendency towards insipid decoration.' Felix Harbord continued to work in this theatrical manner, influenced no doubt by his close friends Cecil Beaton and Oliver Messel. These three shared a fondness for the extravagant and amusing in decoration, which in Harbord's case was underpinned by a sound practical knowledge of the technical aspects of decoration, such as plasterwork and paint finishes.

346

ingly filled with the richly exotic objects and interesting pictures which took her fancy. By the second half of the decade a fashionably baroque feel was the most pronounced element in a mix which included shell grotto furniture, blackamoors and carved Indian pieces alongside the cooler, simplified sofas of Jean-Michel Frank. The arrangements photographed here in about 1938 were by Louis Süe, one of the major figures of French decoration since the days of the 1925 Paris Exposition, and reveal a group of highly decorative and theatrical objects. The similarity to rooms of other, earlier, leaders of taste, such as the Sitwells, is underlined by other surviving photographs of this room. In these there appears on the wall one of the giant heads by the painter Pavel Tchelitchew, who was a firm favourite with the triumvirate in England and an important figure in that section of Parisian artistic society that centred on the Cocteau-Bérard circle.

Philippe and Lucilla Garner

347

Neo-baroque, Paris c.1938

Drawing room in the house of Helena Rubinstein, Paris; decorations by Louis Süe

Helena Rubinstein spent much of her time in the company of the avant-garde painters of Paris, of whom she proved a generous and imaginative patron. She commissioned her portrait from more promising and already successful painters than perhaps any other sitter of recent times, and seems to have been highly receptive to current ideas not just about painting and fashion, but also about interior decoration. Her own house became increas-

347

348

Haut décor late 1930s

Library of Charles de Beistegui at Groussay, near Paris;
architect Emilio Terry; photograph by Cecil Beaton

Cecil Beaton's photograph, taken during the early years of the war, reveals the immensely grand spatial effect of the double-height library in one of the symmetrical pavilions which were added to the Directoire-period château of Groussay by Charles de Beistegui and his architect friend Emilio Terry. The second pavilion housed a private theatre, and was only one of the many extravagant caprices carried out by the millionaire collector with his eye for richness of form, splendour of colour and, especially, baroque magnificence of scale. The Beistegui style has had an immense influence on grand traditional decoration; his arrangements of predominantly neo-classical objects in a theatrically baroque manner inspired decorators such as Geoffrey Bennison and are still widely imitated. In the Groussay library Beistegui placed some of his most splendid pieces. A fine inlaid marble table on griffin supports stood upon the Charles x Aubusson, while the top of every cabinet and each window sill was graced by an antique bust or an over-scaled vase. Against the brilliant red of the walls gilt-framed Regency mirrors and oil paintings hung in ranks right up to the full height of the vast room. At this date the pictures were a mixture of interesting original works, some old, some more recent, and of every quality. Towards the end of his life the great collector became obsessed with the desire to replace his own more interesting collection with copies of his favourites among the more famous works in the major galleries of Europe. Fortunately this aberration had little effect on the overall appearance of the magnificent rooms that he had laid out in the late 1930s and the years after the war.

Cecil Beaton Photograph; Courtesy of Sotheby's, London

349, 350

The beauty of materials and beauty adorned c.1929 and c.1938

Salon of the de Noailles house, the Hôtel Bischoffsheim, Paris; decoration by Jean-Michel Frank

349

350

As the friends and patrons of painters and musicians, the Vicomte and Vicomtesse de Noailles held artistic court in a wholly eighteenth-century manner. Marie-Laure de Noailles especially, herself an interesting painter as well as a passionate collector, extended this enlightened patronage to the brilliant circle of the Parisian avant-garde, centred around the writer and film-maker Jean Cocteau and Christian Bérard, painter and designer of strange sets and costumes, and to the Surrealists. In its starkly modernistic and asymmetrical form the de Noailles' country house at Hyères, designed by Robert Mallet-Stevens, had the appearance of a suburban light-industrial property rather than that of the home of a latter-day Maecenas. In Paris, however, they lived in a fine eighteenth-century house, the Hôtel Bischoffsheim, inherited by Marie-Laure from her grandfather. Some of the interiors were eighteenth-century with *boiseries*, but for others Jean-Michel Frank designed and executed schemes of extreme elegance and cool simplicity, lavish only in the use of unusual and precious materials. The drawing room or principal salon, *c.* 1929, had walls covered in squares of fine vellum, and the doors were of bronze with ivory details. The furniture included such remarkable pieces as a cabinet in shagreen (sharkskin), while most of the chairs and sofas were covered in white leather, complemented by long, low tables in shagreen and lacquer. When first installed the uncluttered beauty of this room was the *dernier cri* in style and chic; but, just as Charles de Beistegui quickly decorated and adorned his empty space by Le Corbusier (pl. 345), so the de Noailles before long began to add pictures and objects from their ever-growing collection to the salon. Frank's walls then became the splendid and sympathetic backdrop for major Surrealist pictures hanging from heavy gold chains, fine early bronzes and an array of other quirkily baroque things, such as the painted chimneyboard figure visible to the right of the chimneypiece. In Beaton's photograph of about 1938 the de Noailles are seen seated to the left of the chimneypiece.

349 *From D. Todd and R. Mortimer,* The New Interior Decoration, *London, 1929*
350 *Cecil Beaton Photograph; Courtesy of Sotheby's*

351

A Surreal office   1930s

Private office of Jean-Michel Frank, Paris,

Jean-Michel Frank was one of the most highly regarded designers of interiors and furnishings working in Paris. Influenced by the style of French furniture popularized by the 1925 Exposition des Arts Décoratifs, he gradually moved towards a greater simplification of forms whilst retaining an obsessive interest in the use of unusual fine materials, including rare woods and veneers, parchment, lacquer and often bronze or ivory for details. The more fantastic (or surreal) elements in his work seem to reflect the influence of his friendship with the architect Emilio Terry and the circle of the de Noailles. An informal view taken in the private office of Frank's shop reveals the various elements which blended to form his unique and glamorous style. The room is panelled in a mad and exaggerated version of the Louis XVI manner, with vertiginously elongated panels picked out in dark against light wood and taken, characteristically, right up to the full height of the space. The lighting is from a classic Frank fitment of white plaster in the form of a human hand supporting an uplighter bowl, which thus combines an up-to-the-minute idea of illumination with a reference to the sort of French

baroque hand or arm sconces so much admired by the Parisian neo-Romantics, Jean Cocteau and Christian Bérard. A Louis XV period library chair stands beside the desk, which seems to occupy a large part of the small room and has upon it both a chic desk set in chrome and an old dinner plate full of cigarette ends. There is one further interesting object, part practical *aide-mémoire* and part delightful surrealistic joke: a hugely over-scaled child's slate with chalk and rubbing-out sponge both attached by a string. It bears a message written by Jean-Michel Frank reminding himself to 'send the umbrella stand to Lady Mendl [Elsie de Wolfe] by Friday at the latest'.

Courtesy of Editions du Regard, Paris

352

English Surrealism   1936

'A corner of a room in Fitzroy Square', arranged by Paul Nash; from Decoration, *June 1936*

In the year in which the Surrealists and the English adherents of the group first showed their work in London, Paul Nash attempted a definition of the ideals of the movement in terms of the decoration and arrangement of objects in rooms (Paul Nash, 'Surrealism in Interior Decoration', *Decoration*, June 1936). He pointed out that the self-professed irrational quality prized by the Surealists, in their lives as well as their work, was almost a contradiction of any established principles of decoration, and in particular he warned that 'once the introduction into the house of what the French describe as *objets trouvés* has begun anything may happen – all the ornaments and bric-à-brac of the Victorian past were never such a threat to man's sanity as *les objets trouvés*'. To illustrate his theme Nash styled a room setting, described as being in the avant-garde location of Fitzroy Square, in which were grouped several interesting English Surrealist pieces. The sheepskin sofa and its cushions were by the rising decorator Duncan Miller, who had just opened a new and by all accounts grand showroom in Lower Grosvenor Place. Next to the sofa stood a small table by the furniture designer Denham Maclaren, with a motif supposed to represent deep fingerprints pressed into the pedestal. A 'vase' by Rupert Lee containing a 'flame of fur' graced the window sill, and, above the rather conventional 1930s bookshelves, the effect was completed with a picture by Edward Burra.

352

353

354

A Surrealist chamber of horrors 1940s

M. Romi with his collection, Paris; photograph from
The Bedside Lilliput, *London, 1950*

A number of the Surrealists and their allies and admirers collected bizarre objects and several, such as Marie-Laure de Noailles, had already begun to discover the eccentric delights of Victoriana and its French equivalent, the kitsch taste of the Second Empire. Here a dedicated collector of such trifles, M. Romi, is seen seated in a classic antler chair surrounded by some of his treasures. 'M. Romi, of Paris, overlooked by a slimly corseted caribou wearing a mantilla, and guarded by an iron snail on wheels, reads a fur-backed novel in his chamber of Victorian horrors....' ran the anonymous *Lilliput* writer's description of this photograph published in 1950. 'He has been gathering such oddments for fifteen years', we are told, which puts this amiable eccentric collector in the very forefront of such 'advanced' taste. The caribou in the mantilla is very similar to the antelope dressed up and placed in his King's Road, Chelsea, shop window by the antique dealer and decorator Roy Alderson to celebrate the coronation of Elizabeth II in 1953. This sort of lightheartedness became a recognizable element of European post-war taste, and is particularly noticeable in the deliberate emphasis on frivolity in the conception and design of the Festival of Britain in 1951.

353

Surrealist interior late 1930s

Drawing by Philippe Jullian from Les Styles, *Paris, 1962*

Philippe Jullian's delightful drawing affectionately parodies the eclectic interiors filled with bizarre objects gathered by the friends and patrons of the Surrealists. Prominent are a 'Mae West's Lips' sofa, which for many was the quintessential Surrealist piece of furniture, and an elaborately framed Dali picture; but the room also includes a number of other highly individual pieces which hint more specifically at the taste of the Vicomtesse Marie-Laure de Noailles, whose collection embraced both modern works of art and eccentric bric-à-brac of the Victorian era.

*Courtesy of Comte Ghislaine de Diesbach and
Editions Plon, Paris*

354

355

356
A Surrealist stair carpet c.1932

Stair carpet leading to Miss Losch's bathroom at Monkton, West Dean, Sussex, designed by Norris Wakefield

At West Dean Tilly Losch's bathroom was approached by a stair and corridor carpeted with a specially woven design resembling her delicate wet footprints. This charmingly surreal conceit was realized for James, as were many of his other whims, by Norris Wakefield, the junior partner in the decorating firm of Mrs Mann. He repeated the idea for James in other parts of Monkton but using the footprints of his patron's dog, which had proved more faithful than his all too fascinating wife. In later years Norris Wakefield observed that in both cases the footprints ought to have been confined to the treads of the stairs, while the risers should have been left plain, but this extra sophistication had not occurred to him at the time of sending the design to the carpet weavers.

Country Life

355
Edward James's bathroom c.1932

Design for the decoration; watercolour by Geoffrey Houghton-Brown

At the time of the construction of Paul Nash's glass bathroom (pl. 359) for his newly acquired wife, Edward James was also planning to have a new scheme of decoration for his own bathroom at Wimpole Street. This time he chose the talented young mural painter Geoffrey Houghton-Brown, who was then still enjoying some measure of popular acclaim for his stylish and inventive wall paintings in the fashionable London restaurant, The Blue Train. For James, Geoffrey Houghton-Brown created the idea of a bathroom with decorations based on the *trompe-l'oeil* architectural murals of Pompeii. The bold designs also have a distinctly modernistic feel, and the visual conundrums of the architectural elements would have appealed to his patron's love of the irrational in the arts.

Michael Parkin Fine Art Ltd, London

356

357

The 'Mae West's Lips' sofa   c.1936

Sofa designed by Salvador Dali and made by Green &
Abbott of 123 Wigmore Street, London; from the
collection of Edward James

Dali's original idea for a sofa in the shape of Mae West's
lips is to be found in his painting *Mae West* of 1934
(Art Institute of Chicago) and a closely related drawing
bearing the title *The Birth of the Paranoiac Furniture*,
1934–5, bought at this time by Edward James, who was a
friend and admirer of the artist. Dali wrote describing his
patron as a 'humming-bird poet [who] ordered aphrodisiac
lobster telephones, bought the best Dalis and was naturally
the richest [of all the artist's friends]'. Several versions of
the sofa were realized: in Paris by Jean-Michel Frank, who
made a pair for Elsa Schiaparelli (though she never took
delivery of them), and in London by John Hill's firm Green
& Abbott, whose premises in Wigmore Street were close to
Edward James's town house in Wimpole Street. Dali
seemed to have specified originally that these sofas were to
be covered all over in shocking pink satin, but the Green &
Abbott version for James was carried out in two tones of
pink felt. A final variant of the idea was included in a set of
designs begun by Dali in 1936 for a Marx Brothers film, but
sadly this project came to nothing.

Brighton Museum and Art Gallery

357

358

358

An English Surrealist's study   1939

Edward James in his study, 35 Wimpole Street;
photographed by Norman Parkinson

Edward James installed much of his curious collection in
the grand town house in Wimpole Street to which he
took Tilly Losch as his bride. In his study a number of
precious marble columns with gilt capitals stood about the
room, enveloped in the baroque folds of a theatrically-
billowing tent. James is seen with his friend Igor Markevitch (lounging with violin), seated at his splendid neo-
classical desk decorated with *verre églomisé*. On the desk
stands a pair of fine ormolu candelabra supported by putti,
and on the floor are strewn copies of the books of poetry
which James published privately from time to time. The
room is dominated, however, by a major work by Picasso.

Courtesy of Christie's, London

359

359
Tilly Losch's bathroom 1932

Bathroom in the house of Edward James, 35 Wimpole Street, London, designed by Paul Nash

The eccentric millionaire poet and patron of the arts Edward James had a kind of creative genius for commissioning work and bringing out the best in artists and craftsmen. On his marriage to the exquisite but difficult Viennese dancer and actress, Tilly Losch, soon to bring him so much pain, James carried out a number of interesting alterations and new decorative schemes in his Wimpole Street house. Paul Nash, whose very English brand of Surrealism went hand in hand with a serious concern for the design of both books and interiors, designed for Tilly's use what rapidly became the most celebrated bathroom of the century. The walls were made from $\frac{1}{4}$ in (6 mm) thick stippled cathedral glass, 'silvered' with a metallic alloy to produce a deep and lustrous mulberry colour, interspersed with panels of peach-tinted mirror glass. The rough surface of the stippled glass did not become disfigured by condensation. On the ceiling was a tilted mirror, and in addition to the sleek fittings in chrome there was also a dance practice barre in the form of a chromed ladder. Lighting was by shaped fluorescent tubes which formed an integral part of the design, and heat was provided by a neatly fitted electric fire.

Architectural Press, London

360
A mirror-glass bathroom 1930–2

Bathroom at Gayfere House, Lord North Street, the London home of Lady Mount Temple, designed by Oliver Hill

Oliver Hill is an unjustly neglected figure whose work in the 1930s combined traditional elements with a feeling for an unaggressive and, many felt, very 'English' Modernism. In a stylish bathroom second only to Tilly Losch's in celebrity, Oliver Hill played on the new 'architectural' potential of glass, using bevelled mirrors to create walls, decorative panels and door architraves in a manner similar to the interior of the Hartnell salon by Gerald Lacoste and Norris Wakefield. Here, as in others of his projects, Hill shows great subtlety in his perfect detailing. He fits the functional elements such as the taps

effortlessly into the unbroken lines of his scheme, and relieves the effect of endlessly reflected vistas with areas of other materials, such as mosaic, which forms the lining of the bath. Such bathrooms as this and Miss Losch's were widely held to be the very epitome of chic right through until the 1960s, when gradually it became smarter to hint at the rich glories of the Edwardian period of plumbing.

Country Life

360

361

An English 'maison de couture' 1934

Norman Hartnell's salon, 26 Bruton Street, London; architect Gerald Lacoste, decoration by Norris Wakefield of Mrs Mann; from Architects' Journal, *1935*

Because of the close connection between fashions in dress and decoration, since the nineteenth century couture houses have always influenced domestic interiors. The Hartnell salon is a fascinating case, for not only was it an important piece of new architecture, but it was also an important project for the decorative firm of Mrs Mann. When Hartnell was setting out on his career as an English couturier all the smartest establishments, such as Lucile's, were decorated in the 'Old French look' in order to suggest a satisfactory connection with the centre of the world of fashion. By 1934 Hartnell had found the funds and the courage to move from his first tiny premises, which had not had a 'look', across Bruton Street to no. 26, a handsome eighteenth-century house built originally for the Marquesses of Hereford. The premises were ideal, for the *piano nobile* retained one very grand room suitable for a salon, while at the rear were modern workshops. Hartnell knew the look he required, just as he knew his clientele. It had to be stylish. It had to hint at tradition, and specifically Parisian tradition, and it had to imply utter modernity and elegance. Gerald Lacoste carried out the structural work, creating a grand staircase and contriving a theatrical proscenium for the main salon. The elaborate glass and mirror panelling, which included the facing of pillars, was executed by the firm of Pugh Brothers. For the decorative schemes Hartnell used the young partner of the Regency revival decorator Mrs Harrington (Dolly) Mann, Norris Wakefield, who had already been involved in the exacting work of realizing the whims and fantasies of Edward James. Together Hartnell and Wakefield came up with the famous one-colour scheme in 'Hartnell green', and acres of plain carpet and velvets for curtains were dyed to the precise shade chosen from a sliver of fabric from the salon matching room. The decorative effect was completed by the crystal that became a hallmark of Hartnell chic. Twelve Regency or reproduction chandeliers hung in the salon and on the stairs, lit night and day. On the opening night, as a *coup de théâtre*, the whole evening show was given by candlelight, but from day to day the image was unchanging. There were always white flowers arranged on low tables in

361

the stylish and novel ways of Miss Constance Spry, and always the effect of the endless mirror glass and the Hartnell green: as Norris Wakefield put it, 'right this year, next year and the next'.

Architectural Press, London

362

362
The all-white room   c.1929–30

Drawing room by Syrie Maugham for her own house in the King's Road, London; from Derek Patmore, Colour Schemes for the Modern Home, *London, 1933*

Syrie's all-white room is beyond doubt one of the two or three most famous and influential schemes of decoration of the century. Celebrated in its own day as a daring statement of a bold new aesthetic, it has been imitated for over fifty years. By the late 1920s the craze for stripping or 'pickling' furniture and the new light palette of colours were becoming widespread, and Syrie Maugham and Elsie de Wolfe were both playing with similar white-on-white ideas for rooms, a notion paralleled in the stage designs of Oliver Messel. Syrie's most successful essay in the look creates a feeling of distinctly modern chic, as much by the use of long, low sofas and tables as by the absence of colour, and in fact there are almost no antique objects or furniture other than a few French chairs. One of the best analyses of

the elements which contribute to the room's success was made by the decorator and writer Derek Patmore, who was a great devotee of the Syrie style. He wrote in *Colour Schemes for the Modern Home*:

> The walls and ceiling are painted dead white; the long settee and the chairs are upholstered in beige satin and the huge rug is in two tones of cream, specially designed for Mrs Maugham by Marion Dorn. Behind the settee is a tall folding screen of narrow panels of mirror glass, set

363

in chromium frames. The low screen which disposes so neatly of the piano is of white lacquer. It will be seen from this scheme that the whole effect has been obtained by the use of the various tones of white. Such a scheme is practical and need not be expensive.

Needless to say, Mrs Maugham thought that the look should be expensive.

363
The all-white room as the quintessence of chic c.1933

Photograph by Cecil Beaton of his sister Nancy in Syrie Maugham's drawing room

Always among the very first to catch a trend, Cecil Beaton here uses Syrie's all-white room as the setting for one of his high-fashion images of his sister Nancy. Boldly placing his model against the astonishing multi-faceted mirror-glass screen, Beaton uses the room itself as much as the dress to create the required statement of chic and modernity, and thereby brings out the sharp and glittering character of the decorative scheme, not always apparent in other views.

Cecil Beaton Photograph; Courtesy of Sotheby's, London

364
A baroque effect 1936

Dining room of the house of Mrs Paravicini, 15 Wilton Street, London, decorated by Syrie Maugham

Syrie's dining room created for her daughter, Mrs Paravicini, was one of the most stylish and successful rooms in her neo-baroque manner. In a house with finely proportioned rooms and some good period detail she chose to play up the drama of the architectural spaces. Rather than elaborate unnecessarily she introduced a few richly sculptural elements, such as the carved chimneypiece and brackets for her daughter's collection of ceramic equestrian figures, and played these elements off against completely plain wall surfaces. The generous forms of the chairs work all the better in this context for being finished in white, and the whole room has a feel of crisp modernity at the same time as suggesting the *Stimmung* of Middle European baroque. This photograph is one of the most interesting shots of any interior of the whole period, for it is without

doubt one of the most conscious attempts to create a visual image in keeping with the style of the room, having been taken using obviously artificial light sources, so placed as to heighten the theatrical effect of the decor. It illustrates the way in which the photography of interiors would progress, from the simple recording of the appearance of rooms to the point where, published in books or magazines, they begin to be an influential factor in the development of taste and fashion in decoration.

Millar & Harris, London

364

365
Cecil Beaton's idyll c.1930

Drawing room at Ashcombe, Wiltshire, 1932

Cecil Beaton wrote lovingly in *Ashcombe: The Story of a Fifteen-Year Lease* (London, 1949) of how he first came upon the magically secluded house in a Wiltshire valley near the home of his friend Edith Olivier. He describes how he brought order to the neglected garden and surrounding land and began to alter and decorate the house with great imagination, if somewhat limited funds. The house was initially old and quite plain. Rex Whistler helped with the designs for new windows and a splendid baroque doorcase, but photographs clearly show that inside the rooms had simple detailing and rough-plastered walls distempered in light plain colours. The interiors that Beaton created were extraordinary, especially for a house in the country. Nearly all the furniture, other than a few quirky pieces new-made for the house, was wildly baroque in feel. Undoubtedly the influence of the Sitwell's Italianate taste was strongest at this time, but there is already another and more personal element discernible here: Beaton's lifelong love of the Second Empire period in French decoration and taste. Thus, alongside the more Curzon Street baroque elements, such as elaborate candle sconces, we can see huge gilt sofas, capacious *fauteuils* and side tables in the most writhingly outrageous neo-rococo style. All this impossibly grand furniture stood on simple tiled floors, and the enormous arrangements of flowers which stood on every available surface and even in huge vases on the floor only served to increase the feeling that the drawing room was just the winter garden of some decayed French château.

Courtesy of Sotheby's, London

365

Fantasy in the country mid-1930s

Wilsford Manor, near Amesbury, Wiltshire, decorated for the Hon. Stephen Tennant by Syrie Maugham

366

The study

367

Drawing room

366

Wilsford was originally a traditional stone-built house by Detmar Blow, completed in 1906 for Sir Edward and Lady Tennant, later Lady Grey (following her second marriage in 1922 to Viscount Grey of Falloden). She was an imaginative and influential patron of the arts who had been instrumental in bringing the Diaghilev ballet to London. Her son, the Hon. Stephen Tennant, artist, poet and aesthete, was a Cambridge friend of Cecil Beaton and perhaps one of his most important early social and artistic mentors. In the 1920s he was already fascinated by the creation of both his own image and that of his surroundings. In Paris he had visited Poiret's shop and for his London bedroom he had put together an extraordinary silver scheme with lots of mirror glass and constant supplies of lilies and other rare flowers. Following Lady Grey's death in 1929, Stephen Tennant inherited Wilsford and set about transforming it into one of the most unlikely country houses in England. Syrie Maugham had already begun to move away from her earlier, straightforwardly neo-Georgian manner and begun to explore the more exciting possibilities of the neo-baroque when she came to work at Wilsford. The drawing room as created by Syrie for Stephen Tennant was a room of ethereal grandeur tinged with a delicious touch of fantasy, in a vein similar to Beaton's own versions of the style at nearby Ashcombe.

367

Subsequently Stephen Tennant continued to alter and add to the decoration, changing the effect entirely and adding ever more bizarre pieces of furniture, such as the baroque table with a mirror-glass top visible in Beaton's photograph of the study taken in the late 1930s.

366   *Cecil Beaton Photograph (late 1930s).*
Courtesy of Sotheby's, London
367   *Courtesy of Millar & Harris, London*

368

368

Cecil Beaton's comic baroque c.1930–2

Circus Bedroom at Ashcombe, Wiltshire, 1932

In a house decorated throughout with humorous and surrealistic theatricality the most amusing and most overtly stagey room was the so-called Circus Bedroom. Beaton's original conception of a room based on circus imagery centred on a bed with twisted brass poles made for him by a manufacturer of merry-go-rounds, but it quickly developed into a *tour de force* of thematic decoration. Apart from a vast pair of Victorian domes of shell flowers, which would have been thought whimsically amusing at that time, the furnishings included side tables draped with fringed curtains and a set of small tables and chairs made like drums: an idea later copied by Ronald Fleming in his scheme for a flat for the actress Gertrude Lawrence (pl. 301). The principal element of the decoration of the Ashcombe circus room was the series of paintings contri-

buted by all the artist friends who came to stay in the house. Each depicted a different circus character, and the various hands were harmonized by a simple but very effective framework of *trompe-l'oeil* niches divided by jolly Salomonic columns. In Beaton's self-portrait, taken in the room at about the time of its completion, he stands to the right of the bed in front of figures of a harlequin painted by himself and a strong woman by Rex Whistler, while to the right the arm of a black man by Oliver Messel is just visible. The circus room was always one of the most popular rooms at Ashcombe, and must have revealed to its many visitors the great influence exerted on Beaton by the taste of his French friends Jean Cocteau and Christian Bérard.

369

369

Cecil Beaton's circus bed c.1930

In the Circus Bedroom at Ashcombe, Wiltshire

The centrepiece of the Circus Bedroom was this delicious confection of 'native baroque' and sheer exuberant bad taste. In some ways it can be seen as the culmination of Beaton's rather English version of surrealism, which flowered elsewhere in the house in the form of solid draperies made from fabric dipped in plaster and light brackets shaped like human arms in the manner of Bérard's settings for Cocteau's film *La Belle et la Bête*. There is, however, another aspect of this seemingly entirely frivolous essay in camp; for such taste is clearly also a reaction against the coolness or even sterility of much of the stripped and minimal aesthetic of the Modern Movement. The reaction against minimalism came in some cases very quickly and was to take many forms in the worlds of painting, architecture and decoration. This *jeu d'esprit* by Beaton seems close in nature to the widespread rediscovery of interest in such forgotten forms as seaside architecture and fairground artefacts, initiated by John Piper and John Betjeman in their pioneering days at the *Architectural Review*.

370

Party decorations at Ashcombe 1937

Studio at Ashcombe, Wiltshire, decorated for the fête champêtre

The high point both socially and in terms of the decoration of Ashcombe came about halfway through the idyllic fifteen years (1930–45) during which Beaton leased the house. Nearly all his efforts during the summer of 1937 were devoted to the immensely elaborate preparations for a vast party in the form of an eighteenth-century *fête champêtre* with fancy dress, music and theatricals. The party decorations were lavish even by the standards of the day for grand entertainments, and included vast quantities of cut and dried flowers and exquisite trophies of gardening implements, hats and ribbons recalling French engravings. The idea of decorating for a party has always been a popular one, and many decorators have become involved in the creation of splendid effects to be enjoyed for just one day or one night. Two of Beaton's designer friends, Oliver

370

Messell and Felix Harbord, were both notable exponents of the genre, while his great socialite friend Charles de Beistegui (pl. 348) became a patron of genius at his celebrated balls in Paris, and most memorably at the Palazzo Labia in Venice.

368, 369, 370 Cecil Beaton Photographs; Courtesy of Sotheby's, London

1945–1960
AUSTERITY AND
THE NEW LOOK

For the most obvious of reasons nearly all decoration came to a halt in Europe in the unsettled period that culminated in the outbreak of war in 1939. In this, as in other areas of the luxury market, things went into abeyance and, with the possible exception of Albert Speer's refurbishment of the principal apartments of the Reichstag (Parliament) in Berlin at this time, no work of any importance was carried out. After 1945 the pattern of gradual resumption of activity is a complex one and, by all accounts, is dominated by the availability or paucity of materials. Post-war reconstruction in many areas of endeavour was largely a matter of inspired opportunism. This was particularly true of a field in which some materials never again became available and others, because of ineradicable changes in the structure of society, effectively ceased to be economically feasible.

In general all good fabrics, the materials from which trimmings, braids and tassels were made, and a host of other things necessary for the traditional operation of the trade, were in short supply and subject to rigorously enforced rationing systems. In England, building materials of all sorts were placed under similar controls, which were aimed at directing scarce supplies to the areas of greatest need, and repairs, alterations and proposed projects for new buildings were controlled by licence. In such a climate, not surprisingly, an attitude of 'make-do and mend' tended to prevail; the virtues of an aesthetic based on extolling the beauty of 'pleasing decay' were readily appreciated and inventiveness flourished. John Fowler, who already enjoyed a unique reputation for understanding how to recreate with sympathy the right sort of wall colours, curtain treatments and other soft furnishings appropriate to the grand English house, found his skills even more in demand as it became more widely known that he was able to get his effects using dyed army blankets for curtain swags, and by washing and touching-up existing paintwork rather than repainting. In fact of such necessity was born the reticent and gentle approach to architectural restoration that lies at the heart of the conservation techniques which are used in historic houses today.

With a gradual return to more normal conditions decorators and designers began to pick up the threads of stylistic development which had been effectively severed by the war. Those working in a modernistic idiom tended, naturally, to build at first on the achievements of the 30s, and only gradually can a distinct new style be seen to emerge, for many projects planned before the war or interrupted by it were only brought to fruition in the late 40s. In the field of High Style and traditional decoration, confidence began to return and a fashionable neo-romanticism, related to similar movements in the cinema and theatre, painting and literature, made itself felt. In 1947 a distinct 'New Look', parallel to the exciting revival of couture, appeared in decoration, too, and the new *House & Garden* magazine, which had begun publication that year, identified the apartment of Mme Yturbe as its epitome (pl. 386). In its deliberately reckless and lavish use of fabric and other materials, and in the utter impracticality in which it revelled in such an austere and practical-minded era, it served to highlight the way in which decoration would gradually sever links with the more mundane world of building, furniture-making and product design, those significant areas of post-war endeavour.

In England the furnishings of the period of rationing, produced according to a rigorous set of standards and known as 'Utility' (in line with clothing and other household goods manufactured under similar controls), proved not only durable but, in their simple attempts to combine an element of tentative modernistic styling with something of the Arts and Crafts attitude to good construction, quite influential. With the lifting of what had amounted almost to a set of sumptuary laws like those of the Middle Ages, a certain self-denying or puritan feeling continued to inform the design of new furniture for the middle range of houses: the most important area of the post-war market for firms such as Gomme & Son, the manufacturers of the ubiquitous 'G-Plan' range.

There was, however, room amid this new seriousness for a certain degree of whimsical fantasy. The perfect expression of this combination was the work produced for the Festival of Britain in 1951, which, playing up the 1851–1951 angle, made constant references to the Great Exhibition of 1851, introducing even into those parts of the project which had been conceived with the greatest seriousness a leavening element of fantasy-Victoriana. To some extent this amusing quality must have tended to allay natural suspicion of the highly radical design solutions which were being framed at this time for housing and other social problems, allowing a design such as the architects Alison and Peter Smithson's 'House of the Future' (pl. 376) to be readily accepted as a piece of fun, in spite of its serious implications for the way in which people would be expected to live in the future in the major cities of the world.

Throughout Europe and America the gap widened between decoration as a luxury activity for an exclusive clientele and commercially manufactured furnishings for the average house. However, because of new economic patterns and rapidly changing market forces, the latter area began to attract designers of a far higher calibre than ever before, and became a recognized arena for the battles of style, taste and fashion. Milan emerged, without doubt, as the most important centre of this new style-conscious furniture industry, and dominated press and public awareness in much the same way as Paris expected to rule in matters of dress. The great figures in serious modern styling of the 40s and 50s include the American Harry Bertoia, and most notably the Turin-based architect-designer Carlo Mollino; but in recent years, possibly because of a renewed interest in the more fanciful elements in decoration and design, the work of the Milanese architect Gio Ponti and his close friend and associate, the designer Piero Fornasetti, has become very highly regarded. Of the two, Fornasetti is the more natural decorator, applying his highly idiosyncratic ornamentation, based for the most part on old black and white prints and arresting images of women's faces, to ceramic plates and large pieces of neo-classical furniture with equal ease and amusement.

Among American designers of the period the greatest stylist was T.H. Robsjohn-Gibbings, who liked to define his particular attitude to design as that of the 'well-read innovator'. His passionate love of the best work of the past, and of the great achievements of the ancient civilizations in particular, was coupled with an equally passionate hate of the cult of antiques and a loathing for 'bric-à-brac-o-mania'. His own furniture and interiors, while based on a profound historical knowledge, were always interpretative renderings. He ended his days in an apartment in Athens which enjoyed a direct view of the Parthenon, his favourite building in the whole history of architecture. His rooms were furnished with only a few Greek antiquities and half a dozen pieces of his furniture designed in imitation of classical beds, tables and the famous *klismos* chair.

In the 1950s virtually all endeavour in the design field came to be lumped together in the public eye under the generic term of 'Swedish Modern'. Swedish designers' contribution to the design of furnishings and the creation of modern room settings in the period is however a distinct and highly important one. It grew out of the earlier design traditions established in the heroic phase by Gunnar Asplund and Carl Malmsten, and first reached a wider public when the exhibition 'Design in Sweden' toured the cities of America and Canada, where its influence was very strong, in the years between 1954 and 1957.

In 1955 the exhibition 'H.55', staged in Helsingborg, brought Swedish system-built and fitted furniture to the attention of the world's furnishing trades, and in particular established the reputation of the designer Bruno Mathsson. Throughout a long career Mathsson maintained a high reputation as a stylist, while also giving Swedish furniture the lead in technical innovations with classics such as his Elipse table with clamp legs of 1960. His most famous piece, the Karin chair of 1968, is used in the celebrated House of Culture in Stockholm.

Such developments in the design, manufacture and marketing of middle-range furnishings had, effectively, no influence whatsoever on the *grand luxe* world of *haut décor*. In France the taste of a coterie centred on Charles de Beistegui, Emilio Terry and the Baron de Rédé set a pattern for the grandiose arrangement of impossibly grand furnishings in an 'old palazzo' style, which evoked both the splendours of seventeenth-century Rome and the glories of Louis XIV's court. Other French designers such as Barroux toyed with the *style Louis Quatorze* in a rather more light-hearted mood, whilst the perennially smart House of Jansen maintained the traditions of its great director, Monsieur Stéphane Boudin, continuing to create exquisite rooms in the '*tous les Louis*' and Directoire manners. In this their only real competitor was Madeleine Castaing, who had made that era her own, showing delightful groups of French and English early nineteenth-century pieces against the perfect cool green walls of her rambling shop, which she had opened on the corner of the rue Bonaparte and rue Jacob, in the decorators' quarter of Paris, during the bleak final days of the war.

In England, John Fowler's pragmatic approach to the faded splendours of English grand houses was at a premium, and for many of a certain generation it represented a desirably patriotic and romantic Englishness. Meanwhile, a younger generation skimming the pages of *The Saturday Book*, rediscovered Victoriana, seaside architecture, garden follies and a number of highly evocative influences which would, in due course, be drawn into the vocabulary of High Style. All these elements contributed to that perfect vision of the English country house which formed John Fowler's mature style and which was to prove so potent, so long-lived and so endlessly adaptable.

The look owes much to Fowler's unique blend of sympathetic understanding of historic styles and knowledge of the practical methods of the past three hundred years, but it seems that it was only as a direct result of his partnership with the American Mrs Nancy Lancaster that his special talents were able to bloom. Mrs Lancaster, who came of an old and distinguished Virginia family, had grown up in the family house, Mirador, and had come to love the qualities of the surviving ante-bellum interiors which she had known as a child. She inherited from her mother, who had very specific ideas about such things as wall-lights and the painting of broken colour, a distinct feel for re-creating the lost grandeur of houses, and when she came to England in the 20s she embarked on the restoration and decoration of a series of famous English houses: Ditchley Park, Kelmarsh Hall and Haseley Court.

Mrs Lancaster bought the somewhat ailing firm of Colefax & Co. during the war, adding to the letterhead, with a characteristic combination of modesty and shrewdness, not her own name but John Fowler's. Together this at first sight unlikely pair embarked on a remarkable run of work which produced, arguably the finest body of decoration undertaken by any one firm. It created in the process the style which has proved the most universally popular of the century.

The 'Vogue Regency' style, which had enjoyed popularity in the 20s and 30s, proved a continuing favourite and was adopted in the 50s especially by those who were theatrical either by nature or by profession. A colourful stage-set version of the style was created by the Surrealist photographer Angus McBean, who aptly christened his interiors 'Fourth Empire'.

Doubts about the amateur status of the decorator and the value of decorating, and increasing concern about abstract notions of the concept of 'the designer' brought about a radical rethink towards the end of this period. A desire to establish the profession on a new and more 'serious' basis led many to call themselves 'interior designers' rather than 'decorators'; or, following the name of the course established by Hugh Casson at the Royal College of Art in London, 'interior architects', ironically a name once popular among the Modernists of the 30s. Among this younger generation several great stylists began to make their very different reputations: Michael Inchbald in London, Keith Irvine, newly arrived in New York, and David Hicks, who in the 60s and 70s would become for many the epitome of the international designer.

371

371

Utility 1942

The 'Cotswold' suite of 'living room' furniture

As a result of wartime shortages of materials and resources the British Government introduced a stringent set of standards for what little manufacturing of ordinary domestic goods still continued. These latter-day sumptuary laws resulted in the set of approved designs and specifications for furniture and other household things known as 'Utility'. The simple, functional, unadorned and therefore patriotic furnishings in the range became celebrated for their soundness, but were in a uniformly dull and debased modern style. With the return to peace, if not immediately to prosperity, and with the gradual increase in the availability of materials, the designers on the Government-appointed Council of Industrial Design tried hard to perpetuate the Utility ethos. However, the public were not happy with this enforced rationality, and as soon as it became possible again to make tables and chairs in the pseudo-Jacobean or neo-Georgian styles customers turned to them in preference to the approved taste. Further 'up-market' reactions were even more positive, and decoration became either richer and grander or, as another response to the earnestness of Utility, turned to a delightful and deliberately irresponsible whimsicality.

BBC Hulton Picture Library, London

372

Post-war reconstruction in England 1954–5

Bed-sitting room furnished with 'G-Plan'; watercolour by Leslie Dandy, designer for E. Gomme & Sons Ltd, High Wycombe, Buckinghamshire

Following the period of extreme austerity during and immediately after the war there was only a gradual move towards the easing of restrictions on the use of materials for furniture and other furnishings. When controls were abandoned some designers and manufacturers reacted against the austere aesthetic imposed by the Utility standards and began to produce lavish and vulgarly ornamented period-style pieces. Others, such as E. Gomme & Sons from High Wycombe, one of the major traditional centres in England of the manufacture of simple country furniture, aimed to continue work in the restrained manner favoured by the official design pundits, making sound materials and craftsmanship in a gently modern style available to all. Gomme's 'G-Plan' range is the epitome of this sort of Welfare State thinking applied to design, and was for a number of years after its launch in 1953 the quintessential suburban furnishing style.

Victoria & Albert Museum, London

373
Wartime gloom dispelled   1947

Suggestions for decorative wallpaper treatments, from Francis Rose, Your Home, *London, 1947*

The much-needed impetus towards reconstruction in Britain in the immediate post-war years took many forms, and not all Government-sponsored projects were in the official watered-down modernistic style. One of the most unlikely publications to appear at this time, when

373

372

building materials were still hard to come by and ingenuity was at a premium, was this little tract on how to brighten up the home. With an introduction by Lord Strabolgi, who played a prominent role in establishing the new and vital public housing policy of the Attlee Government, the text and illustrations were by Cecil Beaton's friend, the painter Sir Francis Rose. Rose was a rather picaresque character, and it is extraordinary to find him making lively water-colours to extol the virtues of newly available coloured plastic bathroom accessories. His ideas for using interesting plants about the house and for artistic and colourful, but inexpensive, wallpaper treatments to dispel the gloom show the influence of Beaton and his other artist friends, and serve as a poignant reminder of how completely decoration stopped during the war years.

374
'Glib sophistication' in America 1946–50

*The Farnsworth House, Fox River, Illinois,
by Mies van der Rohe*

Writing in 1983, at a time when the arguments for and against Mies van der Rohe's reductivist aesthetic were again at their height, Charles McCorquodale adduced two telling contemporary comments on the Farnsworth house (*The History of Interior Decoration*, Oxford, 1983). One anonymous critic in *House Beautiful* described Mies's work as 'elegant monuments of nothingness ... [with] no relation to site, climate, insulation, function or internal activity', whilst perhaps more extraordinarily the owner of the house himself dismissed its design as 'glib sophistication'. There is of course in such schemes no decoration as such, the entire effect being based on the interrelationship of exterior and interior architecture. However, where this basic ideological approach had worked in the houses of Frank Lloyd Wright and others because of the careful underpinning of the spatial arrangements with inherently beautiful materials or subtlety of detailing, in Mies's work

375

there are no such redeeming features. Whilst such buildings were in general admired in the architectural press of the day, their true influence was perhaps much more widely felt in public building projects such as schools, where impoverished materials and levels of finish were disguised as architecturally fashionable functional minimalism. Such buildings crystallized for many the intellectual scheme of things which placed the International Modern style at one end of a spectrum of approaches to living, and 'decoration' firmly at the opposite, and almost antagonistic, extreme.

Photograph Bill Hedrich, Hedrich-Blessing, Chicago

374

375
'Off-the-peg' Modernism 1949

Eames House, Santa Monica, Los Angeles, designed by Charles and Ray Eames

Charles and Ray Eames are remembered today principally for their chair designs, and especially for one classic: the instantly recognizable Eames Chair of 1956, a moulded plywood, leather-cushioned lounging chair with matching footstool, which enjoyed such immense popularity with the designers of modern interiors as to become almost as great a cliché as the Barcelona chair by Mies. The Eameses planned and built their own house in the LA suburb of Santa Monica between 1947 and 1949, using existing or building-trade catalogue materials inserted into a basic and severe steel-grid structure. Of the aesthetic behind what sometimes seem random juxtapositions of architectural elements, Charles Eames has said, 'The house has not been conceived as an abstraction, it is not composed, it is for use rather than contemplation' (quoted in: Arts Council of Great Britain, *10 Twentieth-Century Houses*, 1980). Inside, features such as the acceptance of modern materials unadorned, the introduction of some older artefacts and 'found objects', and the massing of large-leafed houseplants unmistakably point the way to many of the developments in domestic and commercial interior architecture of the 1950s and the earlier 1960s .

Courtesy of Charles and Ray Eames

376
Things to come 1956

'The House of the Future', designed by Alison & Peter Smithson for the 1956 Ideal Home Exhibition

Among the progressive architect-designers working in the 1950s and 60s the Smithsons epitomized the forward-looking ideal of a new interior architecture, as propounded at the Royal College of Art in London by Sir Hugh Casson. It was a period during which many designers felt that a true break with the past was necessary and sought to create an entirely novel aesthetic which would reflect new forms of construction. Commissioned for the Ideal Home Exhibition of 1956, this design for a house of the future has become celebrated as one of the earliest expressions of 'pop architecture'. It proposed a double shell construction, with the inner wall amoebic in form, mass-produced from individual plastic sections or panels in a system analogous to the construction of car bodies. Within this highly innovative basic structure there are a number of ingenious suggestions, including a self-rinsing, thermostatically controlled bath, a unified kitchen module and a table intended to rise from the floor at the touch of a switch. This futuristic movement was not without followers in its time, but ceased to exert much influence after the late 1960s and had come to a dead end by the early 1970s.

Alison & Peter Smithson; photograph John R. Pantlin

376

377

Invention in Milan 1950s

The essence of the inventiveness of the Milanese designers has always lain in their ability to blend humour and excitement with a thorough but unstuffy feeling for tradition. These examples all show an awareness of the way in which the forms of the past can be endlessly adapted and renewed to make vital statements for the day. Each is a visually literate design, each plays with allusions to traditional forms, and yet each succeeds in being a wholly modern design.

377

Dining room by Banfi, Belgiojoso and Peressutti of Milan

In a room mixing old and new pieces this innovative Milanese design partnership used an early version of the long shelving unit (of the kind which became such a cliché of 1960s interiors), wall-mounted, or as a 'room divider'. The dark ceiling and the use of an eclectic group of antique objects juxtaposed with the clean lines of the pale wood unit are both characteristic elements of this emerging style.

378

Fitted wardrobe cupboard and divan bed by Gio Ponti and Piero Fornasetti 1951

379

Secretary with graphic decoration by Piero Fornasetti and Gio Ponti, Milan 1948

Ponti and Fornasetti created a number of delightful schemes and individual pieces in which the main decorative effect came from the use of panels of collage made from old architectural engravings or other more modern graphic images. Later Fornasetti developed a special method, which has still never been successfully imitated, for creating a permanent surface of graphic images on his highly inventive pieces of furniture. This bed of bizarre form and wardrobe which points to the commercial styling of the 1960s were for a bedroom setting at the Triennale Venezia Exhibition in 1951. The secretary was designed for the first Triennale after the Second World War, in 1948.

377 *Private collection*
378 *Collection Bruno and Christina Bischofberger, Zürich*
379 *The World of Interiors; photograph Richard Davies*

378

rent. Designers such as Gio Ponti, Piero Fornasetti and Carlo Mollino produced among their early work at this time bravura pieces in a stylish and sometimes rather surrealistic vein. In a room in the Devalle House dating from as early as 1939 Carlo Mollino played upon the qualities of that much-loved material of the 1930s, black

380

380

Innovative design in Turin 1940

Room with a moveable glass screen and other pieces in the Devalle House by Carlo Mollino

The emergence of Milan and Turin as the leading centres of innovative furniture design in the post-war period has been one of the most important factors in the development of commercial interior architecture. Milanese influence has however been felt only in the smartest domestic interior decoration until relatively recently. The north Italian manufacturers seem always to have been willing to back their judgement with new and untried designers, and this has resulted in a forward-looking and aesthetically stimulating commerical scene, epitomized by the exuberant Milan Furniture Fair held each year. As far back as the late 1930s and 40s interesting experiments with novel forms of furniture and settings were already appa-

381

glass, creating a *trompe-l'oeil* screen, in the centre of which was a working marble chimneypiece flanked by silvered vases of glass flowers. The effect was heightened by the use of quilted satin armchairs and other chairs and tables in a neo-baroque style, made from metal strip. The effect was at once chic and humorous, recalling the rooms of Charles de Beistegui and the de Noailles in pre-war Paris, while at the same time looking forward to much that would become popular in the 1950s as 'Italian style'.

Private collection

381

An obsessive collector 1950s

Peggy Guggenheim in the bedroom of her house on the Grand Canal, the Palazzo Venier dei Leoni, Venice

As a collector Peggy Guggenheim, an American of seemingly limitless fortune and, like many rich Americans before her, a lover of Venice, combined an admirable desire to be a friend and patron to modern artists with that obsessive urge to acquire usually reserved for the buyer of antique things. She once explained her collecting policy with the astounding remark that she had simply 'put herself on a regime to buy at least one work of art every day'. The results of that regime accumulated rapidly in her single-storey house on the Grand Canal in Venice, where gradually she formed the idea of creating a permanent collection open to the public. The collection is an important one, but many visitors are struck as much by the atmosphere and understated interior design of the house as by any one picture or piece of sculpture. Apart from the individual works, nearly every room contains examples of the furnishings which Peggy Guggenheim commissioned from her artists, such as exquisite chimneypieces in a mosaic of broken shards of mirror glass and the bed in which she sits in this picture, made to a design by the sculptor Alexander Calder and carried out in hammered silver. On the wall behind can be seen a part of Peggy Guggenheim's celebrated collection of earrings, all the work of artists and craftsmen whom she admired, which always hung in a glittering display in her bedroom. This way of living with art objects has proved highly influential in both Europe and especially America ever since.

The Photo Source, London

382

382

Fantasy in Milan 1950

Drawing room in the Appartamento Lucano, Milan by Gio Ponti and Piero Fornasetti

In a room typical of the wit and invention of Ponti and Fornasetti in the 1950s, the decoration is based entirely on graphic imagery. The curtains are of silk printed with a design based on manufacturers' labels taken from old periodicals, whilst the seat furniture is all decorated with an extraordinary *trompe l'oeil* fabric in which 'woodgrain' panels and engravings of old books are combined. The wall on the right which also has panels of the 'old library' pattern, is panelled with an extravagant briar wood from Ferrara.

Courtesy of Piero Fornasetti

383

Swedish modern 1951

Living room with furniture by Bruno Mathsson

For all the excitement that centred on the new Scandinavian design of the 1950s, it seems clear in retrospect that most of the major features of the Swedish modern style were to a large degree a continuation of trends of the 1930s. Bruno Mathsson, like Eames, is best remembered for the design of chairs, especially the gracious, curvilinear reclining chair or *chaise longue* to be seen in the far corner of the living room in this his own house. The informal and asymmetrical arrangement of the room is typical of the feel sought by the Scandinavian designers working at this time, and for a while became a key element in 'advanced' interior decoration. The 'feature' fireplace was a popular design element which Robsjohn-Gibbings satirized in *Homes of the Brave*: '... in the "living area" the fireplace, a raised hearth in the middle of the floor with a metal smoke flue suspended from the ceiling, seemed to have such theoretical advantage over the impure hole-in-the-wall type. The whole family anticipated sitting around it in a circle like Indians at a camp-fire. After being smoked like so many herrings all winter, in summer they find that a fireplace cluttering the centre of the living-space is as misplaced functionally as an electric blanket in a Turkish bath.'

Mathsson International, Värnamo

384

New materials, new forms 1950s

Room setting with pieces from the 'Bertoia' Collection by Knoll

It is easy to dismiss the seemingly reckless frivolity of much of the design of the immediate post-war period as illiterate, but there can be little doubt that the new and light-hearted style which emerged in the Britain of the 1951 Festival, and at the same time elsewhere in Europe and America, fitted the mood of the times. For many the desire to create a new order implied the desirability of breaking with traditional forms of architecture and design, and this movement towards an exploratory aesthetic was underpinned by the exciting potential of new materials. The search for novel forms in furniture became a hallmark of the productions of the internationally successful firm of Knoll. These pieces from the 'Bertoia' collection, typical of the colourful and inventive creations of Harry Bertoia and the Knoll design studio in the 1950s, show the almost universal predilection for tapering or splayed legs.

Knoll International, New York

384

385

385

The beauty of materials 1958

Dining room of the Bruno K. Graf House, Dallas, Texas, designed by T.H. Robsjohn-Gibbings with Edward Durell Stone

In his brilliant book *Homes of the Brave* (New York, 1954) the designer and theorist Robsjohn-Gibbings humorously analysed some of the reasons why the International Modern aesthetic met with such resistance from the vast majority of Americans. In particular he suggested that the open-plan 'machine for living in' lacked privacy and was entirely unsuited to the way of life of most people furnishing their houses in the post-war period. Gibbings himself remained firmly committed to the cause of modern design, but chose to work within a more traditional framework, concentrating on the creation of interior schemes and of furniture with cool, clean lines, which alluded to the styles of the past without copying or pastiche.

His ever-popular book, the wickedly funny *Goodbye, Mr Chippendale* (New York, 1944) cloaked a passionate statement of belief in the danger of designers and decorators becoming obsessed with antiques, and of the need for design to be progressive at all times without being 'modernistic' for the sake of fashion alone. In this room, which still echoes the long, low lines of the 1930s, Robsjohn-Gibbings creates a stylish and dignified feeling through the use of fine materials and very simple 'classic' forms, but gives the whole scheme an unexpected twist by placing the chairs and columnar tables on a 'floating island'. Gradually his interests turned more and more to the furnishings and decoration of the ancient world: he designed a number of pieces based on the forms of classical Greek chairs and couches, and finally settled in Athens in an apartment with a perfect view of the Parthenon on the Acropolis.

Ezra Stoller, © *Esto*

386

'The New Look' 1949

Entrance hall of the apartment of Mme Yturbe, near the Champs-Elysées, Paris; from House & Garden, *1949*

As if to underline the connection between *haute couture* and *haut décor*, which had never seemed closer, *House & Garden* gathered a group of images under the title of 'New Look', the phrase coined by Dior for the deliberately ostentatious and extravagant clothes in his first post-austerity collection. The connection with the lavish use of materials in decoration is an obvious one, and the example of Mme Yturbe's apartment was well chosen. In its stylish and very chic clarity of design it suggests the Dior line, and in its daring use of materials it strikes the same novel and sophisticated note. In particular the classic line of the drapery of both window and table point the way towards a look based on opulence rather than fussiness, and the carpet made from a 'specially woven very heavy Scotch tartan cloth' is both visually effective and witty.

Condé Nast Publications Ltd, London

387

386

387

Old and new in provincial France 1950s

Illustration by Philippe Jullian from Les Styles, *Paris, 1962*

In another of the beautifully observed plates from *Les Styles* Philippe Jullian affectionately characterizes that particular blend of the modernistic and the historical that makes so many French provincial or suburban interiors so delightful. An earnestly scribbling husband sits on an aggressively modern and surely very uncomfortable chair, whilst his wife sits knitting in a deeply upholstered chintz armchair of the Second Empire. There is a draped table upon which stand a converted nineteenth-century oil lamp and a number of other such pieces of bric-à-brac, but the present is represented by a splay-legged magazine rack and the inevitable house-plant. All these diverse elements are unified by the modern curly-backed metal chair, which hints at the age of Napoleon III while suggesting the gaiety of French café life. Such chairs had been made by Jean-Michel Frank before the war and continued in vogue throughout the 1950s; indeed, they influenced a whole new generation of furniture makers in the 1980s.

Courtesy of Comte Ghislain de Diesbach and Editions Plon, Paris

388

A perfect writing table 1951

The Marchioness of Bath's desk at Longleat, drawn by Cecil Beaton for her memoir Before the Sunset Fades, *Longleat, 1951*

As a tailpiece to her memoir of life in a great house before, as she put it, so much changed both above and below stairs, Cecil Beaton drew this charming little record of the *objets* adorning the Marchioness of Bath's writing table. It is certainly what *House & Garden* in the 1950s would have described as a 'well-appointed desk', but there is in fact little to distinguish it from the desk of the chatelaine of any English country house of 1910 or 1930 or even 1980, for the elegant and primarily-ornamental writing table has remained one of the most enduring of furnishing clichés, bringing to the room a pleasing suggestion of cultivated leisure.

Courtesy of the Marquess of Bath and the Longleat Estate

388

389

Grandeur and modernity in France 1952

Hall of the Vicomte and Vicomtesse de Noailles, Hôtel Bischoffsheim, Paris; from House and Garden, *June, 1952*

The de Noailles had created stylish interiors which mixed old and new since the late 1920s (see pls 349, 350) and throughout the succeeding years they continued to add both distinguished modern pictures and fine antique objects to the elegant rooms of their eighteenth-century Parisian house, the Hôtel Bischoffsheim, and to their collection in their modern country house at Hyères. This characteristically stylish arrangement in the hall in Paris, which had a beautifully mellow parquet floor, includes some interesting pieces of eighteenth-century furniture, a good pair of busts (made more stunning by being placed on two hugely over-scaled wooden columns) and, as the centrepiece, an important picture by Georges Braque.

Condé Nast Publications Ltd, London

389

Post-war grandeur in England and France 1947–51

It is initially surprising that in the years of seeming austerity that followed the war some remarkably lavish schemes of decoration were carried out in both France and England, where materials remained difficult to obtain for some time. The answer lies of course in the fact that owners of grand houses were anxious to see them return to their ancient glory after the privations and misuse of the war years. For the most part these refurbishments were carried out by rearranging the existing furnishings, as well as by purchasing important antique pieces, on which there were no restrictions and which came on the market in large numbers. On both sides of the Channel a particular form of patrician taste became chic, associated with some of the more socially and artistically minded owners of houses and their friends among the artists, dealers and decorators of London and Paris.

391

390

Long Gallery, Stratfield Saye, Hampshire

Arranged by the seventh Duke of Wellington

Lord Gerald Wellesley, architect, collector, Surveyor of His Majesty's pictures and a founder member in the 1920s of the Magnasco Society, succeeded as seventh Duke of Wellington in 1943, inheriting Stratfield Saye, the house near Reading originally furnished by his ancestor the Iron Duke. After the war he carried out a very sympathetic campaign of restoration and rearrangement of the contents of the house, which brought out the early-nineteenth-century flavour of the private rooms and increased the feeling of grandeur in the hall, gallery and other principal rooms. He made the gallery a splendid and sombre architectural experience by gilding the walls between the fillets of the existing prints to create a black and gold background for a series of bronze busts of victorious generals. These he placed on buhl pedestals and cabinets along the length of the walls, further echoing the effect in the detail and colour of the splendid carpet, made to his own design at the old royal carpet works in Madrid in 1951.

Arcaid; photograph Lucinda Lambton

390

391

The library, Hôtel Beistegui, Paris

Decorated by Charles de Beistegui with Emilio Terry, from House & Garden, *1951*

Charles de Beistegui's own Parisian town house marks the high-water mark of his formidable patrician tastes. The assemblage of vast, over-scaled and impossibly grand neo-classical objects in a wholly new and baroque manner here outshines the effects of even his own Château de Groussaye. Only his redecoration of the state rooms of the Palazzo Labia in Venice could rival this for sheer theatricality.

Condé Nast Publications Ltd, London

392

The library of the Hôtel Lambert, Paris

Redecorated by the Baron de Rédé and others

The Hôtel Lambert, which is one of the two greatest *hôtels particuliers* built on the Ile St-Louis in the middle years of the seventeenth century, came into the possession of the Princess Czartoryski in 1942, when she outbid the city of Paris for the noble but romantically decayed palace. Immediately after the war the family undertook a subtle scheme of redecoration to bring out the mellow glory of the house and to show to better effect their fine collections. The project was overseen by the Baron de Rédé, a popular and intriguing figure on the Parisian social scene. He consulted other connoissseurs such as Charles de Beistegui, who had the finest eye for the creation of rooms in grand and patrician taste, and his friend the architect Emilio Terry. The library is one of the most perfect statements of their personal version of the rich and bold neo-classical style of the Louis Quatorze period, which they in fact created with a mixture of pieces of many periods, including the Empire and even the later nineteenth century. Feeling that the room needed above all one very large piece of furniture to give a sense of monumental scale and grandeur, Beistegui and Terry designed the great bookcase supported on massive columns. Above, on the segmental pediment, can be seen two Michelangelesque figures on whose shoulders the painted beam of the ceiling appears to rest. On the pediment appears the date of the completion of the magisterial project: 1948.

Agence Top, Paris

392

393

The doyenne of Parisian decorators 1950s

Entrance hall decorated by Madeleine Castaing in her own house, the Château de Lèves, near Paris

Mme Castaing first opened the doors of her celebrated shop in the rue Bonaparte during the unpropitious days of the war. Her taste has remained remarkably consistent since those early days, when she grew to love not only Empire and Directoire pieces but also the less highly regarded Charles Dix, the largely ignored delights of the *Style troubadour* and the full-blown glories of the Second Empire. At this date too she developed her distinctive palette of greys, siennas and the ravishing blue-greens that are the leitmotif of all her schemes. Mme Castaing's taste has been a tremendous influence on the way period-style decoration has been thought of in France, and her position and influence in Paris has been not unlike that of John Fowler in England. Her own house in the country near Paris is filled with the kind of pieces she most admires, arranged with a remarkable blend of lightness and formality. Typical is the arrangement of a beautiful set of highly individual chairs in the stone-flagged hall, which is hung with a zany marbled paper and lit by elaborate nineteenth-century light fittings, all with the famous blue-green shades. Elsewhere in the house are rooms with good Empire pieces and a library with elaborate blue and gold shelving and a fine collection of English Regency furniture.

Decorating with antiques 1950s

394

Interior in the Louis Quinze manner by M. Barroux

This remarkably successful room treatment served as the showroom for a '*marchand de tissus anciens*'. Created by the decorator Barroux using green-painted *boiseries* of the period ('from a dining room at Chantilly') and a good red marble chimneypiece, the room avoids the deadness of many such attempts through the masterly scaling and placing of perfectly chosen objects, such as the fine early pair of lustres on pedestals, and through the exquisite combination of drapery and lambrequins at the window, deriving from a design by Daniel Marot.

395

395

Entrance hall in a château in Switzerland; decoration by J. Cornaz

The ability to group objects with style and to mix things of different periods without loosing a coherent sense of design is admirably demonstrated in this strongly architectural arrangement in the hall of a grand Swiss house. Although the architectural bones of the building are neoclassical and of the early nineteenth century, the total effect of the decoration suggests a much earlier period. The use of a bold geometric pattern for the floor, carried out in dark marble strips and bricks, is more reminiscent of the seventeenth century: a note taken up by the plain modern banquettes in a massive style. The fine early eighteenth-century desk and the lavish trophy of musical instruments contribute a sense of richness, but retain a clarity of arrangement very similar to Charles de Beistegui's highly successful excursions into the Louis Treize and Louis Quatorze styles at Groussay, his house outside Paris.

393, 394, 395 Agence Top, Paris

396

'A bodger of genius' early 1950s

Guest bedroom in the Endell Street, London, house of Angus McBean

Angus McBean took some of the finest theatrical portrait photographs ever seen in Britain. His celebrated surrealistic images of the 1940s and 1950s have more recently brought him an even wider, international reputation and now, in his eighties, he is again much in demand by fashion editors. Throughout a long and distinguished career, always close to the theatre world, Angus McBean has consistently created richly theatrical rooms in which to live. He claims to have begun decorating at a very early age and to have continued 'like some bower-bird to embellish myself and my surroundings'. In the 1930s he had experimented with dipped-plaster draperies, masks and other fashionable whims, but by the time after the war when he took the small eighteenth-century house in Endell Street as both home and studio, he had made a particularly quirky version of the French Empire style all his own. Describing himself as a 'bodger of genius', McBean developed an extraordinary talent for mixing the good original pieces which came his way with clever pastiches of his own making. In the Endell Street guest bedroom he placed a fine-quality Empire bed in a prominent position, tented the whole roof space with striped fabric and asked his friend the painter Roy Hobdal to carry out a scheme of *trompe-l'oeil* clouds and seashore vistas. The effect was stylish and led friends to call McBean's style 'Fourth Empire'. At the end of the 1950s he was given the chance to carry out redecorations in his inimitable manner at the Academy Cinema in Oxford Street. Here in the foyer and public areas he created a memorable interior, while upstairs he designed The Pavilion, London's most delightful and visually stylish restaurant of the post-war period. Angus McBean now lives in Suffolk, where for the past twenty years he has concentrated on the creation of furnishings and interiors in his own freely inventive version of the Elizabethan style.

Courtesy of Angus McBean

Versions of the Empire revival mid 1950s

Just as in England the Georgian and Regency styles were endlessly reused at every level of the decoration world, so in France certain looks have predominated. The direct French equivalent of the rather generalized Georgian look is a weak '*tous les Louis*' manner seen at its most blandly

396

uninteresting in luxury hotels, whilst the slightly more chic equivalent of the rather daring 'Vogue Regency' is to be found in the ever-popular Empire or 'Malmaison' look. For the very reason that so much decoration in period style is bland, timid and in fact visually illiterate, examples of the inventive and stylish use of the past have a special quality much to be prized.

397

Empire dining room by Jansen of Paris

The House of Jansen maintained an international reputation for the quality of its decoration in period styles and, under the direction of the designer Stéphane Boudin, carried out celebrated schemes not only in France but also for important clients such as Sir Henry Channon in London (pl. 332). This circular dining room is a classic example of the Malmaison style, so popular in France in the 1950s when the redecoration of the palace was much discussed. The Jansen craftsmen were well known for their abilities to reproduce historic detail and to supply whole sets of furniture 'extended' from a smaller number of pieces, or copied, as in the case of the Channons' Amalienburg suite, from unobtainable originals.

398

The Pelham Place, London, house of Arthur Jeffress

The art dealer Arthur Jeffress was noted for his exquisite taste in houses, furniture, pictures and other desirable objects. In Venice, where he had a pretty house, he expressed his love of perfection and luxury by fitting out his personal gondolier in a livery of white and yellow; but in London he contented himself with gathering a refined collection of French pieces of the Directoire, Empire and Charles X periods. In the dining room of his Pelham Place house he contrived a perfect background for his lavish entertaining with *papiers peints*, richly draped satin curtains and neatly paired objects of the highest quality. A spirited terracotta bust of the young Napoleon presided over the table, giving the necessary spark to the otherwise precisely ordered calm of the room.

397, 398 Agence Top, Paris

397

398

399

Mrs Lancaster's country house grandeur   c.1959

Haseley Court, Oxfordshire, decorated by Nancy Lancaster and John Fowler

After leaving Ditchley Park, Mrs Lancaster looked over 125 houses before finding, in 1954, the derelict and romantic Haseley, with which she immediately fell in love. By this time she had already been in a sort of informal partnership with John Fowler for long enough to establish a working relationship perhaps best described as stimulating and bracing. Certainly the two sparked each other off perfectly, and together they forged an approach to country house decoration that has remained the basis for all subsequent 'period style' work in grand houses. At Haseley Mrs Lancaster's full talent for the creation of grand effects was complemented to perfection by John Fowler's artistic and scholarly eye for colour and detail, making the rooms which they decorated here between 1954 and 1960 among the most perfect expressions of their shared ideal.

399
The Gothic Room

This room, originally arranged as a bedroom for Mrs Lancaster's aunt Nancy Astor, took as the key to its decoration the great Gothic window with simple tracery which reached up to the apex of the hipped roof. John Fowler removed a good deal of indifferent architectural detail from the room and substituted a scheme of exquisitely handled real and *trompe-l'oeil* Gothic decoration. Photographs suggest that the room had a strongly theatrical flavour, with the bed placed centrally in front of the window and heavily draped like a baroque altar.

400
The Palladian Room

Mrs Lancaster had a particular affection for the strongly-architectural quality of this little room. The decoration was based on a fragment of a Chinese wallpaper from the royal palace at Drottningholm, near Stockholm, which had been given to her by the King of Sweden. John Fowler worked up the pattern to fit the spaces, and he and George Oakes, the central figure in the Colefax paint studio, carried out the scheme on small sheets pasted together to simulate the effect of eighteenth-century paper.

399, 400 Country Life

400

401

A theatrical restoration 1960

Drawing room, Flaxley Abbey, Gloucestershire, decorated by Oliver Messel

Oliver Messel is best remembered for the whimsical fantasy of his theatre designs. In the years after the war, and before he went to live on Mustique and designed a series of grandiose beach houses, he was also responsible for two celebrated schemes of decoration. For the Dorchester Hotel he created several rooms, including the 'Messel Suite', which were highly unusual in their theatricality in the context of a seriously grand hotel. The second project, the decoration of the Rayne shoe shop in Bond Street, was in a deliciously light-hearted Vogue Regency manner. It brought this type of stage-set design, which had always been a kind of private joke, to the notice of a far wider public. One customer who bought her shoes at Rayne and became, as John Cornforth in *The Inspiration of the Past* (1985) has recorded, 'captivated' by the Messel style was

Mrs F.B. Watkins, who with her husband had recently acquired Flaxley Abbey. Flaxley had been sold by Sir Launcelot Crawley-Boevey, whose family had owned it for 300 years, and was in considerable need of work. Much of the medieval part of the house retained a strong character, but nothing remained of the seventeenth century, and the eighteenth-century drawing room lacked any detail beyond a cornice and chimneypiece. The Watkinses asked Messel to help with the restoration, redecoration and furnishing of the house, and the result was that over a space of time he created the rich drawing room with its boldly drawn carpet and an entirely theatrical pastiche seventeenth-century bedroom, and he furnished the hall and other parts of the house with appropriate pieces. Ironically, much of the Flaxley decoration seems to have the insubstantial quality of Messel's work while lacking his whimsy. It does not achieve the convincing theatricality of John Fowler's best rooms, and it remained the only large-scale country house decorative project that Messel undertook.

Country Life

...ing Hunting Lodge. Odiham. Hampshire.

'Humble elegance' c.1948

Two watercolours by Alexandre Serebriakoff of rooms at The Hunting Lodge, Odiham, Hampshire, decorated by John Fowler for his own use

402

Sitting room

403

Small red bedroom

John Fowler had a number of the rooms he had decorated painted by Serebriakoff, who also worked for Emilio Terry and Charles de Beistegui in Paris and Venice. His watercolours of rooms at The Hunting Lodge are full of the charm of those early nineteenth-century interiors of which Mario Praz was the greatest connoisseur, and they record the appearance of the lodge just as it was first decorated. Fowler had found the little Gothic gabled brick structure advertised in the pages of *Country Life* and acquired it in 1947. He quickly set about making it the perfect expression of his ideals of 'humble elegance', and it very soon became widely known, admired and influential as the epitome of the 'Fowler style' in its modest, country version. The essence of The Hunting Lodge look was the lightness and prettiness of its decoration and furnishing. Nothing was pretentious and none of the pieces of furniture was very grand in itself, save the good late eighteenth-century Swedish neo-classical commode in the sitting room. Everywhere there was an emphasis on floral themes and patterns, which tied the schemes of the individual rooms to the overall grand design of the formal garden, conceived by Fowler as a sequence of outdoor 'rooms', as well as the setting for his architectural gem. Over the years he discreetly enlarged the lodge, but it is perhaps significant that the basic decoration and arrangements of the house changed hardly at all in the thirty years until his death in 1977.

Courtesy of Stanley Falconer

403

404

The 'buttah-yallah' room c.1958–9

Mrs Lancaster's drawing room, 22 Avery Row, London, decorated by herself and John Fowler

Both Mrs Lancaster and John Fowler had London *pieds à terre* in this delightful Georgian building in Avery Row off Brook Street. The finest room in the house was the great barrel-vaulted studio or drawing office and reception room which the architect Sir Jeffry Wyatville had added, and which, before Mrs Lancaster moved into it in 1958, had served as the main showroom for furniture. Mrs Lancaster called it her 'bed-sitting room', but there can be little doubt that it was one of the grandest rooms in London, with one of the most influential schemes of decoration of the whole period. The butter yellow, or 'buttah-yallah' as Mrs Lancaster's Virginian accent rendered it, was an uncompromising colour, and the rich gloss finish of the walls was

404

heightened by the pale grey marbled paintwork and a profusion of bold and elaborate furniture. The richness of the effects, however, never overbalanced the sense of order in the room. There is a precision and almost graphic clarity in the placing of the major pieces, such as the white-and-gold painted bookcases from Ashburnham House which flank the door, topped by vases linking them with the elaborate gilt-framed looking-glasses above. This pattern was repeated at the far end of the room with two more bookcases from the same set, two more matching mirrors and another pair of large vases, thereby giving not only a sense of balance but a feeling of ordered luxury and profusion to this very grand architectural space. The decoration remained basically unchanged until the summer of 1982 (when this photograph was taken), when Mrs Lancaster gave the room up to be used once again as the showroom for the firm's antique furniture department.

The World of Interiors; photograph James Mortimer

405

405
Scholarly re-creation in America early 1950s

The American Empire Parlor at the Henry Francis du Pont Winterthur Museum, Delaware

Henry Francis du Pont devoted a lifetime of energetic collecting and scholarly endeavour, together with a significant portion of his large fortune, to the creation of his museum at Winterthur, one of the largest and most important sequences of reconstructed rooms and settings of furniture in the world. Du Pont's aim and passion was to document the work of indigenous furniture makers, decorators and upholsterers, from the earliest colonial period through to the end of the classical tradition in American interiors, towards the end of the first half of the nineteenth century, and his collection is rich in both typical pieces and rarities of each era. The house and collection was opened to the public in 1951 and maintains an important role as a museum and research institution, with additions being made to the collection as the opportunity arises. For this reason the decision was taken some years ago to 'freeze' certain of the rooms, in order that Mr du Pont's taste and ideals of scholarly reconstruction, which themselves mark an epoch in American cultural development, might be studied by historians of taste in future years. One such

frozen room, which is already of historic interest for the precise image it presents, is the American Empire Parlor. It was first furnished by du Pont in the 1940s with several important pieces of native furniture and imported artefacts in the French style, which enjoyed popularity in New York, Philadelphia and elsewhere in the States well into the middle years of the nineteenth century. The room has not changed substantially since the opening of the museum.

Courtesy of the Henry Francis du Pont Winterthur Museum

Romantic grandeur in America 1946

Rose Cumming's own New York apartment, 36 East 53rd Street

406

The library

407

The bedroom

One of the best and most individual decorators on the New York scene at this time was Rose Cumming. Her approach to decoration is characterized by a highly personal and romanticized attitude to period style. This led her to arrange rooms in which all-pervading colours and an overall shimmering quality, often achieved by the use of silvered woodwork and other surfaces, create a magical, stage-set feel. Her own drawing room and bedroom were both decorated with an oriental theme. In the bedroom the scheme was based around petrol blues and a deep greyish-silver, which created a mysterious feel enhanced by the use of unusual pieces of furniture such as the Javanese daybed to be seen in the left foreground. The drawing room (frontispiece) by contrast seems to be in a more conventional, or 'European', Chinoiserie style, but even here Miss Cumming's play with a silvery tone pervades the entire scheme. The high-ceilinged library which, in its more robust colours, is the most conventional of the rooms, is based on the grouping of a number of strong pieces of furniture. A magnificent William and Mary period bureau-bookcase sets the theme, and this is answered by an aggressive early Georgian stool and a handsome pair of scarlet lacquer high-backed chairs. The high key of the colour is maintained by the dark saturated green of the walls and the deep glossy blue of the sofa.

Courtesy of Rose Cumming Inc., New York

407

408

Later fantasies at Wilsford 1950s

Wilsford Manor, Wiltshire, home of the Hon. Stephen Tennant

408, 410
Two views of the drawing room

409
Design for a wallpaper frieze by Stephen Tennant 1951

Never one to leave well alone, in decorative terms, as nearly as the first years of the Second World War Stephen Tennant was beginning to recast the appearance of Wilsford in a richer and more densely patterned manner than Syrie Maugham's schemes had allowed (pls 366, 367). His Journal for 2 November 1941 records him musing upon: 'Zebra skin, Cerise-orchid cushion, White fur, sweet-pea pinks, mauves, blues' (quoted in Sotheby's *Catalogue: Wilsford Sale* 14–15 Oct. 1987), which gives a fair hint of what was to come in the next ten or fifteen years of almost constant embellishment, undertaken with the help of various artist friends, decorators and dealers. In 1942 he visited John Fowler for the first time and he has left a rapturous description of the 'great beauty' which he found there: '... such a Handsome pouff – Zebra skin – the sides are brown velvet – the tufts are cream satin, very luxurious: the cord is gold that binds it. 3 or 4 people could sit on it. I was very thrilled – it's a Chef d'Oeuvre. ...' This extraordinary object was given pride of place in the drawing room at Wilsford. As the profusion of gilt looking-glasses, crystal chandeliers and sconces and elaborate draperies increased, so the wall treatments were elaborated with reprinted Empire-style papers and enriched with *trompe-l'oeil* paper

409

410

friezes. Writing to a wallpaper supplier, a Mr Atherton, Stephen Tennant asked him, 'Do you . . . know of a seashell swag border which I could put in my white and gold and apricot dining room? Corals if possible with seashells . . .' (letter of 16 November 1951, now lost). He added a sketch in his typical style to give some further idea of what was

required, but in the event a standard swag pattern had to suffice, pasted below the three-dimensional plaster cornice of scallop shells.

408   *Arcaid; photograph Lucinda Lambton*
409, 410   *Courtesy of Sotheby's, London*

An ever-growing collection mid 1950s

*Drawing room, Avenue House, Ampthill, Bedfordshire,
the home of Sir Albert Richardson*

Photographs taken at successive dates reveal the effects on the rooms of Avenue House of a lifetime of ardent and knowledgeable collecting. Professor Richardson, who bought the house in 1919, continued to add to his remarkable assemblage of furniture, pictures and objects right up to his death in 1964. The house looked exceptionally pure and architectural only for about the first ten years. By the 1930s the rooms were already becoming increasingly full of a more eclectic mixture of things, and as the collection grew so Richardson's taste moved towards a greater richness. He particularly liked objects which cast light on the modes and manners of the eighteenth and early nineteenth centuries, and he had an especial fondness for provenance and the associations of things. In a photograph used for many years as the prospectus for the house, which the Professor allowed the public to view during the summer months, the drawing room has taken on a distinctly Second Empire lavishness. Visible are a splendid rococo Chinoiserie looking-glass and a much grander chandelier, replacing the simpler French Empire one which hung there in the 1920s and 30s. The principal set of seat furniture is part of a suite made in then highly fashionable satinwood for Mrs Fitzherbert, mistress of George IV when Prince Regent, and the plain carpet of the Professor's 1919 arrangement of the room has been replaced by a magnificent large old Aubusson.

Courtesy of Simon Houfe

Theatrical effects by Felix Harbord c.1950

Felix Harbord is the least well-remembered figure in the circle which included Cecil Beaton, Oliver Messel and Martin Battersby, and yet he shared with them a love of theatrically baroque effects, and underpinned that love with remarkable practical know-how and a professionalism that made him a very good decorator. In the 1950s he was in great demand for his ability to realize often quite ravishingly fantastic schemes while working within a small budget.

412

Decorations for a party in London

Harbord carried out the decorations for the first débutante party held in London after the war, given by Lord and Lady Plunket at Hill House, Mayfair, and afterwards was regularly involved in dressing the most fashionable parties of each season. His particularly winning blend of pure fantasy and practical arrangements made him the finest exponent of this entirely ephemeral art form, and a number of his ideas and effects are still copied today by his successors in the field.

Courtesy of Stanislaus Terech

413

Dining room of the School House, Wilton, for the Hon. David Herbert

From House & Garden, *1949*

David Herbert converted the school house in the park at Wilton into a bijou dwelling in 1948–9. The school had been built by his ancestor Lady Georgina Herbert. On to it was grafted a crumbling baroque façade from a folly in the park often attributed to Inigo Jones. Inside Felix Harbord contrived effects of suitably baroque splendour by totally ignoring restrictions of scale, using rich colours, fabrics and gilding and filling the place with carved blackamoors, pilasters and other whimsical details. The resulting interiors may have lacked a certain feeling of permanence, but they certainly did not lack panache.

Condé Nast Publications Ltd, London

412

413

414

Felix Harbord makes a model   1950s

For the decoration of the Westminster house of Michael Berry (later Lord Hartwell)

From time to time Felix Harbord liked to present his ideas in the form of a model showing each of the walls of a room. This section from a model for two interconnect-ing rooms in a pretty eighteenth-century Westminster house reveals just how much trouble he would sometimes take, cutting out windows, creating mirrors of silver paper and painting in spirited *trompe-l'oeil* all the cornices and other architectural enrichments. The decorative panels in rococo frames are intended to be a series of capriccios of London churches, and they are dashed in with a delightfully Venetian bravura.

Victoria & Albert Museum, London

415
Couture extravagance in Paris 1951

The apartment of Elsa Schiaparelli, from
House & Garden, *August 1951*

Elsa Schiaparelli lived, as befitted a leading couturier in Paris, with some serious degree of grandeur; but she did so with the same flashes of wit and outrageous stylishness, spicing up an underlying classicism, as characterized her clothes. In her grand white and gold library-drawing room the bookcases of monumental proportions were topped with flamboyant gilded pennons and sheaves of wheat. A superb eighteenth-century tapestry had been cut, with cavalier disregard, round the white marble mantel and, amid accumulations of personal photographs, and other memorabilia of an intriguing life, leopard skins and purple and scarlet upholstery fabrics created bold splashes of colour. A shared love of such staggering combinations of reds and purples perhaps led Mme Schiaparelli in later years to engage the collaboration of that most confident of modern colourists David Hicks.

Condé Nast Publications Ltd, London

416

415

416
Cecil Beaton's simple grandeur 1950s

The drawing room at Reddish House, Broadchalke, Wiltshire, decorated by Felix Harbord, from
House & Garden, *1962*

This view gives some idea of the richness and very real sense of grandeur achieved by Felix Harbord in his remodelling of the back of the existing house to provide a room 35 feet (11 metres) in length. Divided with white and gold pillars and pilasters, it was hung with wine-red as a background to a collection of the works of Cecil Beaton's many artist friends. In describing Harbord's work at Reddish, however, Beaton maintained that the greatest gain was in the creation of his much-loved conservatory, which opened out of the blue and white guest room, and in which he and his guests passed much of the time.

Condé Nast Publications Ltd, London

Paintings by Martin Battersby

417

Corner of a room at Reddish House; oil painting by Martin Battersby 1950s

418

After a considerable length of time spent searching for a house to replace the much-lamented Ashcombe, Beaton found, through the intervention of his friends Edith Olivier and David Herbert, Reddish, a small and perfect Queen Anne house at Broadchalke in Wiltshire. He immediately began work on the garden and the more confused and unpromising parts of the interior, which were rebuilt in a grander architectural style with the help of Felix Harbord. Hugo Vickers, Beaton's biographer, describes how he was 'soon ... deciding which furniture from Ashcombe fitted the dignity and elegance of his new home,

417

and which should be discarded as frivolous junk'. The brass barley-twist posts of the circus bed (pl. 369) and most of the more madly theatrical and surrealist elements were abandoned, and a more historically correct and distinctly more opulent French Second Empire look was established. Martin Battersby, the talented muralist and *trompe-l'oeil* painter, was at that time working as Beaton's assistant in his theatrical design work (he resigned shortly afterwards, in 1951, after a disagreement, and seems never to have regained Beaton's favour). This little painting therefore recalls a corner of Reddish as Cecil Beaton first arranged it, mixing grand pieces of gilt furniture and lots of mirrors with pretty Frenchified curtain treatments. Highly characteristic too is an arrangement of unusual flowers, for which he had a lifelong passion and which became an essential element in the way he conceived his interiors.

Michael Parkin Fine Art Ltd, London

418

A trompe-l'oeil masterpiece c. 1950

Hall of the house of Duff and Lady Diana Cooper,
Château de St-Firmin, Chantilly; painted decorations by
Martin Battersby

In 1946 the Coopers took a pretty house near the river at Chantilly as a retreat from the bustle of the embassy in Paris, and in fact kept it on for some time after they had been recalled. As a decoration for the hallway Diana Cooper commissioned from Martin Battersby, whom she discovered through Cecil Beaton (for whom he was working), a series of panels which depicted objects, pictures and documents connected with Duff Cooper's family, achievements, honours and interests. The panel on the right, with a grim *memento mori* figure painted bursting through the canvas, is one of the most striking visually, but that on the left is specially interesting for the tiny image shown 'pinned' to the panel. It is a view of the library which was added to the British Embassy in the Hôtel Beauharnais to house the fine collection of books which Duff Cooper had formed, and which he gave to the nation for the embassy. The project involved a number of interesting and influential taste-making figures of the day, for Diana Cooper consulted not only the Duke of Wellington, a pioneer of the Regency revival, but also her artist friends such as Cecil Beaton and Christian Bérard; and Emilio Terry seems also to have offered advice about the suitability of a new version of the Empire style. Eventually the room was designed by Charles de Beistegui and constructed under the supervision of the greatly respected Parisian period decoration specialist Georges Geoffroy.

Ronald Fleming Papers, Archive of Art and Design,
Victoria & Albert Museum, London

419

An architectural solution 1958–9

Entrance lobby created for his own London house by
Michael Inchbald

Michael Inchbald, whose major credits as a designer include the principal rooms of the liner *Queen Elizabeth* and the famous London showrooms of Alfred Dunhill Ltd, inherited a grand but rather gloomy early Victorian Chelsea house at the end of the 1950s, and carried out a series of consistently stylish and inventive remodellings, renovations and decorations. In order to create a suitably imposing entrance he replaced the original but meanly proportioned front door with a handsome pair of polished wood doors, probably of early eighteenth-century date. With the highly skilful use of opposed mirror-glass panels and boldly scaled inlaid flooring he made a space no more than 6 feet (1.8 metres) square into a dazzling architectural capriccio of endless vistas and visual conundrums. In this photograph the two symmetrically placed obelisks are seen reflected over and over again, while the lion mask which seems to float is in fact the handle of one of the outer glass doors, which fold back flat against the mirrored side walls.

Courtesy of Michael Inchbald

419

420

421

Commercialized versions of the Regency revival 1950s

Post-war versions of the Regency revival style, which had been so chic in the 1920s and 30s, tended to play on a very limited number of design clichés. It became one of the first styles to be reduced to the level of a series of visual key symbols, and yet curiously at the very same time undoubtedly 'up-market' schemes were carried out by some of the best decorators using a Regency theme. The quirkier artefacts of the period remained popular with artists and the more influential collectors.

420

Drawing room of the Thurloe Square flat of the decorator Ronald Fleming, London

An accomplished essay in massing rich objects in gilt and bronze against an uncompromising Empire red, this room by Ronald Fleming was one of his most historical schemes until that date, and invites comparison with the creations in a similarly opulent vein by Charles de Beistegui. Although Fleming's collection, which included good modern paintings as well as antique pieces, could not compete in scale with de Beistegui's, it is quite clear that he always had a very good eye for the quality of furniture and pictures, and gathered together a number of very fine things.

Victoria & Albert Museum, London

421

'A formal room'

From Adrienne Spanier, Furnishing and Decorating in Your Home, *London, 1959*

Adrienne Spanier's little treatise on decoration combined a number of stylish English ideas about the use of period furnishing with some serious and practical hints on 'how to do it', rather more in the manner of the DIY manuals popular in the United States. She makes a great number of dogmatic statements of the kind which the inspired decorator will always ignore, captioning this illustration for example with the warning: 'Draped pelmets should not be used except in formal rooms.' Although bold in colour the room is typical of the 'wall-to-wall good taste' of the day, with characteristically under-scaled objects and an emphasis on plain walls, carpets and fabrics.

422

Drawing room of the house of the actor John Mills, Richmond, Surrey

Illustration from the cover of Ideal Home, *1952*

Mr and Mrs John Mills's house in Richmond enjoyed delightful views of the Thames from handsome full-length windows elaborately draped with a classic striped fabric, of the kind which prompted John Betjeman to sigh, 'So Regency, so Regency, my dear.' The red and white or burgundy and white combination became one of the great

clichés of decoration in the Regency manner, still to be found on the chairs of the high street furnishing store versions of the style. Here it has been used in the context of a scheme with nice pieces of white and gold furniture, and creates an appropriately light and cheerful feel suitable for a riverside house – or for the seafront at Brighton, that great bastion of the Regency revival.

Ideal Home

IDEAL HOME

MARCH, 1952 · TWO SHILLINGS · DAILY MAIL IDEAL HOME EXHIBITION NUMBER

The Richmond home of Mr and Mrs John Mills

422

The 'Victoriana' revival 1950s

As early as 1880 Sir Leslie Stephen, the nineteenth-century critic and editor of the *Dictionary of National Biography,* had written: 'One thing is pretty certain: no one will ever want to revive the nineteenth century' (quoted by Jules Lubbock in 'Victorian Revival', *Architectural Review,* March, 1978). But of course even as early as about 1919 *Vogue* had begun to detect an interest in the 'amusing' artefacts of the early Victorian era, often running alongside the more acceptable Regency revival. Then, after the war, the Victoriana craze started to look more like an autonomous fashion. Among fashion people, the architects, artists and writers who founded the Victorian Society, and the circles which centred on some of the smarter curators of the Victoria & Albert Museum, it became the last word to re-create, albeit theatrically, the richness, prettiness and whimsy of the mid-Victorian era.

423

A Victorian revival parlour

Illustration by Osbert Lancaster from Here, of All Places, London, 1959

424

423

Osbert Lancaster's nicely observed drawing of a Victoriana room was one of those he added to the sequel to *Homes Sweet Homes,* which appeared in 1959, in order to keep up with what he saw as the most significant developments in taste in England after the war. (Both volumes were republished together as *A Cartoon History of Architecture* in 1976.) Among the features of the revival which he singled out as the most interesting are the fads for things under glass domes, for the paraphernalia of the fireplace and mantelshelf, and for luxuriant arrays of the ferns favoured in the nineteenth century and housed in elaborated wire plant stands.

John Murray Ltd, London

424

Dining area in the London apartment of the dress designer Digby Morton 1952

Phyllis and Digby Morton's flat in London epitomizes the smart, fashion-world approach to decoration in the 1950s. It was carved out of an unpromising block and suffered from ugly windows and intrusive iron beams. All these disadvantages were concealed by the elegant use of mirrored panels and divisions, and the resulting spaces were filled with a highly eclectic mix of colourful and decorative pieces. Vogue Regency and Victoriana co-existed happily here with neo-baroque elements such as blackamoor figures left over from the 1930s, and the total effect was one of uncluttered whimsicality. Much of the furniture in the flat was Victorian papier-mâché inlaid with mother-of-pearl. At the dining end of the main room Regency chairs were painted with a motif copied from the eighteenth-century marble table-top, which stood on an elaborate mid-nineteenth-century carved and gilded base.

Ideal Home

425

425

Mrs Willie King in her Victorian drawing room, 15 Thurloe Square, London

Viva King was the wife of the curator of ceramics at the Victoria and Albert Museum, Willie King, and a celebrated and popular hostess. Her enthusiasm for the things of the nineteenth century led her to form a fascinating collection of the genre pictures of the Victorian era long before others appreciated or valued such forgotten works of art. In this one of her few serious rivals was Evelyn Waugh. Viva hung her pictures densely, as they had hung in the nineteenth century, and complemented them in the drawing room with a spot-pattern shiny paper, in the taste of the period, and a richly coloured carpet. In this photograph she stands beside a characteristic arrangement of a papier-mâché table bearing a glass dome of wax fruits, and she wears a splendid dress of the 1860s–70s loaned to her by her friend Doris Langley Moore, the collector and authority on costume.

426

Collectors' items   *c.*1953

A dresser arranged with ceramics from the collection of Henry Swanzy; photograph by Edwin Smith from Olive Cook and Edwin Smith, Collectors' Items from The Saturday Book, *London, 1955*

With the increasing fascination of collectors and decorators alike for Victoriana and the simple and delightful artefacts of the Regency, the arranging of such previously unconsidered trifles became a serious preoccupation. The taste for such things was certainly stimulated by the clever picture-essays in the pages of the ever-popular *Saturday Book*, which appeared each year for the Christmas market, to the extent that it is possible to think in terms of a '*Saturday Book* style'. This arrangement of mugs, jugs, teapots and other domestic objects was photographed in the house of the collector Henry Swanzy. It is a kind of grouping that has been endlessly imitated, though not always with such an intriguing mixture of old pieces alongside the more recent, but entirely sympathetic, modern examples by Eric Ravilious. Mr Swanzy's cut-out paper pelmet is also a remarkably stylish additional touch, suggesting wit and flair in the creation of an effect with the simplest of means.

Courtesy of Olive Smith

426

427

427

Old and new 1958–9

Drawing room of Michael Inchbald's house, Chelsea

Michael Inchbald's bold salmon-red drawing room is one of the most accomplished essays in the blending of old and new of its period. Almost unchanged to this day, it remains a successful and still exciting room typical of his consistently inventive and stylish approach to design. Carefully remodelled to provide good proportions, it contains many features then novel, such as the floor inlaid in a stylized neo-classical pattern of different-coloured marbled linoleums. In the main part of the room are arranged a number of beautiful and important objects from Michael Inchbald's very choice collection, while beyond we look into the small conservatory or winter garden added at first-floor level. This winter garden is again very carefully scaled and detailed in order visually to correct original imperfections in the alignment of the house. Michael Inchbald designed and had made the earliest narrow-strip Venetian blind for these windows.

Courtesy of Michael Inchbald

428

David Hicks's first essay in colour 1953

Drawing room of the South Eaton Place house of Mrs Herbert Hicks; from House & Garden, *1954*

David Hicks's career as an interior decorator was launched by a series of photographs published in *House & Garden* magazine showing the rooms he had created in the South Eaton Place house that his mother had bought in 1953, the year after he left art school. Remarkable chiefly for their extraordinarily confident handling of brilliant colours in previously unheard of combinations, these schemes already have much of the Hicks style about them. Old and new things are mixed without hesitation: a gilt neo-Gothic chair of the 1830s is upholstered in bright purple, Victorian lamps are given new cylindrical lamp-shades, prints and drawings in uncompromising coloured mounts are massed in formal patterns on the walls. All

428

these elements point the way towards the look which David Hicks quickly established as his own and which, in its crisp clarity of line and concern for style, clearly marked him as the most important and influential designer of interiors of his generation. For four years Hicks was in partnership with Tom Parr, who later went to run Colefax & Fowler. By 1959 he was established in his own shop in Lowndes Street, and as the 1960s dawned he was attracting not only chic and fashionable urban clients but also those who owned old and grand houses and wished to make a new statement. David Hicks became perhaps the one interior decorator of whom most people in Britain had heard, and one of the first designers to establish a truly international reputation.

Condé Nast Publications Ltd, London

1960–1980
ALTERNATIVE LIFESTYLES
AND REFLECTING SUCCESS

The 1960s and 70s seem to have been dominated by a frenetic search for style. Everyone wanted an 'image' and, having achieved it, proceeded to try to use that look to promote themselves, their cause or their product. The business of designing interiors was intimately connected with this process, and as a result the creation of 'personal spaces' or 'environments' became a major concern for all those who considered themselves visually aware and interested in the workings of fashion and the media.

Interiors in general became more widely accessible, if not in reality then in the burgeoning pages of the glossy magazines devoted to the subject, in newspapers and on television. The lifestyles of the famous were exposed to a far greater degree than in past decades and the interiors of their houses became available for scrutiny. This real-life glamour was imitated and in due course outstripped by 'fictional' settings on television and in films, with the result that a great multiplicity of styles became possible. It was an era in which, it was said, 'anything goes'.

In both Europe and America grand traditional decoration continued to be carried out, though at a soaring cost. In the earlier years of this period the small, highly skilled firms which had traditionally underpinned the decoration industry still continued in business, and in some circles things had changed very little since the end of the war. Thus a figure such as Oliver Messel, whose distinguished work for the stage was much loved and admired, could at this point undertake the decoration of an English country house, Flaxley Abbey (pl. 401). In fact Messel never truly succeeded in any of his domestic projects: his work as a designer of interiors is better represented by his Vogue Regency 'stage-set' rooms at the Dorchester Hotel and his delightful decor for the Bond Street shoe shop Rayne, which survived until only recently.

The varieties of approach to traditional-style interiors

can be seen in American schemes of the early 60s. These range from the elegant restatements of the ideals of the past in the work of T.H. Robsjohn-Gibbings through to the more obviously New York chic theatrical setting, created with Louis furniture and baroque sculpture by the English gentleman-amateur decorator Simon Fleet for the flamboyant Fulco di Verdura, Italian painter, socialite and designer of jewellery for Chanel. At the furthest extreme of this line of development lies the rich, Hollywood exhibitionist style of overblown, bogus historicism epitomized by the delightfully self-parodying Second Empire style and baroque camp of Liberace's California house (pl. 446), one of his several exercises in decorative excess.

Less startling American interiors of the 60s still revealed a love of novel materials and effects: even the most established of New York firms found it necessary from time to time to work in a crisp, modern and colourful style that contrasted with their usual French and English period pieces. Colour is revealed as one of the central obsessions of the early and mid-60s, with bold effects being encouraged both by fashion and by the tremendous advances in paint technology whereby, suddenly it seemed, all the colours previously confined to the designer's paintbox and imagination became available as emulsion and tough gloss finishes for walls.

David Hicks remains the key figure in understanding the decoration of the period. Hicks had burst upon what might almost be called an unsuspecting public as early as 1954, when *House & Garden* showed the remarkable schemes which he had carried out in his mother's London house, his first serious essay in the design of rooms. In these interiors three essential elements of the Hicks style were already to be discerned: his inimitable (and seemingly fearless) colour sense, his feeling for the grouping of objects in telling arrangements, and his long-maintained but then innovative commitment to mixing the best of the old and the best of the new. Over the years David Hicks has held to each of these ideals, emerging as an influential designer of geometric pattern, refining his taste in objects and furniture along increasingly architectural lines and, in the course of a lifetime spent arranging interesting and beautiful things, inventing that minor but perfect art form, the 'tablescape'.

By the mid-60s a number of designers such as François Catroux in Paris and John Stefanidis in London were working with very bright colours, and using entirely novel furniture in wood and plastics as a counterpoint to the large abstract pictures which enjoyed a great vogue at that time. Others, such as David Mlinaric, were already feeling the way towards an entirely eclectic style, in which large and handsome eighteenth-century furniture and objects and Victorian pictures were used in a 'de-contextualized' manner, for their intrinsic beauty or quirkiness of form rather than as period pieces. Characteristic elements of these rooms were huge low sofas, exposed plain floorboards – perhaps sanded and polished – and interesting things such as vast family portraits hung without their frames and picked out by spotlights or the ubiquitous up-and down-lighters of the period.

Among the more adventurous architects and designers at work at this time, whose creations became thought of as part of the movement which *Time* magazine enduringly christened 'Swinging London', were a number, such as Max Clendenning, whose attitudes affected the 'alternative lifestyles' of the young. Clendenning's radical furniture, which included knock-flat pieces in a deliberately space-age style, and more overtly experimental environments such as Alex MacIntyre's 'Trip Box' (pl. 442), both recall the excitement of what appeared in 1967–8 to be the shape of things to come. By the early 70s, however, it had just about vanished beneath a rising tide of nostalgia, encouraged by the seductive grandeur offered in the shops of the emerging dealer-decorators such as Christopher Gibbs and Geoffrey Bennison.

At first the retrospective quality of much that became fashionable in the early 70s was slightly blurred, for the revival of Art Deco, which culminated in London in the widely imitated interiors of the third and largest of the famous 'Biba' shops, bore a sufficient resemblance to the glossy style of New York apartments, and of California houses as portrayed by David Hockney, as to seem part of the same aesthetic and stylistic movement. Only as the back-to-nature elements of the desire for alternative lifestyles began to be reflected in the fitting out of urban kitchens in stripped pine, country cottage style, did it become apparent that not only Modernism but also the more gentle forms of contemporary design in the home were under attack.

As the nostalgic ideal spread down-market another irony emerged: in the wake of the immense popularity of British television costume drama such as *The Forsyte Saga*, and later especially *Upstairs Downstairs* (which enjoyed enormous success in the United States and on the Continent as well as at home), while the rich continued to commission period-style interiors based on the grand apartments of the English country house, the vastly wider section of the population who rely on commercial furnishings were making their rooms resemble the servants' quarters of those very houses.

As custodians of an enormously popular tradition Colefax & Fowler were by the late 70s justifiably proud that their work was often for not just second but sometimes third generation clients. The ideal seems endlessly renewable and still enjoys both prestige and popularity in America, where a number of decorators took the late Fowler style as their starting point. Mario Buatta, the leading exponent of the style in New York is, so to speak, in true canonical descent, having worked for the master for a short time after coming to England to look at English houses and decoration. Keith Irvine, English-born but now living and working in America, whose own style is somewhat more eclectic and at least as indebted to the interiors of Charles de Beistegui as to Fowler, in fact worked with him after graduating from the Royal College of Art in London. Several other of the major figures in America would acknowledge Fowler's influence.

Such was, and is, the demand for traditional 'High Style' decoration in New York that nearly all the established grand firms of the earlier decades continued to flourish throughout this period. Some, such as McMillen Inc., continued to produce interiors almost identical to the ones they had created in the 30s, whilst others, such as Mrs Henry Parish's firm, under the direction of Albert Hadley, increased the range of their activities. And, of course, there was always room for a new talent such as Mark Hampton, who had first worked with David Hicks and rapidly established himself as a key figure on the vibrant New York scene.

In any account of the major areas of activity in the creation of rooms in the 70s, some mention must be made of the work of conservation architects and the decorators who work in this specialized but highly influential field. Again it is necessary to look to the influence of John Fowler, for his seminal work with the National Trust has to an extraordinary degree set the pattern and established the codes of practice which tend to be observed not only in England but in America and elsewhere. Although Fowler worked to some extent by instinct, his knowledge of period detail and materials and his sensitivity to the individual case gave his work a special quality. He could however take the occasional bold decision on the basis of taste alone and at times propose a less than ideal solution. More recent practice has tended towards the use of laboratory tests, paint sections (the scientific analysis of the paint layers present: a more accurate version of the old 'paint-scrape') and a greater use of the surviving historic documentation in order to get as close to the 'correct' result as possible. David Mlinaric, who succeeded Fowler as the Trust's principal adviser, has adopted an approach of extreme reticence. This can be seen in his subtle colouring of the hall at Beningborough, where the intention was to reveal the architectural forms without superimposing any other more overt 'decoration' (pl. 465).

In his work in the magnificent rooms of the British Embassy in Paris, once the house of Napoleon's sister Pauline Borghese, Mlinaric has allowed the richness of the original decoration to suggest the more lavish use of brighter gilding and strong colour appropriate to the Empire period. In this work Mlinaric comes much closer to Continental practice in the restoration of historic interiors, in which the attempt is often made to recapture the brilliance of the decorative scheme through the use of reprinted or rewoven textiles and furniture and other objects brought up to a high finish. This approach can be seen in the work carried out by the French conservation teams at Malmaison (pls 17–24), in the First and Second Empire apartments in the Château of Compiègne, and at its most lavish in the startlingly bright gilding (which is not entirely successful) and lavish textiles in the King's Bedchamber at Versailles.

What might be thought of as the opposite to this approach was that adopted by Peter Thornton (then Keeper of Furniture and Woodwork at the Victoria & Albert Museum) in the restoration of rooms at Ham House, near London (pl. 455). His method, which developed in a period of rather limited funding, might be termed an intellectual or cerebral rather than sensual one. It aimed to use the documents to gain a precise idea of the original furnishings, textiles and paint finishes and then merely to suggest, sometimes almost diagrammatically, the idea of the seventeenth-century appearance, for the most part without the use of materials of equivalent richness. The success or failure of such a method has been hotly disputed. Intriguingly it does not seem to have been taken up as an approach in Russia, where it might be supposed it would find acceptance for a number of economic and ideological reasons. In fact, in Leningrad and elsewhere, work is being carried out on a scale of richness hardly equalled in the time of the Tsars.

429

429

A feeling for architectural values 1966

A library in Kent; drawing showing a scheme of redecoration by David Mlinaric

David Mlinaric has developed over the years a personal aesthetic based on a serious regard for architectural values and a kind of confident reticence. After his original training in architecture at the Bartlett School there followed periods with the decorator and designer Michael Inchbald and in the office of Dennis Lennon, both figures whose work is strongly underpinned by an essential sense of order. In 1965 David Mlinaric set up his own practice, and one of his first important commissions came from an influential patron in whose house in Kent many rooms had been decorated by Colefax & Fowler. Mlinaric recalls that he deliberately set out to make his library different in feel: quieter in tone and suggestive of architectural repose. As the decorator's first essay in a specifically period manner the scheme was a remarkable success, markedly differing from the other rather more hectic rooms in the house, and indicative of the way in which his subtle approach to historic buildings would develop.

Courtesy of David Mlinaric

430

Neo-baroque in America early 1960s

New York apartment of Fulco di Verdura, decorated by Simon Fleet

Simon Fleet was one of those brilliantly inventive amateur decorators whose own eccentric and highly successful interiors and the few commissions which he carried out for friends have had a profound influence on the work of professional decorators. His own residences, a converted army hut (once photographed in all seriousness by *House & Garden*) and his 'Gothic Box', a tiny cottage in Chelsea which he castellated, were both monuments to his whimsical fantasy in decoration and to his extraordinary eye for combining very good objects with others of nothing but amusement value. When he created interior schemes for others he played slightly more seriously with traditional forms and used grander objects, yet never lost the sense of fun which pervades all his projects. For Fulco di Verdura, an Italian duke and painter who lived in New York and designed opulent jewellery for Chanel, Fleet decorated this apartment in about 1960. He made the whole scheme a play on the classic chic style of the 1930s, adding to the obvious elements – long, neutral curtains, plain walls, wall-to-wall carpet and a little white-and-gilt French sofa – a pair of mad, baroque white carved figures on vigorous rockwork bases.

Victoria & Albert Museum, London

431

The Fowler touch 1970

Design for the curtain treatment for the 'best bedroom', Chevening, Kent, presentation drawing by John Fowler

At the time when it was proposed that Chevening should become the official residence of the Prince of Wales, John Fowler was approached to advise on the decoration of the house, and prepared and presented a number of schemes before the entire project was abandoned. Fowler's characteristic method both of showing his ideas for curtains or other details to clients and of briefing the curtain makers and other craftsmen was to give them the roughest of scribbles on odd scraps of paper or (literally) the back of an envelope. When he discovered that

Prince Charles intended to have the support and advice of his uncle Lord Mountbatten at the presentation of the Chevening schemes, Fowler took fright and decided that he would have to take more care than usual in the preparation of his sketches. Thus these curtain treatments are the most finished, and indeed almost the only conventionally tidy, drawings he ever made.

Victoria & Albert Museum, London

430

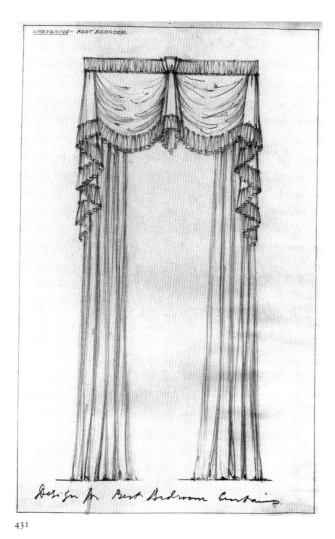

431

432

In the grand manner 1968-9

432

The Saloon, Clandon Park, Surrey; restored by John Fowler

The 1960s and early 1970s were the period of John Fowler's closest connection with and influence upon the National Trust in its preservation and presentation of historic houses. His attitudes to the care of original decoration and its sensitive renewal form the basis of much of the standard conservation practice of the present day. Fowler's unrivalled knowledge of the techniques and materials of early paintwork and his understanding of the decorative use of textiles in interiors earned him a unique position of respect among academics, historians of architecture and the owners of houses. It is sometimes said that his hand can be seen in the appearance of too many of the properties of the Trust, and it is certainly the case that he tended to have a preferred period and style of decoration which led him to try to bring out the early eighteenth-century characteristics of rooms and houses rather at the expense of other aspects of their history and decorative development. He did, however, have an extraordinary ability to pull together the tired and disparate elements in any house and to create convincingly confident schemes with the minimum of repainting (he preferred to wash old paintwork if possible), achieved through attention to small points of historic detail and a great flair for the arrangement of furniture and objects in telling groups. The major campaign of restoration and rearrangement at Clandon in 1968-9 resulted in the complete rethinking of many rooms and a number of bold decisions. The Green Drawing Room had the state bed in it; this was removed to its proper situation and the room was once again furnished as a sitting room. The clutter of drawing room furniture was removed from the saloon, and this important apartment was treated in a far grander and more architectural manner. The walls were repainted, on the evidence of paint sections, in three shades of blue, and the heavy overmantel, previously washed in white, was marbled and picked out in black and white to give it the same strength as the heavy chimney-piece. Happily, Fowler retained the post-war Austerity curtains, made from dyed blankets by the firm of Green & Abbott and now a fascinating period piece, when he found that they complemented his new colour scheme.

The National Trust, London

434

433

Painted ceiling

*Design by Brian Thomas for Paul Paget, Templewood,
near Northrepps, Norfolk*

Templewood was built in an interesting neo-Georgian
style by Seely & Paget for Lord Templewood (Sir
Samuel Hoare) in 1938, incorporating architectural elements salvaged from the Nuthall Temple, near Nottingham
(1754) and from Soane's Bank of England. Pevsner describes it as looking 'in an engaging way like a stage-set for
an Italian eighteenth-century opera, performed in England
in the twentieth'. The great central space of the house is the
saloon, for which Brian Thomas, the celebrated stained
glass designer and decorative artist, designed this ceiling.
Conceived in the Beaux-Arts tradition, the design incorporates a number of wittily depicted references to the life and
thoroughly modern interests of Paul Paget, who commissioned the work, while in overall effect it conforms to the
general composition and palette expected of a painted
ceiling in the grand manner.

Victoria & Albert Museum, London

434

Decorating with antiques early 1960s

Drawing by David Gentleman from Elizabeth Kendall,
House into Home, *London, 1962*

By the early to mid-1960s the fashion for cluttering every
interior with small and decorative antiques was well
established. In England a number of writers, such as Mary
Gilliatt in her admirable study *English Style* which appeared in 1967, even went so far as to stress the essential
Englishness of the so-called eclectic interior. As a result, the
traditional street markets which supplied the antique trade
became much more widely known, and the Portobello
Road in particular became a major element in the myth-
making process which culminated in the proclamation of
'swinging London' in 1966. Popular books on decoration
all stressed the need to 'group things' and make imaginative
juxtapositions. Mary Gilliatt referred quite rightly to the
'cult of the object in the modern interior'.

J.M. Dent & Sons, London

433

435

435
New ways with traditional materials, USA early 1960s

'Dining nook' in an apartment by Roslyn Rosier

The great popularity of the use of 'natural' materials such as wood, stone and exposed brick in the interior architecture of the 1950s and early 1960s has been linked convincingly with notions of a popular search for simple, comforting visual symbols of permanence in an increasingly hostile or transitory world of apartments, bad conversions and poorly built new houses. To some degree the use of such natural materials as marble or rare woods also became an indicator of wealth, and therefore of prestige. Decorators as much as architects found themselves influenced by these considerations, and sought new and interesting ways to use the traditional materials. In a 'dining nook' of an apartment Roslyn Rosier used a natural, clearly grained whitewood with gunmetal grey rubbed into the surface to create this intriguingly graphic effect. The chandelier in thin black metal echoes this linear quality.

Private collection

436

A new eclecticism 1960s

The London drawing room of John French

That most stylish fashion photographer John French and his wife, Vere, were among those who pioneered the development of the Regency taste into the full-blown Victorian revival after the war, along with others such as Hardy Amies, Lady Ashton (Madge Garland), Viva King and, perhaps more surprisingly, Evelyn Waugh. By the late 1950s, however, John French had already begun to eliminate some of the Parian ware figures, vases and other pieces

436

of Victoriana to be seen in the photographs of earlier rooms, in favour of an altogether more spare or 'cool' arrangement of, at first glance, rather heterogeneous objects. There is a definite attempt to blend the old and the new in a newly chic way, and the elements which are gathered here have become to a great extent the ingredients of a classic and international look. Large Chinese paintings, Regency sofas, tall screens and panels of mirror glass, low tables with 'decorator's objects' and lavish arrangements of flowers constitute a look which has been cultivated in London and New York, Florida and California, and as far afield as Sydney.

Courtesy of Vere French

437

A new classicism   1960s

Dining room in the apartment of Mr and Mrs Goulandris, Athens, decorated and with furniture designed by T.H. Robsjohn-Gibbings

The final phase of Robsjohn-Gibbings's career took him to Greece in search of the purest forms of classical architecture and furniture. Working from his apartment overlooking the Parthenon, he carried out a number of projects notable for their extreme austerity, their insistence on the beauty of line and materials, and their almost complete avoidance of any superfluous ornament. Several of the designer's elegant pieces of furniture, all of which were based on ancient prototypes of the classical period, were manufactured commercially by the Widdicombe Furniture Company of Grand Rapids in Missouri. They have remained firm favourites with designers such as Giovanni Patrini of Milan who favour an earlier, archaeological form of neo-classicism.

Private collection

437

438

Design for living 1965

*Room setting by Geoffrey Bennison with Italian furniture,
used to illustrate an article 'Design for living' by Priscilla
Chapman, The Sunday Times, 1965*

This room set dating from the earlier phase of Geoffrey
Bennison's career, at a time when he was still principally concerned with the creation of contemporary schemes
for houses and especially restaurants, and before he
concentrated on antiques, is typical of his stylish and
dramatic use of recent Italian furnishings. Designed to
show off some of the most highly regarded pieces of the day,
the room nevertheless retains a certain unmistakably
Swedish modern influence, revealed particularly in the
prominence accorded to the wood-burning stove, which is
made into what at that time would certainly have been
described as a 'feature'. The furniture includes the 'Bastiano' seating range by Tobia Scarpa and the 'Caori' table by
the celebrated furniture designer Magistretti. The lamp, in
polished steel supported on an arc of spring steel from a
block of marble, is the 'Toio' designed by the brothers
Castiglioni. It rapidly became a classic, and in the mid-
1960s achieved an almost totemic status in the rooms of the
avant-garde from Milan to Los Angeles.

Courtesy of Philippe and Lucilla Garner

438

439

439

Op Art 1969

*Room set with furnishings by Oscar Woollens Ltd from
their promotional calendar for 1970; model Pixie Garvin,
photograph Ronald Bennett*

Commercial furnishing manufacturers in England and
abroad are not always slow to pick up influences and
ideas current in the more avant-garde areas of the design
world. By the mid-1960s the 'alternative lifestyles' of the
self-styled 'underground' movements were becoming a
factor to be taken into consideration even by the high street
retailers, and for a short time highly unconventional
furnishings became quite popular. The renewed interest
around 1966 in the work of Aubrey Beardsley gave a black-
and-white cast to much of the current Art Nouveau revival,
and this found a sympathetic echo in the bold visual effects
of the 'Op Art' painters Bridget Riley in England and Victor
Vasarely in France. In this setting by the astute designers of
the modern ranges at Oscar Woollens, these influences
combine in a deliberately striking way to produce a classic
look of 'Swinging London'.

Oscar Woollens Ltd

440

Drawing room in New York by David Hicks   1966

For the designer Mark Hampton

Boldness, clarity of design and a special feeling for the simple grandeur and scale of the eighteenth century characterize David Hicks's work of the 1960s. Visually inventive and with a strongly developed and highly personal approach to the use of colour, David Hicks's vision was the single most influential factor in the development of the interior during the decade. Hicks's work for a great many socially prominent clients both in England and America, and his series of books which advocated not only the 'Hicks look', but the whole Hicks lifestyle, represent the most carefully thought-out, adept and well-respected exercise in the marketing of taste since the days of Edith Wharton and Elsie de Wolfe.

Courtesy of David Hicks

440

441

Space-age living 1968

Design for a living area by Max Clendenning, drawn by Ralph Adron for an article in the Daily Telegraph Magazine

Max Clendenning was one of the pioneers in the 1960s of a futuristic aesthetic which took as its starting point the smooth forms and pared-down detailing of the 1930s. This design for a living area had much in common with the Smithsons' House of the Future in its use of flowing lines and non-rectilinear forms and modules for the service parts of the structure. Clendenning carried out a number of such schemes at this time for himself, for private clients and as demonstration pieces for television and exhibitions. To some extent, however, such 'futuristic' design rapidly became dated and a stylistic dead end. More influential were the designer's experiments with inflatable furniture and with a range of pieces made from cut-out shapes in wood which slotted together.

Victoria & Albert Museum, London

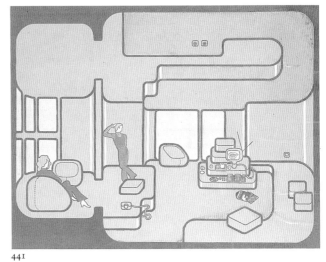

441

442

Alternative lifestyles 1970–1

The 'Trip Box' designed by Alex MacIntyre, installed at Maples, Tottenham Court Road, London

One of the most serious and intriguing reflections of the interest taken by the commercial world in what was happening in the 'underground' culture of the late 1960s was the exhibition *Experiments in Living*. Staged in conjunction with the *Daily Telegraph* by the old-established furnishing store, Maples, it was held at their famous London showrooms in Tottenham Court Road, since the nineteenth century a traditional centre of the high street furnishing trade. For the show a number of avant-garde designers were invited to create deliberately unconventional or 'alternative' environments. These included a rather terrifyingly claustrophobic 'retreat pod' in the form of an egg by Martin Dean, and the Trip Box by Alex MacIntyre, a classic of the 'psychedelic' 1960s. The aim of the Trip Box was to create an infinitely variable and programmable world-within-a-world, in which ready-made hallucinatory experiences could be conjured at will through a sophisticated sound system and images which were back-projected on to any or all of the wall and ceiling panels of 'Makrolon' polycarbonate sheet. MacIntyre was quoted in the descriptive catalogue which accompanied the show as having designed the 'escape pad' for 'rich Americans who like to have the best of both worlds, the old and the new . . .' or 'just for sheer kicks'.

The Telegraph Colour Library, London

442

443

Jet-set glamour   1971

Mr and Mrs Clark and Percy; *acrylic on canvas by David Hockney*

David Hockney's paintings, prints and drawings of the early 1970s captured so precisely the mood and feel of certain kinds of international modernistic decoration that they became a major factor in the popularizing, or glamorizing, of the look and the lifestyle which it expressed. His most complete statement of this period is the large acrylic painting depicting his close friends the fashion designer Ossie Clark and his then wife Celia Birtwell, who has subsequently become established in her own right as a creator of dress and furnishing textiles. They are shown in the first-floor drawing room of their Notting Hill Gate apartment, a large and sparsely furnished room, with a full-length window fitted with louvred shutters opening on to a heavily balustraded balcony. The only visible pieces of furniture are typically early-1970s commercial versions of the Modern movement: a sub-Mies tubular chrome chair and a low, lacquered table; while the 'decorative' elements include a vase of classic white lilies and a piece of left-over 1960s Art Nouveau. The white plastic telephone has equal prominence. Walls and paintwork are in neutral shades and the floor is covered with a square of deep shag-pile carpet, a fashion whose chic did not survive its rapid dissemination as a decorative novelty through the high street furnishers.

© *David Hockney 1971; The Tate Gallery, London*

443

Couture decoration   early 1970s

Zandra Rhodes's Notting Hill flat, London

444
Bedroom

445
Bathroom

Zandra Rhodes's interiors for her own house in London's newly fashionable Notting Hill reflect her designs for dresses, not only in the use of her own printed fabrics, but also in the ways in which fabric and trimmings are put together. This recalls John Fowler's use of dress-maker's detailing in his post-war austerity schemes, but takes the idea a stage further: all the decorations in the Rhodes house are based on fabric that is stuffed, twisted, ruched and draped, almost to the exclusion of any conventional, solid pieces of furniture. Throughout the house there is a tremendous feeling of sensual and luxurious opulence, which results from the use of yards and yards of fabric. The bedroom is tented in very closely and lavishly draped blue-and-apricot printed silk, pattern upon pattern in shimmering layers, and the luxurious quality is further enhanced by heaps of cushions, patterned and quilted in designs reminiscent of, and in a sense alluding to, the Hollywood star's bedroom look of the 1930s. Here and elsewhere in the house are a number of pieces from an extensive collection of modern ceramics by Carol McNicoll. In several rooms specially commissioned pieces by modern craftsmen form part of the interior schemes, while in others pieces of stage-set dressing, such as giant columns and a huge Indian idol in glass fibre, contribute to a more flamboyantly theatrical effect. The bathroom is a dark and glittering subterranean chamber, tiled to Zandra Rhodes's own design and equipped with a shell-shaped basin and other fittings in gold-spangled cast resin.

Arcaid; photographs Lucinda Lambton

445

446

446
Baroque excess in America 1960s

Music room in the California house of Liberace

Liberace, the popular pianist, created for himself a camp, baroque and self-parodying persona, backed up with a lavish display of gaudy finery in his stage costumes and sets, which he carried over into the way he lived in his many 'luxury' houses. With a love greater even than Norman Hartnell's for lavish chandeliers and gilding, Liberace made the most vulgar of grand pianos and a huge candelabrum his tongue-in-cheek trade mark. He gathered what he liked to call his 'pretty things' (that same phrase once used so differently by Lord Clark of Charles Ricketts's collection!) from antique dealers all over the world. Many pieces of his furniture, much of the fine glass and porcelain and some of his examples of ormolu were important French Second Empire rococo revival objects of museum quality, with interesting provenances. In this music room, for example, the piano was reputed to have belonged to Chopin. Its unusual degree of decoration was echoed by the many surrounding pieces of richly carved and gilded furniture, and the whole effect was set off by the splendidly opulent and rather early example of shag-pile carpeting, specially woven with a musical motif.

Courtesy of the James Agency, California

447
60s Victoriana 1969–70

Design for the refurbishment of the Markham Arms, King's Road, London, by Roderick Gradidge with Anthony Ballantine

The domestic interior of the late 1960s and early 1970s was much influenced by developments in the commercial field. One aspect of this trend was the extent to which temporary effects came to play a part as never before in the decoration of houses. Young people who moved house often decorated with a new verve and were not afraid of theatrical effects. A popular scheme which mixed traditional Victorian elements of public house decoration with a feel of the Art Nouveau revival was the work of the architect Roderick Gradidge in collaboration with Anthony Ballantine. Together they recast the interior of this much loved fashionable rendezvous using as a major theme elements drawn from the peacock patterns in Beardsley's *Salome* illustrations. For the walls they created a richly patterned covering in bronzed vacuum-formed plastic, a panel of which was used to frame this rendering. It also proved to be sufficiently translucent to be used in the cylindrical 'Art Nouveau' lanterns. This scheme of decoration survived until 1985: a long run for the decoration of a busy public house. Roderick Gradidge, who also worked from time to time with David Hicks, has subsequently pursued a career involving the sensitive restoration and adaptation of period buildings, including many by architects of the Arts and Crafts and Queen Anne revival movements, Lutyens and others. He created an impressive neo-baroque library in a room at Nicholas Hawksmoor's Easton Neston and recent projects include a new library for Sledmere, the seat of Sir Tatton Sykes, Bt.

Victoria & Albert Museum, London

447

448
A modern 'Wunderkammer' 1970s

Setting featuring 'objects' by Antony Redmile, London

ntony Redmile came to the creation of interiors through his work as a sculptor and creator of his 'objects', a remarkable range of pieces of ever more exuberant fancy. The 'objects' are designed in the tradition of the fabulous and curious artefacts of the seventeenth-century princely collectors' cabinets or *Wunderkammer*. Made from polished metals, cast resins and a variety of other natural and artificial materials, they incorporate, as did *Wunderkammer* objects, such elements as coconut shells, coral and seashells, tortoiseshell and a great many semi-precious stones. Antony Redmile's own rooms have been decorated with these spectacularly quirky pieces, and he has arranged groups of them in suitably exotic settings for other clients who shared his delight in the rich and unconventional. This group includes pieces with elephant tusks, which are no longer available, and sheep horns, which introduce a typically zoomorphic theme to the pair of covered cups on the stands.

Courtesy of Antony Redmile

448

449

450

Tradition, innovation and boldness 1960s

Three rooms by David Hicks

449

Tablescape by David Hicks at his house, Britwell Salome

David Hicks has always taken special delight in the arranging of groups of often disparate objects. He has given such arrangements the name 'tablescapes', which precisely captures their precious quality.

450

Drawing room of David Hicks's house in the south of France

This atmospheric room is a classic statement of David Hicks's ability to use over-scaled objects to dramatic effect. The room has both atmosphere and a typical quality of grandeur achieved by simple means.

451

Entrance hall of an eighteenth-century house

Of this hall David Hicks commented that all it really required was 'pruning'. Clearing away clutter and revealing the spare strength of eighteenth-century architecture is a recurrent theme in the history of taste in decoration, and David Hicks has advocated the emptying of spaces and the use of a small number of appropriately large-scale pieces to great effect in both town and country houses. Here in a country house the architectural qualities have been further played up by painting throughout in a stone colour.

449, 450, 451 Courtesy of David Hicks

452

Italian chic early 1970s

Drawing room of the Casa Brion, Milan, by Franco Albini & Franco Helg; from Casa Vogue, *October, 1972*

In the early 1970s *Casa Vogue* held sway as perhaps the most stylish and influential of the journals devoted to interiors. Certainly it was the one which came closest to establishing its distinctive look on an international basis in the way that *House & Garden* had done in the post-war years and *The World of Interiors* was to do in the early 1980s, taking the lead from *Architectural Digest*. The *Casa*

Vogue style was concerned with the new eclecticism in Italian, and particularly Milanese, design as much as with its traditional inventiveness. It favoured classic arrangements in which a good old tapestry might hang above a sleek black leather and chrome sofa, whilst a novel light fitting cast a pool of light on a fragment of ancient sculpture and a pile of old vellum-bound books. This drawing room by the highly regarded partnership of Franco Albini & Franco Helg, featured in 1972, is a quintessential example of the look which the magazine sought to promote.

Edizione Condé Nast SPA, Milan; photograph Aldo Ballo

452

The dealer-decorator's eye 1970s

The Soho flat of Geoffrey Bennison

453

The hallway

454

An arrangement of objects

Amajor influence on decorating trends in the 1970s, and one which continues to this day, has been the taste of a group of antique dealers which centred, until his untimely death in 1984, on Geoffrey Bennison. Bennison, who was widely revered for his bold and intriguing taste, was held to have one of the finest 'eyes' for a good decorative object, and was universally admired for his great natural gifts as an arranger of telling groups. He had trained as an architect, and as a student had had some minor involvement in the Festival of Britain. In the 1960s he created a number of memorable schemes for restaurants, including one, a Chinese establishment, for which he contrived a huge gilded birdcage containing over-scaled cranes. By the later 60s he had established his antique shop in Camden Passage in the then newly fashionable north London suburb of Islington. By the time he was established in the Pimlico Road in the 70s his name had become a byword for a distinct type of object: things that were grand, large in scale and often slightly decayed appealed most to his theatrical turn of mind, and his window became a source of delight and inspiration to a whole generation of decorators. In his own rooms he tended to favour a dramatic quality, and over the years he kept back for himself an intriguing group of objects. His favourite arrangement, and one which he repeated in more than one of his flats, was based around a huge carved classical head (a copy of the head of Laocoon from the famous classical group). This stood upon a bold pale wood and ebonized seventeenth-century cabinet with robust twisted columnettes which echoed the baroque turn of the head, while all around were heaps of ancient and beautifully bound books and, amongst pieces of coral and seashells, a skull. The complete effect was an entirely theatrical composition reminiscent of a princely cabinet of curiosities.

Photographs Michael Boys

453

454

455
'Intellectual restoration'

late 1970s

The Duchess of Lauderdale's private closet, Ham House, Richmond, Surrey, photographed in 1981

The restoration of the principal rooms of Ham House was carried out in the 1970s by the Victoria & Albert Museum, under the direction of the then Keeper of Furniture and Woodwork, Peter Thornton. As an academic specializing in the seventeenth century, he used his knowledge of the decorative techniques and materials of the era, and the considerable body of surviving documentation

relating to Ham House, its furnishings and other contents, to formulate a style of restoration intended to evoke some feeling of the original decoration of the house, using bright new fabrics and simplified trimmings. As an approach to the treatment of historic interiors the method was controversial, and attracted praise and condemnation in about equal measures. In rooms such as the Duchess of Lauderdale's bedchamber and private closet, the use of strongly coloured fabrics 'paned' (that is, sewn into framed panels) certainly gave an illuminating insight into the ways in which textiles enhanced the architectural feel of a room or a chair. At the same time, however, the actual fabrics were poor and unsympathetic to the surviving paint finishes and pieces of furniture. Critics of the restorations, such as John Cornforth, were quick to point out the irony that it was during the seventeenth century in particular that the 'prodigality' of textiles was crucial to the decorative effect of grand rooms. The restoration of Ham has proved an important landmark in the development of the methods and theories of conservation, both in England and internationally. While few schemes are undertaken with such uncompromising insistence on following written documents rather than surviving visual evidence, there can be little doubt that the intellectual rigour applied to the decision-making process has been an interesting addition to the more usual reliance on taste and feeling.

Victoria & Albert Museum, London

456
An unexpected treasure house   1970s

Drawing room of Andy Warhol's East 60th Street town house, New York

Few people who knew the almost overwhelming public face of Andy Warhol, the quintessential figure of the New York Pop Art world of the 1960s and 1970s, and indeed few of his friends, were aware of the extraordinary and unlikely interiors of the East 60s town house which he had acquired and filled with the plunder of what must have amounted to more than a decade of dedicated shopping. He described the house, which he had repainted in all its original colours, as the kind which 'belonged to somebody's WASP granny', and apparently took a perverse delight in the resulting sepulchral feel, rarely spending much time in the grandest rooms, the drawing and dining

455

rooms, and always sitting and eating in the kitchen. Many of the vast numbers of purchases which he made from dealers all over New York remained unopened, but recent investigations in order to prepare sale catalogues have revealed major collections of American Indian artefacts, Art Deco silver, jewels and furniture, remarkable pictures by friends and contemporaries and a group of very fine Federal and American Empire style furniture, which set the august tone of the 'state rooms'. There were, it appears, no works by Warhol himself in the house.

Photograph Evelyn Hofer

457

A pine interior c.1970

Interior of a barn conversion by Aldington Craig & Collinge

The continued influence of the Swedish modern aesthetic is seen in this barn conversion project with a particularly international feel by the partnership of Aldington Craig & Collinge. The Swedish influence is especially noticeable in the use of features such as the 'ecological' wood-burning stove, but also underpins the entire scheme in its use of untreated timber, horizontal pine boarding and fixed seating with long, low lines. The thick white rug laid on bare polished boards also recalls the 1950s. The furniture includes a number of popular classics of the 1960s, such as the wire chairs. The lighting is by spotlights carefully positioned on lighting tracks.

Arcaid; photograph Richard Bryant

457

458

The democratization of taste 1970s

Bedroom setting from the Habitat Catalogue, 1973

The true 'alternative lifestyle' of the 1960s and 1970s was one in which traditional notions of decoration, 'period' or 'modern', played little or no part. Terence Conran, as design entrepreneur and retailer, brilliantly identified the enormous potential market for a new, bright and economically priced range of furnishings and domestic goods, bringing the idea of 'design' to the high street.

The annual Habitat catalogues, which always show the furnishings in context, have proved a very influential factor in the way vast numbers of people arrange their rooms, and indeed live their lives. The earlier issues tended to reflect Terence Conran's personal taste quite closely. Rooms were often architecturally handsome but treated in a very simple and unhistorical way. Walls were painted rather than papered in white or strong, clear colours, sometimes recalling the 1950s love of colours such as 'beer-froth brown' or 'avocado'. Furnishings were simple in form, with clean lines and no decoration, and often came 'knocked down' for home assembly. Natural woods such as the pale-yellowish beech and, of course, pine predominated, but lacquered finishes, again in strong, clear reds, greens and yellows were also favoured. The room settings tended to show an eclectic mixture of objects, including modern light fittings and ceramics, usually in white. Older artefacts and natural or 'found' objects added character to the arrangements, and so humanized what might otherwise have seemed very stark and austere surroundings. In this bedroom setting a selection of such old and new pieces is arranged on a shelf unit from the 'Lundia' range, while in the foreground is a typical Conran adaptation of a 'classic', a Thonet-style hatstand in natural-finish bentwood. Beyond the screen can be seen a very simple divan and another typical Habitat piece of the period, the white melamine-finish cube-shaped bedside table.

Habitat

458

459

1930s revival in America c.1980

New York apartment by Steven Foreman

This classic New York apartment was created by Steven Foreman in a fashionable mid-town block for one of the most successful directors of big box-office films. The decorative scheme contains elements that are at once chic and modern, charming and nostalgic. There is a great deal of very well-crafted custom joinery which at once echoes the characteristic New York apartment wood floors and recalls the classic Art Deco of American bars and hotels. In one area of the open plan a grand piano is ingeniously included as a flowing built-in feature in a 1930s-style pastiche, while elsewhere this theme is taken up in the use of chrome and mirror glass. In this drinks area chrome cocktail shakers, a drum-shaped table and a stylish hanging lamp continue the theme.

Arcaid; photograph Paul Warchol

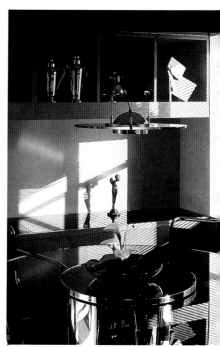

459

460

The English country house look in America   early 1970s

Drawing room in Mario Buatta's own apartment at 117 East 62nd Street, New York

Mario Buatta, a leading decorator and celebrated performer on the New York lecture circuit, first came to England with Stanley Barrow of Parsons' School of Design, and stayed on in London to work with John Fowler, who took him on as an assistant for a short period. In the drawing room of his own apartment in an architecturally distinguished Federal Revival town house on the Upper East Side, Buatta created in the early 1970s a colourful and richly detailed interior, which is at once both a homage to the style of John Fowler and a visual play on a number of the master's mannerisms. The walls, which retain the original panelling, are of a colour reminiscent of Mrs Lancaster's 'buttah-yallah' drawing room in Avery Row (pl. 404) and are densely hung with English dog pictures supported on over-scaled bows. The mixture of patterns, variety of seat furniture and use of the needlepoint rug and gilt wood looking-glass all now seem characteristic of the English style as interpreted in the United States, while the heavily fringed pouffe in front of the chimneypiece is a typically Fowleresque touch.

Victoria & Albert Museum, London

460

461

462
Tradition and romanticism in America c.1979

Design for a bedroom; drawing in pencil by Albert Hadley

Albert Hadley joined the firm founded by Mrs Parish ('Sister Parish') to form the New York partnership of Parish-Hadley. As a designer he works in a variety of idioms, from a crisply modern style right through to the lush romantic manner, juggling with historical elements and allusions, as exemplified by this bedroom, which evokes the magical atmosphere of the mansions of the Old South. Hadley's delightfully fluent drawing style is here used to full effect, playing with scale and details and deliciously suggesting the unreal atmosphere of *Gone with the Wind* with an enormously heightened four-poster bed, pretty window treatment and elaborately draped dressing table. Although this drawing is an idealized scheme of the kind which Albert Hadley delights to invent, it still gives a detailed idea of the types of furniture which, as a designer, he advocates. Apart from much-loved pieces, such as a loose-covered slipper chair, there are a classic Regency stool and a Japanese speckled-lacquer low table: all elements characteristic of the more eclectic version of the country house look current in America.

Victoria & Albert Museum, London

461
Billy Baldwin in retirement 1979

Living room, 22 Hussey Street, Nantucket, Massachusetts

Billy Baldwin had a long connection with that American architectural gem, the island of Nantucket. As a child he had spent happy summers there, and as he grew to appreciate its extraordinary and idiosyncratic buildings he rented various cottages on the island as retreats. He decorated these simple rooms in an appropriately restrained manner, eschewing any richness or gloss in the furnishings and preferring for the most part plain unpolished furniture. When he retired from professional life in 1973 at the age of seventy, he decided to move away from New York and to settle in a charming cottage on Hussey Street, Nantucket. In this last interior which he arranged, white walls and dark wood formed a simple contrast and the unadorned chimneypiece, above which hung a bleached set of antlers, formed a homely focus for a few unpretentious chairs and sofas.

Photograph Ernst Beadle. Copyright © 1979 by The Condé Nast Publications Inc., New York

462

463
The spirit of the age of grandeur late 1970s

Bedroom of David Hicks's London residence, Albany

None of the 'sets' (apartments) in the Albany, the late eighteenth-century development of apartments off Piccadilly, is very large, though most are handsomely proportioned. In his set David Hicks has demonstrated the essential continuity since the 1960s of his approach to the creation of grand interiors. Here he suggests all the sense of occasion and importance of a late seventeenth or early eighteenth-century state bed merely by the placing and bold draping of a simple divan. Other elements in the room similarly evoke the scale and effect of classic decoration. The good marble chimneypiece is surmounted by a looking-glass of exactly the right architectural proportions, but it is unframed, and the cupboards to right and left have no decorative mouldings; instead they make a dramatic point by supporting two large ceramic urns. Altogether the various elements combine to evoke the feeling of important scale and the ambience of period decoration, but are entirely free from the slavish copying of historic detailing.

Courtesy of David Hicks

464
Classical allusions in Paris c. 1979–80

Drawing room of François Catroux's own house, faubourg St-Honoré, Paris

The stylish allusions to architectural forms in this drawing room created for his own house by François Catroux, one of the most highly regarded French decorators, reflect the direction in which his designs have been moving. In the 1960s and early 1970s his work was more influenced by modern American ideas, and he used bright colours, extravagant pieces of modern furniture and large abstract pictures. In his more recent work neutral and stone colours predominate, and good antique and traditional furniture is mixed with architectural pieces which he has designed. In this room, which contains several favourite objects, such as the figure supporting an armillary sphere, there are a powerfully rusticated centre table and an interesting side table with rusticated columnar supports derived from Mannerist architectural forms, both of which are typical Catroux pieces. The carpet, which the designer uses throughout many rooms, is woven in a pattern of *trompe-l'oeil* marble squares and octagons, and is similar to the one created by Lutyens for Lady Sackville (pl. 143) which was later used by Edward James at Monkton.

Photograph Michael Boys

463

1980–1988
THE CULT OF DESIGN AND
THE NEW ORNAMENTALISM

It was the aesthete and critic Thomas Griffiths Wainewright, writing in the early part of the nineteenth century, who most eloquently stated the dangers attendant upon 'noticing the works of contemporaries'. 'I would cut off my forefinger to be impartial,' he continued, 'yet I can never satisfy myself that I am so. Things that spring up under my nose dazzle me; I must look at them through Time's Telescope. . . .'[1]

In spite of this admonition it has become the custom in books which deal with the history of taste in any of its branches, and which have the temerity to come up to the present day, to put forward some interpretation of their own times. This chapter therefore differs to some degree from the preceding six in that, in addition to the visual and descriptive survey of work created during the last eight years, it also offers some elements of more abstract interpretation of what Mario Praz first described in his felicitous phrase as 'la filosofia dell'arredamento'.[2]

We are the inheritors of a classical tradition of Graeco-Roman architecture, ornament and decoration stretching back thousands of years, but which has until recently been viewed, if at all, almost exclusively in terms of eighteenth-century canons of taste or in the distorting mirror of nineteenth-century historicism. For much of this century architecture turned away from tradition, deliberately seeking novel forms and leaving interior decorators alone to make what use they could of the great repertory of historic styles. Some stylists, such as David Hicks, have consistently utilized the past to make elegant restatements of the ideals of harmony and proportion, at once creating an unmistakably contemporary image and demonstrating the endlessly renewable potential of the classical tradition. The physical renewal or conservation of historic decoration is clearly not without its influence in this context, and the interplay between the sensitive practice of conservation and fashionable decoration, as epitomized in the work of David Mlinaric, has enriched both areas of activity(pl. 465).

In a period obsessed with a romanticized nostalgia in decoration, historicism has seldom since the mid-nineteenth century seemed nearer to sweeping away contemporary design, not only in our pretend country house drawing rooms, but, more remarkably, in the kitchen and bathroom too. This overwhelming desire to live in rooms with a 'period feel' has meant that for many the choices in design have been between the different varieties of comfortably domesticated neo-classicism. Of these the perennial favourite, English Regency, is beginning finally to be eclipsed by the increasing popularity of first Austrian and now, more particularly, Scandinavian Biedermeier. Those in the forefront of taste, such as Adriano Magistretti or Laure Welfling, seem, however, to be fleeing from this *gemütlich* (cosy) look and beginning to favour a more austere and visually demanding French Directoire, *néo-grec* or Pompeian classical manner (pls 483–5).

The great traditions of *grand luxe* decoration stretch back not just to the Edwardian era, but to the opulence of imperial Rome and the splendours of courtly life in sixteenth-century Italy or eighteenth-century France. It was palace architecture, the style of princes and great industrialists alike, which was ideally suited to the grand collectors of the nineteenth century such as Sir Richard Wallace (Lord Hertford), or Henry Clay Frick in the early twentieth. It remains the style to which the international 'jet-set' aspires today; but at its best it can also be an expression of the understated richness of fine materials, and the supreme comfort made possible by concentration on faultless plumbing as well as exquisite ormolu and precious marbles.

Between the wars the legendary Monsieur Boudin of the House of Jansen was the greatest exponent of *grand luxe*, working with some degree of fantasy for millionaire clients such as Sir Henry Channon; but at the same time the very perfection of the great Parisian luxury hotels threatened to fossilize the ideal in a *tous les Louis, style Georges Cinq* dreamworld.

Today luxury often has a more reticent or indeed wholly private face. For example few of the magnificent rooms created for Baron Thyssen by Renzo Mongiardino, the Milanese maestro of the 'old palazzo' look, have ever been published. Whilst this remains quintessentially the style of those who wish to impress, many will now choose to do so with immense subtlety, avoiding any hint of the glitter-trash elements so cleverly parodied in contemporary films and television series set in the worlds of glamour and big-business. Today *grand luxe* utilizes more period elements than before, and as in other areas there are distinct fashions in what is revived: currently a rich and exotic version of French Second Empire *orientaliste* taste and anything imperial Russian seem to be much in vogue, while perhaps for the first time *style Louis Quatorze* is in the ascendancy over the Louis Quinze and Louis Seize styles.

The greatest irony of modernity in design is that it dates so quickly. The heroic years of the Modern movement already, for us in the 1980s, have a certain period charm. Many of the more memorable inter-war designs have become classics, or indeed clichés, and chairs and other pieces by Mies van der Rohe, Le Corbusier, Marcel Breuer and Eileen Gray are once again in production,to be used in the creation of chic and up-to-the-moment apartments by designers such as Andrée Putman. But of course the true heirs of the Modern movement are not the firms which make, or the decorators who use, this 'reproduction furniture', but the designers and manufacturers producing their own new pieces today.

In the past, fashions in *moderne* taste veered between a love of austere, clean lines and a concern for the more abstract surface qualities and sculptural values of the individual piece. Today new materials and methods allow an even greater freedom in conception, and a new confidence amongst designers seems at last to have allowed a certain wit and a degree of humorous allusiveness to enter the design process, alongside the more traditional require-ments of function.

Product design, to which the Modern movement is so closely allied, has influenced many, introducing a high degree of accuracy and clarity of thought into the process of design. There remains, however, tremendous diversity in approach, expressed in the differences between the auster-ely beautiful exploratory projections of Jean-Michel Wil-motte and Pascal Mourgue's painterly renderings of pieces of furniture produced in conjunction with his own working prototypes carved in wood.

The other irony of modern design today is that, from a once radical position at the avant-garde edge of taste, challenging the established order, it has become just about the only aspect of decoration and design directly patronized by governments and officially promoted by establishment agencies such as the Design Council in Britain or the admirable VIA in France, established by the Ministries of Culture and Trade to bring designers and manufacturers together.

The world of *haut décor* is above all about the exclusivity of taste; about the look associated with a designer's name; and about the decorator as purveyor of that most elusive quality, chic. The analogy clearly remains with the often overlapping world of *haute couture*, in which the great goal has always been to maintain at all cost the mystique of chic. *Haut décor* must always adhere to this exclusive principle of fashion: the reverse side of that coin being, of course, that as soon as too many people have a thing, or know too much about it, it ceases to be desirable. Then it is time for something new, preferably a little more obscure and almost certainly more expensive. This restless progress can be followed as much in the international social pages as in the glossy architectural magazines for it is as much about personalities as styles.

Haut décor, or 'High Style', seems at the moment to be particularly associated with a grand and theatrical manner deriving from the most expensive and up-market aspects of John Fowler's country house work, but seen as it were through the eyes of Coco Chanel or Mme Schiaparelli. High style draws on the repertoire of the classical tradition and of *grand luxe* but its great exponents, such as Nicholas Haslam, would certainly agree that its essence lies in seeing every room, in Osbert Lancaster's phrase, 'as a setting for a party'(pl. 475).

Haut décor is typified by the methods, reputation and considerable achievements of the great English dealer-decorator Geoffrey Bennison, who died in 1984. He had the most remarkable eye for bringing together the rare and exquisite and massing quirky and over-scaled pieces against a rich backdrop of old and faded textiles. These choice rooms he would assemble for those whom he affected to call 'the happy few', the clients *he chose* to work with each year.

The readiness of decorators to play with, or dissent entirely from, the ideals of the Modern movement has been a source of exasperation to those who would see Modern-ism as a great deal more than just another style. However the story has not been merely one of the triumph of delight over dogma in the way people choose to live, for in following the line of development in Milan for example, from the crucial work of Gio Ponti and Piero Fornasetti through to the utterly serious zaniness of Ettore Sottsass's Memphis group, it can be seen as the most important way forward from the sterile impasse of Modernism.

During the final demise of Modernism as the vital and progressive, if over-dominant, influence in architecture and design, several of the more interesting reactions against it began to gain more attention and to draw closer together, almost aching to become an 'ism'. Post-Modernism was first identified as a coherent movement and defined as a theoretical stance by Charles Jencks, architectural theorist and himself a principal protagonist of the new Symbolic architecture. Jencks's work, which is best seen in the design, ornamentation and furnishing of his own London house (pl. 495), represents a major step in the reopening of the dialogue between interior architecture and decoration. Already a new generation of designers, such as Nigel Coates, Piers Gough and David Connor in England, and Elizabeth Garouste, Mattea Bonetti and Pascal Mourgue in France, begins to emerge, free from inhibitions about symbolism and ornament, indeed happy to play with the past whilst remaining resolutely forward-looking and 'modern'.

As if in reaction to the complacent insipidity of much recent interior decoration and stirred by an almost perversely romantic attitude to the grandeur of the past and to modern urban decay, a number of younger designers and makers seem, either independently or in small groups centred on new galleries in London and Paris, to have arrived at a curiously obscure but exciting and expressive neo-baroque aesthetic. The influences which have come together here are varied, but may well include the popular imagery of Cecil Beaton and the rediscovered taste of the Sitwells, whose own baroque revival enlivened the 1920s and 30s; the neo-romanticism of the war years; and the work of visually obsessive film-makers such as Fellini and, more recently, Derek Jarman. There is too a distinct element which derives from the vigorous street fashion scene. Luxury, or indeed adequate comfort, tends to be eschewed in favour of the visionary, and in the craftwork of the movement all the ordinary notions of scale and of the use of materials are challenged.

This neo-baroque manner restates for the 1980s John Piper's original neo-romantic phrase 'pleasing decay', but with a new forcefulness: its essence now is a new grandeur and a new theatricality; the *mise en scène* a ruined palazzo in a post-holocaust landscape.

To the present author, writing at a moment when perhaps for the first time the New Georgians and the Post-Modernists can each begin to see what the other is about, it seems that any future historian of taste, who might glance into these pages seeking a picture of the age, will see an era remarkably similar to the nineteenth-century age of revivals: a period obsessed with style, or rather with a multiplicity of styles. Our current nostalgic obsession with traditional forms holds some very real dangers for the designer, which the decorator may well help to dispel. For if the past is indeed 'another country', then it is one in constant danger of being spoiled by rapacious and unthinking package-trippers. We should perhaps aim to be better informed about historic style, but less seriously in awe of it. We no longer, as in the nineteenth century, consider Gothic, for example, to be morally superior to rococo, but there are still many design historians and practising designers who hold Bauhaus precepts to be ideologically more sound than Biedermeier. This kind of thinking places an undue strain on our notions of modernity and so-called originality in design, forcing it to become too precious. Decorators see the whole of the past as a playground and the entire repertory of historic ornament as a dressing-up box. It is paradoxically a remarkably confident, fertile and forward-looking ideal.

1. Egomet Bonmot (pseudonym of T.G. Wainewright), 'Sentimentalities on the Fine Arts' in *London Magazine*, March, 1820. Reprinted in W. Carew Hazlitt (Ed.), *Essays and Criticisms by Thomas Griffiths Wainewright*, London, 1880
2. Professor Praz's phrase may be translated as 'the philosophy of furnishings'. It is the title of the original Italian edition of his celebrated book published in England as *An Illustrated History of Interior Decoration*, 1964 (1981)

465

The conservation of historic interiors 1980s

In a decade when attitudes to period decoration have, to an extent hardly imaginable earlier, become a major factor in the look of a high proportion of everyday rooms, the work and ideals of those concerned with the preservation and conservation of historic decoration have assumed a greater importance and influence. In England at the beginning of the 1980s the National Trust, the Historic Houses Association and other preservation agencies and societies all found the basis of their support widening. This reflected a widespread and complex wave of nostalgic interest in 'country house life', which was also expressed in the great popularity of historical drama series on television and in the publication of a huge number of books of memoirs and studies of our vanished or vanishing traditions, such as the very successful *The Country Diary of an Edwardian Lady*. In decoration the actual practice of conservators has been directly influential, and for a far wider section of the population than ever before 'living with antiques' (as it was first called in the 1950s) has become a serious alternative to the natural choice of modern furnishings. In America the high watermark of these attitudes came with the staging in Washington DC in 1985 of the exhibition *Treasure Houses of Britain*, which proved vastly influential.

465

The hall, Beningbrough Hall, Yorkshire

Redecorated under the direction of David Mlinaric for the National Trust and completed in 1979

David Mlinaric, who has succeeded John Fowler as the practising decorator most consulted by the National Trust, continues the process of refreshing old decoration where practicable, and where necessary creating new schemes which respect as far as possible both the original effects and the subsequent history of the house. David Mlinaric's sensitive approach to the redecoration of architecturally and historically important rooms is exemplified in his work at Beningbrough. Eschewing the theatricality of much of John Fowler's work, Mlinaric's respect for the architecture is expressed in schemes of considerable reticence, which may in future years be seen to typify the attitudes of a period in which 'scientific' considerations began to outweigh the rule of 'taste' in the treatment of old buildings. Here the great hall of the house is repainted in a variety of close neutral or stone colours intended to bring out the inherent qualities of the architecture, avoiding any of the kind of 'effects' or 'decorator's touches' which Mlinaric would consider inappropriate for this kind of a project – but which he would deploy with some exuberance in other commissions, such as a recently completed private gaming club in London.

The National Trust

466

466

Proposed rehanging of pictures for Saltram House, Devon

Drawing by Alec Cobbe, 1985

As a restorer of oil paintings, Alec Cobbe also takes a serious interest in the arrangement of pictures. He has been consulted by many private owners of historic houses, as well as the National Trust, for whom he prepares hanging proposals in the form of delightful little water-colour sketches in the manner of the eighteenth century. One of the great virtues of such a way of presenting his schemes is that these quickly dashed-off drawings, each of which represents an enormous amount of measuring and consideration, gives a far more readily appreciable idea of the final effect in terms of scale, pattern and the all-important density of the hang. In recent years the tendency to return to correct, dense 'pattern hangs' in historic rooms has been paralleled in the museum world by the pioneering work of Timothy Clifford during his time as Director at Manchester City Art Gallery This in turn has to some degree affected domestic picture hanging, which can afford to be even more theatrical in approach.

Courtesy of Alec Cobbe

467

Painted sketch for an architectural capriccio

Design by Alan Dodd for the Director's dining room at the Victoria & Albert Museum, London, 1986

The new dining room of the museum, occupying a space which is almost an exact cube of 19 feet (5.8 metres), has been conceived and decorated on a monumental scale. The walls have been painted with *trompe-l'oeil* rustication to the full height of the cornice as a background for the principal decorative elements, a series of five great architectural capriccios by Alan Dodd representing various styles of architecture and decoration. They hang from huge bows, and this massive scale is echoed by a vast wooden chandelier made by the craftsman Neil Trinder, who trained at the museum, and a large ceramic looking-glass by Oriel Harwood, which hangs above the wildly marbled chimneypiece.

Victoria & Albert Museum, London

467

Commercial versions of the 'English country house look' 1980s

The immense popularity of nostalgic decoration, and especially the successful propagation of versions of the 'English country house look' in England, America and elsewhere, has coincided with a widening of the market for stylish decoration. This has had two interesting effects. On the one hand, the always steady demand for the high-quality reproduction furnishings traditionally used for the creation of 'period rooms' has greatly increased, while on the other there has been an extraordinary move among the manufacturers of middle-range and mass-market goods towards 'Georgian', 'Victorian' and 'Edwardian' styles.

468

468

Room setting using co-ordinating paper and fabric 'Chintz' by Zoffany, London

Zoffany is a well-respected firm specializing in the production of furnishings based on traditional patterns. Here a chintz design of about 1800 has been reworked in co-ordinating paper and fabric, and adapted to the prevailing taste of the mid-1980s for a bright and fresh look suggestive of late-Georgian prettiness and elegance. Many of the firm's other papers and textiles are close reproductions of the bolder patterns and colours of the earlier part of the eighteenth century, and the increasing popularity of these more assertive patterns reflects a growing awareness of the decorative possibilities of a serious and confident return to the use of ornament.

Courtesy of Zoffany

469

Room setting for a library-drawing room by Laura Ashley, 1985

The richly evocative interiors contrived by the Laura Ashley designers and stylists in the last three or four years suggest a very close study of the Colefax & Fowler version of the 'English country house look'. They are in fascinating contrast to the earlier, simple style of the late founder of this furnishing empire, in which pretty Indian-inspired single-colour printed cottons were set off with spick-and-span white paintwork. To some extent Laura Ashley's move towards richer, historically inspired looks coincided with her move to a fine eighteenth-century French château. The exploration of the darker and more associative images of the past has continued since her untimely death in 1985, and recent collections include groups of fabrics and papers based on a bold Regency taste, on 'Old French' looks and, most notably, on the sumptuous brocades and damasks of baroque Venice.

Courtesy of Laura Ashley

469

470

470
'Paint magic' 1986

Sitting room decorated by Jocasta Innes using her own stencil designs in her London house

The extraordinary revival of interest in the art of specialist paint effects such as marbling and wood-graining has spawned an enormous number of reprints of old manuals and new works on the subject. The most engaging protagonist in this field, however, has been the design journalist Jocasta Innes. Her book *Paint Magic* (London, 1981) and her television series *Paintability* and the accompanying book (London, 1986) have set thousands of decorators and members of the public on to DIY marbling, stippling and rag-rolling. If the craze is in part merely a rehashing of ideas which all the traditional decorators of the 1950s took for granted, it is none the less well thought out for a new generation eager to revive old skills, and nostalgic for a past which was in itself an historical pastiche. With her partner Stewart Walton, Jocasta Innes has now launched an ingenious range of paint stencils, which are not only carefully contrived to fit the scale of the ordinary domestic house, but also pander stylistically to delusions of architectural grandeur.

Courtesy of Jocasta Innes; photograph Fritz von der Schulenburg

471

buildings. They range from the scholarly, painstaking and reticent restoration of the purists through to the flamboyantly theatrical pasteboard evocations of the spirit of the past thrown together by some of the more extravagant stylists.

471

Front sitting room of the house of the artists Gilbert and George, Spitalfields

The celebrated performance artists and painters Gilbert and George were the first to realize the potential of the Spitalfields houses, moving there well before the conservationists in the 1960s. In their restoration of the house, following fashionable practice, they had the original pine panelling stripped (it would have been painted in the eighteenth century), in order to form a mellow background for an ever-increasing collection of furniture and other decorative pieces by major nineteenth-century architects and designers such as A.W.N. Pugin and Christopher Dresser. Among the furnishings of this room are a number of pieces in the 'reformed Gothic' taste, including a large

The 'New Georgians' in London 1980s

The idea that the 'New Georgians' exist as a club or constitute some kind of a movement is the creation of the label-making journalism of the 1980s. Yet the term serves to identify and give shape to the interesting and extremely diverse theories and activities of a loose-knit circle of friends and acquaintances, in London and elsewhere, who share a passionate conviction about the importance of the great traditions of English domestic architecture of the eighteenth century. For many, living in period rooms and houses is the most effective and most delightful way of ensuring the conservation and preservation of individual buildings of merit and, more importantly, of the essentially domestic fabric and human scale of our towns and inner cities. Central to this ideal has been the New Georgian maxim of 'go where the architecture is'. This has led to the successful saving of important buildings in 'slum' areas, most notably the noble early eighteenth-century houses in Spitalfields, one of the very few surviving enclaves of buildings of such an early date in London. The interiors created by the New Georgians are as various as the

cabinet with an extensive collection of pots by Dresser on its shelves.

Arcaid; photograph Richard Bryant

472

'The Danish Sofa'

Watercolour of his own London drawing room by Glynn Boyd Harte, 1986

The stylishly austere rooms of Glynn Boyd Harte's handsome late eighteenth-century London house represent another version of the New Georgian ideal. The large and empty rooms with bare floorboards, flat-painted walls and well-chosen pieces of furniture evoke the atmosphere of the paintings of Arthur Devis or, more particularly, of the Continental painters of the Biedermeier period, such as Georg Friedrich Kersting. The scene depicted here, a moment of calm during an otherwise hectic New Georgian costume party, the Boyd Hartes' 'Biedermeier Ball', reflects the considerable current interest in the neo-classicism of the Baltic. As an enthusiastic response to the teachings of the influential architectural historian of Peterhouse, David Watkin, this fashion has led to an enormous amount of muslin drapery and bobble-fringe at the windows of plain Georgian houses, and a positive obsession with Karelian birch.

Courtesy of Glynn Boyd Harte and the Francis Kyle Gallery, London

473, 474

Two views of the house of Dennis Severs, Spitalfields, London

Dennis Severs, a Californian who has lived in London for many years, acquired his house in Folgate Street in the late 1970s and, with great inventiveness and tireless enthusiasm, has made it one of the most complete and entertaining statements of the New Georgian ideal. A showman and self-proclaimed 'popular historian', he presents his house and its remarkable, theatrical, DIY period rooms to the public. His guided tours, always given at night-time by the light of candles, recount the history of the area, and include a fictionalized account of the rise and fall of the fortunes of the house and its occupants from the 1720s through to the late nineteenth century. Each room has its themes: characters and events as well as the decoration, way of life and even the sounds and smells of the past are evoked, and the essence of each period is cleverly suggested by the vast assemblage of objects, real and fake, good and bad, which are arranged like elaborate still lifes all over the house.

Courtesy of Dennis Severs

473

474

Dining Hall Lower Belgrave St London SW by Nicholas Haslam

NHIL 12 Holbein Place London SW1

October 1985 730 8623

475

475

The 'Old palazzo' look in Belgravia 1985

Drawing in pen and watercolour by Nicholas Haslam

Nicholas Haslam is the epitome of that most curious phenomenon, the interior decorator as socialite. In the 1960s he lived and worked in America, imbibing both New York and West Coast culture and working in a sharp, colourful and boldly modernistic manner. In England his work has been influenced and mellowed by John Fowler's informal grandeur, and since he opened his own shop in Pimlico his projects have been marked by a stylish eclecticism. In the hall-dining room of a house in Belgravia he creates a version of the currently chic 'Old palazzo' style, using seventeenth-century high-backed chairs, old pewter and eccentric Venetian-looking glasses. There are allusions to the palace style of Daniel Marot in the witty staircase draped with fringed and bowed fabric, but the whole effect is surely influenced too by recollections of the Haslam family house, Great Hundridge (pls 259, 260, 261).

Victoria & Albert Museum, London

Second Empire opulence 1985–8

476

Design for a bedroom in a New York apartment by David Roos 1988

David Roos trained as a designer for the theatre, and brings to his work an extraordinary eye for colour and feel for the dramatic use of fabric in interiors. More unusually among 'theatrical' designers, he places great emphasis on the quality of detailing and finish in his projects. Thus a typical Roos interior will balance richly coloured and subtly patterned curtain treatments and highly original upholstery with the immaculate plain surfaces of walls and paintwork. Roos has designed elaborate interiors which make the most of the possibilities of using highly skilled craftsmen, such as woodcarvers, gilders and painters, achieving a richness of effect hardly equalled by any other decorator. In this bedroom he has used characteristically off-beat colour harmonies and a favourite device of over-scaling pattern by alternating two fabrics to create a grand striped effect on elaborately shaped pelmets.

Victoria & Albert Museum, London

477

The bedroom of Miss Faye Dunaway's London house by David Roos 1985

David Roos's work epitomizes the theatrical aspect of the baroque revival. For the actress Faye Dunaway he created this highly romantic bedroom, which plays with 'Miss Havisham' imagery to suggest something of the opulence of nineteenth-century drapery and upholstery, but at the same time retains a certain knowing modernity. The curtains, with their richly layered structure using alternating translucent and heavy fabrics, are typical of Roos's inventiveness, and the elegant hand-painted shades on tall candlesticks reveal the quality of detailing which underpins the broader theatricality of the effect.

Victoria & Albert Museum, London

476

477

478

478
Playing with tradition   1982

*Entrance hall of a house in Charles Street, London,
painted by Alan Dodd*

Trompe-*l'oeil* painting on a grand scale has never ceased
to occupy an important position at the upper end of
the decoration market, but lately its popularity seems to
have increased even more. One of the largest schemes of
decorative painting carried out in recent years is the vast
mural by Graham Rust for Lord Hertford at Ragley Hall in
Warwickshire, combining both pictorial and architectural
elements. Interest in the figurative – and often capricious –
style of painting seems as strong as that in the more serious
architectural style, and today there are good exponents of
both at work. Alan Dodd's entrance hall for a house in
Charles Street is one of the most impressive schemes of
formal decorative painting carried out in the 1980s, but in
spite of its faultless technique and apparent seriousness of
purpose it contains too that essential hint of whimsicality
and suggestion of irony that marks the more successful
essays in *trompe-l'oeil* done in this century.

Arcaid; photograph Richard Bryant

479
A grand library   1986

*Design by Christian Badin for the Paris house of
Mme Barbara Wirth of David Hicks, France*

Christian Badin, the head of the design team of David
Hicks's French associate company, is a learned stylist
who delights to deploy his great knowledge of past
decorative styles with an entirely modern wit and sense of
chic.

In a library for Mme Wirth he looked to the boldly
colourful and strongly architectural style of the seventeenth
century in France, creating a room immediately suggestive
of the approachable grandeur of the great private palaces of
the Marais or the Ile St-Louis.

Courtesy of Christian Badin and Mme Wirth, Paris

479

480

The 'Old French look', New York 1985

Room in the classic French taste; watercolour by Mark Hampton

Mark Hampton worked for some time with David Hicks before establishing himself as one of the central figures of the New York scene. His influence is felt not only through his work, which is much photographed and published in the design and decoration magazines, but also through his regular and entertaining writings on historic and contemporary trends in decoration, illustrated with delightful little drawings and watercolours. This drawing, one of two which he presented to the Victoria & Albert Museum as examples of his work, shows a room decorated and furnished in the classic Louis Quinze style, as interpreted and loved in America from the days of Elsie de Wolfe onwards.

Victoria & Albert Museum, London

481

481

In the Pompeian style, New York 1986

Sketch with fabric and paper samples for a drawing room by Keith Irvine

Keith Irvine was one of the very first students to take the interior design course instituted by Hugh Casson at the Royal College of Art in London. He then went to work for John Fowler before leaving for America. Arriving in New York in 1959 with only £7 and John Fowler's letter of introduction to the decorator Mrs Henry 'Sister' Parish, for whom he at first worked, he quickly established his own style and reputation. His partnership, Irvine & Fleming, is now one of New York's most respected, with an extensive practice in both the city and the surrounding countryside. For an elderly English client, long resident in New York, Irvine was asked to decorate a large apartment on Central Park in a basically traditional idiom, but with a crisp and dramatic quality. Keith Irvine's solution for the drawing room was to use some existing panelling to articulate a bold red, black and white neo-classical scheme reminiscent of Pompeian decoration. Here all his characteristically rich groupings of decorative objects, varied seat furniture and pictures, and looking-glasses hung against mirror are kept within strict architectural bounds by the formal use of a printed border. The total effect is one of graphic clarity and effortless poise.

Victoria & Albert Museum, London

480

482

482

Colour and pattern 1986

Design for a drawing room in Holland Park, London, by John Stefanidis

Following the boldness of his work in the 1960s, using brash colour, plastic furniture and large modern abstract pictures, John Stefanidis entered an entirely new phase in the 1970s, favouring a restrained palette of colours, neutral and textured materials and a predominance of fine pieces of antique furniture. Only on the island of Patmos, where he has decorated a considerable number of houses and apartments, have the strong light and the traditional painted furnishings and local textiles led him to create vibrant and colourful schemes. More recently, however, and in the forefront of a more general return to a confident use of richer colour and pattern-on-pattern effects, Stefanidis has begun again to use bold combinations of hues in his London work, such as this Holland Park room in pinks, crimsons and purples. This stylish presentation drawing is by a member of John Stefanidis's studio team, Philip Hooper. It shows a comfortable and opulent look appropriate to a mid-nineteenth-century London town house, which in this case takes as its starting-point a fine and rare ceramic chimneypiece.

Victoria & Albert Museum, London

483

A Pompeian scheme, Italy 1980

Design for a dining room by Adriano Magistretti

Before establishing his successful practice in New York and Rome, Adriano Magistretti was a celebrated designer for films, working with many of the great directors such as Fellini and Pasolini. Much of his work as a designer of rooms has the same beautifully judged theatricality, and from the world of total illusion he has brought a number of useful tricks which he deploys with equal delight and success in a domestic context. In order to create just the right sense of richness he will stencil on to a wall a brocade pattern in deepest blues and purples, or create perfect neo-classical floors and carpets by painting a subtle red Greek-key pattern on to ordinary rush matting. In this stylish dining room for the house of Signor Giamelli of Versace, Magistretti has placed neo-classical blond-wood furniture in a theatrical Pompeian setting, playing up allusions to the archaeological revival style which enjoyed such popularity in nineteenth-century Rome and Naples.

Victoria & Albert Museum, London

484

Inspired by the ancients 1986

Design for a room based on Etruscan archaeological motifs, by Giovanni Patrini, Milan

Apart from the central position it occupies in the design world, Milan is also important as a taste-making centre for decoration, with a circle of decorators of the calibre of Giovanni Patrini and Filippo Perego. As in Rome, many of the Milanese decorators look to the glories of ancient Rome and the Renaissance for their inspiration, but Patrini has been among the first to seek ideas and images from further back. His serious interests in ancient art and archaeology have led him to look at the surviving artefacts of the Etruscan civilization, and to create rooms which draw inspiration from this somewhat unfamiliar material. As far back as the earliest discoveries in the eighteenth century there has been an interest in this period: 'Etruscan style' rooms have been created in Italy and in England, where an important attempt by Robert Adam to use such motifs survives at Osterley Park House, Middlesex. Patrini, however, has not merely used conventionalized motifs; on the contrary, in this room setting he has deliberately reflected the uncompromising quality of ancient decoration. On the banquette stand ancient vases, which are one of the designer's favourite inspirations, and a number of the cushions with patterns derived from them for which he is well known.

Victoria & Albert Museum, London

484

485

485

A period re-creation in Milan 1986

Design for a traditional drawing room by Filippo Perego di Cremnago

Filippo Perego is one of the most sensitive and accomplished architect-designers in the Milanese circle which also includes Giovanni Patrini. For a drawing room in a basically featureless modern box in Milan the designer was asked to create a grand traditional effect. Playing up the beamed structure of the space he created a period feel by suggesting a neo-classical order dividing the two halves of the room, and laying floors which echoed the painted ceiling and architectural treatment of the walls. This design drawing shows Filippo Perego's method of presenting his ideas for the main scheme of decoration as a highly finished watercolour 'visual', and of indicating a suggested layout for the individual pieces of furniture and other moveable objects on a transparent film overlay.

Victoria & Albert Museum, London

486

The new architecture in England 1986

Master bedroom on a houseboat redesigned and decorated by Powell-Tuck, Connor & Orefelt

486

In the projects carried out by the partnership Powell-Tuck, Connor & Orefelt there is an interesting tension between the calmer, rational and low-key aspects of Julian Powell-Tuck's ideas and the almost frenzied, 'post-punk' visions of David Connor. As with other newer partnerships, many of their first commissions were to create or redesign spaces in existing buildings, and this has led them, even in their more recent larger architectural undertakings, to maintain a serious concern for the interiors and furnishings of their schemes. Typical of the often off-beat projects which have come the way of the partnership was this commission to completely redesign and decorate a houseboat, normally moored on the Thames at Chelsea. A careful re-arrangement of the internal divisions created surprisingly large and uncluttered spaces, of which the master bedroom beneath the main deck was the main showpiece. Here the crisply delineated skylight set the airy tone for a scheme based on clean lines and pale nautical colours. The main decorative feature is a bedhead which contains storage cupboards and is finished with an abstract pattern of overlapping coloured forms. The essential angularity of the concept perhaps owes most to David Connor's distinctive drawing style, but the precise, ordered use of flat planes and the careful co-ordination of the other features and furnishings reveal Julian Powell-Tuck's hand. The overall effect of the room is curiously like one of the English Surrealist Paul Nash's near-abstract seaside pictures.

The World of Interiors; photograph Clive Frost

487

The room as art 1984

Room set arranged by Marc Chaimowicz for the Arts Council exhibition, Four Rooms

In 1984 the Arts Council organized an exhibition for which four of its favourite artists were invited to design or create a room setting. The extent to which the chosen artists adhered to or flouted conventions about the arrangement and decoration of rooms varied. Perhaps ironically, this, the most deliberately iconoclastic piece of 'installation art' by Marc Chaimowicz, proved to be the most interesting and in some ways most influential of the four. The Chaimowicz room is in fact a perverse homage to the interiors of the 1930s and in particular to the designs of

487

Eileen Gray, several of whose pieces were used as an integral part of the installation. The extraordinary distortions of form and perspective in the room were said to play up the very qualities of geometry which the artist claimed to find and admire in the work of the 1930s designers, but at the same time many were reminded of the famous Expressionist film sets of the silent classic of the Weimar period, *The Cabinet of Dr Caligari*, or of the fairground 'crazy house'. The 'desk' on the left was entitled 'On Decline'. It was manufactured by Pearl Dot Workshops, London, and, like several of the pieces in this and the other rooms, could be purchased from the show.

Arts Council of Great Britain

488
Minimalism   1986

Living area of the designer John Pawson's own flat in West London

The logical outcome of the reductivist tendencies of the Modern movement has been the trend towards a severe minimalism in architecture. The architect John Pawson has taken this to its furthest imaginable extreme in a domestic context in his own London flat. This consists of several interconnecting spaces, each devoid not just of ornamentation but of any detail at all. The 'living' spaces contain practically no furniture or other signs of life, and the gimmick is continued in the sleeping area, where a futon mattress is taken out at night but hidden away during the day in a cupboard concealed in the wall surface. By comparison with these spaces the bathroom contains a riot of visual distractions, with a bath, washbasin made from two different materials, and chrome taps and other fittings. As the very antithesis of decoration, the Cistercian austerity and seclusion of the rooms is completed and emphasized by the exclusion of contact with the outside world by vast, blank expanses of Venetian blind at every window, which create a flat, even light thoughout.

Courtesy of Pawson Silvestrin; photograph Ian Dobbie

488

489

489
Modern French furniture design 1984

Design for an escritoire by Pascal Mourgue

Even among the furniture designers of a nation renowned for its café tables and chairs the work of Pascal Mourgue stands out. His simple and stylish versions of the eternal classics were chosen by the new Cartier Foundation for its own café, and they are also to be found in the showrooms of the excellent VIA, the official agency established by the French Ministries of Culture and Trade to bring designers and manufacturers together. Besides being an architect Pascal Mourgue is also a sculptor, he draws and paints, and his furniture has a certain sculptural and often monumental feel which is clearly the result of his working methods. His studio is divided into two sections: in one space he draws, alongside his wife who is also an architect, while in the second area he works on the actual prototypes of his work, shaping in wood not only the forms of pieces such as this writing desk, but also those which are ultimately to be made in metal. Finally the circle of the design process is often completed by more finished drawings of the pieces and, from time to time, a large painted 'meditation' on the form.

Victoria & Albert Museum, London

490
A modern embassy office 1986

The office of the Ambassador of France in Washington, by Jean-Michel Wilmotte

Contrary to all expectations of Louis panelling and silk-covered *fauteuils*, the French Ambassador in Washington sits in an office of uncompromising modernity. In fact from the days of Pompidou onwards French statesmen, politicians and diplomats have vied with one another to be seen as discerning patrons of the contemporary fine and applied arts. Successive occupants of the Elysée Palace have made their mark there, and this official attitude of encouragement has contributed in no small degree to the buoyancy of the contemporary scene in French design, in both aesthetic and commercial terms. The spare elegance coupled with rich materials in the work of the respected architect-designer Jean-Michel Wilmotte reflects precisely the current French predilection for furnishings in a modern idiom, which seem at last to match the best of the old in their qualities of material and workmanship. Wilmotte makes much use of steel supports, the elegant lines of which are computer-generated in his large office, and which are able apparently effortlessly to support massive slabs of granite or grey and white marble. Here the seats are of leather, as is the central section of the Ambassador's desk, and all the precisely ordered surfaces are in neutral colours, suggesting quiet confidence, a degree of reticence and an unruffled calm entirely appropriate to the office of an ambassador.

Victoria & Albert Museum, London

491
Playing with tradition 1988

Furnishings in the Soho range by Peter Leonard

The idea behind the designer Peter Leonard's Soho shop is in essence a simple one: to take certain basic, traditional English standards and to reinterpret them for manufacture today to retail at economic prices. This almost obvious and yet seldom brought-off strategy has resulted in the creation by Peter Leonard and his in-house associate design team of a number of highly successful pieces, including a stylish variant on the classic Knole sofa, distinguished by clean lines and tall, elegant proportions. Also seen here are a number of pieces in black metallic

490

491

finish: a small 'Gothic' mantel-clock, a 'Gothic' chair, a pair of floor-standing candlesticks and a piece which many would have considered impossible, a 'whatnot' (free-standing shelf unit) or *étagère* for the 80s.

Courtesy of Soho, London

492

493

High-Tech 1980s

The High-Tech aesthetic, a curious and, it would appear, short-lived phenomenon of the 1980s, in many ways recalls the search in the 1960s for 'alternative lifestyles'. It took as its starting point the notion that it should be possible to put together an interesting and supremely practical domestic environment which was appropriate to modern living by using easily available commercial and industrial components (such as hospital sanitary ware or caterer's equipment), rather than conventional kitchen and bathroom fittings which are so poorly designed. The movement rapidly acquired a degree of radical chic and developed a fashionable and surprisingly glossy image, taken up not only by style pundits but also by the media world.

492

Living area by Jan Karlicky and Future Systems for the design journalist Deyan Sudjic

The influential design writer Deyan Sudjic commissioned this deliberately arresting interior for his London flat, in which minimalism, High-Tech and elements recognizable as a Japanese aesthetic are mingled. This view across the surface of a free-standing kitchen 'work-station' shows the eccentric opening, approached by a short metal ramp, which leads to the equally austere bed area.

493

Main seating area in her own apartment by Eva Jirična

Eva Jirična rapidly emerged at the beginning of the 1980s as one of the most accomplished exponents of the High-Tech style. In her own London apartment she created a seating area in the form of a 'living pit' in brilliant green rubber studding, and placed beside it a low dining table surrounded by plastic inflatable cushions. The kitchen and bathroom were both equipped entirely from the standard catalogue lines of commerical fittings manufacturers.

494

494

First London apartment designed by
Eva Jirična for Joseph

Joseph, the owner of the eponymous, highly successful
and increasingly widespread clothing and lifestyle shops,
favours interiors reduced to a fairly austere black-and-
white aesthetic. His interest in functionalism in design

meant that the High-Tech idea held some fascination for
him, and he explored various of its possibilities both in his
own homes and on the merchandise shelves of several of his
shops. His choice of Eva Jirična for both these areas
underlined her already growing status as the high priestess
of the High-Tech cult in England.

Arcaid; photographs Richard Bryant

495

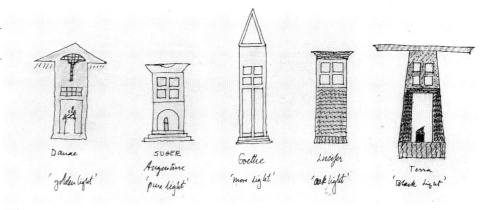

496

Post-Modernism 1980s

It was Charles Jencks, the leading architectural theoretician, who first identified, described and codified the 'Post-Modernist' stance, drawing under the banner, perhaps uncomfortably, a wide and disparate group of reactions against the International Modern style. As he is a practising architect and designer, his projects, mainly houses for himself in Britain and America, form the most eloquent and complete statement of the ideal. His own particular brand of the Post-Modern theory and aesthetic, 'Symbolic Architecture', involves the use of both traditional and novel architectural forms and methods, according to idiosyncratic iconographic programmes.

495

Library and central stairwell designed by Charles Jencks for the 'Thematic House', Holland Park, London

Charles Jencks conceived and designed the Thematic House as his own London residence. It is, strictly speaking, a refurbishment and thorough reconstruction of an existing nineteenth-century villa, standing among listed period houses in a wide avenue in the fashionable Holland Park district. As such, it makes a bold and interesting architectural statement. The house has been reworked by Jencks so that it now functions as a series of principal reception rooms related to the seasons, with specific areas such as the library set aside for one function. On the upper floors are bedrooms and bathrooms. All these spaces are related to a great central spiral staircase which climbs the full height of the house. The shell of this stair impinges upon the library, and its wall is used for architectural and visual games, making plays on the interior/exterior nature of the form and on the layers of the construction 'peeled back' around the large internal window. The library bookcases are typical Jencks designs: each of the individual shelf units, all of which house books on architecture, has a cresting which alludes to different styles or periods of building. The tall, free-standing *aedicule* ('little house') cabinets for photographic slides are constructed from standard metal filing systems, capped with roofs and grained, like the rest of the woodwork in the library, to resemble Biedermeier blond wood. On the desk can be seen a number of the agate and onyx architectural forms which Charles Jencks often incorporates into his furniture.

Arcaid; photograph Richard Bryant

496

Design for table lamps, from a book of drawings called *The Light Sketchbook* by Charles Jencks 1985

Jencks's *Light Sketchbook* is a series of meditations on the theme of light and the symbolic potential of architecture. It includes sequences of table lamps based loosely on the architectural orders and the various historical or mythical figures. The lamp called Danaë is in the form of a tower. At the base is a small plinth on which a piece of iron pyrites symbolizes Danaë, and the 'programme' is completed by the light, representing Zeus, which falls on her. This lamp is one of several pieces by Jencks which have been realized in limited editions by the furniture manufacturer Aram Zeev.

497

The 'Gothic' chair, by Robert Venturi 1982

The Philadelphia architect Robert Venturi has maintained a high profile among the American Post-Modernists for some time. More recently he has begun to enjoy a greater reputation internationally as a result of his selection as architect for the new wing for the National Gallery in London. Despite his avowed respect for the architectural achievements of the past, his work has a certain humour, construed by some as a lightweight attitude. They point to his delightful series of 'Architectural Chairs' as evidence of this. In fact the chairs seem to be a very erudite style game played with a considerable degree of success by an architect whose approach is anything but superficial.

496, 497 Victoria & Albert Museum, London

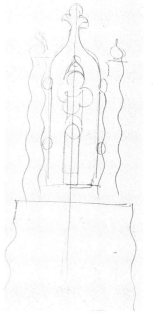

497

498

Chair (the MG2); designed by Michael Graves and manufactured by Sawaya & Moroni, Milan

As in the nineteenth and early twentieth centuries, much of the most interesting furniture, other than that by individual designer-makers, is the work of architects. In England Aram Zeev Designs have consistently approached architects – and, indeed, painters and sculptors. In Milan Sawaya & Moroni have in the past few years brought together in their impressive portfolio the work of a number of major figures, including Jencks, Adolf Natalini and the celebrated American Michael Graves, who designed for them a group of chairs including this example. It seems to hint both at 1930s design and at the elegance of the Biedermeier period. Referring to Graves as one of the 'masters' of American culture, Sawaya & Moroni describe him as 'the personification of the most creative restlessness derived from intolerance of the banality of the International style'.

Courtesy of Sawaya & Moroni, Milan

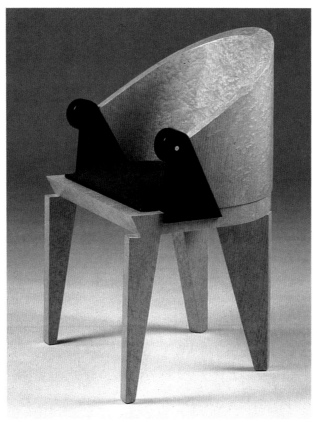

498

Memphis 1981

The radical design group Memphis announced itself to the world at the Milan Fair in 1981. Its leading protagonist is the designer Ettore Sottsass, a major figure in Italian modern design, but one who has, according to Stephen Bayley, 'throughout his career … mixed irony, irreverence and mysticism with the more workaday concerns of being a successful designer for industry' (*Memphis in London*, 1982). Memphis grew to a great extent out of Sottsass' association with the Milanese avant-garde, and in particular, his involvement with the Studio Alchymia, an organization which derived its creative energies from the interaction between performance art, left-wing politics and the designing of bizarre furniture. Memphis, which from its inception was intended to have a serious commercial basis, was funded by the Milan-based design firm Artemide, and showed its designs in a showroom of dazzling white in a grand building in the centre of the city. Sottsass gathered around him an international 'team' of talented young designers, who together evolved a style or aesthetic which, while it owed much to the Sottsass of the 1960s and to the 'mainstream' of Milanese modernism, struck an original, bold and colourful note: a pose of utterly serious zaniness.

499

'Carlton', a shelf unit by Ettore Sottsass

The 'Carlton' was the major piece of furniture in the first Memphis collection, a typically angular and colourful creation using decorative laminate surfaces.

500

'Plaza', a dressing table and stool by Michael Graves

An extravagant piece constructed in briarwood, lacquered wood, glass mirror and brass.

501

'Tawaraya', a seating unit by Masanori Umeda

This conversational seating unit based jokily on the theme of a boxing ring in some ways recalls the 'living pit' of the 1960s. Karl Lagerfeld bought a version for one of his many 'style statement' houses.

Courtesy of Memphis, Milan

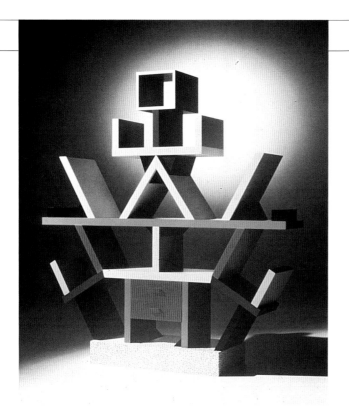

499

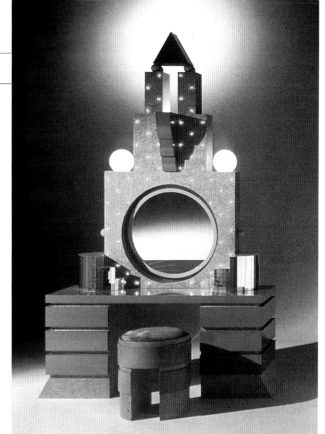

500

501

502

The new Pop Art, Rome 1980s

Designs by Stefano Mantovani

502

Dining room

503

Bathroom

Stefano Mantovani is an accomplished decorator in the grand traditional manner. He creates interiors of great richness and has a sure eye for fine pictures, distinguished furniture and interesting objects. For his own amusement and delight, however, he has for some time designed and produced objects and room settings which recall the Pop Art movement of the 1960s. His objects, beautifully crafted in laminates, are often hugely over-scaled domestic pieces, such as a vast teapot which opens to reveal spaces for cups and has a tea-caddy concealed in the 'knob' of the teapot lid. In his dining room separate tables bear the legends *Breakfast, Lunch* and *Dinner*, a clock points always to teatime, and the light sconces are in the form of giant forks and spoons. The bathroom, which is an even more completely conceived interior, has laminate *trompe-l'oeil* 'drapes' which swing open to reveal cupboards, the hard 'upholstery' of a seventeenth-century-style chair opens up to reveal a cache of necessities, and the looking-glass proclaims comfortingly, 'You look lovely'.

Victoria & Albert Museum, London

504

Post-Modern creative salvage 1980s

The designer's own house, converted and arranged by Tom Brent

While the increasingly popular alternative lifestyle of 'loft dwelling' in the United States and its equivalents in Britain and Europe lay at first entirely beyond the accepted boundaries of decoration, gradually their better ideas began to filter through and to have some effect on mainstream modern design. Two major considerations were brought into play: first, loft dwelling challenged all the usual notions of scale, of the use of floor space and of the 'correct' arrangement of rooms and their proper functions. Second, the reliance of the loft dwellers on salvage or even scavenging for materials, furnishings, lighting and the necessities of kitchens and bathrooms has led to a far more general reappraisal of such possibilities. Tom Brent's imaginative conversion of previously commercial premises as his own residence is regarded as a stylish and eloquent statement of the salvage ethic. In the one large space there are specific areas set aside for various functions. The galleried sleeping area, a typical solution for warehouse living, is here carried out with rather more panache than is usual, with the careful and striking placing of a staircase composed of unusually shaped treads supported on a metal structure.

Arcaid; photograph Richard Bryant

504

Design ideas from the exhibition 'La Mossa del Cavallo' 1986

505

Table, *Il Rilievo*

Designed by Aldo Rossi for Up & Up, 1985

506

Pavement, *Pozzo*

Designed by Adolfo Natalini for the manufacturer Matteo Baldini, 1985

505

One of the most interesting exhibitions devoted to design for interiors of recent years was that which was chosen mainly from Italian sources by the editor of *Casa Vogue*, Isa Vercelloni, with the participation of two other guest curators, Rainer Krause and Vanni Pasca. The show was first seen in Frankfurt in May 1986 and attracted considerable critical interest. The nature of the exhibits chosen was suggested by the title of the show, which translates literally as 'the knight's move' but which, as the chess metaphor suggests, might perhaps be better rendered as 'oblique strategies'. Much of what was chosen was in what has come to be recognized as the Post-Modern style, and the organizers went to some pains to find not merely jokey projects by theoretical architects, but also examples of the work of designers such as Aldo Rossi and Adolfo Natalini, which have already been taken up often by mainstream manufacturers, and put into production. The Rossi table, *Il Rilievo*, was designed in 1985 and realized by Up & Up in the following year. The *Pozzo* floor by Natalini is related to the designer's other areas of activity in furniture and ceramics; it is produced commercially by Matteo Baldini and can be adapted to fit varying architectural spaces.

Up & Up, Massa

506

507

507

'Fairy-tale' opulence in the Near East   1985–6

Entrance hall of a private palace in the United Arab Emirates, by Blanchards plc of London, Alkis Christophorou chief designer

During the years in which Near-Eastern clients were particularly active in the London property market, Blanchards established a reputation for the creation of luxury interiors in an international style, based on rich materials, lavish upholstery and the use of interesting decorative objects both old and new. Recently the success of the firm has been based on major contracts both in England and, more notably, abroad. Of these the most impressive in scale has been the building and decoration from scratch of a substantial private palace in the United Arab Emirates. Such a scheme has given the Blanchards design team, led by Alkis Christophorou, full scope for the creation of a spectacular series of rooms in which 'Arabian Nights' fantasy is underpinned by international-style *grand luxe*. In the entrance hall the entire repertoire of historic ornament has been culled to produce an effect of extraordinary opulence, while this level of luxury is maintained elsewhere with the use of marble, gilding and gold taps in the bathrooms, and Louis Seize-style marble-topped cabinets concealing necessities such as televisions in the family sitting rooms.

Victoria & Albert Museum, London

508, 509

Neo-Palladianism in Portugal 1985–7

Villa Verde, Algarve: the main salon and a sheet of sketches by David Hicks

David Hicks has in the last few years become as much interested in architectural projects and the creation of gardens as in interiors. These interests are revealed in a good deal of his recent writing, which has been concerned more with the architectural solution of interior design problems than with just decoration, and most notably in his discussion of the idea of 'green architecture' in his book on garden design. The project which has given him the most pleasure in recent years, and which, perhaps in consequence, has become one of his finest achievements, is a villa in the Palladian manner which he has built and decorated from scratch in Portugal. Given *carte blanche* by clients with whom he found himself in unusually close sympathy,

508

509

Hicks enjoyed the pleasure, increasingly rare since the seventeenth and eighteenth centuries, of acting as architect, decorator and landscape gardener. The result is a magisterial conception which, while acknowledging a debt to the Villa Rotonda, is nevertheless a building full of incidentally delightful and novel details. This richness of detail is the outcome of a continuous process of drawing, sketching and architectural musing, resulting in the creation during the project of many hundreds of sheets of design ideas, such as this one concerning the arrangement of a vast double-height open loggia.

Courtesy of David Hicks

New architecture: two projects by Nigel Coates 1980s

Nigel Coates has consistently proved to be one of the most interesting of our younger radical, theoretical architects, and is a guiding spirit of the Architectural Association's teaching programmes. His pronouncements and drawings formed the basis for the ideas and activities of the 'NATO' group (Narrative Architecture Today), and he devised and presented a visionary scheme for the South Bank area of London in the exhibition *ArkAlbion*, 1984. More recently Coates has been given a number of important opportunities to realize projects both in Britain and in Japan, where his unique blend of 'post-holocaust' architectural imagery and chic, night-club interior style has become especially appreciated.

510

View across the dining hall to the drawing room

Nigel Coates's own flat, South Kensington, London, 1988

Over the years Nigel Coates's own flat has been one of the most eloquent statements of his ideas and architectural stance. In a high-ceilinged first-floor flat, in which the entrance and all the rooms converge on a central space, Coates has played up the grandeur implied by large doorcases and the feel of a palazzo-like enfilade, placing at the end of one vista a huge blown-up photograph of a Piranesi torchère. All over the flat architectural drawings, mirrors and other objects are leaned against the walls or formed into small arrangements on the handsome nineteenth-century chimneypieces. In the bedroom a more recent feature is a boldly draped swag of bright fabric supported on curving metal strips. This is related to experiments for the decoration of another recent project in London, the interior of a jewellery shop, *Silver*, in which flashes of billowing silk were contrasted with the sharp lines of metalwork by André Dubreuil and elegant chairs by Coates himself.

Arcaid; photograph Richard Bryant

511

Skier's bedroom

Detail from the exhibition project, The Ski Station, *1981*

Of this drawing Nigel Coates writes: 'Instead of overlooking the slopes, the bedrooms look in on themselves – the bed strengthens this because its rococo drapes form a room within the room. But the wardrobe and the WC are in the open, each part hidden behind its own wall.'

Courtesy of Nigel Coates

511

512

A room by David Connor   1985

The London apartment of Marco Pirroni

Marco Pirroni was the lead guitarist with the Ants, the group formed by the singer Adam, for whom Powell-Tuck and Connor had also designed a house. For Pirroni, Connor created one of his most exciting interiors, building things just as they appear in his expressionistic drawings: door frames widening, skirting boards narrowing to a sliver in false perspective and radiators hung halfway up the wall, at an angle and plumbed with a madly spiralling pipe. The total effect is oddly convincing, conforming to a highly idiosyncratic inner aesthetic and logic.

Courtesy of Ilse Crawford

512

The new ornamentalism 1980s

Parallel with the move away from abstraction towards figurative and narrative work in painting and the fine arts there has been a tremendous reawakening in the decorative arts to the potential of ornament, pattern and colour. This is partly due to the influence of a younger generation of art-school-trained and predominantly urban-based craftsmen who, as makers of objects often using skills traditionally associated with a rural aesthetic, have an entirely new appreciation of the way in which their creations can function in a design-conscious and sophisticated market. There has been a consequent interaction between the marketers of interior decoration and art galleries, and a number of recently established exhibition spaces have set out deliberately to blur any remaining distinction between applied art objects and painting or sculpture.

514

513

Inlaid floor

Designed by Jennie Moncur and realized by Forbo Nairn Ltd for the Institute of Contemporary Arts, Carlton House Terrace, London

For the upper landing of the staircase in the architecturally more domestic wing of the ICA Jennie Moncur, a recent graduate of the Royal College of Art, was asked to design for a floor a bold scheme which both struck a contemporary decorative note and respected the nineteenth-century character of the building. Her very successful design took as a starting point existing floor patterns, scaling them right up to fill and enhance the sweep of the stair. The floor was laid in marbled linoleums, a technique pioneered in his own seminal house of the late 1950s by the designer Michael Inchbald.

Courtesy Jennie Moncur and Forbo Nairn Ltd

513

514

Prospectus showing printed textiles by Timney-Fowler, London

Sue Timney and Graham Fowler design printed textiles, she in a freely drawn, often abstract manner, while he uses old engravings and other architectural or sculptural imagery. Their predilection for black and white and the sharp, graphic and highly ornamental quality of their designs touched a sympathetic chord in the mid-1980s and has brought them success internationally. In Japan in particular they are heralded as a part of the 'new wave' of English designers; they enjoy great popularity and their patterns have been taken up by other entrepreneurs as diverse as Joseph and Kingcome Sofas. In addition to designing and selling textiles Timney-Fowler have made a few excursions into the fashion market, and are now producing an increasingly wide range of ceramics with printed designs related to their fabrics.

Courtesy of Timney-Fowler

515

Drawing showing painted silk curtains and metal furniture designed by Carolyn Quartermaine

Carolyn Quartermaine trained at the Royal College of Art in London, specializing in textile design. By the time of her degree show she was already finding that her silk painting technique translated well into other media and she had consistently shown painted vases alongside her hangings and smaller fabric panels. More recently she had turned to furniture, not only painting table tops but also designing metal supports for them, and creating a range of chairs and other pieces in strip metal which reveal her fascination with French garden furniture, and with the elegant forms of the campaign furnishings of the Napoleonic period. In 1986 she was one of the first young designers to be commissioned by Liberty to produce a group of furnishings for its modern department.

Victoria & Albert Museum, London

515

516

'Post-holocaust' 1985–6

Drawing by Ron Arad of the decoration of Bazaar,
South Molton Street, London

Ron Arad creates furniture, objects and entire interiors using rusty metal, stone, cast and fragmented concrete, and glass. At his Covent Garden shop, One-Off, he sells his own designs alongside the work of other designers whom he has chosen as belonging to the 'post-holocaust' aesthetic. Arad makes no distinction between domestic and commercial work, and one of his most completely successful schemes was the sadly short-lived decoration of the clothes shop Bazaar in South Molton Street, then at the height of its importance as a street for fashion shops. Arad's interior for Bazaar looked like an archaeological site where late twentieth-century civilization was being revealed amid the chaos of urban wreckage. The entire back wall was created from vast broken slabs of concrete hung on rusty steel hawsers, while the lighting and other fittings were a seeming tangle of old metal. Each of the racks for the clothes was guarded by a cast concrete figure reminiscent of the victims of the eruption of Vesuvius at Pompeii. All of this extraordinary interior was visible from the street through a plate-glass window, and had an especially striking and rather unreal quality when viewed at night, empty and lit by pin-points of cool light. Ironically, the scheme was almost immediately and quite unthinkingly copied in various ways, such as by one Oxford Street shop which reproduced the monumental steel and concrete 'wall' in polystyrene. Ron Arad's latest project, part of an exhibition at the Pompidou Centre in Paris in 1987, is an 'anti-interior' installation which features a machine for crushing other people's chairs to form cubes of debris with which to 'furnish' a space.

Victoria & Albert Museum, London

516

517

517

Creative salvage   1986

Self-portrait in his own room by Tom Dixon

The creative salvage aesthetic of the mid-1980s represents, ten years on, the coming of age of the punk movement and its fusion with more sophisticated aspects of the English avant-garde. Tom Dixon, who welds salvaged metal into extraordinary new forms, crosses the divide between accepted notions of sculpture and the making of furniture. He has increasingly been commissioned to work in the context of decoration, and has created not only grand set pieces such as throne-like chairs, but also runs of more utilitarian chairs and simple light fittings. More surprisingly, his work has begun to attract the interest of those who are concerned with the more traditional areas of craft.

Victoria & Albert Museum, London

518

Tradition and innovation in furniture   1986

Le clos, design for a commode by André Dubreuil

André Dubreuil came to England from France in the late 1960s and, during a period working for an important London dealer in antiques, became expert in the field of French furniture. Turning next to decoration, he progressed through his interest in the more practical aspects of the work to painting *trompe-l'oeil*. His decoration of the chocolate shop Rococo, in London's King's Road, for Chantal Coady is one of the most successful creations of the period, and it led Dubreuil on to a greater interest in making furniture and other fittings. At this stage he and Tom Dixon were already working together, experimenting with the possibilities of welding metal but, whilst Dixon used 'found' elements for his decorative ends, Dubreuil concentrated on the creation of beautiful forms from curved and welded rods. The pieces which he makes in this way are entirely modern, but they seem always to be inspired in an abstract sense by his detailed knowledge of the forms and styles of the past, and in particular the era of Louis XV. This easy familiarity with the best things of the past has also influenced him in his desire to make new pieces which will equal those of the eighteenth century in the quality of their materials and workmanship. This design for a commode is intended to be carried out in bronze and fine poplar wood. It has two drawers, and the handles are formed by loops of the tendrils which play across the surface.

Victoria & Albert Museum, London

518

519

Barbaric splendour 1981

Design for a room set for Jansen of Paris by Elizabeth Garouste and Mattea Bonetti; drawing by Mattea Bonetti

Elizabeth Garouste and Mattea Bonetti were asked in 1981 by the great Parisian decoration House of Jansen to create a group of their 'barbaric' furnishings to be shown in the unlikely context of a fine Louis Seize panelled room. Garouste and Bonetti, who were at that date at the height of their interest in creating pieces of furniture which verged on sculpture on a Stone Age theme, rose to the occasion and installed, much to the surprise of the patrons and their unusual clientele, chairs and screens made from straw, bound in wire, and hung above the traditional mantel an extravagant rockwork mirror-frame. Subsequent Garouste-Bonetti designs have included jokey ideas for pieces of furniture, such as a table with a grass skirt upon which stands a Second Empire-style candelabrum, which alludes to the death of the Prince Imperial in the nineteenth century at the hands of the Zulus. Most recently the partners' furniture and designs for interiors seem to reflect the influence of Emilio Terry, for whose quirky and inventive designs they share an enthusiasm with the couturier Christian Lacroix, for whom they have recently completed a colourful and highly successful studio and salon in Paris.

Victoria & Albert Museum, London

The 'New baroque' mid-1980s

In a period of strong reaction against the boredom of modernist and minimalist design, the most interesting of all the movements towards a new ornamentalism has been the emergence of a distinct aesthetic which can be identified as the 'New baroque'. The factors which unite the otherwise disparate protagonists of the game are a love of exuberant shapes and details held together by a feeling for an overall architectural form, and a desire to return to and embrace the full decorative possibilities of ornament. Some come to this from a knowledge of historic architecture or decoration, while others seem to arrive at a complementary point having developed their own forms and methods of work. This invites comparison with a similar phenomenon in the late seventeenth century when there coexisted an international avant-garde baroque style and a widely disseminated 'native baroque' based on man's inherent desire to ornament his surroundings and possessions.

520

Chimneypiece in carved stone by Rory Young of Cirencester, Gloucestershire

Rory Young is a stonecarver trained in the traditional methods. He has worked with the carver Simon Verity in the West Country and now has his own workshop in Cirencester, where he is creating a new baroque inner façade in the courtyard of his house. This chimneypiece is a good example of the return to time-honoured traditional forms, and is derived from an original design in the manner of William Kent. It is a work of powerful solidity, confident in its craftsmanship and conservative taste.

Courtesy of Rory Young

521

Design for a chimneypiece, looking-glass and two 'chimney ornaments' by Oriel Harwood; to be executed in glazed ceramic

Oriel Harwood describes herself as an architectural ceramicist rather than as a craftsman. She has consistently explored the possibilities of working on a monumental scale, and uses both historicizing and orginal forms and ornament with a baroque exuberance. Her influences have been mainly Italianate, and are often more architectural and sculptural than ceramic. More recently, however, she has created a series of large tulip vases based on the idea, though not the actual forms, of the Dutch pyramids of the Tulipomania period in the seventeenth century. In this design for a chimneypiece traditional forms are reworked in the mantel and mirror, while the attendant ornamental forms are entirely capricious objects based on the traditional andiron enlarged to a massive scale. A version of the looking-glass in this design forms part of the decoration of the new Director's dining room in the Victoria & Albert Museum (pl. 467).

Victoria & Albert Museum, London

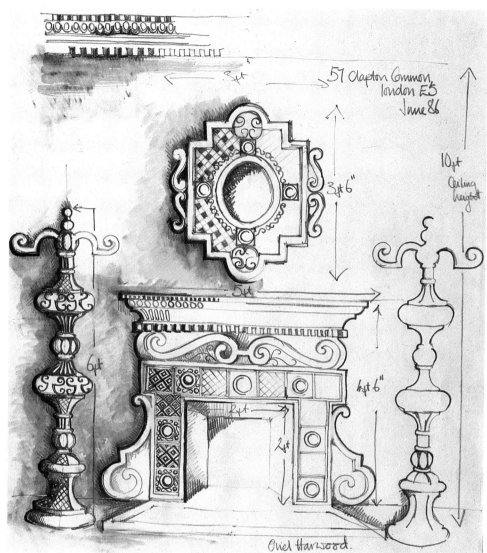

521

522

lighting. The walls are covered with sheets of white drawing paper pasted a little apart to form 'rustication', and all the books on the shelves are bound in vellum or wrapped in white paper. The baroque splendour of the setting is further enhanced by a few pieces of good architectural furniture of the eighteenth century, and completed by busts on splendid pedestals designed by Badin with plaster-dipped draperies.

Courtesy of Christian Badin, Paris; photograph David Massey

523

The 'Old palazzo' look in New York 1987

The main living room in his own New York apartment by John Saladino

There are few figures on the American scene as stylish and at the same time as learned as John Saladino. His thoughtful approach to design seems at all times to be informed by his knowledge of and delight in the great traditions of European Palladian architecture, and animated especially his reverence for the work of the master's great English disciple in the early eighteenth century, William Kent. Saladino's recently completed apartment in New York is an eloquent statement of his ideal, in which the strength and grandeur of the Kentian approach is allied to a slightly whimsical play on the ruined palazzo look which seems to enjoy such popularity in the late 1980s. The room has a high ceiling, elaborate plaster cornice, unpainted walls and a grand Kentian chimneypiece. In this detail the large painting and the long table are draped in a delightful and typically humorous Saladino allusion to the 'off-season' look in a grand palazzo.

Photograph Lizzie Himmel, New York

522

Baroque grandeur in France 1985

Views of a room set for a library by Christian Badin

Christian Badin's sure eye for combining elements of historical styles with a sharply characterized Modernism is revealed in his design for a library, which is one of the most stylish interior creations of its decade. Using huge chunks of plaster cornice, he creates an exciting Mannerist sense of architectural drama, and plays this up with a daring use of a monochromatic scheme and theatrical

523

Invitation card for an exhibition of decorative
arts at Gallery 24, Notting Hill Gate,
London   1986

Courtesy of Gallery 24

Index

A

Aalto, Alvar, pl. 288
Abbotsford, Borders Region, Scotland, 34
Adam, Robert, 374
Adam (of Adam and the Ants), 393
Adie, Button & Partners (architects), pl. 339
Adie, George, pl. 339
Adler, Rose, 163
Adron, Ralph, pl. 441
Aesthetic movement, 29, 59, 60, 76; pl. 6, pl. 32,
    pl. 55, pl. 165
African influence, pl. 115, pl. 116, pl. 187, pl. 288
Alavoine & Co. (decorators), 27, 64; pl. 37, pl. 91
Albers, Joseph, 144; pl. 192
Albert, Prince, 44
Albini, Franco, pl. 452
Alderson, Roy, 273
Aldington Craig & Collinge (architects), pl. 457
Alex Reid & Lefevre, 234
Alexandra, Queen, 33, 34, 259
Alfred Dunhill Ltd, 321
Alhambra Theatre, London, 63
Allied Artists' Exhibition (1914), 137
Allom, William, 83
Alt, Rudolf von, 31, 36
Altman's (department store), New York, 242, 243
Amalienburg hunting lodge, Munich, 256, 305
'American Renaissance', 56, 62
Amies, Hardy, 336
Ancaster, Lady, 122
Anderson House, Brookline, Boston, pl. 89
Anglesey, Marquess of, 267
Anglesey, Minna, 170
Anrep, Boris, 175
anterooms, pl. 25, pl. 26, pl. 105, pl. 132, pl. 224
Arad, Ron, pl. 516
Aram Zeev Designs, 383, 384
Architectural Association, London, 392
Argyll House, Chelsea, London, pl. 167
Ark Albion exhibition (1984), 392
Arlen, Michael, 141
Armstrong, John, pl. 299
Art Deco, 129, 141, 144, 162, 185, 330, 351, 353;
    pl. 182–5, pl. 194, pl. 283
'Art Furnishing', 36
Art Nouveau, 32, 41, 59, 60, 66, 69, 76, 77, 116, 125,
    133, 170, 338; pl. 44, pl. 47–9, pl. 65, pl. 71,
    pl. 95, pl. 443, pl. 447
Artemide, 384
Arts and Crafts movement, 32, 59, 60, 65, 69, 76,
    116, 134, 223, 285, 345; pl. 27, pl. 39, pl. 59,
    pl. 75, pl. 166, pl. 176, pl. 270
Arts Council, pl. 487
Arundel Society, 44
Ashburnham House, London, 311
Ashcombe, Wiltshire, 215, 236, 261, 280, 320;
    pl. 365, pl. 368, pl. 369, pl. 370
Ashley, Laura, 76; pl. 469
Ashton, Lady, 143, 243, 336
Asplund, Gunnar, 144, 286; pl. 153
Astor, Nancy, 306
Åt Solsiden, Stockholm (1910), 61; pl. 95–7
Atelier Elvira, Munich, pl. 47
Atelier Martine, 27, 63, 117, 144; pl. 116, pl. 183,
    pl. 193
Atelier Stenzel, 166
Atget, Eugène, 122
Athens
    apartment of Mr and Mrs Goulandris, pl. 437
    apartment of T.H. Robsjohn-Gibbings, 286
Atherton, Mr, 315
Atkinson, Robert, pl. 166
Au Printemps (department store), Paris, 160
Aubusson carpets, pl. 348
Avenue House, Ampthill, Bedfordshire, 134;
    pl. 159, pl. 411
Axminster carpet works, 267
Ayrton, Maxwell, 180
Aztec influence, pl. 168

B

Badin, Christian, pl. 479, pl. 522
Baer, C.H., 72, 116, 120, 121
Baillie Scott, Mackay Hugh, 65, 69, 70, 72, 77, 116;
    pl. 59, pl. 156, pl. 157
Baker, Sir Herbert, 188
Baker, Josephine, 107
Bakst, Léon, 62, 63, 106
Bal Nègre, 107
Baldini, Matteo, 389
Baldwin, Billy, 216; pl. 335, pl. 461
Ballantine, Anthony, pl. 447
Ballets Russes, 62, 106, 109, 228
Ballo, Aldo, pl. 452
Baltimore
    house of Dr Crim, pl. 54, pl. 55
Banfi, Belgiojoso and Peressutti, Milan, pl. 337
Bank of England, 335
Barcelona chair, 214, 291; pl. 282
Barcelona International Exhibition (1929), 224
'baronial' style, 63; pl. 133, pl. 257
Baroque, 143, 208, 267, 398; pl. 314
    see also under Revivals
Barrow, Stanley, 354
Barroux, 286; pl. 394
Bartlett School of Architecture, London, 332
'Bastiano' seating range, pl. 438
Bath, Marchioness of, 299
bathrooms, 263, 289, 379, 380, 388, 390; pl. 97,
    pl. 200, pl. 202, pl. 355, pl. 360, pl. 445, pl. 503
Battersby, Martin, 317; pl. 339, pl. 417, pl. 418
Battersea, Cyril Flowers, 1st Lord, 79
Bauhaus, 13, 144, 158, 214, 220, 221, 229, 361;
    pl. 188, pl. 282
Bayley, Stephen, 384
Bazaar, South Molton Street, London, pl. 516
Beach House, Worthing, 182, 185, 187; pl. 105,
    pl. 224
Beardsley, Aubrey, 31, 32, 37, 338, 345
Beaton, Cecil, 27, 109, 139, 208, 215, 236, 241, 261,
    268, 280, 289, 317, 321, 361; pl. 262, pl. 263,
    pl. 348, pl. 350, pl. 363, pl. 365, pl. 366, pl. 368,
    pl. 369, pl. 370, pl. 388, pl. 416, pl. 417
Beaton, Nancy, pl. 363
Beaux-Arts, École de, Paris, 335
'bed-sits', pl. 190, pl. 372
Beerbohm, Max, 63
Behrens, Peter, pl. 65
Beisteguí, Charles de, 215, 268, 270, 271, 283, 286,
    295, 301, 303, 309, 323, 330; pl. 391, pl. 418
Beit, Sir Alfred, 216, 256
Bell, Clive, 148
Bell, Vanessa, 64, 136, 137, 143; pl. 169, pl. 170,
    pl. 172, pl. 173, pl. 298
Belter, John Henry, 35
Belvoir Castle, Leicestershire, 34, 165
Beningbrough Hall, North Yorkshire, 331; pl. 465
Benirschke, Max, pl. 68
Benn, H. Pringuer, pl. 140
Bennett, Arnold, 143, 192
Bennett, Ronald, pl. 439
Bennison, Geoffrey, 270, 330, 360; pl. 438, pl. 453,
    pl. 454
Benois, Alexandre, 106
Bérard, Christian, 215, 271, 272, 282, 283, 321
Berndl, Richard, 74; pl. 111
Berners, Lord, 62, 201
Bernhardt, Sarah, 31, 46
Berry, Michael (later Lord Hartwell), 318

Bertie, Lady Jean, 268
Bertoia, Harry, 286; pl. 384
Bethell, Hon. Mrs Guy, 27, 141, 241; pl. 306,
    pl. 307, pl. 325
Betjeman, Sir John, 18, 283, 323
Bianco, Pamela, pl. 180
'Biba' shops, London, 330
Biedermeier style, 60, 216, 359, 361, 472; pl. 95,
    pl. 96, pl. 310
    see also under Revivals
Bing, Samuel, 32, 47
Birtwell, Celiia, pl. 443
Blanchards plc (decorators), pl. 507
Bloomsbury Group, 64, 136, 137, 143, 147, 149, 220,
    234
'Bloomsbury' style, pl. 172, pl. 173, pl. 174, pl. 175
Blow, Detmar, 280
Boehland, R., pl. 135
Boldini, Giovanni, pl. 124
Bonetti, Mattea, 361; pl. 519
Bonnard, Pierre, pl. 293
Borghese, Pauline, 331
Boston
    152 Beacon Street (house of Isabella Stewart
        Gardner), pl. 58
Boudin, Stéphane, 287, 305, 359; pl. 332
boudoirs, pl. 46, pl. 126, pl. 182, pl. 285
Boulestin, Marcel, 63, 64, 109, 137; pl. 118, pl. 200,
    pl. 205
Bourgeois, Djo, pl. 2
Bourguignon, Jean, pl. 21, pl. 22
Boussin, Claude, pl. 112
Boyd Harte, Glynn, pl. 472
Boys, Michael, pl. 453, pl. 454, pl. 464
Braddell, Darcy, pl. 296
Bradley, Catherine, 133
Brangwyn, Frank, 63
Braque, Georges, 107; pl. 389
Breakers, The, Newport, Rhode Island, pl. 79
breakfast room, pl. 64
Brent, Tom, pl. 504
Breuer, Marcel, 144, 360; pl. 189, pl. 191, pl. 290
Brighton, 63, 323
    39 Preston Park Avenue (lodgings of Rex
        Whistler), pl. 342
    40 Sussex Square (house of Lady Sackville),
        pl. 143, pl. 144
Brighton Pavilion, 203
Brissaud, Pierre, pl. 221, pl. 222
British Empire Exhibition (1924), 135
'Brno' chair, pl. 282
Brooklynwood, Maryland, pl. 56
Brown, Mrs Archibald (Eleanor McMillen), 216;
    pl. 219–22
Bruno, K. Graf House, Dallas, Texas, pl. 385
Brussels
    55, rue Mignot-Delstanche, pl. 302
    no. 6, rue Paul-Émile Janson, pl. 48
Buatta, Mario, 330; pl. 460
Bugatti, Carlo, pl. 76, pl. 77
Burges, William, 18
Burlington, Lord, 123
Burlton, Gladys, 239
Burra, Edward, pl. 352
Button, Frederick, pl. 339

C

Cadell, Francis Campbell Boileau, pl. 252
Calder, Alexander, pl. 381
Camden Town Group, 132
Canaletto, Antonio, 196, 267
candelabra, 398; pl. 29, pl. 218, pl. 221, pl. 250,
    pl. 358, pl. 446
candle sconces, pl. 53, pl. 109, pl. 134, pl. 345,
    pl. 365
candle-shades, 64, 191; pl. 164
candlesticks, 31, 196; pl. 34, pl. 129, pl. 180, pl. 259,

pl. 319, pl. 320, pl. 477, pl. 491
Canova, Antonio, pl. 329
'Caori' table, pl. 438
Caravaggio, 259
Carlisle House, Soho, London, pl. 216, pl. 217
Carolean style, 142
Carpaccio, Vittore, 111, 204
carpets, pl. 6, pl. 10, pl. 125, pl. 159, pl. 191, pl. 194,
    pl. 201, pl. 208, pl. 220, pl. 275, pl. 298, pl. 301,
    pl. 303, pl. 306, pl. 310, pl. 318, pl. 320, pl. 323,
    pl. 401, pl. 425
    Aubusson, pl. 411
    faux-marbre, pl. 143
    'Hartnell green', pl. 361
    leopard-skin, 260
    Madrid, pl. 390
    needlepoint, pl. 260
    neo-classical, pl. 141
    oriental, pl. 82, pl. 101, pl. 113, pl. 193
    Persian, pl. 282
    Savonnerie, pl. 346
    shag-pile, pl. 443, pl. 446
    Surrealist, pl. 356
    trompe-l'œil, pl. 464
    wall-to-wall, 273; pl. 430
    Whistler-designed, pl. 344
Carrère & Hastings (architects), 83
Carrington, Noel, 218
Carter, R.C., pl. 74
Cartier Foundation, 378
Casa Batlló, Barcelona, pl. 49
Casa Brion, Milan, pl. 452
Caspar Hrzdil, 70
Casson, Sir Hugh, 263, 287, 291, 372; pl. 303
Castaing, Mme Madeleine, 243, 287; pl. 393
Catroux, François, 330; pl. 464
Cavendish House, St Albans, Hertfordshire, 135;
    pl. 158
Chaimowicz, Marc, pl. 487
Chalfin, Paul, pl. 202
chandeliers, 215, 260; pl. 9, pl. 13, pl. 35, pl. 110,
    pl. 153, pl. 158, pl. 218, pl. 225, pl. 249, pl. 253,
    pl. 332, pl. 338, pl. 346, pl. 361, pl. 410, pl. 411,
    pl. 435, pl. 467
Chanel, Coco, 329, 333, 360; pl. 218
Channon, Sir Henry ('Chips'), 171, 216, 256, 305,
    359
Channon, Paul, 171
Charles, Prince of Wales, 333
Charles X style, pl. 302, pl. 305, pl. 348
    see also under Revivals
Charleston, Firle Park, Sussex, pl. 162, pl. 163
Charters, Berkshire, , pl. 339
Château de Lèves, near Paris, pl. 393
Château de St-Firmin, Chantilly, pl. 418
Chermayeff, Serge, 214, 224; pl. 4, pl. 275, pl. 279,
    pl. 280
Chester House, Clarendon Place, London, pl. 226
Chevening, Kent, pl. 431
Chilham Castle, Kent, pl. 257
chimneypieces, 148, 254, 295, 307; pl. 15, pl. 41,
    pl. 53, pl. 55, pl. 58, pl. 60, pl. 61, pl. 78, pl. 99,
    pl. 131, pl. 138, pl. 148, pl. 149, pl. 158, pl. 160,
    pl. 162, pl. 213, pl. 225, pl. 237, pl. 251, pl. 264,
    pl. 273, pl. 284, pl. 290, pl. 296, pl. 303, pl. 306,
    pl. 316, pl. 318, pl. 319, pl. 331, pl. 339, pl. 341,
    pl. 350, pl. 364, pl. 380, pl. 394, pl. 432, pl. 460,
    pl. 461, pl. 463, pl. 467, pl. 482, pl. 510, pl. 520,
    pl. 521, pl. 523
Chinoiserie, 13, 142, 144, 215, 243; pl. 203, pl. 214,
    pl. 215, pl. 217, pl. 250, pl. 259, pl. 406, pl. 411
Chippendale style, pl. 142, pl. 213
Christophorou, Alkis, pl. 507
Church, Frederick, 35
Clandon Park, Surrey, pl. 432
Clark, Lord, 344
Clark, Ossie, pl. 443
Claude Lorraine, 267

Clendenning, Max, 330; pl. 441
Clifford, Timothy, 363
Clouds, Wiltshire, 135; pl. 41
Clouds Hill, near Dorchester, Dorset, pl. 324
Coady, Chantal, 397
Coates, Nigel, 361; pl. 510, pl. 511
Cobbe, Alec, pl. 466
Coburn, Alvin Langdon, pl. 103
Cocteau, Jean, 175, 271, 272, 282, 283
Codman, Ogden, 53, 61, 62, 82, 86, 94, 129, 142, 168, 169; pl. 78, pl. 79, pl. 80, pl. 92, pl. 94
Colefax, Lady Sybil, 139, 141, 216; pl. 326
Colefax & Co. (decorators), 139, 216, 287, 306
Colefax & Fowler (decorators), 240, 327, 330, 331, 364; pl. 28, pl. 326
Colette, 63
Colonial period, 33, 81; pl. 54, pl. 55
Colony Club, New York, 62, 83, 87, 170; pl. 88
Columbian Exposition (1893), Chicago, 39
Compiègne, Château de, 331
Connor, David, 361, 376; pl. 512
Conran, Sir Terence, 76, 353
Cooper, Sir Alfred Duff, 1st Viscount Norwich, 164, 188, 321
Cooper, Lady Diana, 127, 164, 165, 188, 321
Cooper, Edith, 133
Corfe, B.O., pl. 42, pl. 43
Cornaz, J., pl. 395
Cornelys, Mrs, 174
Cornforth, John, 252, 267, 307, 350
cottage style, pl. 156, pl. 157
Council of Industrial Design, 288
Crawley-Boevey, Sir Launcelot, 307
Crittall windows, 218
Cubism, 107, 228; pl. 290
Cumming, Rose, Frontispiece, pl. 406, pl. 407
Curjel & Moser (architects), pl. 69
curtains, 63; pl. 99, pl. 132, pl. 159, pl. 221, pl. 226, pl. 253, pl. 266, pl. 273, pl. 321, pl. 338, pl. 346, pl. 383, pl. 417, pl. 430, pl. 432, pl. 476, pl. 477
    Casson, pl. 303
    Fowler, pl. 431
    'Hartnell green', 277
    Larsson, 50
    satin, pl. 318, pl. 320, pl. 398
    Second Empire design, 268
    silk, 191; pl. 382, pl. 515
    sun, pl. 252
    swagged, pl. 325, pl. 326, pl. 327, pl. 329, pl. 341
    toile de Jouy, pl. 258
Curzon, Lady, 63
Curzon Street Baroque, 18; pl. 249; pl. 257; pl. 365
cushions, 109, 128; pl. 107, pl. 186, pl. 193, pl. 195, pl. 199, pl. 266, pl. 304, pl. 305, pl. 309, pl. 324, pl. 352, pl. 444, pl. 484, pl. 493
Czartoryski, Princess, 301

D

Dada, pl. 187
Dali, Salvador, 214; pl. 353, pl. 357
Dandy, Leslie, pl. 372
Darmstadt palace, 65, 116, 133
Davis, Sir Edmund, 94
De Feure, Georges, 32; pl. 46
De La Warr pavilion, Bexhill-on-Sea, Sussex, 224
De Molas, Nicolas, 215
De Montesquiou, Comte Robert, 12, 113
'De Stijl' group, 220
De Wolfe, Elsie (Lady Mendl), 20, 21, 29, 53, 62, 81, 87, 94, 141, 142, 150, 168, 169, 176, 213, 216, 259, 272, 278, 346, 368, 372; pl. 86, pl. 87, pl. 88, pl. 209–12, pl. 215
Dean, Martin, 340
Decoration Moderne, 63, 64, 109; pl. 118, pl. 119
Deepdene, The, Surrey, 180, 184
Deering, James, 165
Delaval, Lord, 174

D'Erlanger, Baroness, 63
Deshairs, Léon, 142, 144
Design Council, London, 360
'Design in Sweden' exhibition (1954–7), 286
Deutscher Werkbund, 75
Devalle House, Turin, pl. 380
Devis, Arthur, 367
Devonshire House, London, pl. 214
Diaghilev ballet, 280
Dietterlin, Wendel, 118
Dighton, Richard, 97
Dior, Christian, 298
Directoire style, 81, 99, 287, 302, 305, 359; pl. 108, pl. 110, pl. 221, pl. 348
Dismant, Marion, pl. 177, pl. 178
Ditchley Park, Oxfordshire, 287, 306
Dixon, Tom, pl. 517
Dobbie, Ian, pl. 488
Dodd, Alan, pl. 467, pl. 478
Dolci, Carlo, 200
Dorchester Hotel, London, 307, 329
Dorland Hall, Bayswater, London, 215, 222, 233, 236
Dorn, Marion, 182; pl. 362
Doucet, Jacques, 153; pl. 196–8
Dresser, Christopher, 366, 367; pl. 471
Drian, 171
Drottningholm, Royal Palace, near Stockholm, 306
Du Pont, Henry Francis, pl. 405
Dubreuil, André, pl. 510, pl. 518
Dufour, Joseph, 103
Dufrène, Maurice, pl. 184
Dufy, Raoul, 205
Dunaway, Miss Faye, 369
Duveen, Edward J., pl. 223
Duveen, Joseph, 83, 142

E

Eames, Charles, 296, pl. 375
Eames, Ray, 296; pl. 375
Eames chair, 291
Eames House, Santa Monica, Los Angeles, pl. 375
Eastlake, Charles, 27
Easton Neston, Northamptonshire, 345
Eaton Hall, Cheshire, pl. 1
Écart (furniture manufacturers), 153
Edward VII, King (as Prince of Wales), 33, 34
'Edwardian' style, 364
Edwards, Ralph, 243
Egyptian style, pl. 202
Elden Ltd, 27, 141, 240, 241, 252
Elipse table, 291
Elizabethan period, 123
    see also under Revivals
Elveden Hall, Suffolk, 238
Elysée Palace, Paris, 378
Empire style, 12, 31, 62, 143, 180, 195, 302, 305, 331; pl. 25, pl. 26, pl. 34, pl. 108, pl. 110, pl. 233, pl. 242, pl. 317, pl. 329, pl. 396
    American, 254, 351; pl. 55, pl. 405
Endell, August, 32; pl. 47
Englinger, pl. 184
'English country house look', 364
Ennis House, The, Los Angeles, pl. 168
Epstein, Jacob, 117
Erté (Romain de Tertoff), pl. 186
Esher, Surrey
    house of Mr and Mrs Notley, pl. 303
Essex & Co. (decorators), pl. 27
Etchells, Frederick, 137
'Etruscan style', pl. 484
Eugénie, Empress, 22, 51
Experiments in Living exhibition (1970–1), 340

F

Fairbanks, Douglas, 241

Falling Water, Bear Run, Pennsylvania, 214; pl. 284
Farnsworth House, Fox River, Illinois, pl. 374
Federal style, 33, 81, 101, 351; pl. 9, pl. 10, pl. 54, pl. 55, pl. 316
    see also under Revivals
Fellini, Federico, 361, 374
Festival of Britain (1951), 273, 286, 296, 349
'Field, Michael', 60
fireplaces, pl. 383, pl. 423
Fitzherbert, Mrs, 316
Flaxley Abbey, Gloucestershire, 329; pl. 401
Fleet, Simon, 329; pl. 430
Fleming, Ronald, 111, 173, 187, 213–14, 215, 282; pl. 217, pl. 250, pl. 273, pl. 294, pl. 297, pl. 301, pl. 328, pl. 420
Fletcher, Ronald, 260
Flight, Claude, pl. 199
flooring, 149, 374; pl. 70, pl. 71, pl. 113, pl. 180, pl. 219, pl. 331, pl. 506
    birchwood, pl. 310
    geometric patterning, pl. 129, pl. 186
    inlaid, pl. 221, pl. 300, pl. 321, pl. 513
    linoleum, pl. 231, pl. 427
    painted, 317
    parquet, 9, pl. 82, pl. 99, pl. 209, pl. 210, pl. 389, pl. 395, pl. 472
    'paved', pl. 338
    polished wood, 330; pl. 35
    stone-flagged, pl. 393
    wooden-slatted, pl. 97
flower arrangements, 277; pl. 326, pl. 333, pl. 334, pl. 365, pl. 417, pl. 436
Folifoot, near Harrogate, Yorkshire, 218
Folly Farm, Sulhampstead, Berkshire, pl. 120
Fontaine, Pierre, pl. 19
Forbo Nairn Ltd, pl. 513
Foreman, Steven, pl. 459
Fornasetti, Piero, 286, 294, 361; pl. 378, pl. 379, pl. 382, pl. 435
Fortnum & Mason (department store), 167, 215, 234, 235, 247, 248
'Fourth Empire', 287; pl. 396
Fowler, Graham, pl. 514
Fowler, John, 18, 143, 216, 217, 240, 252, 285, 287, 302, 314, 330, 331, 343, 354, 360, 362, 372; pl. 326, pl. 327, pl. 399, pl. 400, pl. 402, pl. 403, pl. 404, pl. 431, pl. 432
Frank, Jean-Michel, 215, 231, 275, 298; pl. 347, pl. 349, pl. 350, pl. 351
French, John, 243, 336
French, Vere, 336
Frick, Henry Clay, 62, 83, 359
Frick Collection, New York, 62
Frick Mansion, New York, pl. 83
Friedrich, Caspar David, 101
friezes, pl. 27, pl. 67, pl. 69, pl. 117, pl. 140, pl. 159, pl. 186, pl. 222, pl. 236, pl. 293, pl. 409
Frost, Clive, pl. 486
Fry, Roger, 64, 136, 137, 148
Future Systems, pl. 492

G

'G-Plan' furniture, 286; pl. 372
Gaillard, Eugène, 47
Gardner, Isabella Stewart, 56
Garland, Madge, 336
Garouste, Elizabeth, 361; pl. 519
Garsington Manor, Oxfordshire, pl. 165
gasoliers, pl. 5–8
Gaudí, Antonio, 32; pl. 49
Gauguin, Paul, pl. 293
Gaunt, William, 166, 167
Gauthiers-Villars, Henri (pen-name Willy), 63
Gayfere House, Lord North Street, London, pl. 360
Gentleman, David, pl. 434
Geoffroy, Georges, pl. 418
George IV, King, 316

George & Peto (architects), pl. 40
George Webster Ltd, pl. 339
'Georgian' style, 27, 207, 210; pl. 223, pl. 264, pl. 406
    see also under Revivals
German Symbolism, 121
Gesellius, Lindgren & Saarinen (architects), pl. 128
Giamelli, Signor, 374
Gibbon, Michael, 330
Gibbs, Christopher, 330
Gilbert and George, pl. 471
Gill, Eric, pl. 102
Gilliatt, Mary, 335
Giverny (home of Monet), 247
Gizycka, Eleanor, 141
Glasgow School, 59, 65, 66, 69, 117
Gloag, John, 138; pl. 151
Glyn, Elinor, 103
Goethe, Johann von, 104
Gomme & Son (furniture manufacturers), 286; pl. 372
Goncourt, Edmond de, 9, 12
Goodhart-Rendel, H.L., 182; pl. 232
Goodnow, Ruby Ross
    see Wood, Ruby Ross
Goodwin, E.W., 31
Gordon, Lady Duff ('Lucile'), 103
Gordon Russell Ltd, 218; pl. 286
Gore, Spencer Frederick, 133; pl. 155
Gothic style, 18, 32, 37, 361; pl. 471
Gough, Piers, 361
Goulandris, Mr and Mrs, 337
Gradidge, Roderick, 344, 345; pl. 447
Grandchamps, M. and Mme, 237
Grant, Duncan, 64, 136, 137, 143; pl. 161, pl. 162, pl. 169–73; pl. 298
Graves, Michael, pl. 498, pl. 500
Gray, Eileen, 163, 221, 360, 377; pl. 181
Great Exhibition (1851), London, 286
Great Hundridge Manor, Chesham, 62, 111, 368; pl. 259, pl. 260, pl. 261
Greek style, pl. 202, pl. 296, pl. 385
Green & Abbott (decorators), 242, 334
Green's Arctic Lights, 137
Gray of Falloden, Viscount, 280
Grimsthorpe Castle, Lincolnshire, pl. 137
Gropius, Walter, 158, 214, 218, 228; pl. 188, pl. 189, pl. 291
Groscher, Paul, pl. 266
Grosser, Boris, pl. 183
Grosvenor School of Modern Art, 163
Groult, André, 63, 144, 163, 167
Groussay, near Paris, 303; pl. 348
Guggenheim, Peggy, pl. 381
Guhr, Richard, pl. 136
Gunzburg, Baron Niki de, 216
Gustavian style, 60, 101, 131
Gutmann, W., pl. 285

H

'H.55' exhibition (1955), 286
Habitat Catalogue, pl. 458
Hadley, Albert, 330; pl. 462
halls, 74, 262, 300, 307; pl. 11, pl. 12, pl. 30, pl. 67, pl. 70, pl. 83, pl. 87, pl. 89, pl. 103, pl. 111, pl. 120, pl. 136, pl. 140, pl. 175, pl. 187, pl. 219, pl. 224, pl. 245, pl. 300, pl. 315, pl. 322, pl. 336, pl. 339, pl. 386, pl. 389, pl. 393, pl. 395, pl. 418, pl. 449, pl. 453, pl. 465, pl. 478, pl. 507
Ham House, Surrey, 331; pl. 455
Hammershoi, Wilhelm, 61, 101; pl. 152
Hampton, Mark, 330, 339; pl. 480
Harbord, Felix, 283, 320; pl. 346, pl. 412, pl. 413, pl. 414, pl. 416
Hartley, Mr and Mrs, 218
Hartnell, Norman, 182, 214, 248, 260, 261, 276, 277, 344; pl. 336, pl. 361

Harwood, Oriel, pl. 467, pl. 521
Haseley Court, Oxfordshire, 287; pl. 399, pl. 400
Haslam, Nicholas, 360; pl. 475
Haslam, William Heywood, 111, 203, 204
Haslam family, 62
Havinden, Ashley, 231
Haweis, Mary Eliza, 18
Hawksmoor, Nicholas, 345
Haynes & Co. (decorators), pl. 264, pl. 265
Heal, Ambrose, pl. 176
Hearst, William Randolph, 205, 208
Hearst Castle, San Simeon, California, pl. 267,
    pl. 268, pl. 269
Heil, Graf von, 119
Helg, Franco, pl. 452
Helleu, Mme, pl. 53
Helleu, Paul-César, 53; pl. 53
Helmsley Palace Hotel, New York, 56
Henry, Hélène, 221
Henry, Mrs Sedan, 186
Henry Francis du Pont Winterthur Museum,
    Delaware, pl. 405
Hepplewhite period, 125
Hepworth, Barbara, pl. 290
Herbert, Hon. David, 320; pl. 413
Herbert, Lady Georgina, 317
Herbst, René, 221
Hereford, Marquesses of, 277
Hertford, Lord, 370
    see also Wallace, Sir Richard
Hess, Otto, 276
Hesse, Grand Duke of, 65, 116, 133
Hicks, David, 287, 319, 329–30, 345, 359, 370, 372;
    pl. 428, pl. 440, pl. 449, pl. 450, pl. 451, pl. 463,
    pl. 508, pl. 509
Hicks, Mrs Herbert, 327, 329
'High Style', 215–16, 259, 287, 330, 360
High-Tech style, pl. 492, pl. 493, pl. 494
Highpoint I, Highgate, London, pl. 295
Hilberseimer, Ludwig, pl. 277
Hill, John, 275; pl. 310, pl. 318
Hill, Oliver, 214; pl. 214, pl. 360
Hill House, Helensburgh, 73; pl. 63
Hill House, Mayfair, London, pl. 412
Historic Houses Association, 362
Hoare, Sir Samuel, 335
Hobdal, Roy, pl. 396
Hockney, David, 330; pl. 443
Hoffman, F. Burrall, Jr, pl. 202
Hoffmann, Josef, 59, 70, 73, 157; pl. 66, pl. 67,
    pl. 71, pl. 72
'Hollywood Hispanic' style, 244
'Home Exhibition' (1917), Liljevalch Gallery,
    Stockholm, 144
Hommes, Robert, pl. 130
Hookham, John, pl. 259
Hooper, Philip, pl. 482
Hope, Thomas, 62, 99, 182; pl. 230
Hoppen, Col. Francis, pl. 82
Horta, Victor, 32; pl. 48
Hortense, Princesse, 22
Hôtel Beauharnais (British Embassy), Paris, 321,
    331
Hôtel Beistegui, Paris, pl. 391
Hôtel Bischoffsheim, Paris, pl. 349, pl. 350, pl. 389
Hotel Cecil, London, pl. 50
Hôtel Lambert, Paris, pl. 392
Hotel Parr, Vienna, 256
Houghton-Brown, Geoffrey, 215; pl. 297, pl. 355
House of Culture, Stockholm, 286
'House of the Future', 1956 Ideal Home Exhibition,
    286, 340; pl. 376
houseboat, pl. 486
Howarth, A.E., pl. 73
Hudson River School, 35
Hunting Lodge, Odiham, Hampshire, pl. 402,
    pl. 403
Hussey, Christopher, 180, 182, 185

Hutchinson, Mrs St John, 147
Huxley, Aldous, 138
Huysmans, Joris Karl, 12, 31, 36, 37
Hyères (de Noailles country house), 271, 299

I

Ideal Home Exhibition (1934), 254
Ideal Home Exhibition (1936), 241
Ideal Home Exhibition (1956), 291
Ilsted, Peter, 61; pl. 106, pl. 107
Imbert, M., pl. 313
Impressionism, 31, 132
Inchbald, Michael, 287, 332, 394; pl. 419, pl. 427
inglenook, pl. 61
Innes, Jocasta, pl. 470
Institute of Contemporary Arts, London, pl. 513
International Modern movement, 74, 144, 158, 383;
    pl. 385
Ionides, Basil, 142, 188, 198; pl. 213, pl. 239, pl. 240,
    pl. 241, pl. 246, pl. 247, pl. 248
Iribe, Paul, 63, 144, 162
Irvine, Keith, 287, 300; pl. 481
Irvine & Fleming (decorators), 372
Isabella Stewart Gardner Museum, Boston, 56
Islington, Lady, 141
'Italian style', 295

J

Jacob, Georges, 102; pl. 22
Jacobean style, 123, 208
    see also under Revivals
Jagger, Serjeant, pl. 296
James, Anne Scott, 216
James, Edward, 127, 214, 215, 233, 267, 274–7, 356
James, Henry, 61; pl. 98
Jansen, House of, Paris, 88, 142, 256, 286–7, 359,
    398; pl. 218, pl. 234, pl. 235, pl. 397
Japanese prints, 32, 37; pl. 32
japonisme, 60
Jarman, Derek, 361
Jazz Modern, 129; pl. 236, pl. 289, pl. 296
Jeffress, Arthur, pl. 398
Jekyll, Gertrude, 42
Jencks, Charles, 361, 384; pl. 495, pl. 496
Jiřična, Eva, pl. 493, pl. 494
Joel, Betty, pl. 304
Jones, Mrs George Frederick, 38
Jones, Inigo, 317
Jones, Owen, 166
Joseph, 381
Josephine, Empress, 22
Jourdain, Francis, 221; pl. 185
Jourdain, Margaret, 122, 142
Jugendstil see Art Nouveau
Jullian, Philippe, pl. 33, pl. 114, pl. 353, pl. 387

K

Kandinsky, Wassily, 158
Karin chair, 286
Karlicky, Jan, pl. 492
Kaufmann, Edgar J., 225
Keebles (decorators), 109, 122, 142; pl. 26, pl. 217
Kelmarsh Hall, Northamptonshire, 287; pl. 307,
    pl. 325
Kelmscott Manor, Oxfordshire, 41, 60
Kelso (decorators), 217, 233
Kent, William, 122, 123, 125, 127, 399, 400; pl. 138
Kersting, Georg Friedrich, 101, 367
Keynes, John Maynard, 137, 147
King, Mrs Willie (Viva), 325, 336; pl. 425
kitchens, 214, 267, 291, 330, 388; pl. 71, pl. 280,
    pl. 281, pl. 492
Klee, Paul, 158
Klimt, Gustav, pl. 66
klismos chair, 286

Knoblock, Edward, 61, 97, 99, 104, 135, 185, 187,
    192; pl. 224, pl. 229
Knole, Kent, 126, 142, 251
Knoll International, pl. 384
Knothe, Paul, pl. 203
Knox, Archibald, 76
Koch, Alexander, 59, 65, 70, 115, 118
Kozma, Ludwig, pl. 131
Krause, Rainer, 389

L

Laboureur, Jean-Émile, 167; pl. 119, pl. 204
Lacoste, Gerald, 276; pl. 361
Lacrois, M., 221
Lacroix, Christian, 398
Lagerfeld, Karl, 384
Lajoue, Jacques de, pl. 331
Lamb House, Rye, Sussex, pl. 103, pl. 104
lamps, pl. 7, pl. 176, pl. 206, pl. 207, pl. 318
    desk, pl. 291
    gas, 34; pl. 80
    hanging, pl. 132
    oil, pl. 35, pl. 80, pl. 160, pl. 220, pl. 387
    shaded, pl. 123
    skirted, pl. 141
    standard, 142; pl. 126
    table, pl. 118, pl. 160, pl. 177, pl. 496
    'Toio', pl. 438
    Victorian, pl. 428
lampshades, 144, 150; pl. 248, pl. 249, pl. 428
Lancaster, Lady, 216
Lancaster, Mrs Nancy, 240, 287, 354; pl. 399,
    pl. 400, pl. 404
Lancaster, Osbert, 18, 62, 106, 143, 201, 214, 360;
    pl. 115, pl. 227, pl. 249, pl. 270, pl. 288, pl. 289,
    pl. 423
Land's End, Newport, Rhode Island, pl. 78
Lansdowne House, Holland Park, London, pl. 99,
    pl. 100
lanterns, pl. 160, pl. 230, pl. 231, pl. 338
Largillière, Nicolas, 196
Larsson, Carl, 60, 61, 101, 131; pl. 95, pl. 96, pl. 97,
    pl. 285
Larsson, Karin, 60, 61, 92
Lauderdale, Duchess of, 350
Lauren, Ralph, 76
Laurencin, Marie, 167; pl. 204
Laver, James, 12–13
Lawrence, Edith, 163
Lawrence, Gertrude, 233, 236, 282
Lawrence, T.E., 251
Le Corbusier, 214, 215, 218, 220, 228, 271, 360;
    pl. 345
Lee, Rupert, pl. 352
Lefevre Gallery, 234
Lefuel, Henri, 102
Legrain, Pierre, 162
Leighton, Lord, 31, 35, 36
Leighton House, London, 31
Leleu, Jules, pl. 302
Leningrad, 331
Lennon, Denis, 332
Lenygon, Francis, 83, 122, 142
Lenygon & Morant (decorators), 64, 109, 122, 142,
    174, 206
Leonard, Peter, pl. 491
Léopolda, La, near Villefranche-sur-Mer, pl. 92
Lepape, Georges, pl. 117
Lerma, Duchess of, 205
Leverson, Ada, 61
Lévy (publisher), 46
Levy, Sir Albert, 173
Lévy, Mme Mathieu, pl. 181
Lewis, Wyndham, 27, 144; pl. 164
Leyland, Frederick, 31
Leys, The, near Elstree, Hertfordshire, pl. 61
Liberace, 329; pl. 446

Liberty, Arthur Lasenby, 47, 60, 76
Liberty & Co., London, 32, 60, 77, 395; pl. 75
Liberty style, pl. 73
libraries, 263, 321, 345; pl. 81, pl. 171, pl. 172,
    pl. 173, pl. 291, pl. 330, pl. 331, pl. 348, pl. 391,
    pl. 392, pl. 406, pl. 429, pl. 469, pl. 479, pl. 495,
    pl. 522
lighting, 215, 397; pl. 50, pl. 99, pl. 159, pl. 194,
    pl. 315, pl. 393, pl. 452
    electric light bulbs, 127; pl. 130, pl. 230
    sconces, pl. 502
    spot-lights, pl. 457
    strip lights, pl. 187
    wall-lights, 287; pl. 336
Linder, H.E., pl. 127
Liselund, Denmark, pl. 107
Little & Brown (decorators), pl. 89
living rooms, pl. 95, pl. 153, pl. 168, pl. 261, pl. 383,
    pl. 523
lobby, entrance, pl. 419
Lobden, near Malvern, Worcs., pl. 274
loft dwelling, pl. 504
loggias, 391; pl. 266
London
    Academy Cinema, Oxford Street, 304
    Albany, off Piccadilly (apartment of David
        Hicks), pl. 463
    3 Albert Gate, Regent's Park (house of Mrs St
        John Hutchinson), pl. 171, pl. 173
    16 Arlington Street (house of Duke of Rutland),
        pl. 145
    22 Avery Row (house of Mrs Lancaster), 354;
        pl. 404
    5 Belgrave Square (house of Sir Henry Channon),
        pl. 330, pl. 332
    Bruton Street (house of Victor Stiebel), pl. 337
    Cambridge Street, Pimlico (house of Aubrey
        Beardsley), 31–2, 37
    Carlyle Square (house of Osbert and Sacheverell
        Sitwell), 144; pl. 255, pl. 256
    Charles Street, pl. 478
    13 Crawford Street (house of H.L. Goodhart-
        Rendel), pl. 232
    Edith Terrace, Chelsea (studio of Charles
        Shannon), 37; pl. 32
    Edwardes Square ('a small London house'),
        pl. 160
    Endell Street (house of Angus McBean), pl. 396
    Fitzroy Square, pl. 352
    Folgate Street, Spitalfields (house of Dennis
        Severs), pl. 473, pl. 474
    46 Gordon Square (John Maynard Keynes's
        house), pl. 169, pl. 170
    50 Gordon Square (house of Clive Bell), pl. 172
    Gower Street (house of Lady Diana Cooper),
        pl. 201, pl. 237
    15 Kensington Palace Gardens (house of Sir
        Alfred Beit), pl. 331
    King's Road, Chelsea (house of Syrie Maugham),
        213; pl. 362, pl. 363
    Lower Belgrave Street, pl. 475
    Marble Arch (house of Lord Battersea), pl. 76
    Mecklenburgh Square (house of William
        Nicholson), pl. 101
    11 Montagu Place (house of Edward Knoblock),
        pl. 229
    Notting Hill Gate (flat of Zandra Rhodes),
        pl. 444, 445
    Notting Hill Gate (house of Mr and Mrs Clark),
        pl. 443
    31 Old Burlington Street (showroom of Francis
        Lenygon), pl. 138, pl. 139
    17 Park Square East (house of H.J. Venning),
        pl. 225
    Pelham Place (house of Arthur Jeffress), pl. 398
    73 Portland Place (apartment of Gertrude
        Lawrence), pl. 301
    Portman Square (flat of Sir Geoffrey Fry), pl. 292

Regent's Park (house of Lady Katharine Somerset), pl. 253, pl. 254
Restaurant Boulestin, Covent Garden, pl. 204, pl. 205
Restaurant Français, Leicester Square, 167
Rutland Gate (house of Mr and Mrs Anthony Sewell), pl. 321
Soho (flat of Geoffrey Bennison), pl. 453, pl. 454
South Eaton Place (house of Mrs Herbert Hicks), 329; pl. 428
South Eaton Place (house of Clough Williams-Ellis), pl. 243, pl. 244, pl. 245
South Kensington (flat of Nigel Coates), pl. 510
South Molton Street, Bazaar, pl. 516
South Street, Mayfair (house of the Hon. Henry McLaren, later Lord Aberconway), 213
Spitalfields (house of Gilbert and George), pl. 471
Thurloe Square (flat of Ronald Fleming), pl. 420
15 Thurloe Square (house of Mrs Willie King), pl. 425
11 Titchfield Terrace (house of Lord Gerald Wellesley), pl. 230, pl. 231, pl. 258
Tite Street (studio-house of James McNeil Whistler), 31
Upper Belgrave Street (house of Lady Jean Bertie), pl. 346
42 Upper Brook Street, pl. 275
The Vale, Chelsea (house of Whistler), 31, 133
Vale Avenue, Chelsea (house of Miss Ethel Sands), pl. 175
8 Wellgarth Road, Hampstead Garden Suburb (house of Mrs Friede Slater), pl. 199
15 Wilton Street (house of Mrs Paravicini), pl. 364
Wimpole Street (house of Edward James), 214; pl. 344, pl. 355, pl. 358, pl. 359
long galleries, pl. 209, pl. 210, pl. 390
Longhi, Pietro, 205
Longleat House, Wiltshire, pl. 388
Loos, Adolf, 33, 59, 130, 220; pl. 70, pl. 187
Losch, Tilly, 214, 274, 275, 276
Louis XIII style, 303
Louis XIV style, 18, 286; pl. 268, pl. 392
see also under Revivals
Louis XV style, 53, 397, 398; pl. 123, pl. 351
see also under Revivals
Louis XVI style, 53, 196, 390; pl. 176
see also under Revivals
Lovel Dene, near Windsor, Berkshire, 34; pl. 336
Lowry, Robert, 251
Lubbock, Jules, 324
Lubetkin, Berthold, 231
Lucile's (couturier), 103, 277
Lutyens, Edwin, 33, 63, 111, 126, 207, 214, 232, 249, 345, 356; pl. 40, pl. 120
Lutyens, Mary, 249

M

McBean, Angus, 287; pl. 396
McClelland, Nancy, 216; pl. 315
McCorquodale, Charles, 290
McEvoy, Ambrose, pl. 237
MacIntyre, Alex, 330; pl. 442
McKenna, Reginald, 232
McKim, Mead & White (architects), 56, 87; pl. 9, pl. 11, pl. 12, pl. 81
Mackintosh, Charles Rennie, 59, 65, 70–73, 117, 129; pl. 62, pl. 63
Mackintosh, Margaret MacDonald, pl. 62
Maclaren, Denham, pl. 352
McMillen, Eleanor, *see* Brown, Mrs Archibald
McMillen Inc. (decorators), 216, 330; pl. 219, pl. 220
McNicoll, Carol, pl. 444
Macy, Louise, pl. 335
Magistretti, Adriano, 359; pl. 438, pl. 483
Magnasco, Alessandro, 27, 200

Magnasco Society, 202, 300
Magritte, René, 215
Maison de l'Art Nouveau, La, Paris, 47
Maison Gouffé, Paris, 227
Maison Martine, Paris, pl. 195
Makart, Hans, 31, 36
Mallet-Stevens, Robert, 221
Malmaison, château of, near Paris, 13, 51, 104, 115, 165, 182, 187, 245, 305, 331; pl. 17–24
Malmsten, Carl, 131, 144, 286; pl. 154
Mann, Mrs Harrington ('Dolly'), 62, 97, 256, 260, 267, 274, 277
Mannerism, 118
see also under Revivals
Mantegna, Andrea, 32; pl. 34
mantels, 63, 81; pl. 6, pl. 8, pl. 9, pl. 53, pl. 165, pl. 213, pl. 214, pl. 221, pl. 290, pl. 415, pl. 423
Mantovani, Stefano, pl. 502
Maples & Co. (furnishers), 340; pl. 50
Marbury, Bessie, 170
Marie, Crown Princess, 116
Marie-Antoinette, Queen, 39
Markevitch, Igor, pl. 358
Markham Arms, King's Road, London, pl. 447
Marlborough, Consuelo, Duchess of Vanderbilt, pl. 124
Marlborough House, London, 33, 259; pl. 29
'Marlborough House Set', 33
Marmottan, Paul, 102, 103
Marot, Daniel, 368; pl. 394
Marshall, T. Hayes, pl. 320
Mary, Queen, consort of George V, 127
Massey, David, pl. 522
Mathildenhöhe, Darmstadt, pl. 65
Mathsson, Bruno, 286; pl. 383
Mathsson, Karl, 296
Maugham, Syrie, 29, 63, 141, 213, 214, 216, 245, 314, 372; pl. 362, pl. 363, pl. 364, pl. 366, pl. 367
Mayan influence, pl. 168
Melchett, Lord and Lady, 232, 233
Memphis Group, 361, 384
Mendelsohn, Erich, pl. 280, pl. 283
Messel, Oliver, 268, 278, 283, 317, 329; pl. 368, pl. 401
Metropolitan Museum of Art, New York, pl. 272
Mewes & Davis (decorators), pl. 90
Meyer, Baron de, 63
Mies van der Rohe, Ludwig, 214, 291, 360; pl. 282, pl. 374, pl. 443
Milan, 286, 292, 294, 374
Appartamento Lucano, pl. 382
Milan Fair (1981), 384
Milan Furniture Fair, 294
Miller, Duncan, pl. 291, pl. 352
Mills, Mr and Mrs John (later Sir and Lady), 323
Mills, Waymer, 186
minimalism, 398; pl. 488, pl. 492
Mirador, Virginia, 287
Mlinaric, David, 330, 331, 359; pl. 429, pl. 465
mock-Tudor style, 129
see also under Revivals
Modern Architectural Research Group (MARS), 215
Modern Movement/Modernism, 13, 71, 144, 213, 214, 215, 216, 221, 224, 228, 243, 254, 283, 287, 330, 360, 361, 377, 384, 398; pl. 2, pl. 153, pl. 285, pl. 286, pl. 324, pl. 345, pl. 360, pl. 375, pl. 443
Modigliani, Amedeo, 192
Moholy-Nagy, Laszlo, 144, 158; pl. 189
Molesworth, H.P., 210
Mollino, Carlo, 286; pl. 380
Molyneux, Edward, 261
Moncur, Jennie, pl. 513
Monet, Claude, 247
Mongiardino, Renzo, 360
Monkton, West Dean, Sussex, 214, 215, 356; pl. 356

Monnoyer, Jean-Baptiste, pl. 16
Montegufoni Castle, near Florence, 143, 205
Moore, Doris Langley, 325
Morant (upholsterer), 122
Morgan, J. Pierpont, 33, 82, 83
Morrell, Lady Ottoline, 138
Morris, Jane, 41, 60
Morris, Marshall, Faulkner & Co., 27, 42, 247, 251; pl. 99
Morris, May, 60; pl. 39
Morris, William, 27, 32, 41, 59, 60, 127, 251
Mortimer, Raymond, 143, 148, 220; pl. 174
Morton, Digby, 243; pl. 424
Morton, Phyllis, pl. 424
Moser, Kolo, 73, 129, 157; pl. 64
Mossa del Cavallo, La, exhibition (1986), pl. 505, pl. 506
Mottisfont Abbey, Hampshire, pl. 341
Mount, The, Lenox, Mass., pl. 82
Mountbatten, Lord, 333
Mourgue, Pascal, 360, 361; pl. 489
Mower, Martin, pl. 58
Mucha, Alphonse, 31; pl. 44, pl. 45
Mucha, Jiri, 46
Mulberry House, Smith Square, London, pl. 296
Munstead Wood, Surrey, pl. 40
music rooms, 243; pl. 58, pl. 59, pl. 62, pl. 214, pl. 298, pl. 446
Muthesius, Hermann, 59, 69, 94

N

Nantucket
22 Hussey Street (house of Billy Baldwin), pl. 461
Napoleon Bonaparte, 331; pl. 21
Napoleon III style, pl. 387
Nash, John, 262
Nash, Paul, 214, 215, 274, 376; pl. 352, pl. 359
Nast, Condé, 173
Natalini, Adolfo, pl. 506
National Gallery, London, 149
National Trust, 331, 334, 362, 363
'NATO' group (Narrative Architecture Today), 392
neo-baroque style, 62, 143, 144, 215, 216, 280, 361; pl. 76, pl. 131, pl. 136, pl. 245, pl. 249, pl. 251, pl. 255, pl. 256, pl. 257, pl. 263, pl. 267, pl. 308, pl. 309, pl. 322, pl. 331, pl. 337, pl. 338, pl. 345–8, pl. 364, pl. 430, pl. 446, pl. 477
see also under Revivals
neo-classicism, 42, 74, 303, 337, 374; pl. 80, pl. 95, pl. 96, pl. 231, pl. 258, pl. 348, pl. 358, pl. 402, pl. 485
see also under Revivals
neo-grec style, 359
neo-Romanticism, 361
Neuilly
villa of Jacques Doucet, pl. 196–8
'New Baroque', 398; pl. 520, pl. 521, pl. 522
New Georgians, 361, 366; pl. 472, pl. 473, pl. 474
new ornamentalism, 394, 398
'New Look', 285; pl. 386
New York
121 East 21st Street (house of Stamford White), pl. 57
36 East 53rd Street (apartment of Rose Cumming), pl. 406, pl. 407
East 55th Street (house of Elsie de Wolfe), pl. 16
East 60th Street (house of Andy Warhol), pl. 456
East 8oth Street (apartment of Mario Buatta), pl. 460
7 East 96th Street (house of Ogden Codman), pl. 94
884 Park Avenue (apartment of Edith Wharton), pl. 80
1040 Park Lane (house of Condé Nast), pl. 215
Villard houses, 56
West 25th Street (house of Mrs George Frederick Jones), pl. 35

New York School of Architecture and Decoration, 196
New York School of Fine and Applied Art, 142
Nichols, Beverley, 213
Nicholson, Ben, pl. 290
Nicholson, Mabel, 105; pl. 101
Nicholson, William, 62, 105; pl. 101, pl. 105, pl. 224
Nicholson, Harold, 251
Nid, Le, near Darmstadt, 116
Noailles, Comtesse Anna de, pl. 123
Noailles, Vicomte de, 215, 221, 271, 272, 295; pl. 389
Noailles, Vicomtesse Marie-Laure, 215, 221, 271, 272, 273, 295; pl. 350, pl. 389
Nuthall Temple, near Nottingham, 335

O

Oakes, George, pl. 400
Oberkampf, J., 195
objets trouvés, 215, 272
Oetzmann (furniture manufacturers), 59
offices, pl. 338, pl. 351
Olbrich, J.M., 73
'Old French look', 53, 62, 81, 277, 364; pl. 14, pl. 84–7, pl. 92, pl. 94, pl. 109, pl. 110, pl. 176, pl. 208, pl. 480
'Old palazzo' style, 286, 360; pl. 346, pl. 475, pl. 523
'Olde English' furniture, 64, 129, 215
Olivier, Edith, 280, 320
Omega Workshops, 13, 64, 136, 137, 143, 148, 163, 234, 246–7
One-Off, Covent Garden, 396
Op Art, pl. 439
Orchard, The, Chorleywood, Hertfordshire, pl. 60
ornamentalism, new, 394, 398
Orpen, William, pl. 101
Oscar Woollens Ltd, pl. 439
Osterley Park House, Middlesex, 374
Otte, Benita, pl. 191
Oud, J.J.P., 218
overmantels, pl. 14, pl. 78

P

Paget. Paul, 335
paintings
mural, 171; pl. 236, pl. 343, pl. 355
trompe l'œil, pl. 136, pl. 238, pl. 293, pl. 340, pl. 341
Palais Royal, Paris, 99, 104, 180
Palais Stoclet, Brussels, pl. 66
Palazzo Ricci, Via Guilia, Rome, pl. 329
Palladianism, 11; pl. 138, pl. 139, pl. 508, pl. 509
see also under Revivals
Palladio, Andrea, 33, 214
panels/panelling, 127, 167; pl. 16, pl. 27, pl. 35, pl. 62, pl. 81, pl. 94, pl. 128, pl. 132, pl. 136, pl. 169, pl. 170, pl. 214, pl. 223, pl. 240, pl. 259, pl. 260, pl. 261, pl. 306, pl. 351, pl. 360, pl. 382, pl. 418
canvas, 148
'correctly' proportioned, pl. 87, pl. 264
dark-stained, pl. 43
framed, 350
glass, pl. 105, pl. 224
hanging, pl. 298
and heating, pl. 226
lacquered, pl. 165
Louis Quinze, pl. 82
Louis Seize, 398
mirror, pl. 14, pl. 15, pl. 218, pl. 361, pl. 362, pl. 419
mural, pl. 66
rectilinear, pl. 130
stripped, 213–14, 366
sub-rococo, pl. 8
three-quarter-height, pl. 140

veneered, pl. 304
white-painted, pl. 61
Pannini, Giovanni, 216
papiers peints, 180, 181; pl. 110, pl. 398
Paragon, The, Richmond, 60
Paravicini, Mrs, 245
Paris
  Avenue des Champs-Elysées (apartment of
    Charles de Beistegui, 215; pl. 345
  Avenue des Champs-Elysées (*salon* of Mlle Sorel),
    pl. 122
  rue Cambon (Coco Chanel's premises), 175
  faubourg St Honoré (house of François Catroux),
    pl. 464
  29 faubourg St Honoré (home of Coco Chanel),
    pl. 218
  rue de Lota (apartment of Mme Mathieu Lévy),
    pl. 181
  2 rue Louis-Boilly (house of Paul Marmottan),
    pl. 108
  rue Val de Grâce (studio of Alphonse Mucha), 31;
    pl. 45
Paris Exhibition (1900), 47
Paris Exhibition (1925), 228, 233
Paris Exhibition (1937), 223
Paris Exposition des Arts Décoratifs (1925), 144,
  155, 161, 272; pl. 182–5
Parish, Mrs Henry ('Sister Parish'), 216, 330, 355,
  372
Parkinson, Frank, 263
Parkinson, Mrs Frank, 263
Parkinson, Norman, pl. 358
parlours, 134, 62, 143, 144; pl. 5–10, pl. 31, pl. 54, pl. 55, pl. 80,
  pl. 104, pl. 155, pl. 259, pl. 405, pl. 423
Parr, Tom, 327
Parsons, Frank Alvah, 142, 151, 216, 330; pl. 206,
  pl. 207
Parsons School of Design, New York, 168, 354
Pasca, Vanni, 389
Pasolini, Pier Paolo, 374
Pater, Walter, 12
Patmore, Derek, 176, 215, 230, 231, 234, 238, 239,
  242, 278; pl. 312
Patrini, Giovanni, 337, 375; pl. 484
Paul, Professor Bruno, 63; pl. 125, pl. 132, pl. 135
Paulsson, Gregor, 144
Pavillon Colombe, near Paris, pl. 208
Pawson, John, pl. 488
Payne, Jack, 223
Pearce, C. Maresco, pl. 293
Pearl Dot Workshops, London, 377
Pel Ltd, Birmingham, 229
Pepler, Marian, 218
Percier, Charles, pl. 19
Perego di Cremnago, Filippo, 374; pl. 485
Peter Jones (department store), 216, 253
Pevsner, Nikolaus, 13
Phillips, R. Randal, 172, 181, 188, 189
Philpot, Glyn, 265; pl. 236, pl. 296
Picasso, Pablo, 107, 214; pl. 358
Pickford, Mary, 241
Pinsent, Cecil, 62
Piper, John, 283, 361
Pirroni, Marco, 393
Plank, George, 63
Plas Newydd, Anglesey, pl. 343
Platt, J.B., pl. 228
Plunket, Lord and Lady, 317
Poe, Edgar Allan, 35, 254
Poiret, Paul, 27, 63, 106, 111, 113, 115, 144, 280;
  pl. 116, pl. 117, pl. 118, pl. 183, pl. 186, pl. 193,
  pl. 195
Pompeii, 274
Pompeiian style, 27, 359; pl. 111, pl. 481, pl. 483
Pompidou Centre, Paris, 396
Ponti, Gio, 286, 294, 361; pl. 378, pl. 379, pl. 382
'pop architecture', pl. 376
Pop Art, 350

see also under Revivals
Port Lympne, Kent, pl. 236, pl. 340
Portmeirion, North Wales, 192
Portois & Fix, Vienna, 70
Post-Impressionism, 64, 136, 143
Post-Modernism, 361, 383, 389; pl. 504
Powell-Tuck, Connor & Orefelt (architects), 393;
  pl. 486
Powell-Tuck, Julian, 376
'prairie houses', 225
Praz, Mario, 102, 216, 254, 309, 359
Pre-Raphaelites, 31, 76, 127
Prutscher, Professor Otto, pl. 126
Pryce-Jones, Alan, 201
Pugh Brothers, pl. 277
Pugin, A. W. N., 366
punk movement, 397
Purkersdorf Convalescent Home, Vienna, 71
Putnam, Andrée, 153, 360

Q

Quartermaine, Carolyn, pl. 515
Queen Anne style, 18
  see also under Revivals
Queen Elizabeth (liner), 321
Quennell, Peter, 143

R

Raffalovich, André, 37
Ragley Hall, Warwickshire, 370
Ranken, W.E., pl. 239, pl. 246, pl. 247, pl. 248
Rationalism, 215
Ravilious, Eric, 215, 325; pl. 292
Read, Herbert, 214; pl. 290
Rebel Art Centre, 137
Récamier sofa, 182
Reddish House, Broadchalke, Wiltshire, pl. 416,
  pl. 417
Rédé, Baron de, 286; pl. 392
Redmile, Antony, pl. 448
Regency style, 34, 62, 143, 144, 180, 195, 302, 325;
  pl. 98, pl. 101, pl. 143, pl. 158, pl. 221, pl. 231,
  pl. 243, pl. 244, pl. 252, pl. 256, pl. 258, pl. 260,
  pl. 300, pl. 317, pl. 319, pl. 320, pl. 328, pl. 329,
  pl. 348, pl. 361, pl. 436, pl. 462
  see also under Revivals
Reich, Lilly, pl. 190
Reichstag, Berlin, 285
Renaissance period, 37, 111, 208; pl. 6, pl. 43, pl. 58
Renishaw, Derbyshire, 143, 241; pl. 263
'Renoir boudoir', 243
Restoration period (French), pl. 313
retour d'Égypte style, 180; pl. 105
Revivals
  'age of satinwood', 18
  ancien régime, pl. 37
  Art Nouveau, pl. 447
  Arts and Crafts, 345
  Biedermeier, pl. 125, pl. 126, pl. 132, pl. 495,
    pl. 498
  Carolean, 142
  Charles X, 18
  Chippendale, pl. 142, pl. 213
  Curzon Street Baroque, 18; pl. 249, pl. 257,
    pl. 365
  Directoire, 81, 105; pl. 106, pl. 112, pl. 194
  Edwardian, 364
  Egyptian, pl. 202
  Elizabethan, 142; pl. 178, pl. 396
  Empire, 13, 61, 162, 176, 321; pl. 36, pl. 50,
    pl. 117, pl. 182, pl. 194, pl. 202, pl. 220, pl. 228,
    pl. 233, pl. 234, pl. 235, pl. 247, pl. 302, pl. 317,
    pl. 321, pl. 396, pl. 397, pl. 410
  Federal, 354
  Gothic, 27, 361; pl. 428, pl. 491, pl. 497
  Greek, pl. 202, pl. 296, pl. 385

Gustavian, pl. 154
Hepplewhite, 125
Jacobean (pseudo), 288
Louis XIII, 303
Louis XIV, 303, 360; pl. 392
Louis XV, 53, 88, 90, 360; pl. 46, pl. 80, pl. 82,
  pl. 113, pl. 480
Louis XVI, 53, 118, 360; pl. 90, pl. 109, pl. 351
Mannerist, pl. 464
neo-Baroque, 143, 215, 216, 243, 317, 329, 345,
  361, 364; pl. 76, pl. 131, pl. 136, pl. 245, pl. 249,
  pl. 251, pl. 255, pl. 256, pl. 257, pl. 259, pl. 263,
  pl. 308, pl. 309, pl. 322, pl. 331, pl. 337, pl. 338,
  pl. 345, pl. 346, pl. 347, pl. 366, pl. 367, pl. 369,
  pl. 380, pl. 413, pl. 424, pl. 446, pl. 477
neo-classical, 359, 374; pl. 5, pl. 51, pl. 106,
  pl. 129, pl. 141, pl. 258, pl. 302, pl. 330, pl. 358,
  pl. 427, pl. 485
neo-Georgian, 143, 167, 207, 215, 232, 280, 288,
  304; pl. 99, pl. 140, pl. 141, pl. 193, pl. 213,
  pl. 245, pl. 264, pl. 273, pl. 312, pl. 435, pl. 468
'Olde English', 64, 129, 215
Palladian, pl. 523
Pop Art, pl. 502, pl. 503
Queen Anne, 345
Regency, 97, 118, 135, 143, 195, 215, 216, 256,
  262, 267, 287, 304, 321, 322, 324, 359, 364;
  pl. 225, pl. 229, pl. 230, pl. 236, pl. 296, pl. 303,
  pl. 310, pl. 320, pl. 330, pl. 422, pl. 436
Renaissance, pl. 41, pl. 81, pl. 111, pl. 236
Restoration (French), pl. 302
rococo, 361; pl. 250, pl. 315, pl. 330, pl. 365,
  pl. 414, pl. 511
Second Empire, 344, 360, 398; pl. 476
Sheraton, 66, 116, 125, 133
'Stockbrokers' Tudor', 18; pl. 270
Tudor, 142, 215; pl. 270
Victorian, 364; pl. 327, pl. 423–6
Wedgwood, pl. 312
William and Mary, pl. 309
Rhodes, Zandra, pl. 444, pl. 445
Richardson, Professor Albert E., 101, 134, 135, 143,
  180, 210; pl. 159, pl. 411
Richardson, H.H., 225
Richmond
  house of Mr and Mrs John (later Sir and Lady)
    Mills, pl. 422
  The Paragon (house of Edith Cooper and
    Catherine Bradley), 133
  Spring Terrace (home of Charles Ricketts and
    Charles Shannon), pl. 98
Richter, H. Davis, pl. 253
Ricketts, Charles, 31, 36, 44, 60, 133, 344; pl. 98,
  pl. 99, pl. 100, pl. 257
Riemerschmid, Richard, 75
Rietveld, Gerrit, 220
Riley, Bridget, 338
Robert Graves & Co., 39
Roberts, William, 137, 144, 200
Robsjohn-Gibbings, T.H., 33, 286, 296, 329;
  pl. 385, pl. 437
rococo, 344, 361; pl. 8, pl. 250
  see also under Revivals
Rococo, King's Road, London, 397
Rodin, Auguste, 63
Rogers, Mrs Millicent, 176
Romantic movement, 11
Rome
  apartment of Mario Praz, pl. 25, pl. 26,
    pl. 329
Romi, M., pl. 354
Romney, George, 262
Romney House, Hampstead, London,
  pl. 338
room dividers, pl. 292, pl. 377
Roos, Christian P., pl. 36
Roos, David, pl. 476, pl. 477
Rosa, Salvator, 200, 267

Rose, Sir Francis, pl. 373
Rosier, Roslyn, pl. 435
Rossetti, Dante Gabriel, 31, 247
Rossi, Aldo, pl. 505
Rothenstein, Sir William, 33n, 60, 133; pl. 102
Rothermere, Lady, 196
Rotterdam
  living room by Mart Stam, pl. 276
Rousseau, Clément, 163
Royal College of Art, London, 237, 287, 291, 330,
  394, 395
Royère, Jean, pl. 287
Rubens, Peter Paul, 31
Rubinstein, Helena, 269
rugs, pl. 107, pl. 134, pl. 153, pl. 262, pl. 318, pl. 319,
  pl. 362, pl. 457
  bearskin, pl. 9
  flat-weave, pl. 95
  fur, pl. 35
  khilim, pl. 290
  needlepoint, pl. 460
  oriental, 41; pl. 123
  Persian, pl. 99, pl. 251
  Samarkand, pl. 321
  striped, pl. 285
Ruhlmann, Jacques-Émile, 144, 237; pl. 182
Runge & Scotland (architects), pl. 134
Ruskin, John, 31, 44, 111
Russborough, Co. Wicklow, Eire, 256
Russell, Mrs Gilbert, 265
Russell, Gordon, 214, 218, 223; pl. 286
Russell, R.D. (Dick), 218
Russian Ballet style, 63; pl. 114, pl. 115, pl. 186,
  pl. 195, pl. 203
Russian Empire style, pl. 236
Rust, Graham, 370
Rutland, Violet, Duchess of, 34, 127, 165

S

Saarinen, Eliel, 116
Sackville, Lady, 27, 63, 83, 111, 126, 127, 137, 168,
  207, 251, 356
Sackville-West, Vita, 62, 63, 126; pl. 323
Saladino, John, pl. 523
Salon des Artistes-Décorateurs (1923), 153
salons, 103, 214, 260, 261, 276, 398; pl. 18, pl. 90,
  pl. 92, pl. 195, pl. 211, pl. 218, pl. 278, pl. 325,
  pl. 349, pl. 350, pl. 361
Saltram House, Devon, pl. 466
Sander, Bertha, pl. 151
Sands, Ethel, 149
Sassoon, Sir Philip, 188, 265
Sawaya & Moroni (furniture manufacturers),
  pl. 498
Scarpa, Tobia, pl. 438
Schiaparelli, Elsa, 275, 360; pl. 415
School House, Wilton, pl. 413
Schrijver, Herman, 305; pl. 309
Schuyler van Rensselaer, Mrs, 56
Scott, Geoffrey, 62, 111, 186, 201, 203; pl. 261
Scott, Sir Giles Gilbert, pl. 226
Scott, M.H. Baillie, 59
Scott, Sir Walter, 34
screens, 41, 153, 173; pl. 7, pl. 11, pl. 199, pl. 218,
  pl. 362, pl. 363, pl. 380, pl. 436
Seal, Ethel Davis, 142
Second Empire period, 53, 215, 268, 273, 302, 329,
  331, 344; pl. 50, pl. 365, pl. 387, pl. 411,
  pl. 417
  see also under Revivals
Seely & Paget (architects), 335
Serebriakoff, Alexandre, pl. 402, pl. 403
Sert, José-Maria, 175, 188, 263, 265
Sert, Misia, 175
Severini, Gino, 201
Severs, Dennis, pl. 473, pl. 474
Sewell, Mr and Mrs Anthony, 249

Sezession movement, 70, 71, 74, 116, 157; pl. 67, pl. 68
Shannon, Charles, 37, 44, 60, 133; pl. 32, pl. 98, pl. 99, pl. 100, pl. 257
Shapland, H.P., 124, 125
Shaw, Mrs George Bernard, 251
Shaw, Richard Norman, 33
Sheraton period, 125
    see also under Revivals
Sheringham, George, pl. 214
Sickert, Walter, pl. 293
Sissinghurst Castle, Kent, pl. 323
sitting rooms, pl. 147, pl. 241, pl. 243, pl. 244, pl. 251, pl. 314, pl. 402, pl. 470
Sitwell, Edith, 27, 62, 143, 202, 241, 280, 361; pl. 263
Sitwell, Sir George, 143
Sitwell, Sir Osbert, 27, 62, 107, 143, 188, 202, 280, 361; pl. 255, pl. 256
Sitwell, Sacheverell, 27, 62, 107, 143, 202, 280, 361; pl. 255, pl. 256
Slater, Friede, 163
Sledmore House, Humberside, 345
Smith, Edwin, pl. 426
Smith, Freeman, 142
Smithson, Alison and Peter, 286, 340; pl. 376
smoking rooms, pl. 128, pl. 135, pl. 185
Snowshill Manor, Gloucestershire, 214; pl. 271
Soane, Sir John, 143, 193, 335
Somerset, Lady Katharine, 198
Sommerard, Alexandre du, 37
Sorel, Mlle, 112
Sottsass, Ettore, 361; pl. 499
'Souls, The', 29, 42, 127
Spanier, Adrienne, pl. 421
Spanish style, 314
Spealls (decorators), 27, 63, 126, 137
Speer, Albert, 285
Spry, Constance, 252, 277; pl. 333, pl. 334
staircases, 277; pl. 47–9, pl. 60, pl. 216, pl. 475, pl. 495, pl. 504, pl. 513
Stam, Mart, pl. 276
Stefanidis, John, 330; pl. 482
stencil designs, 374; pl. 470
Stephen, Sir Leslie, 324
Stiebel, Victor, pl. 337
Stile Liberty *see* Art Nouveau
'stockbrokers' Tudor', 18; pl. 270
Stockton, California
    George Gray house, pl. 31
Stone, Edward Durell, pl. 385
Storey, W.R., 244, 245; pl. 314
Strabolgi, Lord, 289
Strachey, Lytton, pl. 175
Stratfield Saye House, Hampshire, 184; pl. 390
Stuck, Franz von, pl. 51
studies, pl. 43, pl. 290, pl. 291, pl. 294, pl. 324, pl. 358, pl. 366
Studio Alchymia, Milan, 384
studios, 398; pl. 338, pl. 370
style troubadour, 302
Sudjic, Deyan, 380
Süe, Louis, pl. 347
surrealism, 214, 215, 271, 272, 287, 376; pl. 351–4, pl. 356, pl. 359, pl. 369
Sutherland, Graham, 228
Sutton Place, New York, pl. 221, pl. 222
Svenska Slöjdforeningen (Swedish Society of Industrial Design), 144
Swanzy, Henry, pl. 426
Sweden, King of, 306
'Swedish Modern', 286; pl. 383, pl. 438, pl. 457
Sykes, Sir Tatton, 345
'Symbolic Architecture', 383

T

Talbot, Suzanne, *see* Lévy, Mme Mathieu
Tate Gallery, London, 264

Taylor, Imogen, pl. 28
Tchelitchew, Pavel, 201, 214, 269
Templewood, Lord, 335
Templewood, near Northrepps, Norfolk, pl. 435
Templier, Raymond, 221
Tennant, Lady (later Lady Grey), 280
Tennant, Sir Edward, 280
Tennant, Hon. Stephen, 215, 261, 280, 281; pl. 366, pl. 367, pl. 408, pl. 409, pl. 410
Terry, Emilio, 215, 268, 272, 286, 309, 321, 398; pl. 348, pl. 391, pl. 392
Thedlow Inc. (decorators), pl. 317
Thematic House, Holland Park, London, pl. 495
Thomas, Brian, pl. 433
Thomas, Rodney, 295
Thonet, Michael, pl. 277, pl. 458
Thornton, Peter, 12, 331; pl. 350
Thornton Smith, 143, 216
Thyssen, Baron, 360
Tiffany, Louis Comfort, pl. 11
Tilden, Philip, pl. 236, pl. 240
Timber House, Sevenoaks, Kent, pl. 291
Timney, Sue, pl. 514
Timney-Fowler (textile and ceramic designers), pl. 514
Todd, Dorothy, 143, 148, 220
'Toio' lamp, pl. 438
Tonks, Henry, pl. 52
tous les Louis manner, 304
Towndrow, Frederick, pl. 150
Townshend House, Regent's Park, 201
Treasure Houses of Britain exhibition (1985), 362
Tree, Mrs Ronald, 240, 252
    see also Lancaster, Mrs Nancy
Triennale Venezia Exhibition (1951), 292
Trinder, Neil, pl. 467
'Trip Box', pl. 442
Trollope's of Belgravia, 27, 142
trompe l'œil, 314, 320, 397; pl. 136, pl. 215, pl. 219, pl. 231, pl. 232, pl. 238, pl. 293, pl. 300, pl. 340, pl. 341, pl. 355, pl. 368, pl. 380, pl. 382, pl. 396, pl. 399, pl. 414, pl. 418, pl. 435, pl. 464, pl. 467, pl. 478, pl. 503
Troost, P.L., pl. 129
Truex, Van Day, 216
'Tudor' style, 27; pl. 270
    see also under Revivals
Tugendhat House, Brno, pl. 282
Tuileries Palace, Paris, 24
'Tulipomania', 399
Turin, 286, 294
Turin International Exhibition (1902), 79
Turkish style, 27
Tzara, Tristan, 157

U

UAM (Union des Artistes Modernes), pl. 278
Umeda, Masanori, pl. 501
'Utility' furnishings, 285, 288; pl. 371

V

Valpy, Canon, 44
Van de Velde, Henry, 158
Vanderbilt, Cornelius, 80
Vanderbilt, Mrs William K., 111
Vanderbilt Mansion, New York, 83
Vasarely, Victor, 338
Vaux, Calvert, 35
Venice
    Palazzo Labia, 283, 301
    Palazzo Venier dei Leoni (house of Peggy Guggenheim), pl. 381
Venturi, Robert, pl. 497
Vercelloni, Isa, 389
Verdura, Fulco di, 329, 333
Verity, Frank, 134

Verity, Simon, 399
Vernet, Claude-Joseph, 267
Veronese, Paolo, 268
Versace
    house of Signor Giamelli, pl. 483
Versailles, 331
VIA, 360, 378
Vickers, Hugo, 320
Victoria, Queen, 34
Victoria and Albert Museum, London, 243, 331
    Director's dining room, 399; pl. 467
Victorian Society, 324
Victoriana, 143, 192, 210, 214, 240, 243, 254, 287, 330, 336, 337; pl. 255, pl. 256, pl. 260, pl. 318, pl. 319, pl. 326, pl. 327, pl. 447
Villa Corne d'Or, Cannes, pl. 234, pl. 235
Villa Hochstetter, Vienna, pl. 71
Villa Karma, Lake Geneva, pl. 70
Villa Rotonda, Vicenza, 391
Villa Savoye, Poissy, 218
Villa Stuck, Munich, pl. 51
Villa Trianon, Versailles, pl. 209–12
Vizcaya, Miami, pl. 202
Vogue Regency style, 13, 61, 143, 216, 260, 287, 305, 307, 329; pl. 227, pl. 233, pl. 303, pl. 320, pl. 336, pl. 424
Vorticism, 137, 144
Voysey, C.F.A., 59, 76, 77; pl. 60, pl. 166
Vuillard, Edouard, pl. 38

W

Wade, Charles Paget, 210, 214
Wadsworth, Edward, 137
Wagner, Otto, 71, 74
Wainewright, Thomas Griffiths, 27, 359
Wainwright, Shirley B., pl. 146–9
Wakefield, Norris, 276; pl. 336, pl. 356, pl. 361
Wallace, Sir Richard, 62, 83, 359
wallpapers, 41, 60, 63, 81, 133, 142–3, 151, 173, 216; pl. 6, pl. 14, pl. 27, pl. 32, pl. 36, pl. 78, pl. 80, pl. 110, pl. 132, pl. 135, pl. 194, pl. 201, pl. 206, pl. 207, pl. 213, pl. 230, pl. 231, pl. 294, pl. 328, pl. 342, pl. 373, pl. 393, pl. 400, pl. 409, pl. 410, pl. 468
Walpole, Horace, 138
Walton, Allan, 167, 215; pl. 300, pl. 319
Walton, George, pl. 61
Walton, Stewart, 365
Warchol, Paul, pl. 459
Warhol, Andy, pl. 456
Waring & Gillow (furnishers), 27; pl. 322
Warner, Lady Leucha, 231
Warren, Dorothy, 62, 186, 203
Warren, Edward, 98
Washington, D.C.
    office of the Ambassador of France, pl. 490
Washington Irving House, New York, pl. 13–15
Watkin, David, 367
Watkins, Mrs F.B., 307
Waugh, Evelyn, 141, 325, 336
Webb, Philip, 135; pl. 41
Webster, Geoffrey, pl. 339
Wedgwood style, pl. 312
Weissenhofsiedlung, Die, Stuttgart, 220
Welfling, Laure, 359
Wellcome, Syrie, *see* Maugham, Syrie
Wellesley, Lord Gerald, 62, 135, 143, 180, 182, 185, 249; pl. 225, pl. 230, pl. 231, pl. 238, pl. 258, pl. 330, pl. 331
Wellington, Duke of, 184
Wellington, Lord Gerald Wellesley, Duke of, 321; pl. 390
Wells, Trenwith, 180
West, Mae, 241, 275
West Dean, West Sussex, 127
Wharton, Edith, 9, 38, 53, 61, 62, 80, 86, 94, 129, 168, 346, 368; pl. 80, pl. 82, pl. 208

Whistler, James McNeill, 31
Whistler, Rex, 188. 214, 215, 263; pl. 340–44, pl. 365, pl. 368
White, Stanford, 17, 87; pl. 57
White Allom, 142
White House, Washington, D.C., 13
    'Green Room' (Parlour), pl. 5–10
    Hall, pl. 11, pl. 12
Widdicombe Furniture Company, Grand Rapids, Miss., 337
Wiener Werkstätte, 59, 70, 71, 75, 151, 166
Wilde, Oscar, 11, 27, 31, 33n, 37, 61, 133, 135
William and Mary period, 203; pl. 241, pl. 406
    see also under Revivals
Williams, Elydr, pl. 321
Williams-Ellis, Clough, 143, 167, 203; pl. 243, pl. 244, pl. 245, pl. 338
Wills, Trenwith, pl. 238, pl. 330, pl. 331
Wilmotte, Jean-Michel, 360; pl. 490
Wilsford Manor, Wiltshire, 215, 261; pl. 366, pl. 367, pl. 408, pl. 409, pl. 410
Wilson, Elsie Cobb, 216; pl. 316
Wimperis & Simpson (architects), 213
Winchester
    3 The Close (house of Canon Valpy), pl. 42, pl. 43
Winckelmann, Johann, 104
Windsor, Duke and Duchess of, 90
Wirth, Mme Barbara, 370
Withers, F.C., 35
Wood, Ruby Ross, 62, 216; pl. 335
'Wrenaissance' style, 33, 123; pl. 120
Wright, Frank Lloyd, 214, 290; pl. 168, pl. 284
Würzler-Klopsch, Paul, pl. 133
Wyatville, Sir Jeffry, 310
Wyndham, Hon. Percy, 42

Y

Young, Rory, pl. 520
Yturbe, Mme, 285; pl. 386

Z

Zoffany, John, pl. 468
Zola, Emile, 36